The Cornwallis Papers

The Campaigns of 1780 and 1781

in

The Southern Theatre of the American Revolutionary War

Volume V

Arranged and edited by

Ian Saberton

The Naval & Military Press Ltd

Published by
The Naval & Military Press Ltd

Unit 10 Ridgewood Industrial Park,
Uckfield, East Sussex,
TN22 5QE England

Tel: +44 (0) 1825 749494
Fax: +44 (0) 1825 765701

www.naval-military-press.com
www.military-genealogy.com
www.militarymaproom.com

Documents hitherto unpublished © Crown copyright 2010

Documents previously published in which Crown copyright subsists
© Crown copyright

Introductory chapters, footnotes and other editorial matter © Ian Saberton 2010

The right of Ian Saberton to be identified as author of the introductory chapters, footnotes and other editorial matter in this work has been asserted in accordance with sections 77 and 78 of the UK Copyright, Designs and Patents Act 1988

ISBN Volume I   9781845747923
ISBN Volume II   9781845747916
ISBN Volume III 9781845747909
ISBN Volume IV   9781845747893
ISBN Volume V   9781845747886
ISBN Volume VI   9781845747879

Printed and bound in Great Britain by
CPI Antony Rowe, Chippenham and Eastbourne

CONTENTS

Editorial Method		v

PART TEN
THE VIRGINIA CAMPAIGN
20 May to 22nd July 1781

49.	Introduction to the rest of Part Ten	3
50.	The Phillips Papers	
	1 – Between Phillips and Clinton	7
	2 – From Phillips to Cornwallis or Craig	64
	3 – Other letters	70
51.	Letters to or from New York or London	
	1 – Between Cornwallis and Clinton	71
	2 – From Arbuthnot or Graves to Cornwallis	144
	3 – From Clinton or Graves to Leslie	147
	4 – From Germain to Cornwallis	150
	5 – From Robertson to Cornwallis	152
52.	Letters to or from Portsmouth	
	1 – From von Fuchs or Rochfort to Cornwallis	154
	2 – Between Cornwallis and Leslie	160
	3 – Between Haldane and Major England	196
	4 – From Connolly to Cornwallis	200
53.	Correspondence etc with naval officers in Virginia or South Carolina	
	1 – With naval officers	205
	2 – Desultory water operations	219

54.	Miscellaneous correspondence etc relating to Virginia or Maryland	
	1 – Between Cornwallis and Simcoe or Tarleton	224
	2 – Between Cornwallis and Lafayette, Heth or Steuben	229
	3 – With or concerning the Troops of Convention	241
	4 – Intelligence	249
	5 – Intercepted letters	257
	6 – Other letters	265
55.	Correspondence relating to the Carolinas	
	1 – Between Cornwallis and Balfour	271
	2 – Between Cornwallis and Rawdon	286
	3 – Between Cornwallis and Gould or Stewart	294
	4 – From Cornwallis to Craig	300
	5 – From Craig to Balfour	302
	6 – Proposed enlistment of prisoners at Charlestown for the West Indies	314
	7 – With the public departments	320
56.	Letters from Georgia or East Florida	
	1 – From Sir James Wright	324
	2 – From Clarke	328
	3 – From Tonyn	337
	4 – Between Brown and Balfour	357
	5 – From Kirkland	362
Index		363

Editorial method

Subject to the following modifications, the editorial method remains the same as described in volume I.

Omitted papers

Though belonging to the period covered by this volume, the following papers in the series PRO 30/11/- are omitted on the ground that they do not relate to the southern campaigns or are too inconsequential: 3(24); 5(10); 6(7), (10), (12), (13), (186), and (202); 71(21); 95(46); 104(7), (9), and (11); 105(3), (32), (34), (36), (38), and (50); 275(11); and 277(8).

Footnotes

As a general rule biographical footnotes on persons who are not the subject of such notes in this volume will be found in one of the preceding volumes.

Titles of works cited in abbreviated form in footnotes

Appletons'
   Appletons' Cyclopædia of American Biography (New York, 1888-)

Army Lists
   A list of the general and field officers... (London, 1754-77), together with *A list of all the officers of the army...* (London, 1778-)

Boatner, *Encyclopedia*
   Mark Mayo Boatner III, *Encyclopedia of the American Revolution* (D McKay Co, 1966)

Cashin, *The King's Ranger*
   Edward J Cashin, *The King's Ranger: Thomas Brown and the American Revolution on the Southern Frontier* (Fordham University Press, 1999)

Charnock, *Biographia Navalis*
   John Charnock, *Biographia Navalis: or Impartial Memoirs of the Lives and Characters of Officers of the Navy of Great Britain from the Year 1660 to the Present Time* (London, 1794-98)

Clark, *Loyalists in the Southern Campaign*
   Murtie June Clark, *Loyalists in the Southern Campaign of the Revolutionary War*, volume I (Genealogical Publishing Co, 2003)

Coldham, *Loyalist Claims*
   Peter Wilson Coldham, *American Loyalist Claims* (National Genealogical Society, 1980)

DAB
> *Dictionary of American Biography* (New York, 1928-1958)

DCB
> *Dictionary of Canadian Biography* (University of Toronto, 1967; also available on internet)

Davies ed, *Docs of the Am Rev*
> K G Davies ed, *Documents of the American Revolution 1770-1783,* volumes XVI, XVIII and XX (Irish Academic Press, 1976-9)

DeMond, *Loyalists in NC*
> Robert O DeMond, *The Loyalists in North Carolina during the Revolution* (Duke University Press, 1940)

DNB
> *Dictionary of National Biography* (London, 1885-1901)

Ewald, *Diary*
> Johann Ewald, *Diary of the American War: A Hessian Journal,* translated and edited by Joseph P Tustin (Yale University Press, 1979)

Garden, *Anecdotes* (1st Series)
> Alexander Garden, *Anecdotes of the Revolutionary War* (Charleston, 1822)

The Greene Papers
> *The Papers of General Nathanael Greene,* volumes VI-IX, edited by Richard K Showman, Dennis M Conrad, Roger N Parks, et al (University of North Carolina Press, 1991-7)

Gwathmey, *Historical Register*
> John H Gwathmey, *Historical Register of Virginians in the Revolution 1775-1783* (The Dietz Press, 1938)

Hay ed, *Soldiers from NC*
> Gertrude Sloan Hay ed, *Roster of Soldiers from North Carolina in the American Revolution* (Reprint, Genealogical Publishing Co Inc, 1988)

Heitman, *Historical Register*
> Francis B Heitman, *Historical Register of the Officers of the Continental Army during the War of the Revolution* (Reprint, Clearfield Publishing Co Inc, 2000)

Johnson, *Traditions*
> Joseph Johnson, *Traditions and Reminiscences chiefly of the American Revolution in the South* (Charleston, 1851)

Johnston, *Commissioned Officers in the Medical Service*
> William Johnston, *Roll of Commissioned Officers in the Medical Service of the British Army: 20 June 1727 to 23 June 1898* (Reprint, The Wellcome Historical Medical Library, 1968)

McCowen Jr, *Charleston, 1780-82*
    George Smith McCowen Jr, *The British Occupation of Charleston, 1780-82* (University of South Carolina Press, 1972)

McCrady, *SC in the Rev 1780-1783*
    Edward McCrady, *The History of South Carolina in the Revolution 1780-1783* (The Macmillan Co, New York, 1902)

ODNB
    Oxford Dictionary of National Biography (Oxford University Press, 2004)

Raymond, 'British American Corps'
    W O Raymond, 'Roll of Officers of the British American or Loyalist Corps', *Collections of the New Brunswick Historical Society*, ii, 1899

Ross ed, *Cornwallis Correspondence*
    Charles Ross ed, *Correspondence of Charles, First Marquis Cornwallis*, volume I (London, 1859)

Royal Regiment of Artillery
    List of Officers of the Royal Regiment of Artillery from the Year 1716 to the Year 1899 (London, 1900)

Sabine, *Biographical Sketches*
    Lorenzo Sabine, *Biographical Sketches of Loyalists of the American Revolution* (Boston, 1864)

Simcoe, *The Queen's Rangers*
    John Graves Simcoe, *A Journal of the Operations of the Queen's Rangers* (Exeter, 1787)

Stevens, *Clinton-Cornwallis Controversy*
    Benjamin Franklin Stevens, *The Campaign in Virginia 1781: the Clinton Cornwallis Controversy* (London, 1887-8)

Syrett and DiNardo ed, *The Commissioned Sea Officers*
    David Syrett and R L DiNardo ed, *The Commissioned Sea Officers of the Royal Navy 1660-1815* (Navy Records Society, 1994)

Tarleton, *Campaigns*
    Banastre Tarleton, *A History of the Campaigns of 1780 and 1781 in the Southern Provinces of North America* (London, 1787)

Tyler, *Encyclopedia*
    Lyon Gardiner Tyler, *Encyclopedia of Virginia Biography* (New York, 1915)

Va Military Records
    Virginia Military Records (Genealogical Publishing Co Inc, 1983)

Valentine, *The British Establishment*
>Alan Valentine, *The British Establishment, 1760-1784: An Eighteenth-Century Biographical Dictionary* (University of Oklahoma Press, 1970)

Wheeler, *Historical Sketches*
>John Hill Wheeler, *Historical Sketches of North Carolina from 1584 to 1851* (Reprint, Clearfield Company Inc, 2000)

The Cornwallis Papers

PART TEN

The Virginia Campaign

20th May to 22nd July 1781

CHAPTER 49

Introduction to the rest of Part Ten

Cornwallis arrived at Petersburg in the morning of 20th May. Under his command were his own corps of some 1,780[1] men, Phillips' of 3,500, and a reinforcement of 1,700[2] concurrently arriving from New York. Opposed to him on the north side of James River was a Continental corps of a little over 800 rank and file under the Marquis de Lafayette, supported by militia. On 10th June it would be joined by about the same number of the Pennsylvania line under Wayne and on the 19th by 450 Continentals newly raised by Steuben in Virginia.

Cornwallis did not stay at Petersburg for long. Within four and a half days he had crossed James River – two miles wide – at Westover, and while awaiting the passage of the bulk of his combined corps, he dispatched Leslie, with a reinforcement, to command the garrison at Portsmouth. Then, having dislodged Lafayette from the vicinity of Richmond, he moved to Hanover Courthouse before crossing the South Anna River. Advancing slowly towards the Point of Fork, which lay some forty-five miles west of Richmond, he detached Simcoe to destroy the arms and stores there and at the same time dispatched Tarleton on the Charlottesville raid to disturb the revolutionary assembly and also wreak destruction. Cornwallis played his part too, but not wishing to engage in further operations which might interfere with Clinton's plans, he retired gradually to Williamsburg to await dispatches from the Commander-in-Chief. He arrived there on 25th June. As he retired, Lafayette had generally kept about twenty miles from him, but on the 26th a detachment of the enemy was repulsed when it attacked Simcoe at Spencer's Ordinary. On the same date Clinton's dispatches of the 11th and 15th arrived. Much to Cornwallis's dismay they ruled out solid operations in Virginia during the sickly months of summer.

---

[1] This figure is for all ranks.

[2] The figures of 3,500 and 1,700 are for effectives – an expression which excludes officers – and are given in Clinton's letter of 30th April. That they are for effectives is confirmed in his letter of 11th June, where the combination of the two figures is revised to 5,304.

Threatened by a siege of New York, Clinton requested the return of 3,000 troops and artillery unless Cornwallis was minded to adopt Clinton's ideas of operations in the upper Chesapeake (which Cornwallis was not). The rest of the troops Clinton desired to be used for desultory water excursions, a defensive, and the establishment of a station, preferably at Yorktown or Old Point Comfort, under cover of which 'large ships as well as small may lie in security during any temporary superiority of the enemy's fleet'.

On viewing Yorktown and Gloucester, Cornwallis saw that it would require a great deal of time and labour to fortify them, both posts being necessary to secure a harbour for vessels of all sizes. Yet fortification was not an option, as assistance would have been wanted from some of the troops now being requisitioned by Clinton. And even if it had been an option, 'they would have been dangerous defensive posts, either of them being accessible to the whole force of this province, and from their situation they would not have commanded an acre of country.' Under these circumstances he advised Clinton on 30th June of his decision to pass James River and retire to Portsmouth that he might arrange the embarkation for New York.

On 4th July Cornwallis quit Williamsburg and three days later completed his crossing of the river from Jamestown Island. While waiting to pass, he had been attacked by Wayne, but it was an inconclusive affair named after the Green Spring Plantation nearby.

On the 8th, while at Cobham, Cornwallis received Clinton's dispatch of 28th June. In it Clinton appeared to forget the threat to New York and announced his intention to raid Philadelphia. For this purpose he repeated his requisition of troops and artillery, to which was subjoined a requisition of vessels, twelve waggons, horses, and an engineer with entrenching tools etc for 500 men. Cornwallis immediately advised Clinton that he would comply, but went on to question the utility of a defensive post in Virginia. It is clear that he had Portsmouth in mind, as indeed is confirmed by Clinton in his reply of the 15th[3]. In Cornwallis's eyes such a post 'cannot have the smallest influence on the war in Carolina and... only gives us some acres of an unhealthy swamp and is for ever liable to become a prey to a foreign enemy with a temporary superiority at sea. Desultory expeditions in the Chesapeak may be undertaken from New York with as much ease and more safety whenever there is reason to suppose that our naval force is likely to be superior for two or three months.'

On the 9th Cornwallis began to march to Suffolk, where he expected to arrive in four or five days. From there he intended to send to Portsmouth the troops destined for the embarkation. As he began his march, he dispatched Tarleton on a raid to Prince Edward Courthouse and New London in Bedford County with orders to destroy supplies for Greene's army and to intercept any detachment coming from it. Tarleton marched hard but achieved little, as the supplies had been sent south a month or more earlier and no northward detachment had been made. He rejoined the troops in Suffolk fifteen days after his departure.

It was on 12th July that Cornwallis, now in Suffolk, received Clinton's letters of 29th May, 8th June, 19th June, and 1st July. The first informed Cornwallis how much Clinton was displeased with his move to Virginia, but otherwise the first three letters were mostly superseded by Clinton's of 28th June, upon which Cornwallis was now acting. The fourth

---

[3] See vol VI, ch 58.

simply confined itself to the timing of the embarkation for the raid on Philadelphia. Cornwallis immediately replied, confirming that every exertion would be made to fit out the expedition in the completest manner without loss of time and that, as apparently requested by Clinton, Leslie would accompany it.

Like a bolt out of the blue Cornwallis received at 1 am on the 20th Clinton's brief dispatch of the 11th countermanding the expedition, directing that Cornwallis remain on Williamsburg Neck or, if he had quit it, that he return should it be expedient, and desiring that at all events Old Point Comfort be held so as to secure Hampton Road. On the 21st Clinton's dispatches of the 8th and 11th arrived stating his reasons, the gist of which was that Cornwallis had misinterpreted his intentions and that a station protecting ships of all sizes was so important on Williamsburg Neck that one should be possessed even if it occupied all the force at present in Virginia. He accordingly requested that Old Point Comfort be examined and fortified without loss of time and that, if it could not be held without possessing Yorktown, the latter be occupied too.

Clarity was not Clinton's hallmark. As to his volte-face in countermanding the embarkation, there may have been other considerations besides the establishment of a station on Williamsburg Neck. Clinton had just received Germain's letter of 2nd May,[4] in which he stressed the importance of recovering the southern provinces and of prosecuting the war from south to north, made known his mortification at withdrawing troops from the Chesapeake, and conveyed the King's pleasure that all available troops be employed on southern operations. He did qualify his remarks by saying that during the sickly months of summer troops might be withdrawn for offensive operations north of the Delaware, particularly on the Hudson or in New England, but as Philadelphia lay on the west side of the river, it is uncertain whether such a dispensation extended there.

Later in this Part developments in the Carolinas are described in considerable detail. By mid May Forts Watson and Motte had fallen to Lee and Marion, Fort Granby to Lee, and Greene was about to lay siege to Ninety Six. Cruger, who was a tougher nut to crack, maintained a valiant defence until relieved by Rawdon one month later. The post was abandoned, so that in South Carolina the British were confined within the boundaries of the Santee, Congaree and Saluda.

In Georgia Brown was less fortunate than Cruger. Besieged by Lee and Pickens, he courageously held out for two weeks against overwhelming odds before surrendering on 5th June. Only the Low Country remained under tenuous British control.

This Part provides further evidence that, as stated in chapter 44[5], it would have been perfectly feasible for Cornwallis to have returned overland from Wilmington to South Carolina. According to the commissary, Captain Gregory Townsend, 'It appears by the returns from thence [*Wilmington*], 26th March, there are for 6,000 men *bread and flour sixty nine days, pork and beef thirty three days, rum 69 days*, and a good supply of salt, which I

---

[4] Published in Stevens, *Clinton-Cornwallis Controversy*, i, 464.

[5] See vol IV, p 101.

hope with the help of cattle from the country will make up the deficiency of salt provisions.'[6] So, sufficient was in store to supply Cornwallis for a short stay in Wilmington and for an overland march with 1,780 men to South Carolina — the same number that he took to Virginia. As to the practicality otherwise of the march, Balfour commented as follows: 'In my dispatch by a schooner which I had purchased for the purpose of communicating with your Lordship I had mentioned your coming into this province by the way of George Town and that I had placed a vessel with provisions there for the use of the army, as also had provided boats and flatts and stopped Watson's corps for a short time in order to support your passing the ferrys. McArthur with his corps at the Eutaws was also ordred to join you when he heared of your approach. This vessel being unfortunately taken, and not being able to procure any mode of safe conveyance to you at that critical period, was most distressing, as your return would then, I presume, have been determined upon when you knew that it might have been so easily effected from these asistances.'[7] Yes, Cornwallis did not receive Balfour's letter, but it should not have been beyond the wit of a perceptive commander to realise that he could have relied on support from South Carolina, even if he had felt it necessary to call on it himself.

As this Part concludes, the scene is set for the occupation of a place soon to be ignominious in British military history.

§ - §

Principal papers and works consulted in the writing of this chapter

Mark Mayo Boatner III, *Encyclopedia of the American Revolution* (D McKay Co, 1966)

The Cornwallis Papers (UK National Archives, Kew)

Sir John Fortescue, *A History of the British Army*, volume III (Macmillan and Co Ltd, 1902)

The Papers of General Nathanael Greene, volumes VIII and IX, edited by Dennis M Conrad, Roger N Parks, Martha J King et al (The University of North Carolina Press, 1995 and 1997)

Banastre Tarleton, *A History of the Campaigns of 1780 and 1781 in the Southern Provinces of North America* (London, 1787)

Christopher Ward, *The War of the Revolution* (The Macmillan Co, NY, 1952)

Franklin and Mary Wickwire, *Cornwallis: The American Adventure* (Houghton Mifflin Co, 1970)

§ - §

---

[6] See p 320.

[7] See p 275.

CHAPTER 50

The Phillips Papers[1]

1 - Between Phillips and Clinton

Clinton to Phillips, 10th March 1781[2]   95(9): LS

Head Quarters
New York
March 10th 1781

Major General Phillips

Sir

You will be pleased to proceed with the troops embarked under your command to Chesapeak Bay and there form a junction as soon as possible with Brigadier General Arnold, whom, and the corps with him, you will take under your orders.

---

[1] These papers came into Cornwallis's possession on his arrival in Virginia. They are in the order they were written or received by Phillips.

[2] An extract, omitting the last three paragraphs, is published in Stevens, *Clinton-Cornwallis Controversy*, i, 347. There are no other material differences.

Should any unforeseen accident prevent your forming an immediate junction with Brigadier General Arnold, you will, however, exert every endeavor to communicate with him, and as the principal object of your expedition is the security of him, the troops at present under his orders, and the posts he occupies upon Elizabeth River near the mouth of James River in Virginia, you will of course use every means to attain this very material purpose. The properest methods to be pursued on this occasion cannot be exactly pointed out to you, but they must be left to your discretion.

When you shall have formed your junction with Brigadier General Arnold, if you find that general acting under the orders of Earl Cornwallis, you will of course endeavor to fulfill those orders. If this should not be the case, after receiving every information respecting his probable situation, you will make such movements with the corps then under your orders as can be made consistent with the security of the post on Elizabeth River or you shall think will most effectually assist his Lordship's operations by destroying or taking any magazines the enemy may have on James River or at Petersburg on the Appamatox. After which, if it should be thought necessary, you will establish a post or posts at such stations on James River as shall appear best calculated to open the way for, and secure the safety as far as possible of, a rapid movement of troops, to give jealousy for Upper James River, and to interrupt the course of supplies to the Carolinas.

The object of co-operation with Lord Cornwallis being fulfilled, you are at liberty to carry on such desultory expeditions for the purpose of destroying the enemy's public stores and magazines in any part of the Chesapeak as you shall judge proper.

If the Admiral, disapproving of Portsmouth and requiring a fortifyed station for large ships in the Chesapeak, should propose York Town or Old Point Comfort, if possession of either can be acquired and maintained without great risk or loss, you are at liberty to take possession thereof, but if the objections are such as you think forcible, you must, after stating those objections, decline it 'till solid operation take place in Chesapeak.

As to whatever relates to the people of the country, their being received and armed, or being more for the King's Service that they should remain quietly at their houses, or respecting the oaths that should be offered to them, or for your general conduct in matters of this kind, I refer you to my instructions to Major General Leslie and Brigadier General Arnold[3], copies of which will be given to you.

And concerning your return to this place, you will receive either my orders or Lord Cornwallis's as circumstances may make necessary.

'Tis presumed his Lordship will be able to spare troops to station at Portsmouth etc, but should that not be the case, you are at liberty to leave either the Regiment of Prince Hereditaire or the 76th or both for that purpose under any officer, being a general officer, Lord Cornwallis may chuse to appoint, but if it should be an officer of your own appointing, with the rank of lt colonel, I think Lt Colonel Dundas, as being acquainted with the spot, should remain.

---

[3] *my instructions..*: see vol II, p 50, and vol III, pp 23 and 55.

It is probable, whenever the objects of this expedition are fulfilled and that[4] you have strengthened the present works and added such others as you shall think necessary, that you may return to this place. In which case you must bring with you Brigadier General Arnold, the light infantry, Colonel Robinson's corps[5] or the 76th, and, if it should be possible, the Queen's Rangers.

The moment you have communicated with Lord Cornwallis and heard from his Lordship, you are to consider yourself as under his Lordship's orders untill he or you shall hear further from me.

Some blank warrants for holding general courts martial were delivered to Brigadier General Arnold, which you will of course receive from him, and I do hereby authorize and impower you to approve of the several sentences of said courts, unless in such cases as are capital or may extend to the cashiering of commissioned officers, which are to be transmitted to me for my consideration.

Five thousand pounds sterling is shipped on board the *Richmond*, which on your arrival at the place of your destination is to be paid into the hands of such person as you shall appoint to act as Deputy Paymaster and be subject to your orders.

In order that I may be furnished with every information necessary to be communicated to the Secretary of State to be laid before the King, I am to request that you will from time to time transmit to me such intelligence as you may think interesting to His Majesty's Service.

Most heartily wishing you success, I have the honor to be, sir,
Your most obedient and most humble servant

H CLINTON

Clinton to Phillips, 14th March 1781[6]   *95(1): LS*

Half past 2
March 14th 1781

Major General Phillips

Dear Phillips

By the inclosed from the Admiral you will see that the want of intelligence has again lost us a fair opportunity of giving a 'mortal blow'. I hope, however, he will still overtake them

---

[4] *that*: the meaning is 'when'. As in modern French, a subordinate conjunction, if repeated in 18th-century English, was often replaced by 'that'.

[5] *Robinson's corps*: the Loyal American Regiment.

[6] Annotated: 'Received by Noble at 6 in the morning, March 15th.' The letter, omitting the last two sentences of the postscript, is published without the enclosure in Stevens, op cit, i, 352. There are no other material differences.

before they reach Chesapeak. They sailed in a snow storm on Wednesday and I fear he was not out of Gardiner's Bay till Saturday. He was, however, left pursuing on the 11th with all his coppers and a fair wind. I think, if he does not overtake them at sea, they will not risk an action in Lynhaven Bay and will therefore proceed with their *whole* fleet to York, as I told the Admiral they would, and there perhaps lay and, I had almost said, *fascinate* the Admiral till another fleet arrives. If from Europe, it ought not to come without a hint from thence; from the West Indies, it will not probably come unaccompanied by our friend Sir George. 'Tis possible it only means to see the transports off the Chesapeak and then proceed to the *West Indies* with the fleet of men of war. 'Tis possible also that the whole is gone to the West Indies, for it is a bold move to evacuate Rhode Island and proceed to the Chesapeak so encumbered, liable to be followed by an unencumbered superior copper fleet. God send our old Admiral success. I depend on early information from you and shall prepare for every possible event. Recollect that we have not a single transport 'till you send some.

With every wish for your health and success, believe me, dear sir,
Your very humble obedient servant

H CLINTON

[*Subscribed*:]

The schooner shall attend you, tho we can ill spare her. As often as possible communicate by these vessels. They work their passage better than the frigates.

PS

I have received your letters.

In addition to what I have written above, pray observe me well in what I am saying.

I think, if the French are gone to Chesapeak, they will shelter themselves in York River. The Admiral will immediately hold his usual language — that he waits for the army. That from South Carolina cannot come, as Colonel Balfour has very injudiciously sent home the transports. I cannot move a man till you send back transports, but if he proposes any thing to you, he must first declare in writing positively what he thinks his fleet will do, or at least attempt, before you can decide, and then, after consulting your officers, let me know your opinion what can be done and what land force it will require to do it. If *all* agree that they will be unattackable in that station, it must be blocked, and then we must do our best to assist Lord Cornwallis's operations or carry on desultory expeditions in Chesapeak till some other plan can be settled, but all must be settled in formal council. Beware of verbal conversations. He will forget them and deny all he says.

Enclosure
Arbuthnot to Clinton, 8th March 1781   99(30): C

Royal Oak in Gardiner's Bay
the 8th of March 1781

His Excellency General Sir Henry Clinton KB etc etc etc

Sir

I delay not an instant to forward the inclosed intelligence to your Excellency which I have just received from an undoubted hand. I have already communicated Captain Hudson's orders to you, and your Excellency's fiat will give effect to their execution.

I expect to sail with the squadron from this bay tomorrow morning.

I have the honor to be
Your Excellency's most obedient and most humble servant

M[T] ARBUTHNOT

Clinton to Phillips, 24th March 1781[7]   95(13): LS

New York
March 24th 1781

Major General Phillips

Dear Sir

I believe that Lord Cornwallis has finished his campaign, and, if report says true, very handsomely, by taking all Green's cannon and recovering the greatest part of his own men who had been made prisoners by Mr Green. If that should be the case and Lord Cornwallis does not want any cooperation to assist him, and you see no prospect of striking an important stroke elsewhere, I shall probably request you and General Arnold to return to me with such troops as I have already named in my instructions; but all this will depend on the information I shall receive from you and your opinion respecting the post at Portsmouth and such others as you propose to establish on James River, with their importance considered either as assisting Lord Cornwallis's operations or connected with those of the navy.

When you return, you will be pleased to bring with you a full proportion of howitzers, mortars, cohorns etc, so placed in the vessel in which they are embarked as to be ready to land directly, as it is very likely we may proceed upon some operation immediately on your arrival.

---

[7] Published in Stevens, op cit, i, 373. The only material difference is in the second paragraph, where Stevens has 'small' instead of 'full'.

I believe Fayette is entrenched at Anapolis and that his corps does not now exceed 900 men tho' he started with 1300. You may possibly attempt him in earnest. He will at all events serve as a mask to your return to us.

You will probably hear from Lord Cornwallis before you determine on any attempt at a distance from him. I wish much to know what force he thinks he can spare from the troops under his Lordship's immediate orders, for, till I do, 'tis impossible to fix any plan. Three compleat regiments will, I hope, arrive at Charles Town in the course of a few days if Captain Elphinston should think it too early in the season to come directly here, and three more are hourly expected from the West Indies, both which divisions will, of course, join me.

The French certainly expect an early reinforcement. If it comes from Europe, we must, I think, hear from thence long before it arrives. If from the Havannah, copper bottomed sloops or frigates which the Admiral will doubtless have on the look out will announce their arrival and give you time to determine what in that case will be best to be done. And here I take the liberty of hinting to you that (from the appearance on the map), when you have once obtained a naval force in Curratuck and Albemarle Sounds, by holding the bridges of Pequimans and Pasquotank Rivers you secure a short passage accross the Albemarle Sound and communication with Lord Cornwallis, or by destroying the bridges on those rivers you prevent the enemy's approach by the bridge at North West Landing. Upon those hints I request your opinion in cypher as soon as possible. In the meantime I shall prepare for what may probably be your determination after talking with Brigadier General Arnold.

I beg you will be so good to forward the inclosed to Lt Colonel Moncrief[8] by the first opportunity to Charlestown, and that you will bring Mr Fyers of the Corps of Engineers with you when you return to this place.

I have the honor to be, dear sir,
Your most obedient and most humble servant

H CLINTON

PS

Pray send Brigadier General Arnold here by the first good opportunity if you should not have particular occasion for his services.

---

[8] *the inclosed..*: no copy.

Phillips to Clinton, 29th and 30th March 1781

5(137): C

Portsmouth, Virginia
March 29th 1781

His Excellency General Sir Henry Clinton

Sir

By the *Medea* frigate your Excellency will have received my several letters of the 26th and 27th instant and the inclosures they contained. I hastened on the morning of the 27th to land the 76th Regiment, which was effected, and they arrived early in the day at Norfolk. The wind, which had been unfavourable, changed and carried the transports by four o'clock up to Hampton Road. It was my intention to have pushed up the light infantry transports, covered by some sloops of war, to above *Newport News* ready to have assisted Lt Colonel Dundas in his attempt near Williamsburg, but on my going on board the *Guadaloupe*, Captain Robinson, I was informed Lt Colonel Dundas was returned to Portsmouth, and Brigadier General Arnold, who arrived soon after, acquainted me that the dark and stormy night had prevented all possibility of pursuing the object of the intended expedition, which was to have surprized a body of militia assembled at Williamsburg. Upon this I decided for the transports going up to Portsmouth, which they did yesterday, but the weather has been and continues this morning so extremely stormy and raining that it will prevent any arrangements being made for the troops, and indeed it will require time to prepare *hutts* and *wigwams* for those which came with me before they can be all disembarked, but knowing, sir, your desire of having transports sent you, I have directed that ten of those which have been here of some time may proceed instantly to Hampton Road and I shall be able to add five to them, and in a few days these transports will proceed for New York.

I went yesterday morning to Captain Robinson and took with me the Brigadier. We found that gentleman ill but, however, he assured us there should be nothing wanting on his part to assist in and co-operate with the King's Service. We had as much conversation as could be, considering his ill state of health, and knowing that La Fayette's corps was by the last intelligence at Anapolis, where two sloops of war blocked them, I pressed for two other sloops being sent to Potowmack, in which idea I had General Arnold with me, which Captain Robinson consented to and we parted. Immediately on my arrival here I writ to that naval officer on the subject, a copy of which letter[9] I inclose, but have not yet received any answer, but imagine there can be no doubt of my requisitions being complied with. I have not on the instant mentioned any thing concerning James River as I think it adviseable to not open on that scene to the navy until I shall be ready by a settled plan with the Brigadier to propose *effectually*.

The naval force left by the Admiral under the command of Captain Robinson is as follows:

Frigates ⎡ *Guadaloupe* 28 guns
⎣ *Thames*   32

---

[9] *a copy of which letter*: if Phillips retained his own copy, it is missing.

        Bonnetta   18

        Hope   18

        Monk   18

        Savage   18

        Vulcan   18

        Swift   18

and, should I suppose it necessary, the *Foy* also, of 20 guns.

I really think this a sufficient naval force and of the nature best calculated for the Chesapeak. I do not mention the armed vessels as your Excellency knows there are four - three only effective, as *one* went unarmed some time since with a flag of truce and has been detained. If the sea and land service fortunately shall agree, and I will do all in my power to attain so very desireable an end, I think we cannot fail in naval strength. The force the enemy have against us cannot be exactly ascertained, but by the latest intelligence Brigadier General Arnold has been able to obtain there is about three thousand militia at and near *Suffolk* and the North West Bridge under Brigadier General Muhlenberg. General Weedon[10] commands at Williamsburg and the neighbouring districts on *Chickahominy, York, Hampton* etc etc with about fifteen or sixteen hundred militia. It may be presumed these troops will retire on their being certain of the reinforcement arrived here. I say being certain, for the Admiral having gone out of the Capes and returning made the country conceive an idea of the French having taken possession of this bay. I was glad to convince *Princess Anne* that it was not so by marching a battalion in their view, and our fleet of ships of war and transports appearing in Hampton Road soon after must prove to the deluded inhabitants that we are masters at sea and of the Chesapeak.

I am sorry to inform you, sir, that Brigadier General Arnold has not been able to procure any intelligence of or from Lord Cornwallis. It is presumed his Lordship may be at *Hillsborough* and that Green is on this side the branches *Dan* and *Staunton* of the *Roanoke*. General Arnold has sent within this last month several expresses to endeavour at a communication with Lord Cornwallis. Whether any have reached his Lordship is uncertain. I shall dispatch a small express boat to Wilmington as the seeming surest means of being able to send intelligence to his Lordship. I shall do this immediately on its being determined when to act upon James River in favour of the operations of the southern army.

---

[10] A pre-war innkeeper of Fredericksburg, Virginia, George Weedon (1734-1793) was a Continental brigadier general and had seen service during the New York, New Jersey and Philadelphia campaigns before going on to take part in the Battle of Germantown. Having become dissatisfied over a question of seniority, he had obtained leave of absence in autumn 1778. He was now active again, commanding a brigade of Virginia revolutionary militia, and would invest Gloucester with it later in the year. For an extended account of his involvement in the revolution, see Harry M Ward, *Duty, Honor, or Country: General George Weedon and the American Revolution* (American Philosophical Society, 1979))

I had little conversation with the Admiral. His concern at not having been more successful, his hurry for sailing in pursuit of the French fleet without knowing where they were, and indeed my pressing him for certain objects for this place rendered it almost impracticable to enter deeply on the subject of this post as it respected the navy. Upon the whole I am inclined to believe he does not wish to connect himself with any operations here more than to supply a naval force for security and for movements in these waters, as he observed that it was the business of *his fleet* to guard the Chesapeak and that he had nothing to do with any thing higher up than *Lyndhaven Bay*. This sort of converse and opinion the Admiral held also with General Arnold, who agrees with me that the Admiral does not wish or mean to give an opinion upon any post in Chesapeak. In this case I shall so soon as possible make a formal and official requisition from Captain Robinson for his ideas as a naval and the commanding officer here respecting that part of your Excellency's instructions to me which connects the opinion and, as far as can be, the decision of the navy officers upon the use of this or any other post here taken in a naval view of security and cooperation.

In my conversation with the Admiral I took a free liberty of observing that the cruizers hovered much in the latitudes near the Capes of Chesapeak, but that I hoped also that he detached his frigates for intelligence both to the southward and northward, even so far as Georgia and Rhode Island. I found a frigate had gone southward but none to the northward. He seemed determined to look into the *Delaware*, conjecturing it possible the French, being disappointed of landing their troops in Chesapeak, might do it there and march them by La Fayette's route. I believe this idea was given to the Admiral by General Arnold, and I think it not an unlikely one, but I suggested to the Admiral that the same plan might take place in Albemarle Sound or Cape Fear and hoped he would be prepared for such an event. He seemed to be of opinion that, if the French steered southward, they would go to the West Indies. This is all I can inform your Excellency of respecting my interview with the Admiral. The French fleet was seen on the 18th instant two days after the action in the latitudes of the Capes at some distance, I think by the *Medea* frigate. Of the action itself[11] it is too (very much so indeed) melancholy a subject to talk upon, and your Excellency will hear enough of it.

A *proper person* has been dispatched over land to *Edentown* to collect intelligence from *Albemarle Sound*. He may be expected back in six days.[12]

My time has been much employed. The fleet arrived on the 26th instant, which day was taken up in attendance on the Admiral. The next day we got to Hampton Road and arrived here yesterday. Tomorrow I hold a consultation with Brigadier General Arnold, Lt Colonels Abercrombie, Dundas and Simcoe, and on Saturday with the engineers and commanding officer of artillery, and shall pursue in consequence of the lights[13] and information I shall receive such measures as may seem best calculated for effecting the purpose of your

---

[11] *the action itself*: that of 16th March between Arbuthnot and Destouches off the Capes of Virginia. The French squadron, which had sailed to support Lafayette, retired to Rhode Island.

[12] See enclosure (2), p 30.

[13] *lights*: opinions.

Excellency's instructions and orders. In doing this I shall consult General Arnold, whose chearful intelligence and active zeal cannot be too much commended. I have, indeed, found in him every thing I could have wished to meet in an able second.

I have received your Excellency's dispatch by Andrew Coulter, serjeant of the 17th Dragoons, and you may depend, sir, from my attachment for you, from my fidelity to the King, from my love and veneration for my country, that I will pay the utmost attention to your Excellency's instructions, to the matters contained in your several letters, and to your orders.

I have called for all necessary returns and reports and will collect every information in my power to make the subject of a second letter as soon as possible.

Six o'clock in the morning
March 30th 1781

I had written the foregoing part of this letter yesterday but kept it open for any further matter I might think it necessary to send your Excellency as the tide would not favour the going out of the express boat until midnight, but I have been prevented dispatching of it until this day at noon, when it will undoubtedly sail.

The flag of truce vessel which the rebels had detained came back to us yesterday evening with Lieutenant Hare[14] of the navy, whose reports from intelligence he gained at Williamsburg and other places seems to be of the utmost importance. I inclose for your Excellency's perusal a sketch of this report as delivered by Lieutenant Hare to Major Damer, as also several letters I have written to the Admiral in consequence of it.

I will freely own to you, sir, to imagine that parts of this intelligence are fictions, calculated for the meridian of Williamsburg and the other posts of the enemy to keep their people in spirits, and also perhaps aiming to alarm us. The action said to have been between Lord Cornwallis and General Green was on the 15th instant near Guildford Court House, which I understand from conversations with your Excellency to lay between the *Haw* and the *Yadkin* Rivers, in which case Lord Cornwallis must have retired from Hillsborough. Green is said to have had upwards of four thousand men with him, and Lord Cornwallis only fifteen hundred. Now, as his Lordship's force was on his passage over the Dan more than double that number, one cannot account for the decrease of his army unless it may be supposed his Lordship had made large detachments to Cape Fear River, and it may be conjectured so if the rebel accounts are true that his Lordship, altho' master of the field of battle, did not pursue them. The rebels allow a loss of two hundred men and four pieces of (being all) their cannon, but make the loss of Lord Cornwallis much more considerable. Indeed, if it be true that one hundred and forty men were butchered in the enemy's retreat, it must be so. Another part of the intelligence is that Lord Cornwallis had taken post upon the *Regulators'* ground, which I apprehend to be Hillsborough, in which case his Lordship must have again advanced and might, if his Lordship pleased, have opened a communication with any detachment he

---

[14] Apart from belonging to the *Swift* sloop of war, Hare has not been identified. No lieutenant with his surname is listed by Syrett and DiNardo as serving in the Royal Navy at this time.

may have made to Cape Fear River and with Wilmington. This leads me to the second part of Lieutenant Hare's intelligence, namely, the French having landed two thousand four hundred men from their fleet at Cape Fear. It is to be imagined from instances of the same kind this may be false and that the enemy, having indeed received a very severe blow from Lord Cornwallis, raised this report in opposition to it, but should it be true, we may hope that Lord Cornwallis, receiving early intelligence of the event, may be able to push down and give the French, before they can be guarded against it, a severe check. I must refer all this to your Excellency's judgement, observing only that Lieutenant Hare is very positive in his declaration of having gained this intelligence. He says he has had very intimate conversations with a number of people at and about Williamsburg, with Baron Stuben and Monsieur La Fayette, the latter of whom is to command in this district whenever his troops now at Anapolis, said to be eighteen hundred men, shall arrive. They understood immediately upon our arrival here what we were, told Lieutenant Hare that Major General Phillips was arrived at Portsmouth with the light infantry and Grenadiers, in all about two thousand four hundred men.

I will now conclude, sir, with only one observation, that if the French troops are really landed as reported, they can have but one of two objects, either to attempt a junction with Green and act against Lord Cornwallis in the Carolinas or to attempt this post, under which last description the force opposed to us will be the French, Fayette's Continental corps, and the militia of this country, which under such circumstances will be very numerous. It is for you, sir, to determine whether Portsmouth is to be sustained, whether in that case a reinforcement may not be necessary. I submit it entirely to your Excellency's decision, having only one request to make upon the occasion, that if you shall think it necessary to send any troops to me, they may be from the corps your Excellency was so good to give me the high honour of commanding.

The consultation I mentioned in the body of my letter will take place this day at one o'clock. It will go in the first instance to the security of this post and in the next to the fulfilling the first object of your Excellency's instructions to me. Your Excellency is well acquainted with the activity, military knowledge and zeal of the several officers in question, and you may depend, sir, I shall join with them in every possible exertion for the good of His Majesty's Service.

Six o'clock in the evening
March 30th 1781

I have been prevented from sending away Serjeant Coulter as I proposed to do, and it gives me the opportunity of observing a little more upon the intelligence respecting the French landing at Cape Fear. I find that from the bar going in from the sea to Brunswick to Wilmington, where the King's troops had possession under the command of Major Craig, is forty miles, and if the necessary landing of provisions and artillery is brought into contemplation, it is scarcely possible to conceive there could be time for so full an operation as that described in the intelligence, for, taking into consideration the time from the French fleet being seen after the action off the Capes of Chesapeak by the *Medea* frigate on the 18th instant to the 27th, the day on which La Fayette received his intelligence at Williamsburg, it does not seem probable the French could have landed and taken possession of Wilmington, for, allowing three days for the express going from that place to Williamsburg, a distance of three hundred and twenty miles, there will remain only five days and an half for the French fleet compleatly refitting at sea, sailing to Cape Fear, debarking troops, provisions, artillery and stores, forcing and gaining possession of Wilmington, and Monsieur de Lausun sitting down to pen an account of his success from thence to La Fayette at Williamsburg. It surely must be an invention of the enemy. Give me leave to venture an idea: why may it not be the three regiments from England, which, arriving at Charlestown, would in course be sent directly to Cape Fear to reinforce Lord Cornwallis? Lieutenant Hare, who is now gone to the Admiral, mentioned to me his having heard that the French landed from transports. I knew the French fleet had none with them, but I put it down to a common mistake arising from so great a distance, but I am possessed now with a contrary idea and live in the hope that *the troops did* land from transports and that they were *British troops*, that La Fayette did receive intelligence of this landing from some American friend and chose to call it from the Duke de Lausun, who conceived the troops without further examination to be French, for such is the infatuation of these southern people that they have supposed from the moment the French left Rhode Island they were to possess the sea and land to the southward of New York. Thus, sir, I submit my conjectures to your Excellency. If they serve no other purpose, they will, I hope, convince you, sir, that we do not feel here much apprehension from the *present* French fleet or army in America.

I have examined the map of North Carolina with Mr Corneill[15], whom 'till this day I did not know was here. I was right in my description of the situation of Guildford Court House, but that gentleman informs me it is there what is usually termed the *Regulators*' ground, tho' it extends in a common acceptation as far as Hillsborough, and from Guildford as well as from Hillsborough is a great leading road to Cross Creek upon Cape Fear River, so that my idea of Lord Cornwallis having detached may still be just.

In your Excellency's letter to me of the 24th of March you are pleased to mention, sir, that Lord Cornwallis, as was reported, had retaken the prisoners taken by Green, meaning, I apprehend, those captured by Morgan in the unsuccessful action of Lt Colonel Tarleton. Had Lieutenant Torianno[16] of the 20th Regiment, an exchanged officer of the troops of Convention, been admitted to your Excellency's presence, he would, I believe, have informed you, sir, that he saw at Winchester, Frederick County, in Virginia between the Blue and the North Ridges the remains of the 7th and the 71st Regiments which Morgan had taken and which Lord Cornwallis would have retaken in his pursuit of Green had not the overflowing of the Staunton branch of the Roanoke prevented his crossing that river.

---

[15] The Hon Samuel Cornell was familiar with the Regulators' ground (to which Phillips later refers), having been wounded at the Battle of Alamance. A friend of Governor Tryon and a member of HM Council during Governor Martin's administration, he had been a wealthy merchant at New Bern, North Carolina, owning three vessels and engaging prominently, but only partly, in the slave trade. On the fall of the royal administration in 1775 he chose to repair to England, from where he returned to New Bern in December 1777 under a flag of truce to settle his affairs. He was allowed ten days to do so. Before departing for New York, he conveyed his estates by deeds to his children, but it was all to no avail. The property was later confiscated by the revolutionary authorities. There is a portrait of him among the Tryon Palace collection at New Bern. (DeMond, *Loyalists in NC*, 56, 188-9; Sabine, *Biographical Sketches*, i, 335-6; Charles Christopher Crittenden, *The Commerce of North Carolina, 1763-1789* (Yale University Press), 97)

[16] Commissioned an ensign in the 3rd Regiment (the Buffs) on 26th December 1770, Charles Torriano had been promoted to lieutenant in the 20th Regiment on 14th November 1775. (*Army Lists*)

I have had the consultation twice mentioned in this letter and have found such unanimity, such an evident desire of contributing to the utmost of their power, under those parts of your Excellency's instructions and orders which I opened to them, for His Majesty's Service that I have every reason to hope for the greatest assistance from the well intentioned exertions of these gentlemen.

The transports so much desired by your Excellency will be ready to sail, as far as depends on me, in three or four days, and it is with real pleasure I can inform your Excellency that I believe you, sir, will have a sufficient number sent to New York to transport at this season of the year. allowing one ton and an half per man, for three thousand men.

I now really conclude a very long letter, and I do it with assuring of you, sir, of my most perfect attachment, of my sincere respect and regard, and of my being, dear sir,

Your Excellency's most obedient and faithful humble servant

W PHILLIPS

Enclosure (1)
Intelligence, 29th March 1781   *5(130): C*

Minutes of intelligence by Lieutenant Hare of the Swift sloop of war, who came in on Thursday at six o'clock in the evening, March 29th 1781, from Williamsburg

That while he was sitting with Count Dillon[17], Monsieur de Charlieu[18] came in from the Marquis de la Fayette and delivered the following message to the Count: that La Fayette had just (Tuesday morning 27th instant) received an express giving him an account of the French fleet having landed the Grenadiers, Chasseurs and Lauzun's Legion, in all 2400 men. The Duc de Lauzun[19] commands the whole. That their intention was to attack our post at Wilmington consisting of 400 men under the command of General Prevost.

---

[17] Arthur Comte de Dillon (1750-1794) was serving in the Duc de Lauzun's Legion, which had arrived at Newport with Rochambeau's expeditionary force in July 1780. After the war he would become Governor of Tobago, a lt general, and a member of the Estates-General. One of the most brilliant aristocrats in Louis XVI's court, he was a sincere champion of liberty, but his political views did not extend beyond a constitutional monarchy. He took a notable part in defeating the Prussians in 1792-3 but was falsely accused of holding a correspondence with the enemy. Found guilty by a revolutionary tribunal, he was guillotined. (James Breck Perkins, *France in the Revolution* (Corner House Publishers, 1970), ch xvi; Marie-Nicholas Bouillet and Alexis Chassang, *Dictionnaire universel d'histoire et de géographie...* (Paris, 1878); Pierre Larousse, *Grand Dictionnaire universel du XIXe siècle* (Paris, 1866-1879))

[18] Charlieu has not been identified.

[19] Armand Louis de Gontaut-Biron, Duc de Lauzun (1747-1793), was commander of the Legion which bore his name. A mixed force of some 1,000 men, it comprised infantry, cavalry, and artillery. With it he would form part of the troops investing Gloucester during the siege of that place and Yorktown. A member of the Estates-General in 1789, he supported the revolution and as a lt general commanded the revolutionary armies of the west against the Vendéan insurgency. When he was led to resign by the insubordination of his troops and the suspicions of his political supervisors, he was accused of treason, found guilty by a revolutonary tribunal, and guillotined. (Marie-Nicholas Bouillet and Alexis Chassang, op cit; *Encyclopædia Britannica* (11th edition))

The date of the arrival of the French fleet off Cape Fear Mr Hare does not know. He imagines the express would not require more than 48 hours to reach Williamsburg (where he, Mr Hare, then was) from Cape Fear.

From the similarity of Mr Hare's dress to the rebel uniforms or regimentals, he was in general taken by them for one of their officers; and particularly at the time the above message was delivered, Monsieur de Charlieu, who delivered it, was under that deception.[20]

Mr Hare further says that Count Dillon, Monsieur de Charlieu and another French officer, who had joined Monsieur de la Fayette as volunteers upon a supposition the French would have landed their troops in the Chesapeak, had set out for Rhode Island before he left Williamsburg. The Marquis de la Fayette was the only officer of distinction he left at Williamsburg.

Mr Hare likewise mentions that intelligence had been received of an action on the 15th instant between Lord Cornwallis and General Green in which we had taken four pieces of brass cannon and had kept the field but had not pursued them. This last circumstance was much dwelt upon. It was said that Lord Cornwallis had detached 300 men to possess themselves of two pieces of cannon, which they effected. Green detached Colonel Howard to retake the cannon, which Colonel Howard accomplished, but Lord Cornwallis, moving a large body of troops, took the cannon a second time and drove Colonel Howard. In his retreat Colonel Howard thought proper to put 140 prisoners to death[21], saying that he had been taught to skiver by General Grey[22].

Mr Hare likewise adds that Green was supposed after this action to be without cannon. The action of the 15th instant happened one mile from Guildford Court House, and at the time the express left the rebel army Lord Cornwallis was on *Regulators*' ground.

The above taken by me from Mr Hare.

G DAMER[23], Major, 87th Regiment

---

[20] The message was false.

[21] This report about the killing of prisoners and of John Eager Howard's involvement in it was false. An exceptionally gifted and humane officer, who greatly distinguished himself in the Carolinas, he was Lt Colonel of the 2nd Maryland Continental Regiment.

[22] Charles Grey (1729-1807) had come out to North America as a major general in 1777 and taken part in the Philadelphia campaign. On 21st September 1777, in a surprise attack by night on sleeping troops of Anthony Wayne near Paoli, he ordered his men to remove their flints and use bayonets. The enemy lost 150 men, of whom 53 were killed and 40 badly wounded. The action earned Grey the sobriquet of 'No-flint' and was represented by the revolutionaries as a massacre. One year later, at Old Tappan, he conducted by night a similar surprise attack, which was equally successful. A hardline officer who initially favoured the fullest prosecution of the war, he became disillusioned that British arms could succeed and eventually resigned, returning to England in early 1779. He died an earl and was buried at Howick, Northumberland. (*ODNB*; Boatner, *Encyclopedia*, 828-9, 1085-6)

[23] A nephew of Lord George Germain, the Hon George Damer (1746-1808) was the second but first surviving son of Lord Milton (1718-1798), who in 1792 would be created the Earl of Dorchester. Educated at Eton and Cambridge, he embarked on the grand tour in 1764 but had to flee Italy, having killed a coachman in a drunken

Enclosure (2)
Phillips to Arbuthnot, 29th March 1781[24]   *5(132): C*

Portsmouth
March 29th 1781

His Excellency Vice Admiral Arbuthnot

Sir

A flag of truce vessel which had been detained by the enemy is returned and the officer, Mr Hare of the *Swift* sloop of war, is just arrived. He gives me such very material intelligence as engages me to send him to your Excellency that he may by word of mouth explain all he knows, which cannot be so fully communicated in writing.

If the French have landed their troops southward of *the Chesapeak*, it will be indeed a most alarming event to both Lord Cornwallis and to this post and will prove that my apprehensions were not ill founded when I suggested a possibility of such an event happening.

It is not for me, sir, to presume pointing out any mode to be pursued in this most interesting situation, but will take only a liberty, I hope a decent liberty, of observing that unless it can be ascertained where the French fleet are and what have been the operations of that fleet since the sea action of the 16th instant, it will be impossible for the King's troops here to hazzard any operations either in favour of Lord Cornwallis or offensive against the enemy in the Chesapeak.

Mr Hare informs me of an action between Lord Cornwallis and the rebel General Green. We are uncertain of the event. At any rate a corps of French troops being landed southward must prove, as I have before observed, of the most serious and perhaps fatal consequences.

I must refer, sir, to your Excellency's clear judgement in this critical circumstance of affairs and have no doubt but your Excellency's decision will be guided by mature deliberation and the most active operations.

It will give me great satisfaction to know your Excellency's determination, upon which we shall depend, upon which we shall govern our conduct, upon which our future operations will, I must say can or cannot, be pursued.

---

      street fight. He went on to serve in the Commons between 1768 and 1774 as the Member for Cricklade and chiefly voted with the opposition. By 1776 he had amassed debts large enough for him to 'retire' to France but returned before 1778 and was re-elected to the Commons as the Member for the Anstruther East Burghs. On 5th October 1779, with the help of Germain, he was commissioned one of the two majors in Lord Chewton's 87th Regiment and came out to North America. Now the Member for Dorchester, he returned home in time to vote in 1783 against Shelburne's peace terms and for Fox's India Bill. Having opposed Pitt in 1784, he proceeded to become Chief Secretary in Ireland and relinquished a seat in the Commons only when he succeeded to the Earldom of Dorchester on the death of his father. He died while Lord Lieutenant of Dorset. (Valentine, *The British Establishment*, i, 235-7; *Army Lists*)

[24] Annotated: 'Dispatched at half past six o'clock evening by Lieutenant Hare of the *Swift* sloop of war.'

I rely on your Excellency's goodness to send Mr Hare back to me directly as I have not taken any information from him respecting his mission with the flag of truce, conceiving the intelligence he carries to your Excellency of the *first* consequence.

Perhaps your Excellency may not think it improper to send an express with the utmost dispatch to Sir Henry Clinton with this important intelligence.

I have the honour etc

W PHILLIPS

Enclosure (3)
Phillips to Arbuthnot, 29th March 1781[25]   *5(145): C*

Portsmouth
March 29th 1781

His Excellency Vice Admiral Arbuthnot

Sir

I have the honour to inclose to your Excellency a duplicate of a letter sent by Mr Hare, Lieutenant of the *Swift* sloop of war, returned this day with a flag of truce vessel from the rebels and gone by land to Lyndhaven Bay with directions to make such signals as will, I trust, have been observed by the officers of Your Excellency's ship, and that in consequence a boat may have been sent for him, but lest any accident may have prevented that communication, I have sent an express boat with this letter, and on its arrival, should Lieutenant Hare not be with you, I entreat Your Excellency will have the goodness to send a boat for him, and I will take the liberty of requesting that Mr Hare may be sent back to me immediately as some part of his intelligence seems of so serious a nature that upon a further investigation may lead me to pursue an immediate operation against the enemy.

I am extremely fearful of giving offence or of giving an opinion on matters which it cannot be supposed I am perfectly acquainted with, but feeling as I do the utmost anxiety in this very critical situation of affairs, particularly respecting the French fleet, I hope your Excellency will kindly excuse my solicitude and that you will, sir, not take ill my submitting to your Excellency's consideration the seeming necessity there appears for exploring the present situation of the French fleet, and I will with the utmost deference and respect for you, sir, offer it as my opinion that Albemarle Sound and Cape Fear should be most thoroughly examined, and I will hope whatever report may be made from such examination may be immediately communicated to me and that, if your Excellency should be sailed from Chesapeak, that the persons you entrust with such commission may communicate with me upon the occasion.

---

[25] Annotated: 'Dispatched at half past 9 at night by an express boat under the care of John King of the Queen's Rangers.'

If I have trespassed upon your Excellency's patience, I hope you will impute it to the true cause, an anxious zeal for the King's Service.

I have the honour to be etc

W PHILLIPS

Enclosure (4)
Phillips to Arbuthnot, 30th March 1781 5(147): C

Portsmouth
March 30th 1781

His Excellency Vice Admiral Arbuthnot

Sir

My endeavours to send letters to your Excellency last evening and last night proved ineffectual. Lieutenant Hare, who went by land, could not communicate with your fleet in Lyndhaven Bay and the express boat could not make the passage, but I still think it necessary to send Lieutenant Hare to your Excellency that you may gather from his own mouth the intelligence he brings.

I have been considering upon the subject of Mr Hare's intelligence and will offer to your Excellency some little remarks I have made respecting time. The French fleet were discovered by the *Medea* frigate, as your Excellency informs me, after the action and on the 18th instant 20 or 30 leagues off at sea in the latitudes of the Capes of the Chesapeak. The intelligence is said to have arrived to the Marquis de la Fayette on the 27th instant, which gives, exclusive of the 18th, nine days for the execution of the following operations: first, the refitting of their fleet to enable them to sail, of which you, sir, will be a competent judge; second, the time it would require for sailing to Cape Fear, which depending on winds, the log books of your Excellency's fleet may possibly assist in the calculation; third, the necessary time to make the debarkation; and lastly, the time necessary for sending an express to Williamsburg on James River, which I will take the liberty of deciding upon by giving three entire days for the express to travel that distance, so that there will be six days for your Excellency to form a judgement upon the operations in question, and I shall take it as a singular favour if you will have the goodness to give me your opinion upon them.

I most earnestly supplicate your Excellency to have the goodness to pardon the trouble I give you, but I am assured your anxious solicitude in all matters which concern the King's Service will incline you, sir, to excuse that which I may shew upon the present occasion.

Should it really be true that the French have landed their troops to the southward, the fleet will in course pursue some other object or perhaps return, having compleated one, that of a reinforcement to the rebel armies southward, to Rhode Island, but of the destination of the French fleet as also whether any French troops are landed to the southward or in the Delaware

I make no doubt but that your Excellency will be informed by your frigates and with great respect entreat of you, sir, to have the goodness to give me the earliest intelligence of these interesting events, which you must be sensible, sir, will materially affect the operations of the King's troops in the Chesapeak. I request you will have the goodness to send back Lieutenant Hare immediately.

I have the honour etc

W PHILLIPS

Phillips to Clinton, 3rd and 4th April 1781[26] 5(155): C

Portsmouth, Virginia
April 3rd 1781

His Excellency General Sir Henry Clinton

Sir

The troops are disembarked. The light infantry with Simcoe's corps are canton'd in Princess Anne County, making Kemp's Landing the head of the cantonements. The 76th Regiment is at Norfolk, attached to the duties of this place, where the 80th and Hessian regiments with Robinson's corps form the garrison. I have from the moment of my landing here pursued the first object of your Excellency's instructions, 'the security of the post upon Elizabeth River near the mouth of James River', and your Excellency may be assured I shall use every means to attain this very material purpose, so necessary and which alone can enable me, with four thousand militia in our front and near us, to pursue the second part of your instructions, sir, a move in force upon the enemy's communications between Virginia and North Carolina at Petersburg in assistance to Lord Cornwallis, and I shall do this the moment it may be possible, consistent with the security of the post on Elizabeth River.

I send you, sir, a sketch[27] of the different works with some little additional strength for the security of the flanks. I have given 300 men for the works exclusive of fascine making and other necessary business, and I am taught to believe a very little time will render this post, with such force as I shall on moving leave in it, capable of resisting and repelling any attack by coup-de-main.

It is unlucky for us that we know so little of Lord Cornwallis, in favour of whom and his operations we are directed by your Excellency to exert our utmost attention. I shall do all in my power to assist and cooperate with his Lordship and shall, from inclination as well as in obedience to your Excellency's instructions, do all I can to effect this most desireable end.

---

[26] Extracts containing inconsequential differences are published without the enclosures in Stevens, op cit, i, 377.

[27] *a sketch*: no extant copy.

I apprehend from various rebel accounts that Lord Cornwallis, although he kept the field, has suffered very much after the action of the 15th ultimo and to be fortifying to the west of the *Haw* River near Guildford, which seems a good position, having that river in front of the communication quite down to *Crosscreek* and *Cape Fear*. Should his Lordship want support, he must in course draw it from Charles Town to Cape Fear River by directing Lord Rawdon to abandon the frontier and keep only a garrison in Charles Town. I have not any belief in the report of the French being landed any where to the southward, and if they had been left in the Delaware I must ere this have heard it.

Your Excellency will perceive by certain intelligence I have had that La Fayette's corps was still at Anapolis on the first instant. 'Tis reported they are to march. If Green is pressed, I should suppose they would join him; if not, come against this post. I embrace your idea, sir, that should La Fayette remain at *Anapolis*, which must proceed from the enemy's fear of being attacked in Maryland, it will be possible to carry him, Anapolis and Baltimore, and if you will send me the British grenadiers and 42nd Regiment, I will with almost certain hopes of success go upon the attempt and will make an expedition in Virginia at the same instant as shall effectually prevent any support from thence to Maryland. This leads me, sir, to observe that at this season the troops cannot be so well as when employed. The corps I brought here are much improved in health. So would those your Excellency might send me and, having performed the material service I mention, would be ready to rejoin you, sir, in May or might take possession of the lower counties of Delaware and act in cooperation or move from thence to form a junction with your Excellency. Should you, sir, incline to reinforce me for this evident essential purpose, the troops ordered might arrive, if sent instantly, about the time the expedition up James River would return and need not disembark but proceed on the instant to the attack of an unprepared enemy.

I beg now, sir, your attention to the situation we are in here as it respects a view towards Carolina. If you intend to preserve this post as a station to which Lord Cornwallis may retire or come to should he be very successful, it must be taken up upon a more extensive plan. It will be necessary perhaps to have a post fortified at some good point in Nansimond near to Suffolk, and on our left the *North West Landing* must be possessed in the same manner. The first will prevent any erruption in force from the rebels while we are masters of the sea, and the having North West Landing gives support and communication to an armament sent into Curratuck and Albemarle Sounds and all the depending waters, in which latter sound a stationary squadron should be ordered in consequence, which would effectually secure with Cape Fear River and the inlet of Ocacoke the whole waters of North Carolina. In this case it would require full the force at present here to support so large a plan, but with this force, supposing the Chesapeak secure, it would be scarcely possible for any numbers of the enemy to assail us with success. It comes then into consideration whether upon so very uncertain a communication with Lord Cornwallis as appears to us to be the case your Excellency will lock up 3,400 men at Portsmouth and its dependencies, which I think might extend occasionally even so far as Albemarle Sound. Lord Cornwallis can best, indeed can only, inform your Excellency of his situation, but as a matter of opinion I will imagine his Lordship *cannot*, possibly may not, have intended to pass the Roanoke but will be content with fixing himself along the *Haw* from Guildford to Cape Fear River and Wilmington. If his Lordship finds the country, as has been supposed, ready to arm in his favour, and if they are to be armed, his Lordship's posts will be protected by their assistance and his Lordship may then (about June) move northwards with a corps of troops to act in Chesapeak. Should the country not arm in favour of Government, I imagine Lord Cornwallis will not pursue his movements through the back of the Carolinas but take up three great posts, probably Charles Town, somewhere on Cape Fear River, and in Albemarle Sound, which will give him, with a reserve of troops to be sent on water expeditions, a communication with, and in a degree the possession of, all the great waters of the Carolinas. In this case it may also be in Lord Cornwallis's power to move a corps of troops (in June) to act in the Chesapeak. Thus, sir, you have my *creed*. I give it freely but with the utmost respect to you, sir, and to your Excellency's judgement, and you will find by *this creed* that I do not suppose it probable that a corps of troops stationed here will be able to assist his Lordship's operations other than by breaking upon the enemy's communications between James River and the Roanoke. To offer any view of the situation northward or what might be effected there would be arrogant for me to presume doing. If you, sir, incline to have the Chesapeak explored, Maryland attacked, a post established for security to the left of any corps of troops to be thrown on the neck between *Elk* and *Christian* Rivers, I hope you will have the goodness to consider these cannot be effected unless you are pleased, sir, to send directly the reinforcement I mention or, with the British grenadiers, some other corps equal to the 42nd Regiment.

In your Excellency's instructions you are, sir, pleased to direct that whenever the objects of the expedition are fulfilled I may probably return to New York and that I must bring with me General Arnold etc etc, but in several letters you have, sir, been pleased to write to me is contained a desire that General Arnold may be sent so soon as possible. I give your Excellency my strong assurances that I will not keep General Arnold a moment longer than shall be necessary, but it will be impossible to part with him at any rate untill after the James River expedition is compleated and untill it shall be determined by Your Excellency whether it may be an object of your contemplation to reinforce me for the purpose of effecting an expedition in great force against Maryland. Brigadier General Arnold is an officer of great utility here. His entire knowledge of all water enterprizes with his useful information respecting this country render him necessary here some little time longer. I certainly will not keep him from your Excellency but as short a time as possible.

I come now to the particulars of this post, and as it is not possible in so short a time to go through the proper form of a regular report of the commanding engineer who came with me, I will, untill that can be done, very freely offer my opinion that it has not been, I should imagine, properly explained to your Excellency by Generals Matthew[28] and Leslie. The object of the post, from its situation respecting James River and the Chesapeak, with its connections with the waters to and in Albemarle Sound and the consequent connections it may have with an army in the Carolinas, are subjects I do not think myself at liberty to touch upon. I mean to confine myself merely to the locality of the post itself, and under that description I declare I think the present situation not calculated for a post of force or for one for a small number of troops. In the first idea I think three points should be taken as at *Mill Point* and *Norfolk* positively. The third must depend on more examination of the Elizabeth River than I have yet been able to give. These points taken would mutually assist the navy

---

[28] Edward Mathew (1729-1805) had occupied Portsmouth in May 1779 during the highly successful expedition to Virginia commanded by himself and Commodore Sir George Collier. He had come out to North America in 1776 as a brigadier general commanding a brigade of Guards and had taken part in the New York campaign. Promoted to major general in 1778, he saw action at Springfield, New Jersey, in June 1780 before returning to England not long afterwards. He died a full general. (Boatner, *Encyclopedia*, 685, 1149)

stationed here, which might lay within and be protected; and one *point* forced, a retreat is left by the other two; and your Excellency will immediately observe that it must require a large force indeed to attack the three points at once.

Should it be required by your Excellency to merely keep a post here without intending more than a station, I think *Mill Point*, where the old fort stood, well calculated for such purpose and would require not more than a strong battalion equal to 600 men, effective rank and file, to be the garrison.

In both instances the Chesapeak must be secure[29], for, even allowing every exertion of defence against an enemy's fleet, it would be difficult to preserve the river under the first idea of an extensive plan. Under the latter I consider it scarcely possible to be done. Old Point Comfort shall be explored, as it seems a point which a small force might defend and the shipping have scope to act in and by trying various methods of winds and tides would be able possibly to escape from even a superior naval force, whereas, once blocked up in Elizabeth River, the ships must at last fall with the post.

I come now to the Norfolk and Princess Anne Counties, where we cannot much depend for assistance. They are timorous, cautious, at best but half friends, and perhaps some, if not many, concealed enemies. Supposing them perfectly ours, we should not be able to arm more than 5 or 600 men, who would become a charge to us while we remained and, being left, would be undone. At present they act a sort of saving game but are of no use to us.

Upon the whole, sir, it may be perceived that I lean in favour of a small post where the army can assist the navy and the latter have a chance of escaping, supposing a superior force to arrive in the bay, and where the post can be maintained with 500 or 600 men for some time, even perhaps until some reinforcement, *naval* and *land*, might be sent to raise a siege.

I am now, sir, to request your pardon for giving you the trouble of reading so long a letter and for offering so freely my sentiments to your Excellency. It is an honest zeal which speaks. It is a confirmed attachment for you which has led me on. It is ardent desire of serving my country and King that prompts me to hazard my opinion, which I submit with every possible respect and deference to your judgement.

I request most anxiously that you will not, sir, imagine that I ask for more troops from a desire of parading a consequence to myself. I do assure you I do not. If you mean only little enterprizes in the vicinity, we are enough. If you wish a strong and serious cooperation with Lord Cornwallis and a positive blow struck in Chesapeak leading to a more enlarged plan of establishing a corps on the *lower counties*, it cannot be done with the force I now have. It may be, I trust, with that reinforcement I have before mentioned. It all depends on your Excellency's judgement and orders, to which I shall cheerfully submit, and you may depend, sir, on my utmost exertions as well for your honour as my own and for the publick service.

I have a favour to ask, which is that you will, sir, have the goodness to let me know your Excellency's intentions so soon as convenient to you, as the being certain whether I am to

---

[29] *must be secure*: i.e needs to be secured by British ships of war.

pursue contracted or enlarged plans will render it in my power to not delay in either.

I began this letter yesterday but have not been able to finish it before this day, the 4th instant. I send your Excellency a letter writ to me from the commanding engineer and my answer to it and also this evening's report of the state of the works[30], which may serve to shew your Excellency the present situation. The engineer has omitted to mark the Negro's employed on two damms to raise the waters of the creeks, which appear strong in the plan but are indeed of very little real strength.

The Negro's I mention are to the number of 250, who have come in and have been given to Captain Frazer of the Pioneers to be distributed to the several publick departments and for the works. These people have been clothed by order of Brigadier General Arnold but are not yet put on any establishment of pay. I really think a Corps of *Black Pioneers* may prove of real use, but then they should have a very small pay and out of that furnish themselves with clothing. I request your Excellency's orders on this. These Negro's have undoubtedly been of the greatest use.

There should be commissions of some sort sent for the masters of armed vessels. I should suppose your Excellency's commissions the best, otherwise letters of marque. There are already four armed vessels and I believe it will be in my power to arm two more. This leads me to report that there are twelve very fine boats which will be compleat in six days, capable of carrying 1,000 men and 14 days' provisions, and twelve more will be got on as fast as possible. They are the best boats I have seen on the American Service, and I sincerely wish your Excellency had one hundred of them, including gun boats, boats for cavalry, and for infantry.

I send your Excellency copies of all the material correspondence I have had with the Naval Department[31] and you will perceive by it, sir, that I have been at times dissappointed in the assistance I have requested and expected from them.

By the letters from the Admiral will be shewn that he first intended sailing to the northward, then to the southward. He certainly sailed on the evening of the 2nd instant.

The Admiral sent me an extract of your letter, sir, to him dated the 27th ultimo. I sometimes imagine it was *our fleet* the master of the Liverpool ship saw, as we were on the 21st ultimo at noon in latitude 39°: 30 steering, the wind having just then changed, north west, but the longitude not the same by three or four degrees. I was sorry to not have heard from Your Excellency by the *Kitty*.

I have the honor to be etc

W PHILLIPS

---

[30] *this evening's report..*: no extant copy.

[31] *the material correspondence..*: if Phillips retained copies, they are missing.

Enclosure (1)
Intelligence from Anapolis, 3rd April 1781   5(165): C

Minutes of intelligence by Lieutenant White

Lieutenant John White[32] of His Majesty's Sloop of War the *Hope* left her off Anapolis the 1st instant in the afternoon. When he came away, a body of the rebels lay encamped to the left of Anapolis Court House to the amount of 1,500 men under the command of the Marquis La Fayette, the Marquis himself at that time being absent at Williamsburg. From the best intelligence received on board the *Hope* they were much in want of provisions, their supply cut off by water by the position of the *Hope* and *General Monk* sloops, and Baltimore the only place from whence they can receive provisions of any sort.

Within the harbour of Anapolis: the *Nesbit* armed brig of 18 guns, six and nine pounders; the *Porpoise* sloop of 16 guns, nine pounders; two schooners of 8 guns each, supposed 4 pounders; and about sixty sail of small craft which brought the rebel troops.

The entrance of the harbour is defended by two forts, one on each side. That on the left contains 4 pieces of cannon, supposed to be eighteen pounders; that on the right, two pieces lately brought down and calibre not known.

At Baltimore there are two armed brigs of 16 and 18 guns, 4 and 6 pounders.

In general there was the greatest apprehension of the men deserting from Anapolis, evident from the commanding officer of the rebel troops refusing to grant a certain number of men for the protection of the ship which was burnt in the West River, and from the general precautions taken such as the militia taking the duty of advanced guards upon certain bluff points where otherwise it would be natural for detachments of this corps to be posted.

On Kent Island opposite Anapolis, and about six miles distant, the militia have turned out, but very reluctantly, and it is certain from the intelligence given by the ferry man and others that no resistance would be made by them to any party of ours that chose to land there. The mere necessity they are under of turning out and the heavy fines they are subjected to in case of refusal are their only motives for being in arms.

Taken Tuesday, 3rd April 1781

G DAMER
Major, 87th Regiment

---

[32] Apart from belonging to the *Hope* sloop of war, John White has not been identified. No lieutenant with his name is recorded by Syrett and DiNardo as serving in the Royal Navy at this time,

Enclosure (2)
Intelligence from Currituck, 2nd April 1781 5(163): C

A B sayeth that on Thursday afternoon he passed the South Branch[33] and got to the Great Bridge a few minutes after the drum beat, tarried there about half an hour, and upon his leaving the above post the captain on guard ordered two shots to be fired over his head to drown suspicion. Came up with a rebel centry a little after day break on the Friday morning, posted about half a mile on this side the North West Bridge. On the other side there is a breast work thrown up, and opposite the bridge are three single threes and one single four cannon. The bridge is about half a quarter of a mile from General Gregory's encampment. The General has about three hundred and fifty men with him, not more, tho it is said he has six hundred. Many of the former number are very young and exceedingly ill armed, many of them having no musquets but only bayonets fixed upon sticks. The Great Bridge twelve miles distant from the North West Bridge. It was said at General Gregory's that Colonel Parker[34] had moved from Edmond's Hill to Suffolk with 450 men, as the deponent has been credibly (as he thinks) informed. C D gave the deponent this information and that relative to the strength of General Gregory's party.

That as the deponent was standing near the General's (Gregory) marquee, he overheard a discourse between him and some officers relative to the action between Lord Cornwallis and Green (a week last Wednesday). The account they gave was that neither kept the field, that Green had 350 killed, Lord Cornwallis 700, and that the latter sent to the former to take care of the wounded as he was not able to do it.

He was asked what number of troops were in this place[35], they not having heard for certain of the reinforcement[36] having come in. He told them he did not know, as he never had an opportunity of getting near them, but believed 1,500. The General asked him whether he had ever been concerned in the war. The deponent said he had not, upon which the General said he had notwithstanding given a good guess, as he did not believe them to be above 1,100.

---

[33] *the South Branch*: of Elizabeth River.

[34] Josiah Parker (1751-1810) was born at 'Macclesfield', his family's estate on James River in the northern part of Isle of Wight County. A member of his county's committee of safety, he went on to serve as a field officer in the Virginia Continental line, taking part in the actions at Trenton and Princeton and in the Battle of Brandywine. He resigned his commission in July 1778 for family reasons. By 1781 he had been elected for two terms in the Virginia revolutionary assembly and was now a colonel commanding Virginia revolutionary militia south of James River. After the war he was awarded 6,666 acres and appointed naval officer at Portsmouth before serving between 1789 and 1801 as a representative in Congress, where he took a keen interest in naval affairs and spoke against slavery. He was buried at 'Macclesfield' in an unmarked grave. (Joel D Treese and Dorthy J Countryman, *Biographical Directory of the United States Congress 1774-1996* (Cq Pr, 1996); Heitman, *Historical Register*, 426; Gwathmey, *Historical Register*, 604)

[35] *this place*: Portsmouth.

[36] *the reinforcement*: Phillips' corps.

As they were suspicious of a reinforcement having arrived, and as they took him for a deserter from a gun boat at Great Bridge, he was asked many questions relative thereto. One of the officers observed his reason for not believing any reinforcement had arrived was that he did not suppose the English were able to give one.

At 10 o'clock in the morning of Friday, soon after the above conversation, he left the encampment and travelled to C D's, got there about half after four in the afternoon. C D informed him an express had gone by from Halifax sent by Governor Nash, that the news he (C D) heard was that Lord Cornwallis was at Guildford Court House, Green ten miles from him towards Halifax, that Lord Cornwallis, expecting to be attacked, marched out six miles and met General Green, that the former lost 700 men, the latter 350. The next day Lord Cornwallis buried his dead and then returned to Guildford Court House. The action happened on Wednesday week last past. Green retreated to his post ten miles from Guildford Court House.

And likewise the same express carried orders to Colonel Jarvis[37] to draft every fifteenth man to reinforce General Green, and in consequence eighty five were drafted in Curratuck County to serve one year.

There is also another draft to be made to relieve the men at the North West Bridge. That an Act has passed whereby all the inhabitants of Curratuck are required to give in a fifth of all the provisions, stores, or cattle or live stock they may have in their possession. That a report of the French having landed at Powel's Point C D knew to be false as well as their having landed any where to the southward as low down as Cape Fear. The latter part he knew from a boat that came from Occacock, the former from his own knowledge.

That from C D's he went down to the Curratuck shore and from thence into Princess Anne County, where he heard of some youngsters who belong to [the] neighbourhood of Doge's Bridge and make a frequent practice of coming there for clean cloathes and are the people whom he supposes to have shot one of our horses in that neighbourhood.

That General Gregory's people are supplied with fresh beef from Nott's Island, where they make a frequent practice of going and where there is plenty of cattle.

---

[37] Samuel Jarvis (1736-?) was a leading revolutionary of Currituck County, North Carolina, which he had represented in the Provincial Congress and the upper house of the revolutionary legislature. In September 1775 the Congress had appointed him to the colonelcy of the Currituck revolutionary militia, an office which he still held. (Wheeler, *Historical Sketches*, i, 65, 78, 85; Hay ed, *Soldiers from NC*, 502; Heitman, *Historical Register*, 318)

Enclosure (3)
Rochfort and Fyers to Phillips, 3rd April 1781 96(11): LS

Portsmouth, Virginia
3rd April 1781

Major General Phillips etc etc

Sir

In compliance with the orders we had the honor of receiving from you this morning, we have consulted on the artillery necessary for the defence of the redouts and lines as they will be when compleated, and are of opinion that there is a necessity for adding to the artillery already mounted the following: one 18 pounder, eight 12 pounders, four 6 pounders, four howitzers.

For the disposition of these pieces we beg leave to refer you to the plan[38], and have the honor to be, sir, with great respect

Your very humble and most obedient servants

G ROCHFORT[39]
Captain commanding Royal Artillery

W^M FYERS[40]
Lieutenant, Commanding Engineer

---

[38] *the plan*: no copy.

[39] George Rochfort (*c.* 1741-1821) entered the Royal Regiment of Artillery as a cadet on 12th May 1756 and was commissioned a 2nd lieutenant some two and a half years later. A 1st lieutenant on 27th February 1761, he was promoted to captain lieutenant five years later and to captain on 25th May 1772. He was now commanding the artillery detachment at Portsmouth and would still be doing so when Cornwallis entered Virginia in May. As the senior artillery officer during the siege of Yorktown, he would be in command of an artillery detachment of 218 men and receive a mention in Cornwallis's dispatch following the capitulation. He was again commended by Cornwallis in a letter of 15th February 1783 to the Duke of Richmond, the Master General of the Ordnance, and one month later was promoted to major. He died a lt general. (*Royal Regiment of Artillery*, 8; *Army Lists*)

[40] William Fyers had been commissioned a 2nd lieutenant in the Corps of Engineers on 11th November 1773 and promoted to lieutenant on 7th May 1779. (*Army Lists*)

Enclosure (4)
Fyers to Phillips, 4th April 1781   *96(13): ALS*

Portsmouth, Virginia
4th April 1781

Major General Phillips etc etc etc

Sir

As the plan of Portsmouth[41] which I have the honor of sending you requires some farther explanation, I beg leave to accompany it with the following remarks.

The most essential closed works require nine hundred and fifty men for their defence. I presume the reserve you are pleased to allow will be capable of sparing a number of men sufficient to defend the fleches and the several batteries.[42] The stockaded house is consider'd as a barrack as well as a point of defence.

It is necessary to note that the creeks on each flank, described in the plan as at high water, are almost dry at low water and consequently do not afford that security which they apparently give the place in the drawing. For this reason and the disadvantageous situation of the post, every auxiliary defence shou'd be employ'd for its protection. An important one may be obtain'd by mooring an arm'd vessel, with six guns on a side, at the mouth of the creek on the left to serve as an enfilading battery for the same and to deter an enemy from attempting its passage.

The water is too shallow at the mouth of the creek on the right to admit near enough any vessel larger than a boat, as will appear by the soundings mark'd on the plan, but this point is well secured by a formidable direct and intersecting fire of cannon and musquetry.

I have the honor to be with the utmost respect, sir,
Your most obedient and very humble servant

W^M FYERS
Lieutenant, Commanding Engineer

---

[41] *the plan..*: no copy.

[42] In the margin is the following annotation: "950
                                                    180*
                                                  1,130

*These to be given out of the reserve.

WP."

Enclosure (5)
Phillips to Fyers, 4th April 1781   *96(15): C*

Portsmouth
April 4th 1781

Lieutenant Fyers
Engineer

Sir

The one hundred and eighty men which you desire for the fleches and batteries, independent of the inclosed works, which, with nine hundred and fifty required for the latter, amounts to the number of 1,130 specified in your plan, shall be supplied as you mark from the reserve.

The ordnance ship *Tartar* shall cover the left flank, as you desire, with ten 9 pounders, and a gun boat with a 12 pounder carronade shall be added to the defence, tho' already a good one, of the right flank.

I am, sir, etc

W PHILLIPS

Phillips to Clinton, 15th April 1781[43]   *96(21): C*

Portsmouth in Virginia
15th April 1781

His Excellency General Sir Henry Clinton

Sir

I had the honour of writing to your Excellency on the 3rd instant, sending with that letter a variety of inclosures. It was delivered to Captain Shads[44], who sailed with the *Roebuck* from Hampton Roads on the 5th, left the Capes of Virginia the next day with a fair wind, and must have arrived, I trust, three or four days after at New York.

---

[43] Extracts containing material differences are published without the enclosure in Stevens, op cit, i, 407.

[44] Commissioned a lieutenant in the Royal Navy on 7th March 1759, Henry Chads (?-1799) had been promoted to commander on 18th September 1779, a rank which carried with it the courtesy title of captain. He would normally have commanded a smaller vessel such as a sloop of war, but if he did so, it has not been ascertained. The *Roebuck* frigate, with which he had now sailed to New York, was commanded by an officer of higher rank, the post-captain John Leigh Douglas. Chads would attain that rank on 14th April 1783. He died at Chichester. (Syrett and DiNardo eds, *The Commissioned Sea Officers*, 77; *The Cornwallis Papers*)

Finding the putting this place in a proper state of defence rather beyond the calculation in point of time, I made up that deficiency by numbers of men between seven and 800 for some days, which rendered the state of the several redoubts and lines so tolerably compleat as to enable me, without any probable risk, to move with two thousand troops upon that expedition first directed to be undertaken by your Excellency's instructions and orders to me.

The demand I made from Captain Robinson for sailors with a request for his co-operation was most readily complied with. The *Foy* ship of war was to have accompanied me, Captain Palmer[45] of the *Vulcan* to conduct the fleet of boats, and every thing was prepared and ready for a movement on the 11th instant. Unfortunately the winds blew directly contrary and very strong on that day and every one after until yesterday, when it changed in a degree to allow some transports with troops to go down to Hampton Road, and I had ordered the light infantry and Queen's Rangers to march from their cantonments to embark in the boats prepared for them at Norfolk, when a most violent storm of wind and rain obliged me to postpone moving the troops. The same weather still prevails and it is impossible until it subsides to pursue the expedition. The moment of fair weather shall certainly be seized and I hope in forty-eight hours to have the troops embarked and in motion.

I have imagined it right to give the enemy a general jealousy and therefore in addition to two sloops of war stationed off Anapolis I sent the armed brig *Defiance*; the sloops *Savage* and *Swift* with a small armed vessel to cruize in Potowmack; the sloop *Bonetta* at the mouth of York River; the *Formidable* and *Spitfire* armed vessels off Newport Neus to check the enemy in James River; the *Vulcan* fire ship stationed at Portsmouth as a guard ship; and the commanding naval officer in the *Guadaloupe* with the *Thames* frigate in Hampton Road.

I had sent a very particular request to Captain Thomas[46] commanding the *Hope* sloop off Anapolis to watch the motions of La Fayette's corps and to send me immediate intelligence of any thing they might make. Such intelligence was sent me as your Excellency will see by the inclosed letter[47], which was sent without being signed by Captain Thomas, and the copy of my answer will mark to your Excellency my sense of that gentleman's conduct. Since then, his intelligence respecting the movement of La Fayette to Baltimore has been seconded by some other, which inclines me to believe it to be true. La Fayette's corps, a strain from Washington's army, was certainly intended to operate in conjunction with the French fleet and army against this place, and probably after destined against Lord Cornwallis. As it is, I am of opinion they will either remain at Baltimore or return to Washington's army, for I will freely declare that I do not conceive they will dare to cross the Potowmack and the

---

[45] George Palmer (?-1834), who was commanding the *Vulcan* fireship, had been commissioned a lieutenant in the Royal Navy on 23rd April 1778 and promoted to commander on 1st December 1780. Bottled up at Yorktown, the *Vulcan* would be set afire by red-hot shot from the enemy's batteries on the night of 10th to 11th October and be totally destroyed. Palmer survived and died an admiral of the white. (Syrett and DiNardo eds, op cit, 344)

[46] William Thomas (?-1800) had been commissioned a lieutenant in the Royal Navy on 2nd February 1761 and promoted to commander on 8th March 1780. He would rise no higher in the service. Now commanding the *Hope* sloop of war on the Chesapeake station, he would transfer with it to the Charlestown station later in the year. While conveying dispatches from Balfour to Clinton in late September or early October, the *Hope* would be lost, probably taken by de Grasse's fleet off Virginia. (Syrett and DiNardo eds, op cit, 435; *The Cornwallis Papers*)

[47] *the inclosed letter*: no extant copy, nor of Phillips' reply.

Rappahanock and venture themselves into this country, by which they will be totally cut off from Mr Washington, of whose army they are the élite.

I must refer your Excellency to my former letters, particularly my last letter, for my sentiments upon what may be attempted against La Fayette, against that quarter in the Chesapeak, and the consequent operations leading to the opening of the campaign after the first object of your Excellency's instructions and orders shall be accomplished; but this must depend upon a reinforcement in force or all enterprizes here will be merely dissultory, which may in a degree annoy the enemy but answer, I apprehend, no great object.

I am extremely fearful, sir, of incurring your displeasure, or at least your suspicion, when I mention a reinforcement, from perhaps a conclusion that I wish to add a pride of situation without a positive advantage to the King's Service, but I rely on your goodness of heart to judge of mine and hope you will be assured that I have only in view the common good connected with an obedience to your orders and a desire of doing every thing possible to gain your esteem and approbation.

I have the honour to inclose you a letter I have written to Lord Cornwallis[48], whom I believe to have been victorious in his late action with General Green but still not in a state to make any great advantages of his victory. The letter went on the 9th instant with a fair wind. I conceive myself restricted from pursuing any movements over the Roanoke, and indeed with the present force it would be not possible for it to be done, but perhaps with a reinforcement and your Excellency's permission and orders a junction might be made, at any rate a co-operation, with Lord Cornwallis which would force Mr Green from the power of giving any interruption to his Lordship settling the situation of affairs in North Carolina so as to permit him to be connected in a nearer manner with your Excellency's campaign.

I send you, sir, a letter I have written to the commanding engineer, who has been so ill as to be of no use to me since my arrival, but, being now on the recovery, I hope he will be able to execute the orders I have given him. I am free to declare Portsmouth to be a bad post, its locality not calculated for defence, the colateral points necessary to be taken up so many that altogether it would require so great a number of troops as no general officer I imagine would venture to propose to a commander in chief to leave here for mere defence. A spot might be found, I apprehend, for a post for five hundred men should it be necessary to have one in Elizabeth River.

I will trouble you, sir, with papers[49] respecting the seizure by Captain Robinson of a brig which came down James River with an intention, as has been presumed, of coming into this port. I hope my letter to Captain Robinson will prove I have given all the attention in my power in this affair. The issue must be left to your Excellency and Admiral Arbuthnot.

I should do injustice to the troops if I did not report to your Excellency that they have most willingly executed every labour the service has required.

---

[48] *a letter..*: of 8th April (p 64), it miscarried. See Craig to Cornwallis, 2nd May, vol IV, p 167.

[49] *papers*: no extant copies.

I found upon my arrival here a regular establishment formed by General Arnold for a garrison as an independent post, which, the General having reported to your Excellency, I have not thought it proper to make any alterations upon. Indeed, the establishments seem necessary and go pointedly to the service.

I very much wish to hear from your Excellency upon the first great objects of my letters of the 29th and 30th ultimo and of the 3rd instant, and I hope you will, sir, have the goodness to give me answers when convenient to your Excellency respecting the detail matters contained in those letters.

I have the honour to be, sir, with the highest respect
Your Excellency's most obedient and most humble servant

[W PHILLIPS]

Enclosure
Phillips to Fyers, 15th April 1781 *96(17): Df*

Portsmouth
April 15th 1781

Lieutenant Fyers

Sir

As I hope your health is by this time tolerably well established so as to enable you to do small dutys, I will request of you to give the labouring part of the service to Lieutenant Stratton[50] in compleating the works at Portsmouth and that you will turn your thoughts generally and particularly upon the situation of Elizabeth River and its several branches as a post to be fortified and taken by His Majesty's troops.

In doing this, sir, you will examine it in two points of view, the one as supposing it to be taken in force upon a permanent station in which you are to connect affording a security for ships of war and transports. And you are to combine a mutual assistance of navy and army in the defence of such post under the circumstances of a determined attack by siege on land and a supposition that the enemy may be in force sufficient in the Chesapeak in naval strength to oblige our ships of war to retire into the protection of the post.

You will please to give your report whether Portsmouth, as it is now fortified or as it might be fortified, taking in by redoubts or otherwise such distant points as at present seem to threaten from their situation the station at Portsmouth, is the proper spot to answer the ends I have described, and what number of troops it would require to defend the post against any probable attack of an enemy. You are to consider also whether the narrowness of the river may not be such as to hazard the shipping, even tho' the post might be preserved.

---

[50] James Stratton had been commissioned a 2nd lieutenant in the Corps of Engineers on 2nd February 1775. (*Army Lists*)

You will endeavour by a review of all the points within Elizabeth River to discover whether it may not be possible to take up two points, perhaps three, and form regular establishments upon them, giving to the two or three points I mention that number of troops which you shall report necessary for the security of Portsmouth and its dependencies. These points must be so situated, I should imagine, as to allow of the shipping coming above two of them so as to render it necessary for an enemy to possess these points to disturb the shipping at their moorings above them. I will not hesitate to give it as an opinion of mine that Mill Point, Norfolk or the Distillery near that place might be two of the points in question and, being taken in force, would permit shipping to lay in the bason above. A third point, if necessary to be taken at all, will require your particular attention to form a judgement upon.

You will observe, sir, that the second idea of taking up Elizabeth River and two or three separate points can only come into contemplation from your being perfectly convinced that Portsmouth would always prove an inferior post in strength to such others I have mentioned, to which it may not be unnecessary to add that the latter idea may possibly comprehend a fewer number of troops for its defence in force than Portsmouth — an object [which] you cannot be ignorant is of the greatest importance.

The second point of view in which you are to pursue your reflections is to examine where best a small post may be formed which shall be in a little time rendered so strong as to repel, with a garrison composed of a battalion of five hundred men, an assault by coup de main and also to be able to hold out against a regular approach for twenty or thirty days. In the examination of this second object you will try to gain such a point as may have its approach by land very contracted and where the depth of water also near it may be if possible such as not to permit ships of war to approach near enough to batter the works in flank or rear.

You will be so good, sir, in forming your report of these several objects, to give sketches of the works you would propose constructing on the occasion and the time required for compleating them, and in particular that last delineated, *a post for five hundred men*.

I apprehend you will naturally suppose I shall submit your report with my observations upon it for the consideration of his Excellency, the Commander in Chief.

I am, sir, etc

W PHILLIPS

Clinton to Phillips, 5th April 1781　　　　　　　　　　　　　　　　95(15): LS

New York
5th April 1781

Major General Phillips

Dear Sir

I am favored this day with your dispatches of the 29th and 30th March. The letters you mention to have wrote to me by the *Medea* are not yet arrived.

As I do not wish to lose a moment in answering them, I shall not enter into a long detail, which you may naturally expect from me. From all the intelligence I have been able to collect, the French ships of war had only 1,500 men embarked under Baron Viominy. From ships of the line, supposing that time and distance made it possible, troops cannot land in Cape Fear, nor, if they did, could they penetrate as far as Wilmington without an armed naval force of small draft to cover them, supposing that our naval force in that river is (as it of course will be) on their guard. I therefore perfectly agree with the opinion given in the latter part of your letter that, if troops are really landed from transports at Cape Fear, they must be of some other corps than that at Rhode Island, probably the three regiments expected from Corke. In short, I have no uneasiness with respect to Cape Fear, much less to Albemarle Sound. Those are navigations little calculated for Monsieur Destouches' squadron[51], which I have reason to believe arrived in Rhode Island on the 27th ultimo.

By the inclosed extracts from General Washington's intercepted letter dated before he knew the failure of the French expedition to Chesapeak (for we have taken another rebel mail), you will see his hopes, his fears. As to his hopes, I shall say nothing, but his fears, I flatter myself, will be reallised by your operations.

With respect to the action of the 15th near Guildford Court House you will perceive by the inclosed hand bill[52] that from their owning so much we have reason to believe the victory has been complete, and tho' they do not own it, I am persuaded they were followed to the ford and all those troops they mention to be missing were probably made prisoners there. But these are mere opinions and will not of course operate to prevent your doing every thing in your power to favor Lord Cornwallis, which perhaps may not be better done than by striking at the rebel corps at Williamsburg or those near Suffolk, of which, however, you, being on the spot, will be the best judge, for you will always consider that the principal object of your expedition is to favor his Lordship's operations.

With regard to your establishing another naval station in Chesapeak for large ships I need only refer you to my instructions, which started that idea only on the supposition that the Admiral or naval commanding officer should require it for a security to the King's ships, but if they do not seem to wish it, there is no necessity at present of entering further upon that subject as such a proposal will of course come first from them.

I have the honor to be, sir,
Your most obedient humble servant

H CLINTON

---

[51] Admiral Charles-René-Dominique Gochet, Chevalier Destouches had succeeded the Chevalier de Ternay, who died on 15th December 1780. Commanding the French squadron at Newport, he sailed south to support Lafayette in Virginia but withdrew after the action off the Capes on 16th March. In May he was succeeded by the Comte de Barras. (Boatner, *Encyclopedia*, 329)

[52] *the inclosed hand bill*: not extant.

Enclosure
Washington to Harrison, 27th March 1781[53]   *105(8): C*

Head Quarters
New Windsor
27th March 1781

Hon Benjamin Harrison Esq[54]

Dear Sir

On my return from Newport I found your favor of the 16th of February with its enclosures at head quarters. I exceedingly regret that I could not have the pleasure of seeing you, not only from personal motives but because I could have entered upon the subject of your mission in a much more free and full manner than is proper to be committed to paper.

I very early saw the difficulties and dangers to which the southern States would be exposed for resources of cloathing, arms and ammunition and recommended magazines to be established as ample as their circumstances would admit. It is true they are not so full of men as the northern States, but they ought for that reason to have been more assiduous in rasing a permanent force to have been always ready, because they cannot draw a head of men together as suddenly as their exigencies may require. That policy has unhappily not been pursued either here or there, and we are now suffering, from the remnant of a British army, what they could not in the beginning accomplish with their force at the highest.

As your requisitions go to men, arms, ammunition and cloathing, I shall give you a short detail of our situation and prospects as to the first, and of our supplies and expectations as to the three last.

Men

By the expiration of the times[55] of service of the old troops, by the discharge of the levies engaged for the campaign only, and by the unfortunate dissolution of the Pennsylvania line I was left, previous to the march of the detachment under the command of the Marquis de la Fayette, with a garrison barely sufficient for the security of West Point, and two regiments

---

[53] Endorsed: 'On Public Service – General Washington to the Hon Benjamin Harrison Esq, Speaker of the House of Delegates, Richmond, Virginia'. A copy of the letter is published in Davies ed, *Docs of the Am Rev*, xx, 97-8. It contains no differences other than those mentioned in notes 55 and 56 below.

[54] The Hon Benjamin Harrison (1726-1791) of Berkeley plantation, Charles City County, Virginia, had served for many years in the colonial House of Burgesses before taking part in the Virginia revolutionary convention in 1775. A member of the Continental Congress from 1774 to 1777, he was a signer of the Declaration of Independence. On resigning his seat in Congress, he was chosen Speaker of the Virginia House of Delegates, of which he was also a member, and would hold office until 1782. At that time he was elected Governor of Virginia and served for two terms. An intimate acquaintance of George Washington, he was father of the 9th President of the United States and great-grandfather of the 23rd. (Joel D Treese and Dorthy J Countryman, *Biographical Directory of the United States Congress 1774-1796* (Cq Pr, 1996))

[55] *times..*: Davies has 'terms'.

in Jersey to support the communication between the Delaware and North River. The York troops I had been obliged to send up for the security of the frontier of that State. Weak, however, as we were, I determined to attempt the dislodgement of Arnold in conjunction with the French fleet and army and made the detachment to which I have alluded.

In my late tour to the eastward I found the accounts I had received of the progress of recruiting in those States had been much exaggerated, and I fear we shall in the end be obliged again to take a great proportion of their quotas in levies for the campaign instead of soldiers for three years or for the war. The regiments of New York having been reduced to two, they have but few men to raise. Jersey depends upon voluntary inlistments upon a contracted bounty, and I cannot therefore promise myself much success from the mode. The Pennsylvania line, you know, is ordered to compose part of the southern army. General Wayne is so sanguine as to suppose he will soon be able to move on with 1,000 or 1,200 men, but I fancy he rather over rates the matter.

You will readily perceive from the foregoing state that there is little probability of adding to the force already ordered to the southward, for should the battalions from New Hampshire to New Jersey inclusive be compleated (a thing not to be expected), we shall, after the necessary detachments for the frontiers and other purposes are made, have an army barely sufficient to keep the enemy in check in New York. Except this is done, they will have nothing to hinder them from throwing further reinforcements to the southward; and to be obliged to follow by land every detachment of their army, which they always make by sea, will only end in a fruitless dissipation of what may now be called the northern army. You may be assured that the most powerful diversion that can be made in favor of the southern States will be a respectable force in the neighbourhood of New York. I have hitherto been speaking of our own resources. Should a reinforcement arrive to the French fleet and army, the face of matters may be intirely changed.

Arms

I do not find that we can at any rate have more than two thousand stand of arms to spare, perhaps not so many, for should the battalions which are to compose this army be compleat or nearly so, they will take all that are in repair or repairable. The two thousand stand came in the *Alliance* from France and I have kept them apart for an exigency.

Ammunition

Our stock of ammunition, tho' competent to the defensive, is by a late estimate of the commanding officer of artillery vastly short of an offensive operation of any consequence. Should circumstances put it in our power to attempt such an one, we must depend upon the private magazines of the States and upon our allies. On the contrary, should the defensive plan be determined upon, what ammunition can be spared will be undoubtedly sent to the southward.

Cloathing

Of cloathing we are in a manner exhausted. We have not enough for the few recruits which may be expected, and except that which has been so long looked for and talked of from

France should arrive, the troops must next winter go naked unless their States can supply them.

From the foregoing representation you will perceive that the proportion of the Continental Army already allotted to southern service is as much as from present appearances can be spared for that service[56], and that a supply of arms, ammunition or cloathing of any consequence must depend in great measure upon future purchases or importations.

Nothing which is within the compass of my power shall be wanting to give support to the southern States, but you may readily conceive how irksome a thing it must be to me to be called upon for assistance when I have not the means of affording it.

I am with the greatest regard, dear sir,
Your most obedient and humble servant

G^O WASHINGTON

Clinton to Phillips, 5th April 1781[57]   96(37): C

April 5th 1781

I need not say how important success in the Highlands would be.

I beg you will without loss of time consult General Arnold upon the subject. I beg I may have his project, and your opinion as well as his respecting it, as soon as possible. When I have considered it, and if I determine to undertake it, I will send for him if operation should be at a stand in Chesapeak at the time. I will request you also to be of the party. The proportion of artillery I desired you to make will of course be ready.

H CLINTON

PS

If General Arnold does not think it expedient at this time to attempt it, which, however, I shall be sorry for, perhaps a combined move between us against Philadelphia may take place, you by landing at head of Elk, I at Newcastle or Chester. If the first, General Arnold must let me have his plan as soon as possible and be ready to follow it himself or may bring it if you can spare him.

---

[56] *service*: Davies has 'purpose'.

[57] Published with a material difference in Stevens, op cit, i, 392.

Phillips to Clinton, 16th April 1781[58] 96(27): Df

Portsmouth, Virginia
16th April 1781
2 o'clock pm

His Excellency General Sir Henry Clinton

Sir

This day at noon the adjutant of the Queen's Rangers arrived at this place with your Excellency's dispatches of the 5th instant. His report[59], which I enclose, will give the causes why he was so many days on his voyage with an almost constant fair wind.

Your Excellency will receive at the same time with this my dispatch dated yesterday, and I am sorry to inform you, sir, that the bad weather which followed the change of the winds still remains. It is squally, strong blasts of wind and very heavy rain, and I can not think of exposing troops in boats to such inclement season, as I think that waiting twenty four hours for fair weather can not be of a material consequence equal to that which must attend the King's troops should I expose them at first to the chances of the winds and the violence of such rains. The first instant the weather breaks, the troops, which are all ready, shall move according to the description I had the honour to give your Excellency.

I will now take the liberty of answering some parts of your Excellency's letter to me of the fifth instant and will begin by returning you, sir, my sincere thanks for the quickness with which you have been so good to make answers to my letters of the 29th and 30th ultimo. I have of some time been entirely free from any apprehensions of French troops to the southward. I did imagine it probable they might land them in the Delaware, but your letter, sir, convinces me they are safe arrived at Rhode Island.

I am clear that Lord Cornwallis pursued the enemy to the ford with great slaughter, for I observe the enemy industriously give an account only of their Continentals, not their militia. There is therefore reason, as you observe, sir, to believe the victory to be compleat, but forgive me for thinking that he may have bought it dear and that his Lordship remained a little crippled after the action. The move of these troops, as I hope tomorrow, cannot fail of being a most useful cooperation with that army, and should your Excellency have judged it necessary to reinforce me, it may be in my power from a communication with Lord Cornwallis to join in the dispersing Mr Green's army.

I am confirmed in my idea, from reading the intercepted letter of General Washington, of what I took the liberty of mentioning yesterday to your Excellency respecting La Fayette, and that he will never venture to move southward, and it leads me to suppose that he remains at

---

[58] A short extract from this letter is published in Stevens, op cit, i, 407. Other short extracts, combined with one from Phillips' later letter of the 16th (p 47), appear, op cit, i, 409. None contains material differences.

[59] *His report*: no copy.

Baltimore waiting events. Should an expedition proceed against him, he possibly may retire to Washington, in which case *Maryland* and the *Susquehana* to *York Town* and from thence back to *Frederick Town* on the *Potowmack* with that river would in a degree be in our power. Should he on the contrary remain to protect Baltimore or Anapolis, he certainly may be carried with his troops, but the attempt, sir, can not be made with the force at present here, for it would be incompatable with the situation of Portsmouth to take from its defence for so distant an operation more than 16 or 1800 men.

I can not sufficiently express my extreame joy at reading Washington's letter. It is such a description of distress as may serve to convince that, with a tolerable reinforcement from Europe to enable your Excellency to determine upon an offensive campaign, the year 1781 may probably prove the glorious period to your Excellency's command in America of putting an end to the rebellion.

Mr Washington observes very plainly that he can only act on the defensive and by keeping as much force as he can upon the North River endeavour at preventing your Excellency from acting upon it, but can by no means prove an impediment to your sending troops into Chesapeak, which Washington allows to be the most distressing thing that can happen to him, as he should be obliged to make detachments by *land* from his army, which would, as he marks, 'only end in a fruitless dissipation' of it.

He says also that he speaks only of their own resources and that 'should a reinforcement arrive to the French fleet and army, the face of matters may be entirely changed'. This has been so frequently the subject of conversations which I have had the honour to hold with your Excellency that I need say nothing upon it, but a certain swelling of the heart urges me to observe that, had the British fleet the other day acted with that *good fortune* which British fleets heretofore have been accustomed to, the face of matters would indeed have been entirely changed.

I could not have conceived it possible the state of arms and amunition in the rebel service to be such as Mr Washington describes, and it must have given your Excellency great pleasure to have read that part of his letter where he mentions 'the long looked for and talked of assistance from France' and the effect a disappointment from thence will produce to the rebel cause.

The instructions contained in your Excellency's letter written in cyphers shall be strictly adhered to. The project with my opinion upon it shall be sent to your Excellency immediately after the James River expedition and if possible by General Arnold. I think, as it strikes me on the instant, that the expedition connected with my landing at the head of Elk might take place after the enterprize upon Baltimore or Anapolis, and it does not appear to me that the combination need go *so high* as that your Excellency mentions. I should imagine a naval assistance with a very small detachment of troops might suffice in the Delaware. I really will submit my opinion to your Excellency that the first great object you mention is of so important a nature that it should be pursued and I own to think it would be attended with success. I do not yet know what General Arnold's idea is respecting time, but I will freely give my own for the begining of June.

You may perceive, sir, from the tenor of my letters that I do not conceive it to be likely that I shall have a personal communication with Lord Cornwallis, and it has led me to call upon the intelligence of my own mind respecting those operations detailed by your Excellency to me from your great book the day before I left New York. I have drawn General Arnold into loose conversations on the matter. I shall now do so particularly, having your Excellency's authority for it in your cypher letter. I really believe he and I think nearly the same and that it will go fully to that important blow your Excellency leans to. The previous operations in Chesapeak tending towards the lowers counties I have written upon. Forgive me, sir, for once more observing that without a reinforcement to this corps of troops little can be done, except plundering of tobacco, which is not an object of mine. With a reinforcement I think a great deal may be done by the end of May.

I return you, sir, my most sincere thanks for all your goodness towards me, particularly for communicating so immediately with me. I always am anxious for your orders as it is an ardent desire of mine to obey them to your satisfaction.

I have the honour to be, dear sir, with most perfect attachment and great respect
Your Excellency's most faithful and obliged humble servant

[W PHILLIPS]

Clinton to Phillips, 13th April 1781[60]   *95(22): LS*

New York
April 13th 1781

Major General Phillips

Dear Sir

I am favored with your dispatches by Captain Chads and lose not a moment to inform you that the Admiral arrived with his fleet off the Hook the 10th instant.

The *Lapwing* dispatch boat carried you two letters from me of the 5th instant, duplicates of which are sent herewith. In addition to what I have said in those letters I scarce need mention that I am persuaded you will not delay to make such movements in favor of Lord Cornwallis as you judge best with the force you will have left after garrisoning the different works at Portsmouth, which, after reading the report of your engineer, I flatter myself will be perfectly secure with six or eight hundred men. In that case you will be at liberty to act with the remainder, being as good troops as any in this country, in such operations as you shall judge most conducive to assist those of his Lordship.

---

[60] An extract from the second paragraph is published in Stevens, op cit, i, 405. It contains no differences.

Inclosed is a letter to Lord Cornwallis[61] inviting him to meet you in the Chesapeak as soon as his presence in the Carolinas can be dispensed with.

I wait with impatience for your answer to my letter of the 5th, nor shall I determine positively about reinforcements until I receive it.

Faithfully, dear sir,
Your obedient humble servant

H CLINTON

[*Subscribed*:]

After reading the inclosed to Lord Cornwallis, you will be so good to dispatch it to Cape Fear River in one of the runners[62], with a letter to Major Craig likewise, with positive orders to return to you as soon as possible; and if you could by sending an officer to Major Craig establish a cypher with him, so much the better.

Arnold to Phillips, 16th April 1781 96(35): ALS

16th April 1781
9 o'clock evening

Major General Phillips

Dear Sir

I have the honor to inclose your letter and a copy of one from the Commander in Chief respecting the opperations of the campaign. If you wish to see me this evening upon the subject, I will wait on you any hour you please.

I have the honor to be, dear sir,
Yours sincerely

B ARNOLD

---

[61] *a letter..*: of 13th April, p 94.

[62] The runner was captured and the letter sunk. See Craig to Cornwallis, 2nd May, vol IV, p 167.

Enclosure
Clinton to Arnold, 13th April 1781 96(39): C

New York
13th April 1781

Brigadier General Arnold

Sir

Can we hope for success in a coup de main against the fort in the Highlands? Washington, I imagine, has about four thousand Continentals there. What force etc etc do you think requisite, recollecting the numerous supply of troops that can be thrown into him? In what time could the fort be compleatly invested, and how? Pray answer the above questions, and if you are of opinion on reading Washington's letter that an attempt should be made, apply for a safe frigate and come yourself or send your plan of operation as soon as possible. I have been preparing for some weeks.

If you do not, all things considered, think advisable to attempt the fort by regular siege, I shall probably reinforce General Phillips for such operations as he shall judge best to assist Lord Cornwallis and annoy the enemy 'till after consulting Lord Cornwallis may determine upon others.[63]

H CLINTON

Phillips to Clinton, 16th April 1781[64] 96(31): C

Portsmouth in Virginia
16th April 1781
8 o'clock evening

His Excellency General Sir Henry Clinton

Sir

Mr John Watson, master of the schooner *Swallow*, who left New York with your Excellency's dispatches for me on Friday last the 13th instant, is arrived within this hour at this place and has delivered me your Excellency's letter of that date with the letter for Lt General the Earl Cornwallis and also a duplicate of Your Excellency's dispatch to me of the 5th instant. The master of this express boat seems to have made very considerable dispatch notwithstanding some damage his main mast has received, which, requiring repair, prevents me from immediately sending him back to New York. You will perceive, sir, that this last express boat has arrived in eight hours after that dispatched the 6th instant.

---

[63] Annotated in margin: 'I or he or we?'

[64] See p 43, note 58.

In your letter, sir, you are so good to do me justice in being persuaded I shall not delay the movements to be made in favour of Lord Cornwallis. Had the winds and weather permitted, it would have been done on the 11th instant. As it is, it must depend upon a favourable change of the weather, which I trust will happen tomorrow or next day at the farthest.

I have in all my letters taken the liberty to remark that I think this post cannot be perfectly secure without a great number of troops, but taking into consideration the sort of enemy, tho' numerous, in our front — that the movement I shall make will probably occasion one from them — I am of opinion the post will be secure with the troops I shall leave in it, which amount, including the post at the Great Bridge and a guard upon the General Hospital at Norfolk, to 900 men, and there will be about 300 left sick in the General and Regimental Hospitals. In the effective numbers I do not include the artillery, armed artificers, nor sailors.

I shall send your Excellency's letter to Lord Cornwallis to his Lordship immediately by a small vessel under care of an officer, but I am fearful I shall not have time to compose a cypher for Major Craig, and it perhaps may not be positively necessary as letters going by sea are generally sunk previous to any vessels being taken. By land it would certainly be impossible to correspond otherwise than under the secret of a cypher.

I candidly acknowledge, sir, that in reading your letter to me written in cyphers I did not conceive it required a full answer previous to our returning from the expedition in favour of Lord Cornwallis. Still less did I imagine the matter of a reinforcement depended on such answer, but as you seem, sir, in your letter of the 13th just received to be impatient to hear from me in answer to your Excellency's letter of the 5th instant, I have desired General Arnold to meet me this night, when we will consult upon the subject and will write to your Excellency the result of our conversation.

This instant, while I am writing at 9 o'clock, I received the following note from General Arnold:

...[65]

Your Excellency's letter to the General opens so large a field for consultation that it must be deferred until the morning, when I shall have the honour of again addressing your Excellency.

I have the honour to be, sir, with the highest respect
Your Excellency's most obedient and most humble servant

[W PHILLIPS]

---

[65] Phillips quotes virtually verbatim Arnold's letter of the 16th, p 46.

Phillips to Clinton, 19th April 1781[66]   96(41): ADfS

Hampton Road on board the *Maria*
April the 19th 1781
5 o'clock morning

His Excellency General Sir Henry Clinton

Sir

In my way down to the assembly of transports and boats yester evening this vessel which I am in run on ground, and while I was waiting for a swell of the tide, an express boat arrived to me with a letter from Lord Cornwallis[67] which the *Amphytrite* had brought. I enclose to you, sir, a copy of the letter.

I have red the copy of the dispatch to your Excellency[68] alluded to, and it is a plain tale of many difficulties and distresses, great perseverance and resolution, and honour. The action of the 15th was glorious, but, as I feared, that sort of victory which ruins an army. I most sincerely hope the *Medea* frigate is already with Lord Cornwallis or at least will be soon. I imagine your Excellency's letter will cause his Lordship, joined to the not being able to move his army immediately, to set out for the Chesapeak. I shall be sincerely glad of it, as in that case your Excellency will have the assistance of his Lordship's council and cooperation.

The face of affairs seem changed and the Carolinas like all America are lost in rebellion. My letters of the 15th, 16th and of yesterday[69] will go now in the *Amphytrite*, for I stoped the express boat last night. I have nothing further to add than that I conceive Lord Cornwallis will not have it in his power to bring with him many troops. It will depend on your Excellency, from his Lordship's letters and from those of Brigadier General Arnold and me, whether you shall think it proper to have an operation in force in Chesapeak. If yes, the troops here are too few; if no, too many.

I hope to hear from your Excellency directly, and perhaps it may not be so well to trust such a serious dispatch as your next, sir, will probably be to an unarm'd vessel but that a frigate will be sent.

---

[66] Published in Stevens, op cit, i, 412. There are inconsequential omissions, which Stevens supplies later.

[67] *a letter..*: Cornwallis to Phillips, 10th April (85(29)), vol IV, p 114.

[68] *the dispatch..*: Cornwallis to Clinton, 10th April, vol IV, p 109.

[69] *My letters..*: of that of the 18th there is no copy, but Stevens, op cit, i, 412, contains an extract. In it Phillips and Arnold outline possible operations if reinforced with up to 2,000 men. On the one hand, they could take a post in force at Petersburg, disrupting Greene's communications with Virginia and otherwise cooperating with Cornwallis. On the other, they could strike at Lafayette, Baltimore and Anapolis, possibly destroying all magazines and shipping in Maryland. If completed in May, the expedition could then take post in the lower counties of Delaware, attempt Philadelphia, or return to New York to act with Clinton. They recommend a base other than Portsmouth for operations in the Chesapeak.

The operation I had proposed against Williamsburg shall take place to morrow morning, but I think it my duty to call a council of war, circumstanced as Lord Cornwallis is, to judge whether an attempt on Petersburg may now be proper.

I have etc

W PHILLIPS

Clinton to Phillips, 25th April 1781   95(24): LS

New York
April 25th 1781

Major General Phillips

Dear Sir

I have read the papers you have sent me respecting the brig *Unity* seized by Captain Robinson, but it is impossible for me to determine the propriety or legality of the capture, which must be left to the decision of a Court of Admiralty. I will, however, speak to Admiral Arbuthnot on the subject, with whom I have already had a general conversation on that of the prizes taken by the King's ships in conjunction with the troops.

As it is your opinion that the establishments formed by Brigadier General Arnold at Portsmouth are necessary and pointed to the service, there is no occasion to alter them, but as you are left at liberty to reduce that post if you should find it requisite to do so, the establishments will of course be reduced in proportion.

The corps of black pioneers which you propose forming (as mentioned in your letter of the 3rd instant) I leave entirely to your discretion, to be placed on what establishment you judge proper, as I do the augmenting the mounted of the 80th to the number you desire.

I have the honor to be, dear sir,
Your most obedient and most humble servant

H CLINTON

Clinton to Phillips and Arnold, 26th April 1781   95(26): LS

New York
April 26th 1781

Major General Phillips and Brigadier General Arnold

Gentlemen

I had the honor to receive your joint letter of the 18th instant containing your opinions and observations respecting the proposed attack of the forts in the Highlands and the corresponding operations on the side of Chesapeak, but as certain reasons have occasioned my suspending those considerations for the present, it becomes unnecessary for me to give you any further trouble thereon than to return you my thanks with assurances of my being with great regard, gentlemen,

Your most obedient and most humble servant

H CLINTON

Clinton to Phillips, 26th and 30th April 1781[70]   95(32): LS

New York
26th April 1781

Major General Phillips

Dear Sir

Your letters of the 15th, 16th, 18th and 19th instant were delivered to me on the 22nd by Captain Biggs of His Majesty's Ship *Amphitrite*, and I should have now entered largely into, and given a detail answer (agreeable to your desire) to, the several subjects thereof if I had not from the purport of Lord Cornwallis's letter of the 10th and yours of the 19th judged it to be unnecessary at present to give either you or myself that trouble.

What you say in your letter of the 15th instant respecting the post at Portsmouth and the choice of another somewhere else on Elizabeth River you will find fully answered in mine to you of the 11th, which accompanies this, for (tho' written above a fortnight since) I had no safe opportunity before the present of sending it to you.

Lord Cornwallis's arrival at Wilmington has considerably changed the complexion of our affairs to the southward, and all operations to the northward must probably give place to those in favor of his Lordship, which at present appear to require our more immediate attention. I know nothing of his Lordship's situation but what I have learnt from his letter to me of the 10th, which you have read, and as I have the strongest reason to believe that he had above 3,000 men (exclusive of cavalry and militia) when he entered North Carolina, I am totally at a loss to conjecture how his numbers came to be reduced before the day of the action to 1,360[71] infantry except by supposing (as you have done) that he had previously weakened his army by detachments. Of this, however, I shall probably be informed when I receive the copy of his Lordship's letter to the Minister; and I shall most likely be at the same time

---

[70] Published in Stevens, op cit, i, 437. There are no differences except a point of punctuation in the seventh paragraph.

[71] Because of the similarity in the ways in which '3' and '8' were written in the 18th century, it is at times easy to confuse the two. A copyist may well have made this mistake when preparing for signature Cornwallis's letter of 10th April to Clinton (vol IV, p 109). In that event the correct figure would have been 1,860, which, if it excluded artillery, correlates with the figure of 1,924 (including 50 artillery) given in the third return in chapter 42 (vol IV, p 63).

informed what prospects he may still have of arming the numerous friends we were taught to expect his finding in the districts he has visited in his march to and his retreat from Guildford, without whose assistance we shall, I fear, hold those provinces by a very precarious tenure.

I had great hopes, before I received Lord Cornwallis's letter, that his Lordship would have been in a condition to have spared a considerable part of his army from Carolina for the operations in Chesapeak, but you will observe from it that, instead of sending any part of his present force thither, he proposes to detain a part of the reinforcement coming from Europe for his more southern operations, even though they should be defensive. I shall therefore take the opinions of the general officers near me upon the present state of our affairs and I propose afterwards to send you such a further detachment from this army as we may judge can be done with tolerable security to this post, at least while we remain superior at sea.

With so large a force as you will then have I flatter myself that you will be able to make the most effectual exertions either directly or indirectly in Lord Cornwallis's favor as far as your efforts on the shores of the Chesapeak can cooperate with what he may be doing in Carolina. What these, however, may be, you as being upon the spot must certainly be the best judge until you either hear further from or see his Lordship.

In yours and Brigadier General Arnold's joint letter you mention that from 1,600 to 2,000 more men would enable you to take a post in force at Petersburg, from whence you might break up Mr Green's communications with Virginia and in cooperation with Lord Cornwallis probably disperse the rebel army, and that you could, moreover, with this increased strength attempt Fayette's corps, Baltimore and Anapolis with great probability of success, and finally attempt Philadelphia, and take post in the lower counties of Delaware, for which you apprehend your force would then be sufficient.

The security of the two Carolinas is certainly an object of the greatest importance and should at all events be first attended to. Success also against any considerable corps of the enemy which may be collected any where within reach and the taking or destroying their public stores, magazines etc are undoubtedly very important advantages, but there is in my humble opinion still another operation which, if successfull, would be most solidly decisive in its consequences and is therefore well worth our consideration. It is the trying the same experiment (which has hitherto unfortunately not succeeded to the southward) in other districts which have been represented as most friendly to the King's interests. Virginia has been in general looked upon as universally hostile, Maryland has not been as yet tried but is supposed to be not quite so much so, but the inhabitants of Pennsylvania on both sides of the Susquehannah, York, Lancaster, Chester and the peninsula between Chesapeak and Delaware are represented to me to be friendly. There, or thereabouts, I think this experiment should now be tried, but it cannot be done fairly until we have a force sufficient not only to go there but to retain a respectable hold of the country afterwards should it be judged necessary. I wish that our numbers were competent to the occupying two corresponding stations at Baltimore and Elk River agreeable to what I mentioned to you in the conversations we have had together on this subject, to which that you may be able on occasion to refer I have committed the substance of them to writing and send them to you inclosed. This I should have done sooner had I had a safe opportunity before. I have now the greater reason to be convinced that the opinions I then gave you were right from a conversation I have since had with a very intelligent friend of ours[72] from the country, known to Colonel Simcoe, who goes to you by this opportunity and will be able to give you the fullest information thereon.

April 30th

I expected that the *Medea* would have been sent to Lord Cornwallis and that Captain Duncan would have been appointed by the Admiral to conduct the naval operations in the Chesapeak, for which he is particularly qualified from his knowledge of those waters and his having had the management of that business in Lord Howe's command; but the Admiral has just wrote to me that he cannot possibly at present spare Captain Duncan and that he has appointed Captain Hudson of the *Richmond* to carry my dispatches to Chesapeak and Cape Fear and afterwards attend this service. My dispatches will therefore go in her under the charge of Lord Chewton, and as we both know Captain Hudson's great zeal to cooperate with the troops on all occasions, I hope every thing will go on under his direction perfectly to your satisfaction.

I have the honor to be, dear sir,
Your most obedient and most humble servant

H CLINTON

Enclosure (1)
Clinton to Phillips, 11th April 1781[73]

95(18): LS

New York
April 11th 1781

Major General Phillips

Dear Sir

Your letter of the 3rd instant by Captain Chads, which I am this day favored with, makes me apprehensive lest you may have misconceived my intentions with regard to the order in which I wished that the different objects recommended to you in my instructions should be attended to, and that your having in consequence proposed to commence with strengthening the works at Portsmouth may occasion some delay of the operations desired to favor those of Lord Cornwallis, whose situation after the action of the 15th ultimo might not only derive the greatest advantage from, but indeed might possibly be so critical as even to require, a timely exertion of the troops under your command.

You will therefore have the goodness to forgive me if I request you to recollect that at the time those instructions were drawn up General Arnold was partly invested by a considerable

---

[72] *a very intelligent friend of ours*: Colonel William Rankin. See p 59, note 79.

[73] Published in Stevens, op cit, i, 401. There are no differences.

body of militia and threatned with an attack from the French armament from Rhode Island and Fayette's corps then on their march to Virginia, which naturally pointed out the *security of him, the troops under his orders and the posts on Elizabeth River as the principal object of your expedition*, which words were certainly intended to mean no more than relieving them from their supposed danger by either forming a junction with General Arnold or taking such measures against the enemies opposed to him as might most effectually enable you to throw into his lines an immediate supply of provisions and men, for how could I imagine that the post at Portsmouth, which General Arnold had but just informed me in his letter of the 27th of February[74] he could defend against the force of the country and 2,000 French troops until a reinforcement arrived from hence, would require additional works for its security after you had joined him with so considerable a reinforcement or was acting against the rebel stations in its neighbourhood? And I could not but suppose that you yourself comprehended what I intended to be the first object of my instructions when you tell me in your letter by Serjeant Coulter that the proposed consultation would go '*in the first instance to the security of this post* and in the *next* to the fulfilling the *first object* of your Excellency's instructions', which (excuse me for repeating it) has been invariably, in all my instructions to the general officers sent to the Chesapeak, *operation in favor of Lord Cornwallis*. But if you will have the goodness to read those I gave you once more, I am sure you will perceive that what I have said about *strengthening the present works on Elizabeth River and adding such others as you shall think necessary* is placed subsequent in order to most of the other objects recommended to you, and they were of course designed to have been taken into consideration after those had been accomplished and you were upon the point of returning to me with part of your present force.

I am always happy to receive your opinions respecting the different operations of the war in this country, particularly those immediately connected with your own station. I therefore of course shall pay every attention to what you say about the post at Portsmouth and feel myself greatly obliged to you for the trouble you have taken to investigate its good and bad properties. My ideas of a post on Elizabeth River have continued uniformly the same since I first took a view of it, having always considered it merely as a station to protect the King's ships, which might occasionally sail from thence to cruize in the waters of the Chesapeak and command its entrance. I therefore only wished to have there such a number of troops as might be sufficient for its defence and which, being occasionally reinforced as circumstances should require and our abilities admit, might act offensively in distressing and embarrassing the measures of the enemy in its neighbourhood, for God forbid I should think of burying the elite of my army in Nansemond and Princess Ann! These ideas I communicated to the general officers I sent on that service and they each adopted such as appeared to them best calculated to answer the intended purpose. My own opinion indeed was that we should possess a close work at *Mill Point* (which Fyers fortified by my order in 1776, as he will remember), another at Norfolk, and a third somewhere on the *opposite side* of the river, but as I had been there only for a very short time, I could not of course but be influenced by the representations of the general officers and engineers on the spot, who had more time and better opportunity to examine all the different positions on that river. General Leslie therefore having informed me that he had with the unanimous suffrage of the sea and land officers on the expedition made choice of Portsmouth, which probably he did with a view of putting our

---

[74] *his letter..*: published in Stevens, op cit, i, 329.

friends of Princess Ann etc under cover and protection (but by your account a small house, I fear, will be sufficient for them all), and his engineer, Captain Sutherland, having in consequence begun a work there which he was of opinion could in a few days be in a state to be perfectly secure with a small garrison, I was induced to recommend to General Arnold the occupying the same ground, and tho' I must do the justice to that general officer to acknowledge that he gave me in his letter of the 23rd of January[75] a very different representation of the post at Portsmouth from the one given me by Major General Leslie, circumstances became so critical at the time I received it, in consequence of the French preparations at Rhode Island and the numerous militia who were collecting in Virginia and North Carolina, that I thought it an improper time to change the station because, good or bad such as it was, it must for the present be defended. I accordingly thought it right to defer to some more proper occasion the writing to General Arnold on the subject, and I was afterwards happy to find by his letter to me of the 27th of February that his works there were in such forwardness and that he was even preparing to send up James River an expedition of 500 men. All these circumstances considered, I was led to suppose that the post at Portsmouth was now rendered an eligible one by the manner in which it was fortified. However, as I intimated before, it is by no means a position of my choice, and if you and General Arnold have such good reasons to condemn it, it may be right to return to our original object, *a station to protect the King's ships which is capable of being maintained by a garrison of about five or six hundred men*, and if Mill Point will answer these purposes without Norfolk and the corresponding station on the opposite side of the river, I can have no objection but leave it to you to act as you judge best for the King's Service.

I am, dear sir,
Your most obedient and most humble servant

H CLINTON

Enclosure (2)
Substance of conversations between Clinton and Phillips[76]   95(28): DS

Substance of several conversations had with Major General Phillips on the subject of operations in the Chesapeak before his embarkation on his expedition thither

Untill I know Lord Cornwallis's success to the southward and what force can be spared from the Southern District for further operation, and untill the reinforcements expected to this army arrive, such troops as are in the Chesapeak may be employed first in assisting his Lordship's operations and then in either establishing a permanent post near the entrance of that bay (if the naval commander does not approve of the one in Elizabeth River), where large ships as well as small may lie in security during any temporary superiority of the enemy's fleet, or, if such a post cannot be found, in employing what remains of the season in carrying on desultory expeditions against such towns, stations, magazines etc as the enemy may have

---

[75] *his letter..*: a relevant extract is published in Stevens, op cit, i, 322.

[76] Published in Stevens, op cit, i, 430. There are no differences.

there — to convince those people more by what we can do than what we really do that they are in our power — and finally in pursuing the same plan (supporting friends) in a more northerly and healthy climate.

With regard to a station for the protection of the King's ships, I know of no place so proper as York Town if it could be taken possession of, fortified and garrisoned with 1,000 men, as, by having 1,000 more at a post somewhere in Elizabeth River, York and James Rivers would be ours and our cruisers might command the waters of the Chesapeak. Troops might likewise be spared from these posts to carry on expeditions during the summer months when probably nothing can be risked in that climate but water movements. But if the heights of York and those on Gloucester side cannot be so well and so soon fortified as to render that post *hors d'insult* before the enemy can move a force etc against it, it may not be adviseable to attempt it. In that case something may possibly be done at Old Point Comfort to cover large ships lying in Hampton Road (which is reckoned a good one and not so liable to injury from gales at north-east as that of York, particularly in winter). If neither can be secured, we must content ourselves with keeping the Chesapeak with frigates and other armed vessels, which will always find security against a superior naval force in Elizabeth River. As our operations in proper season may recommence in the Upper James, perhaps a station might be found at the entrance of the narrows of that river that may be of use in future day and held with a small force. James Town seems a proper spot for such a station, as does the place where the narrows and windings begin.

At a proper time of the year operations must still go northward either by a direct movement — stationing your supplies in the navigable rivers which lye favorable for it — in which you are, however, exposed to a temporary naval superiority of the enemy, or by proceeding up the Chesapeak if a force equal to the attempt can be collected, for, when it can, I should propose to take a station threatening all the provinces bordering on Chesapeak with a desultory war [and] prevent those provinces from being succored by menacing communications and availing ourselves of a supposed numerous band of friends, who otherwise may be forced to arm against us. Had we a force sufficient for two movements, that would be best, 4,000 men to proceed in transports up to Baltimore, taking a station within a certain distance of the Susquehannah and having vessels always ready for a rapid move with part or even the whole to a corresponding station in the Eastern Neck, while a corps of 10,000 men or more (according to the force that can be brought against you) occupies the Eastern Neck and can in its turn succor the western corps. Whether the eastern corps acts alone or in cooperation, it must be in very great force for reasons obvious. I do not know enough of this neck to say what force, or whether any, can be placed in security. The most advanced station would certainly be the best, particularly at first, to enable our friends, who we are told are at Lancaster, Little York Town and Chester, to join us. Iron Hill may perhaps be it, and as marshy creeks run up from Delaware and Chesapeak, the heads of which are not far asunder, many good posts may be found for corps of different strength, for while we command those bays, there can be no danger of operation against our flanks and rear, and if the enemy should be superior in one, he cannot be so in both. We should therefore have always a communication open. This corps should be very strong indeed, or there should be one acting in favor of it in Jersey. The preference must be given to that plan against which Washington can bring the least force. He undoubtedly can bring a greater force into Jersey than anywhere, as the New England troops may be prevailed on to go there, and they cannot so easily be drawn into the Eastern Neck or even over the Delaware. Besides, if Washington moves into Jersey, his meal and flour have both but a short portage, but, once deprived of the eastern counties, his cattle in that case coming chiefly from New England will increase his difficulty of subsistence, for, as we may under those circumstances attempt to occupy King's Ferry, he will be reduced to the detour. I therefore should prefer a single corps in the Eastern Neck, sufficient, however, for the purpose. As the French have added considerably to Washington's force, I do not think an army less than Sir William Howe had could be sufficient — 15,000 men! But where are they to be found? My whole force, rank and file fit for duty, is nearly 24,000. It is presumed Lord Cornwallis will be content with 6,000 for the southward; 2,000 we suppose in the Chesapeak; 12,000 are required for New York. There remains only 4,000 for that operation. I did expect 10,000 men as an augmentation to my present army. Had they come, this project might have taken place, but I am now told I am to expect only 4,000, which will not be sufficient. However, once convinced that the French will not send reinforcement and that we shall be permanently superior at sea and have an active co-operating naval commander, I should be tempted to try, but until all this combines, I dare not, and if it is delayed too long, our friends in Pennsylvania may be forced from us or cajolled.

If we could hold the Chesapeak by the posts on Elizabeth and York Rivers, Oxford and Port Penn, and the two eastern on the sea coasts, and threaten our enemies of Virginia and Maryland and protect our friends of all these countries, I think we should in that case leave the French little to induce them to support the war.

26th April

These, however, I give you merely as my opinions at the time we talked on this subject, and they will influence you, of course, no further than as they correspond with your own now.

H CLINTON

[*Subscribed*:]

With respect to the number and disposition [of] friends in Pensilvania I am telling you more what I wish than what I expect to find, for we have been too often deceived by representations of sanguine friends.

Clinton to Phillips, 30th April 1781 99(32): C

New York
30th April 1781

Sir

I have been favoured with your dispatches by the *Amphitrite*, and my answers to them will go to you on Tuesday or Wednesday by the *Richmond* man of war, who will also carry my letters to Cape Fear.

In the mean time I think it right to send an advice boat with the inclosed intelligence, that you may be on your guard.

...[77]

As it is necessary I should always have a number of these boats ready, I must request you will send hither all those now with you, except one, which may be kept for any emergency, and that in future you do not detain more than one but send them back with all convenient dispatch, whether you have any information to communicate or not.

I have the honor to be, sir,
Your most obedient humble servant

H CLINTON

PS

As the wind has been contrary for two or three days, probably the French fleet have not yet sailed.

Enclosure
Intelligence, 29th April 1781   *99(32): C*

New York
29th April 1781
5 o'clock am

J S, who was dispatched the 24th instant to gain intelligence from Rhode Island, is just return'd and reports that he crossed the sound from Oyster Ponds to the Rope Ferry the 26th at night, that he there met his friend from Rhode Island, who had come off on purpose to get an opportunity to send the following intelligence to us: that the whole of the French navy and some transports with 2,500 troops on board were to sail at farthest on this day (the 29th), and it was imagined for the Chesapeake, supposing our fleet so disabled as not to be able soon to follow them.

The French troops had marched to Providence for a few days, then returned and immediately embark'd.

That this day sevennight 20 transports sailed from Rhode Island loaded with provisions, supposed for the West Indies, but does not know what convoy they had.

---

[77] A paragraph consisting of two lines in Arnold's cipher. It is not decoded.

Clinton to Phillips, 30th April and 2nd and 3rd May 1781[78]   95(40): LS

Secret and most private   New York
   30th April 1781

Major General Phillips

Dear Phillips

I cannot judge from Lord Cornwallis's letter whether he proposes any further operations in the Carolinas, what they may be, and how far you can operate in his favor. If I was to give a private opinion from reading his letter, I would say I cannot conceive from it that he has any offensive object in view. He says that North Carolina is a country in which it is impossible for an army to act or move without the assistance of friends. He does not seem to think we have any there — nor do you. I shall give no opinion respecting that at present or until I receive his Lordship's account of the state of the province and of his winter's campaign.

His Lordship tells me that he wants reinforcements. With nine British battalions and detachments from seven more (besides those from the artillery and 17th Dragoons), five Hessian battalions and a detachment of Jagers, and eleven Provincial battalions exclusive of the cavalry and infantry of the Legion and the Provincial light infantry, I would ask: how can that be possible? And if it is, what hopes can I have of a force sufficient to undertake any solid operation?

To be brief, if his Lordship proposes no operation to you soon and you see none that will operate for him directly (that is, before the first of June), I think the best indirect one in his favor will be what you and General Arnold proposed to me in N° 10 of your joint letter of the 18th instant (beginning with the attempt on Philadelphia etc). The only risk you run is from a temporary superiority of the enemy at sea. Land and naval reinforcements from France are talked of. If they come immediately from Europe, we must have some information of them, and they will, I hope, be followed; if from the West Indies, I hope the same. It is, however, an important move and ought (in my opinion) to be tried, even with some risk. If our friends are as numerous and hearty as Colonel Rankin[79] represents them to be, with their assistance added to what you carry thither you will be able to maintain yourself, but if, after having given the experiment a fair trial, you find it will not do, you may either retire to Portsmouth or by transports and boats in Delaware pass to Jersey, where at all events I must

---

[78] Published without the enclosure in Stevens, op cit, i, 450. There are no other material differences.

[79] Born to Quaker parents in Bathgate, West Lothian, William Rankin (1739-1833) is thought to have migrated in the early 1760s to York County, Pennsylvania, where he became a Justice of the Peace and colonel of militia. As the revolutionary war progressed, he organised a covert association of loyalists in his locality and entered into a clandestine correspondence with the British high command. Eventually found out by the Pennsylvania revolutionary authorities, he was attainted and his estate confiscated. He died at Mill Hill, London, having spent part of his later life in Canada, where his son James settled in 1796. He is not to be confused with several others in Pennsylvania who shared the name William Rankin during the revolution. (Information from Linda Burkell, a descendant of Rankin, 3rd August 1999 and 4th & 7th May 2001; Sabine, *Biographical Sketches*, ii, 569)

pick you up by receiving you at or near Mount Holly. Give me timely notice of your intended move, and if possible I will follow you into Delaware with such a small reinforcement as I can at the time spare.

As my invitation to Lord Cornwallis to come to the Chesapeak was upon a supposition that every thing would be settled in the Carolinas, I do not think he will come. If, however, he determines to do so as a visitor, he will get Barkley or some other to bring him, for the Admiral has this day only ordered a ship for the purpose and the one he has ordered cannot (I apprehend) get over the bar of Cape Fear.

Our Admiral is grown if possible more impracticable than ever. He swears to me that he knows nothing of his recall; to others he says he is going home immediately. If the next packet does not satisfy me in this particular, I shall probably retire and leave him to Lord Cornwallis's management, to whom it will be my advice to try the only experiment that (in my opinion) can operate if the one in Carolina has failed. As to Virginia, I know none which can reduce that province in one campaign. Tho' it is certainly a great exertion, the only one that appears to me is the above. If I stay, it shall be tried. Without a cooperating naval chief, the risk is doubly great. It would be sufficiently so with one. But if it succeeds, its consequences must be very decisive.

May 2nd

The reinforcement is embarked and fallen down to Staten Island, where they wait only the Admiral's pleasure for their proceeding to Chesapeak. Two days ago he offered to take them thither under the escort of his fleet. To day he writes to me that he thinks he cannot be justified in losing a moment to proceed off the Chesapeak, but if I think it of greater consequence to land the reinforcement of troops proposed to be sent there than to intercept the enemy, he will take the transports with him, otherwise he shall certainly leave them behind until it is known where the enemy's fleet is lodged, of which he will transmit the earliest information to me, and then appoint a convoy to bring them on. In answer I have acknowledged the very great importance of intercepting the French fleet, but that it is also of importance that this reinforcement should join you immediately, and leave to him (as being the best judge) the properest mode of accomplishing it with safety. Thus the matter rests.

May 3rd

As I am (from the Admiral's strange conduct) doubtfull when or whether the reinforcement will ever join you, I do not now send Colonel Rankin to you as I at first proposed but I inclose his proposals. You will see by them that he is not much of an officer, but he appears to be a plain, sensible man worth attending to, and Simcoe can explain a thousand things respecting him and his associates which I cannot in a letter. As you seemed to think (before you received Lord Cornwallis's letter) that all direct operation in favor of his Lordship would cease by the end of May, should the expedition not sail from hence before the 20th instant, and I do not hear further from you, I will not send it, for in that case I think the experiment on the peninsula may be tried to more advantage up Delaware than round by Chesapeak, in which case I shall expect General Arnold and you with such troops as you can spare to meet me at the head of Elk or Bohemia and form a junction. I can certainly spare more troops from hence for such a move than I can send to Chesapeak for reasons obvious. Pray let me receive General Arnold's and your opinions upon Colonel Rankin's proposals as soon as possible. I confess I am not sanguine, but if the experiment can be tried without any other risk than from the enemy's superiority at sea, I should wish to do it. Therefore, if General Arnold and you like it, I shall be reconciled to it, and it shall be tried after I know your opinions on it and the inclosed proposals and, if you approve, about what time you think the attempt may take place. I am persuaded that on application Captain Hudson will give you a frigate for your dispatches. If we move up Delaware, Captain Duncan (Lord Howe's captain) will conduct us. I have already talked to him on the subject and he approves.

If Lord Cornwallis proposes any thing necessary for his operations, you of course must adopt it if you can, letting me know your thoughts thereon, but should his Lordship determine on a defensive in the Carolinas, he surely cannot want any of the European reinforcement and will of course send it to you and all such other as shall arrive. Thus reinforced, if, after leaving a sufficient garrison in Elizabeth River, you can proceed to the peninsula, I think we shall be in force to give this a fair trial, and I may leave you in the command there unless things should take a more favorable turn in the Carolinas and Lord Cornwallis's presence there be no longer necessary, for, until they do, I should imagine he will not leave Carolina.

You will think me long winded, but as safe opportunities are not frequent, I must make the best use I can of this. I refer you for more information to Lord Chewton, who is the bearer of my dispatches.

Sincerely yours

H CLINTON

Enclosure
William Rankin's proposals   *102(11): C*

That two thousand of the British forces be landed at Chester or the Wilmington, at either of which places one thousand ought to keep post and the remainder march to the upper part of the Chesapeak. That ten thousand stand of spare arms, artillery and a sufficiency of ammunition for the use of the inhabitants be sent with this expedition; that four thousand of these be lodged at Wilmington or Chester and the remainder be conveyed to the upper part of the Chesapeak aforesaid. That the inhabitants be permitted and encouraged to rise in arms by companies under officers chosen by and from amongst themselves, and that they also be permitted to seize all magazines and every officer civil or military in their power acting under usurped authority. That on the inhabitants joining the King's forces, civil officers of justice be appointed in the country with proper authority to execute the laws on delinquents, and that associators be permitted to return to the country from whence they came for the protection of these ministers of justice, where they are to remain as a militia and act in conjunction with the royal army or by themselves, as circumstances may require, on the shortest notice when called upon during this rebellion. That blank commissions be granted for the officers chosen by the inhabitants, to be filled up occasionally as I have not brought the return of their names with me. That an address to the people be published on our commencing hostilities, in English and German, declaring our intentions etc, as there are many left who will make good soldiers and could not be entrusted with our combination. That where unavoidable occurrences shall make it necessary to take from any loyalist provisions, horses, waggons or other requisites, they receive assurances of pay for such articles.

I hope no recruiting parties from any other regiments excepting from those employed on this expedition will be suffered to inlist any of the associators, and that his Excellency will give such of the associators as have distinguished themselves in this affair and are properly qualified for the purpose the exclusive priviledge of raising any corps on the Provincial establishment that may be wanted, if they desire it.

Clinton to Phillips, 11th May 1781　　　　　　　　　　　　　　95(44): ALS

May 11th

Dear Phillips

I was in hopes that the fleet would have sailed long since, but altho the Admiral dates his letter 10th off Sandy Hook, I fear he is still within.

Report says that the French had not sailed from Rhode Island a few days ago. They might, however, have sailed yesterday. The only news we have is a riot at Phi——— and all paper money refused in payment. It works finely.

No news from Lord Cornwallis since his letter of the 10th April.

Washington some days since called in Burgoyne. By a letter from him this day, that is countermanded or suspended. Their councils seem a little unsetled. 'Tis reported and believed that the French troops are to join Washington, and now on the route.

Faithfully

H C

[*Subscribed*:]

Lord Chewton sailed 3 days since for Lord Cornwallis.

Memorandum by Clinton, May 1781　　　　　　　　　　　　　　102(14): D

Canada – The General has applied in vain to the Admiral for convoy to send with troops and victualers.

Ethan Allen has increased in his demands, extended his district, and is wavering – seems waiting for events to deside.

Washington's army is about 5,000, increasing daily with six months' men. Difficult to raise for the war.

West Point much strengthened since Arnold left it.

The General has a very good correspondance.

Sends a copy of Rankin's proposals. Refers to Simcoe for particulars.

Washington's letter.

Burgoyne recalled. The General has offered the Cedars[80] and to make up their own tariff from officers our prisoners.

Near a year's provisions in store.

Six regiments coming by way of the West Indies. General Vaughan is directed not to employ them.

At a time when the General thought it likely Lord Cornwallis would have finished his operations in the Carolinas, the General would have wished him to have conducted them in the Chesapeak.

The General applied in the strongest terms to the Admiral for Captain Duncan. He promised but has since appointed Captain Hudson, who has upon all occasions shewn great zeal and desire of hearty cooperations with the army.

The general tenor of the dispatches.

Connolly recommended to be sent with an expedition on the Ohio — important while operations are going on in the Chesapeak.

The object of the French last year was on the arrival of their reinforcements to have attacked this place if possible — if not, Halifax and Penobscot.

That reinforcement sailed and is now in the West Indies.[81]

By the information Government have received they think it likely they may send one this year.[82]

---

[80] *has offered the Cedars*: presumably as a place for commissaries of prisoners to meet.

[81] Clinton adds in his own hand: ''Tis so to prove.'

[82] '- to the French' is added in Clinton's hand.

To General Phillips on present uncertain state. Say the 20th to General Phillips instead of the 15th May.[83]

Lord Cornwallis the first object.

Head of Elk, Baltimore, lower countys on Delawar.

§ - §

2 - From Phillips to Cornwallis or Craig

Phillips to Cornwallis, 8th April 1781[84] 　　　　　　　　　　　　　　　　　*5(191): C*

Portsmouth, Virginia
April 8th 1781

Lt General the Earl Cornwallis

My Lord

Under the extreme uncertainty of your Lordship's situation and from the variety of reports respecting your good and ill success I am render'd unable to even guess where your Lordship may be and what are your present operations. You will do us the justice to be assured that every man here is ready to sacrifice his life in endeavouring to persue the instructions and orders of the Commander in Chief, which go strongly and principally to a cooperation with your Lordship's intentions for His Majesty's Service, and I am directed both publickly and secretly to give your Lordship every assistance which the corps of troops here can afford. How chearfully I shall obey these orders of Sir Henry Clinton I need not describe. My sincere attachment for you, my Lord, connected so strongly with the King's Service, will convince you that no exertions shall be left untried upon this occasion.

I send to you, my Lord, a variety of papers which may serve to explain every thing which I should otherwise be obliged to make the subject of a long letter. I send to your Lordship an officer, Lieutenant Rutherford of the 82nd Regiment, who can detail almost every publick matter here. He has my directions to use every means for reaching your Lordship. He has orders to destroy this dispatch at sea if it shall be necessary, and I have writ to the commanding officer at Wilmington not to hazard these letters should it be unsafe. I hope, however, there will be a possibility of your Lordship receiving this intelligence.

---

[83] This paragraph is written in Clinton's hand.

[84] This letter miscarried. See Craig to Cornwallis, 2nd May, vol IV, p 167.

The works here will be in a state to allow of a movement on the 12th instant and it will be made with a force of 2,000 effective men, the garrison being left in a situation to resist any attempt from the mass of militia in our front. The plan will be to break up the communication from Virginia to Carolina and it may possibly call upon Green to fall back, in which case it will allow your Lordship to persue such operations as you may judge necessary, but should the distance be so great as not to affect Green as I describe, he will assuredly receive no reinforcement of militia except perhaps from the lower part of Roanoke, where the enemy have ordered a large draught to be made from that militia in aid to Green. The time I shall be able to remain above cannot be ascertained. It will depend on what La Fayette does. If he moves from Anapolis with his corps of Continental troops (1,500 men) sustained by a numerous militia, it will oblige me to return here to guard this place and in doing so I shall destroy every publick store, all vessels, boats and the corn and other mills so as to render the country as much incapable of acting as possible. Should it be possible for me to have communication with your Lordship, I shall then consider myself under your Lordship's orders and obey them to the utmost of my power. A personal communication with your Lordship is most ardently to be wished for many reasons, for some which I must refer your Lordship to my *secret* letter[85] to explain. How this may be brought about is not in me to describe, but I am ready to undertake any thing your Lordship may conceive necessary to order on this and every other occasion. Whenever all hopes of communicating with you, my Lord, are over and that[86] the expedition up James River shall be finished, I am left at liberty by the Commander in Chief to persue such operations as may appear eligible to me and wait for being recal'd to New York, and this leads me to observe to you, my Lord, that Sir Henry Clinton means at all events that I and Brigadier General Arnold with the light infantry and the Loyal Americans should join his immediate army for the operations of the campaign. The rest, I imagine, will be left to a cooperation with your Lordship or to act immediately under your orders.

After what I have thus written, taking also the contents of my *secret* letter, I need not urge the consequence it will be to the service that I should hear from your Lordship. It will appear so necessary that I make no doubt but you will, my Lord, send to me if possible an officer of trust and confidence and that I shall have explained to me what are to be your Lordship's future operations: whether you intend coming into Virginia and by what route that I may assist your movement; whether you intend, my Lord, to connect your different posts in the Carolinas and move this way by water; or whether it may be your Lordship's intentions to confine your operations solely to the Carolinas, in which latter case it might be well to detail something of the manner that I may form an idea how best to assist your Lordship with the troops here. My intentions are, when I can no longer operate for *your Lordship*, to do so for myself by expeditions in Chesapeak and the waters of that bay, but I must observe to you, my Lord, that assisting your army is the first great object of my wishes, founded on the instructions and orders of his Excellency the Commander in Chief.

---

[85] Annotated: 'The secret letter was wrote by the General and no copy made of it.

GEO VALLANCEY
Secretary to Major General Phillips'

[86] *that*: the meaning is 'whenever'. See p 9, note 4.

The *Roebuck* ship of war, carrying my dispatches to Sir Henry Clinton, sailed from the Capes on Fryday noon the 6th instant with a fair wind for New York, and as it has continued so, I conceive it must reach that place tomorrow, and I make no doubt but I shall have answers from his Excellency on the instant. From Sir Henry Clinton's determination respecting a reinforcement and from a communication with your Lordship I am to calculate and judge what may be done best for His Majesty's Service. I apprehend that the first or second week in June must terminate all movements in the Carolinas and in Virginia from heat of weather and the climate, at which time the campaign will in course open to the northward.

I cannot conclude without doing justice to the ability, activity and zeal of Brigadier General Arnold, who with a small corps of troops effected a very essential move up James River, has sustained a rather weak post here, and carried on a variety of objects with great success.

Lieutenant Rutherford, who carries this dispatch, is an active, good officer. As such I recommend him to your Lordship's favour.

I have desired the commanding officer at *Wilmington* to open this publick letter, but the *secret* papers and *secret* letter to be conveyed if possible to your Lordship.

I have the honour to be, my Lord, with the most perfect attachment
Your Lordship's most obedient much obliged humble servant

WILLIAM PHILLIPS

Phillips to Craig, 9th April 1781[87]   5(205): C

Portsmouth, Virginia
9th April 1781

Major Craig

Dear Sir

I send Lieutenant Rutherford of the 82nd Regiment with dispatches for his Excellency Lt General the Earl Cornwallis. The two publick ones you are at liberty to open, and having read them, you will immediately dispatch the vessel back to me here with such remarks as you may be able to make upon my letters and every information it may be in your power to give me respecting the present situation of Lord Cornwallis and what you know of his Lordship's future intentions.

You will be so good, provided you have a communication with Lord Cornwallis, to send Lieutenant Rutherford with my dispatches to his Lordship, and as you may naturally imagine my *secret dispatch* to be of the greatest consequence and that it must not on any account be

---

[87] This letter miscarried with Phillips' of 8th April to Cornwallis.

suffered to fall into the hands of the enemy, you will please to send such an escort with Lieutenant Rutherford as may secure him from a possibility of being taken.

I need not recommend dispatch to you, as I am sure your zeal for the service will prompt you to use the quickest with the securest means of forwarding Lieutenant Rutherford (if you have any communication with Earl Cornwallis, as I before observed) to his Lordship, and that you will dispatch the express boat back again with all the intelligence you can give me from your own information and knowledge.

I recommend Lieutenant Rutherford to you as an officer very much in credit here, as has been reported to me by Lt Colonel Dundas and Brigadier General Arnold, and I refer you to him for further particulars.

I am, dear Craig, with great regard
Your sincere friend and humble servant

W PHILLIPS

Phillips to Cornwallis, 18th April 1781[88]

5(227): C

Portsmouth, Virginia
18th April 1781

His Excellency Lt General the Earl Cornwallis

My Lord

I have the honour to inclose your Lordship a letter which came to me from the Commander in Chief to be forwarded to Cape Fear, which I do by Lieutenant Anderson of the 82nd Regiment.

I take for granted that the particulars alluded to in the letter has been or will be detailed fully to your Lordship.

I trust my last dispatch sent you, my Lord, by Lieutenant Rutherford has reached Wilmington and that it may have been forwarded to your Lordship from thence. To that dispatch I most impatiently wait for the answer.

In answer to my letters to the Commander in Chief of the 29th, 30th ultimo and the 3rd instant, of which I sent your Lordship copies, I have not any determined plan given me, nor his Excellency does not say what he intends further upon those subjects. He defers taking into consideration my proposal for a reinforcement untill he shall receive answers to some queries he has put to Brigadier General Arnold and to me. Those answers go off in an express boat this night, as shall that intended for Cape Fear if the wind will permit.

---

[88] This letter, enclosing Clinton's of 13th April to Cornwallis (p 94), miscarried. See Craig to Cornwallis, 2nd May, vol IV, p 167.

The movement intended to be made in favour of your Lordship up James River to Petersburg has been delayed by contrary winds, storms and rain ever since the 11th instant. The winds have changed this morning and the troops will embark and proceed this evening upon the expedition. Allowing for every cross accident and the resistance the enemy may make at the strongholds upon the river, I conclude we must be at Petersburg in eight days.

How far I may be of use to you with the 2,000 men I take from hence will depend upon a communication with you and your orders either by land or by water. Should I unfortunately not hear of or from your Lordship, I shall return here by the first of May in order to pursue such other operations as the Commander in Chief may please to dictate.

The personal interview desired by the Commander in Chief between your Lordship and myself I most ardently hope may take place, for I believe it is equally the Commander in Chief's wish as it will be for the good of the service that your Lordship's sentiments may be given through me upon the operations of the ensuing campaign.

I beseech you, my dear Lord, to let me hear from you as soon as possible.

I have the honour to be, my Lord, under every description of consideration, attachment and affectionate regard
Your Lordship's most faithful humble servant

WILLIAM PHILLIPS

Phillips to Cornwallis, 19th April 1781[89]   70(5): CS

Hampton Road in Chesapeak
April 19th 1781

His Excellency Lt General the Earl Cornwallis

My dear Lord

The *Amphytrite* sent me last night your Lordship's letter of the 10th instant and the inclosures. I lament your Lordship's situation at the same time that I glory in your conduct and success. I perfectly agree with you, my Lord, on the present state of our affairs and think them very critical. I agree with your Lordship respecting the drain New York is to us, but I fear it is too great a weight in the political scale to throw away. It might affect not only America but Europe.

I understand the *Medea* is sent for you and I make no doubt but you will embrace the opportunity of coming here and I do assure you, my dear Lord, that I shall feel infinite pleasure in being superceded.

---

[89] This letter miscarried.

Under the expectation of seeing your Lordship I will not delay the express boat going to your Lordship.

I lament from my soul poor Webster and the other losses your Lordship has sustained.

With an ardent desire of meeting you, etc

WILLIAM PHILLIPS

Phillips to Cornwallis, 6th May 1781[90]　　　　　　　　　　　　　6(58): CS

On board the *Maria* off Burrell's Ferry, James River
Sunday May 6th, ½ after 10 am

Earl Cornwallis

My dear Lord

A teazing indisposition prevents my using my own hand, but I will not loose one moment in answering your letter dated the 24th April[91], which I received an hour ago. La Fayette is upon the James River with ten, twelve or fifteen hundred men, for the accounts are various, but this corps I can easily keep in subjection, and should you not apprehend danger from any other, there will not be the least difficulty in your making a junction with me if you please, and for which purpose I will do every thing in my power to communicate with your Lordship from Petersburg, but I foresee many — very many — difficulties in doing it.

I was returning to Portsmouth from a successfull expedition up James River to Petersburg and Manchester, having destroyed all the State armed vessels, merchant ships, privateers etc etc etc up the river, a great quantity of wheat, flour, and corn, and tobacco to the amount of six thousand hogsheads. I am now sailing back with a fair wind and shall reach Petersburg probably tomorrow, certainly the next day, and it will give me infinite satisfaction if this corps of troops proves of service to your Lordship's operations. Had you been, my dear Lord, *positive* of coming to the Roanoke, I would have made a forced march to have met you, but at an uncertainty I do not dare venture the movement.

I will communicate with you by sending letters in cypher continually, but I greatly fear this mode of conveyance will miscarry, as the country keeps so good a look-out. I wish you every possible success, and am, my dear Lord,

Your most sincere and obedient humble servant

W PHILLIPS

§ - §

---

[90] This letter miscarried.

[91] *your letter..*: see vol IV, p 116.

3 - Other letters

Phillips to von Fuchs, 6th May 1781　　　　　　　　　　　　　70(7): CS

On board the *Maria* off Burrell's Ferry, James River
Sunday May 6th 1781, ½ after 10 am

Lt Colonel de Fuchs

Sir

I was proceeding down the James River to Portsmouth when I received some dispatches which have occasioned me to return. Upon my departure from Portsmouth I left a vessel laden with twenty days' provisions. I desire you will immediately dispatch that vessel after me under convoy of the *Rambler* and that you will direct also all recovered men belonging to the light infantry and Queen's Rangers to be put on board the vessels which will come up the [river] to me.

I have the honour to be etc

W PHILLIPS

Extract, Vallancey to Phillips, 8th May 1781　　　　　　　　　　99(33): C

When the *Mercury* sailed from New York, the fleet was at Staten Island and the captain of the vessel thinks they sailed yesterday.

A report prevailed when he came away that the French fleet had sailed from Rhode Island. Admiral Arbuthnot is to convoy the fleet.

The strength is as follows of those already embarked:

17th Foot	243
43rd	392
1st Anspach	617
2nd ditto	598
Convalescents and recruits for this army	200
	2,050

§ - §

CHAPTER 51

Letters to or from New York or London

1 - Between Cornwallis and Clinton[1]

Clinton to Cornwallis, 2nd January 1781　　　　　　　　　　　　　　　　*5(21): LS*

New York
January 2nd 1781

Lt General Earl Cornwallis

My Lord

I have perused your Lordship's proclamation of the 16th September last respecting the sequestration of rebel property and have the honor to intimate my approbation of your humane intention therein, which I have no doubt is perfectly consistent with your Lordship's local knowledge of affairs in Carolina.

Lord George Germain having transmitted to me the copy of a petition which had been presented to the King by the merchants trading to South Carolina, which appears to me likewise to relate in some degree to the subject of that proclamation, and his Lordship having signified to me His Majesty's pleasure respecting the same, I have the honor to send your Lordship copies of the petition and the Minister's letter, together with my instructions to the trustees in consequence; and I request that your Lordship will be pleased to give such additional instructions to the persons intrusted with the management of rebel property as you

---

[1] Clinton's letters from 2nd January to 8th March 1781 (pp 71-87) formed a bundle conveyed to Charlestown by the *Jupiter* merchant ship under the care of Captain Amherst, aide-de-camp to General Dalling. They arrived early in April but did not reach Cornwallis until June, when he records receiving a letter forming part of the bundle (Stevens, *Clinton-Cornwallis Controversy*, i, 85). As stated in the Editorial method (vol I, p xiii), the rest of the letters are, as elsewhere, not in chronological order but in the order that they were written or received by Cornwallis.

may judge most likely to answer the King's intentions, consistent with the state of matters in that province, of which your Lordship must have a more competent knowledge than I possibly can at this distance.

I have the honor to be
Your Lordship's most obedient and most humble servant

H CLINTON

Enclosure (1)
Germain to Clinton and Arbuthnot, 3rd August 1780   99(15): C

Whitehall
August the 3rd 1780

Sir Henry Clinton KB and Vice Admiral Arbuthnot

Gentlemen

The merchants trading to South Carolina, to whom many individuals in that province are largely indebted, having put into my hands an humble petition to the King, I have had the honor to lay it before His Majesty, who was pleased to receive it very graciously and to command me to transmit it to you and to signify to you His royal pleasure that you do take the prayer of it into consideration and give all the relief and facility in your power to the petitioners, and all other His Majesty's faithful subjects residing in Great Britain in the like circumstances, in recovering and receiving satisfaction for their just demands against the inhabitants of that province.

I am happy to find that the motives which induced you to restrain the exportation of effects from Carolina until their property and destination should be ascertained by the Commissioners you had appointed for that purpose are done justice to by the petitioners, and I have no doubt the very measures prayed for will have already been taken by that Board in consequence of your instructions. But as the petitioners' case requires very particular attention and to be treated with the utmost tenderness, it will be proper for you to instruct the Board to be extremely circumspect in their investigations and carefully to distinguish what is really the property of rebels from what may be only apparently theirs but ultimately that of the British merchants, for you will readily conceive that, although the person in whose possession effects may be found has borne arms against the King and no British merchant has any demand against him, yet if the merchant in Carolina to whom he is indebted be himself indebted to the British merchant and unable to pay him unless he is paid by the revolter, the confiscation of the effects in the revolter's possession must prove ultimately the loss of the British merchant, which would be the greatest cruelty, hardship and injustice to men who have struggled with every difficulty the suspension of their trade and the stoppage of their remittances have laid them under, since the rebellion broke out, without murmur or complaint, and therefore entitled to the fullest protection and most liberal consideration of Government.

I am, gentlemen,
Your most obedient humble servant

GEO GERMAIN

Enclosure (2)
Petition to the King, undated   *99(21): C*

To the King's Most Excellent Majesty in Council

The petition of the merchants trading to the province of South Carolina most humbly sheweth

That Your petitioners being informed that Sir Henry Clinton, Commander in Chief of Your Majesty's army in North America, having given orders to stop and detain indico and other property of the people in the province of South Carolina in order to prevent the same being applied to the payment and discharge of foreign debts or other improper uses, appointing at the same time Commissioners to examine and take under their care and direction such indico and other property so stopped and detained in order that the good intentions of the Commander in Chief might be carried into full execution

And Your petitioners having received certain information that the officers of Your Majesty's troops and navy have taken, stopped and detained books of accounts, papers, indico and other property, and on application being made by the proprietors to the Commander in Chief, praying to have them restored, have received for answer that the same must be determined by Your Majesty in Council, and whereas the taking and detaining of such books of accounts, indico and other property will be attended with consequences exceedingly injurious and distressing to Your Majesty's petitioners, who are already sinking under their accumulated misfortunes

Your petitioners do therefore most humbly pray that Your Majesty will be graciously pleased to give effectual orders that such books of accounts, papers, indico and other property as have been or may be taken, stopped and detained be immediately restored to the proprietors on their giving security that the same shall be applied to the discharge of British debts or such other good purposes as may be truly correspondent with the interest of Your suffering petitioners, or to grant such other relief as to Your Majesty in Your royal wisdom shall seem meet.

GREENWOOD & HIGGINSON	CHAMPION & DICKASON
RICHARD SHUBRICK	LANE, SON & FRASER
JOHN SHOOLBRED	JOHN NUTT
	GEORGE BAGUE

Enclosure (3)
Clinton to the Trustees of Captured Property, 2nd January 1781

99(19): C

New York
January 2nd 1781

The Trustees of Captured Property

Gentlemen

You receive inclosed the copy of a petition which has been presented to the King from the British merchants trading to South Carolina and transmitted to me by the Secretary of State for the American Department, who has signified to me His Majesty's pleasure that I should take the prayer of it into consideration and give all the relief and facility in my power to the petitioners, and all others His Majesty's faithful subjects residing in Great Britain in the like circumstances, in recovering and receiving satisfaction for their just demands against the inhabitants of that province.

I do therefore in obedience to the King's commands require that you will be extremely circumspect in your investigations and carefully distinguish what is really the property of rebels from what may be only apparently theirs but ultimately that of the British merchants.

Wherefore the better to fulfil the prayer of the petition it may be proper for you to collect all claims of the petitioners and of such others in the like circumstances and to transmit them by every opportunity to me that the King's commands may be taken for the payment of such as shall by His Majesty be thought *just* demands. You will likewise be pleased to transmit to me from time to time full accounts of all your transactions in all these matters and communicate your thoughts to me upon what other steps you judge expedient to be taken to relieve such of the petitioners and others whose claims appear to be properly founded.

I have the honor to be, gentlemen,
Your most obedient and most humble servant

H CLINTON

Clinton to Cornwallis, 3rd January 1781

5(31): LS

New York
January 3rd 1781

Lt General Earl Cornwallis

My Lord

I had the honor of writing to your Lordship on the 13th of last month[2], a duplicate of which letter is herewith transmitted. I have now the honor to inclose for your Lordship's

---

[2] See vol III, p 31.

information the copy of a declaration[3] which Vice Admiral Arbuthnot and I thought necessary to publish at this time as Commissioners, a copy whereof is likewise transmitted to Lt Colonel Balfour in order that a number of them may be struck off and circulated.

By the report of a privateer just arrived from the Chesapeak it seems probable that the expedition under Brigadier General Arnold entered that bay on the 27th, but I have not yet received any official accounts from him.

Vice Admiral Arbuthnot, who has been here for a short time on the business of the Commission, intends to return to day to rejoin his fleet at Gardiner's Bay, where it lies to watch that of the French at Rhode Island, the commander of which (Monsieur de Ternay) died a few days since at that place.

The French troops (except Lauzun's Legion, which moved lately to Lebanon) remain also at that Island and continue to add to its fortifications.

I have the honor to inclose to your Lordship the copies of several letters that were intercepted a short time since in a rebel mail, some of which you will perceive are very interesting.

Your Lordship will also receive herewith the copy of some intelligence lately received respecting Ethan Allen, and as I have received corresponding accounts of this event by other channels, I think there is great probability of the truth of this report.

I have the honor to be
Your Lordship's most obedient and most humble servant

H CLINTON

Enclosure
Intelligence concerning Ethan Allen etc   *104(5): C*

Information received on the 29th December 1780

That Ethan Allen had been to General Haldimand and reported on his return that it was engaged on the part of the Crown to make Vermont a separate government at the end of the war. That he had begun to fortify Bennington, the Vermonteers concurring with him. That a body of British had taken post at Ticonderoga to support the Vermonteers.

On this intelligence the Connecticut Assembly was called. The informer was at Hartford while they were deliberating on the motion to go against the Vermonteers last Monday sennight. High debates for several days. The motion not carried. Most people out of doors and some within declared that the Vermonteers had done well and that it would become the whole colony to follow their example.

---

[3] *copy of a declaration*: of this and the later enclosures, only the intelligence concerning Ethan Allen is extant.

Clinton to Cornwallis, 5th February 1781[4]

5(69): CS

New York
February 5th 1781

Lt General Earl Cornwallis

My Lord

I have the honor to inclose to your Lordship the copy of a letter I have lately received from Brigadier General Arnold, by which you will perceive that with scarcely 1,000 men (for several of his transports that had been separated on the voyage had not then rejoined him) he penetrated to Richmond, the capital of Virginia, and has rendered important service by destroying a valuable founderie, a considerable quantity of public stores, cannon etc etc as per the copies of his returns, which I have the honor to transmit herewith to your Lordship. Indeed the whole of his operations upon this occasion appear to have been conducted in a manner which strongly marks his character of a very active and good officer, and I sincerely hope, my Lord, that this important stroke will essentially aid your Lordship's operations.

By this precarious conveyance I shall only add that

I have the honor to be
Your Lordship's most obedient and most humble servant

H CLINTON

Enclosure (1)
Arnold to Clinton, 21st January 1781[5]

99(23): C

Portsmouth, Virginia
21st January 1781

Sir

I do myself the honor of embracing the first opportunity which has presented (since my arrival here) of transmitting to your Excellency an account of our proceedings since the army under my command left New York.

On the 26th and 27th December a hard gale of wind at north west separated the fleet, which joined again off the Capes of Virginia and arrived in Hampton Road on the 30th, except three transports and one armed vessel, with upwards of 400 troops on board, which did

---

[4] Published without the enclosures in Stevens, op cit, i, 324. There are no other material differences.

[5] Published without enclosures (2) and (3) in Davies ed, *Docs of the Am Rev*, xx, 40-3. There are no other material differences.

not arrive until the 4th of January. Some of the vessels were damaged in the gale of wind. About one half of the cavalry horses were lost. The *Swift* sloop of war and *Rambler* armed brigantine threw part of their guns overboard. The *Sally*, an ordnance ship, was very near foundering.

On the 31st December embarked the troops which had arrived in small vessels and boats (part of which were captured on our first arrival) and proceeded up James River with the *Hope* and *Swift*. On the 3rd of January at 7 o'clock pm, anchored at Flour de Hundreds about half a mile from Hood's Fort, which kept up a brisk fire upon us from a battery of 3 eighteen, one 24, pounders iron and one brass 8 inch howitzer, which killed one man. Lt Colonel Simcoe with a detachment of 250 men landed and took possession of the battery without opposition, spiked the iron guns and brought off the howitzer. On the 4th the fleet weighed at 7 o'clock, and at 10 anchored off Westover, the seat of the late Colonel Byrd, about 170 miles from the Capes of Virginia. We began immediately to disembark the troops and artillery, which was rendered tedious for want of proper boats, and it was 3 o'clock pm before the artillery, horses etc were landed, at which time came on a heavy shower of rain, but as the distance we had to march to Richmond and Westham (the objects in view) was 33 miles (in the heart of the enemy's country), no time was to be lost. The troops were therefore immediately put in motion and at 11 o'clock next morning reached Richmond without opposition. The militia who had collected fled at our approach. Lt Colonel Simcoe with his own corps, the flank companies of the 80th Regiment, the Yagers and York Volunteers were ordered to proceed to Westham, seven miles above Richmond, where they burnt and destroyed one of the finest founderies for cannon in America, 26 pieces of cannon, 310 barrels of gun powder, a large magazine of oats, and stores of various kinds, and returned to Richmond the same evening.

On my arrival at Richmond I was informed there was in stores a large quantity of tobacco, West India goods, wines, sail cloth etc. There was between 30 and 40 sail of vessels loaded with tobacco between Westover and Richmond. As the navigation of the river above Westover was intricate, the season critical, and many difficulties attending the removal of the goods, a proposal was made to the merchants who remained at Richmond, to prevent the destruction of private property (and at the same time to prevent the public from deriving any advantage from it), that, upon their delivering the whole of the goods enumerated on board His Majesty's fleet in James River, that one half the value should be paid to them. The approbation of their nominal Governor, his passes for their ships, and hostages for performance were required, and they were allowed until the next morning to obtain an answer from Mr Jefferson[6], who was in the neighbourhood. The next morning at ten o'clock I was informed by the merchants that their agent, sent to Mr Jefferson, was not returned, that from the delay no favorable answer for them was to be expected. As Mr Jefferson was so inattentive to the preservation of private property, I found myself under the disagreeable necessity of ordering a large quantity of rum to be stove, several ware houses of salt to be destroyed. Several public store houses and smiths' shops with their contents were consumed

---

[6] A signer and primary author of the Declaration of Independence, Thomas Jefferson (1743-1826) had been serving as Governor of Virginia since June 1779. Criticised by some for incompetence, he would be replaced by Thomas Nelson Jr in June 1781. A man of many parts, he would go on to become the 3rd President of the United States. (*DAB*; Boatner, *Encyclopedia*, 553-8)

by the flames. A very fine rope work full of material (private property) was burnt without my orders by an officer who was informed it was public property. A large magazine with quarter master's stores, sail cloth etc etc was burnt. A printing press and tipes were also purified by the flames.

The wines, of which there was a large quantity, and other goods (private property) were left unmolested. I did not think it good policy to destroy the tobacco or vessels, as they are always in our power, and the public can avail themselves of no advantage of either, and I have reason to believe that great part is the property of subjects well affected to His Majesty's Government. On the same principles the vessels and tobacco at Petersburgh were spared. The public stores at that place were not thought a sufficient object for our attention. The ships went up within six miles of Petersburgh and brought off some vessels. Most of them were sunk. Five very fine brass 6 pounders field pieces were taken and brought from Richmond, which place the troops evacuated at 12 o'clock and marched that night to Hudson's, 13 miles from Richmond, where they arrived at 7 o'clock. The excessive heavy rains prevented the troops from proceeding here[7]; they were without cover the whole night.

At 9 o'clock on the 7th they began their march, and at 3 o'clock pm returned to Westover. The excessive heavy rains in the night of the 6th and on the 7th rendered the roads, which are in some places a stiff clay, almost impassable. The troops (who with an ardor and firmness which would have done honor to veterans) performed a march of 66 miles in three days in an enemy's country where they were some times retarded hours by the destruction of bridges, and were detained upwards of one day in Richmond on severe duty.

The 8th in the evening Lt Colonel Simcoe was detached with 42 cavalry to Charles City Court House 9 miles from Richmond, where with his usual gallantry he surprised about 200 of the enemy's cavalry and foot, killed about 20, and brought off 8 prisoners with the loss of one man killed and 3 wounded. Captain Shanks[8] of the Queen's Rangers behaved on this as on every other occasion with great bravery.

On the 9th we were joined by the troops who were in the missing transports, and all the troops were reimbarked. On the 10th we fell down the river as low as Flour de Hundreds, when we were informed there was a party of 6 or 800 rebels under the command of Baron Stubens. At 7 o'clock, landed 120 Rangers, 170 Loyal Americans, 50 Yagers and 30 Artillery, when the boats returned for the 80th Regiment. 300 men under the command of Lt Colonel Simcoe were ordered to march about 2 miles to the Cross Roads where the enemy

---

[7] *here*: Westover.

[8] David Shank (?-1831) was a Scot who had migrated to Virginia before the revolution. Now a captain in the cavalry of the Queen's Rangers, he had entered the corps as a lieutenant in November 1776 and served in its infantry until 25th August 1780. During this period he had taken part in the Battles of Brandywine, Germantown, and Monmouth and in the Charlestown campaign. He would now remain with the Queen's Rangers in Virginia and capitulate with them at Yorktown. At the close of the war he was placed on the British half-pay list but returned to active duty in 1791 when the Queen's Rangers was reconstituted in England for service in Upper Canada. After serving there until 1799, he came back to Britain. He died in Glasgow, a lt general. (Sabine, *Biographical Sketches*, ii, 279; Donald J Gara, 'Biographical Sketches on Cavalry Officers of the Queen's American Rangers 1779-1783' (*The On-Line Institute for Advanced Loyalist Studies*, 8th April 2006); Raymond, 'British American Corps')

were posted and attack them. The vanguard was commanded by Captain Hatch[9] of the Loyal Americans, who with great gallantry attacked a picquet of the enemy and drove them to their main body. A very heavy fire from the rebels killed 3 men, wounded Captain Hatch, Ensign Sword[10] and about 20 privates of the Loyal American Regiment, whose conduct on this occasion does them great honor. They charged the enemy with such firmness and resolution that they instantly fled on all sides and were pursued for about 2 miles. The darkness of the night, badness of the roads, and heavy shower of rain which fell about this time prevented our pursuing the enemy any further. On our return 3 pieces heavy and some light cannon with a quantity of tobacco, biscuit etc were taken on board and the troops embarked at 4 o'clock next morning. On the 11th, fell down the river. On the 12th, anchored at Cobham and discharged a ware house of flour and tobacco. On the 13th, fell down to Williamsburgh. On the 14th, anchored at Harding Ferry and landed the troops, horses, artillery etc. On the 15th the army marched to Smithfield on Pagan Creek, 17 miles from Harding's Ferry, where a quantity of provisions etc was collected. On the 16th Lt Colonel Simcoe with a party of 200 men was detached to Mackay's Mills, 3 miles from Smithfield, to dislodge about 200 of the enemy who had taken post there, and who fled upon his approach. Major Gordon[11] was thrown over the creek at the same time with a party of 200 men to cut off the retreat of the enemy, who fled to the woods. 17th, the army moved to Mackay's Mills, the 18th to Sleepy Hole, ten miles further on Nansemond River. Lt Colonel Simcoe with 200 men crossed in the evening. At 2 o'clock in the morning on the 19th the troops began to cross the ferry and

---

[9] Christopher Hatch (1754-1819) was a Bostonian who had been commissioned a captain in the newly forming Loyal American Regiment on 28th March 1777. Now wounded, he would recover and serve till the close of the war, at which time his regiment was disbanded and he was placed on the Provincial half-pay list. Proscribed and banished by the revolutionary authorities in Massachusetts, he settled in New Brunswick, first at St John, then at Campobello Island, where he engaged in mercantile business, and finally at St Andrews, where he became a magistrate and colonel of militia. (Treasury 64/23(3), WO 65/164(37), and WO 65/165(3) (National Archives, Kew); *Saint Croix Courier* (St Stephen, New Brunswick), 12th July 1894; W O Raymond, 'The Loyal American Regiment', *A Raymond Scrapbook* (Fort Havoc Archives CD), i, 37; Sabine, *Biographical Sketches*, i, 522)

[10] Richard Swords (1762-1781) had been commissioned an ensign in Christopher Hatch's company of the Loyal American Regiment in April 1778. Born in Maryborough, Ireland, his father, Thomas (1737-1779), served in the 55th Regiment during the Seven Years' War and after the assault on Fort Ticonderoga in July 1758 was commissioned a lieutenant from the ranks. After the war he settled on a fine farm near Saratoga, but with the onset of the present conflict he fell foul of the revolutionaries for his loyalism, was imprisoned for a time, and was eventually allowed to repair to New York City, where he died. His farm was confiscated. Richard, his son, would soon meet an untimely end, dying of wounds received in the action which Arnold now relates. (Polly Hoppin, 'The Thomas Swords Family: A Perspective on the Loyalists of the American Revolution' (Internet, 12th April 2006); Raymond, 'British American Corps')

[11] James Gordon (?-1783) had entered the newly forming 80th Regiment (the Royal Edinburgh Volunteers) on 16th December 1777 as the senior of two majors. Now accompanying his regiment as part of Arnold's expedition, he would be present with it in Virginia when Cornwallis arrived there in May. According to Samuel Graham, a captain in the 76th Regiment and a friend of Gordon's, his 'military ability was justly appreciated by Lord Cornwallis, at the same time that it somewhat excited his surprise, as his Lordship had known him twenty years before in the gay circles of London.' On 6th July, 'mounted on a very tall horse', he would lead the 80th as part of Dundas's brigade in the action at Green Spring. Among the troops who capitulated at Yorktown, he was not one of the officers selected by lot to remain on parole with the men, but offered to take the place of Lt Colonel Gerard Lake, a Guards officer, who had 'expressed himself in such a manner' on being so selected. The offer 'was joyfully accepted'. He remained with the division quartered first at Fredericktown, Maryland, and then at Lancaster, Pennsylvania, until the troops were freed in June 1783. Promoted by brevet to lt colonel, he died soon afterwards at Morris's House and was buried with military honours at New York. (Colonel James John Graham ed, *Memoir of General Graham...* (Edinburgh, 1862), 31, 51-2, 54, 64, 71-5, 104-7; *Army Lists*)

were all over at 11, and marched 15 miles to 5 miles from Portsmouth, where Lt Colonel Simcoe by a forced march arrived at 10 in the morning to prevent the town from being burnt, as was threatned by the rebels.

On the 20th in the morning the whole army, to the great joy of the inhabitants, marched into Portsmouth in good health and high spirits. The troops upon this expedition behaved with a firmness, perseverance and spirit that would have done honor to veterans. The Yagers, York Volunteers and flank companies of the 80th Regiment have been very useful indeed. The officers commanding corps have been indefatigable in their duty and deserve every possible encomium.

I am greatly indebted to Commodore Symonds for his great attention and to the other gentlemen of the navy, who gave us every assistance in their power. Captain Evans[12], who left his ship and proceeded up the river with us, contributed greatly to our expedition.

We were very deficient in pilots for the river and owe our success in getting up with so much expedition in a great measure to the industry, attention and knowledge of Captain Wm Goodrich[13], who was the only pilot that we could depend upon and took unwearied pains by day and night.

I do myself the honor to enclose a return of stores, arms, ammunition etc etc taken and destroyed.

I beg leave to refer your Excellency for further particulars to Brigade Major Brabazon[14], who will have the honor of delivering my dispatches. He is very intelligent and has great merit.

I have the honor to be etc

B ARNOLD

---

[12] Commissioned a lieutenant in the Royal Navy on 27th September 1762, Henry Francis Evans was promoted to commander on 12th November 1777 and to post-captain some five months later. He would be killed in action on 21st July. (Syrett and DiNardo eds, *The Commissioned Sea Officers*, 147)

[13] William Goodrich was a mariner of Norfolk, Virginia. By October 1784 he had removed to England and was living in London. (Coldham, *Loyalist Claims*, i, 217)

[14] Commissioned a lieutenant in the 22nd Regiment on 16th January 1759, Edward Brabazon was promoted to a captaincy there on 7th December 1772. He was now acting on secondment to the Adjutant General's Department as a major of brigade, having previously served with the 22nd as part of the garrison at Newport, Rhode Island. (*Army Lists*)

Enclosure (2)
Return of captured arms and ammunition etc

Return of Ordnance, Ammunition, Stores, Small Arms etc taken and destroyed at Richmond and Westham in Virginia, January 5th 1781

AT RICHMOND

Brought off:

6 pounders brass, French	5

Spiked and left:

32s iron	8
18s ditto	3
12s ditto	2
9s ditto	3
6s ditto	1
4s ditto	6

Garrison carriages burnt and destroyed:

32 pounders	6
24 ditto	1
18 ditto	1
12 ditto	2
9 ditto	4
32s land, unfinished	3
18s for gondaloes	3
Carriage of a new construction for a 32 pounder	1

Burnt and destroyed:

Small arms	2,200
Large casks with new French musket locks containing each 2,000	2
Bolts of canvas	50
Cordage	10 cwt
Hemp	3 cwt

Shot thrown into the river:

32 pounders	1,600
24	500
18	400
12	600
6	4,000
4	1,200
3	200
1 grape	20,000
8 inch shells	31
8 inch fuzes undrove	2,621

AT WESTHAM
by a detachment commanded by Lt Colonel Simcoe

Spiked and the trunions broke off:

6 pounders iron	24
4 pounders ditto	4

Stores destroyed:

Cartridge boxes and bayonets	1,800
Barrels of powder	330
Hogsheads of brimstone	19
Chests of musquet cartridges	19
Chests of flints	3
Chests of 6 pounder cartridges	11
A foundery for casting iron cannon, a magazine, mill etc	

FROM HOOD'S FERRY, JAMES RIVER

Taken and brought off:

8 inch howitzer brass with carriage compleat	1

Shells for ditto empty	42
24 pounders iron	1
18 ditto	2

All the public store houses, magazines of oats etc with the armourys and work shops

A great number of other military articles which could not be taken an account of

A large rope work with a great quantity of cordage and sails in it

---

Enclosure (3)
Return of destroyed stores   *99(29): C*

> *Return of Stores destroyed at Richmond in Virginia by the Troops under the command of Brigadier General Arnold, Richmond, January 5th 1781*

Destroyed:

Hogsheads of rum	503
Warehouses full of salt	2
Bushels of wheat	120

E BRABAZON
Major of Brigade

Clinton to Cornwallis, 2nd and 8th March 1781   *68(1): LS*

New York
March 2nd 1781

Earl Cornwallis

My Lord

   Your Lordship may probably hear that the army and navy in Chesapeak are blocked up by a superior French naval force to that under Captain Symonds. The first account I had of it was from General Arnold dated the 14th February and I sent it immediately to the Admiral at Gardiner's Bay. A day or two afterwards I had it confirmed that they were part of the fleet from Rhode Island, which, I have heard since, sailed from thence on the 9th ultimo. Notwithstanding which, I greatly fear he has not sent a naval force to relieve them. Washington has detached some New England troops under La Fayette and Howe that way. If so much time is given I cannot answer for consequences. Portsmouth is safe at this season against any attack from the Suffolk side, but not so from a landing in any of the bays to the eastward of Elizabeth River. I have much to lament that the Admiral did not think it adviseable to send there at first, as Brigadier General Arnold's projected move in favor of your Lordship's operations will have been stopt, and if the Admiral delays it too long, I shall dread still more fatal consequences. I have troops already embarked in a great proportion to that of the enemy, but to send them under two frigates only, before the Chesapeak is our own, is to sacrifice the troops and their convoy.

I inclose[15] to your Lordship all the news I have been able to collect. Ethan Allen has, I think, quitted Congress and put them at defiance. Your Lordship will see his plan by the news paper of the 28th February, said to be genuine. Discontents runs high in Connecticut. In short, my Lord, there seems little wanting to give a mortal stab to rebellion but a proper reinforcement and a permanent superiority at sea for the next campaign, without which any enterprize depending on water movements must certainly run great risk. Should the troops already embarked for Chesapeak proceed and, when there, be able to undertake any operation in addition to what Brigadier General Arnold proposes, I am confident it will be done. Major General Phillips will command this expedition.

Till Colonel Bruce arrives, I am uncertain what reinforcements are intended for this army. The Minister has, however, assured me that every possible exertion will be made.

I shall tremble for our post at Portsmouth should the enemy's reinforcement arrive in that neighbourhood before the force which I *now* flatter myself the Admiral will order a sufficient convoy for arrives.

March 8th

I have received a letter from General Arnold dated the 25th ultimo wherein he tells me that the French left him on the 19th, and in another letter of the 27th[16] he says he has not the least doubt of defending his post against the force of the country and 2,000 French troops until a reinforcement can arrive from New York, and that he proposed to send five hundred men under Colonel Dundas up James River to make a diversion in favor of your Lordship.

The Admiral informs me of the return of the French ships to Rhode Island and of their having taken the *Romulus* and carried her into that place, but as the Admiral in his letter of the second instant seems to think that the whole or at least a great part of the French fleet

---

[15] The enclosures are not extant.

[16] *another letter..*: published in Stevens, op cit, i, 329.

sailed for Chesapeak on the twenty seventh, and that[17] he was at that time ready to sail, I flatter myself he is either gone there or has sent a sufficient force to clear the Chesapeak.

The troops under General Phillips have been embarked some time and are now at the Hook waiting for the Admiral or a message from him. General Phillips commands, and I am sure you know his inclinations are to cooperate with your Lordship, and you will be pleased to take him under your orders untill your Lordship hears further from me.

I have the honor to be
Your Lordship's most obedient and most humble servant

H CLINTON

Clinton to Cornwallis, 5th March 1781[18]

5(103): LS

New York
March 5th 1781

Earl Cornwallis

My Lord

I was honored with your Lordship's dispatches[19] dated the 18th of November, the 3rd, 4th, 6th, 7th, 22nd and 29th December, and 3rd, 6th and 18th of January by the *Halifax* sloop of war on the 16th ultimo. And by the *Mercury* packet, which will sail in a day or two for Europe, I propose to transmit copies of such of them to the Minister as may be necessary for His Majesty's information.

What your Lordship observes in your letter of the 4th December I am very sensible of, and am fully persuaded that no representation I can make will have any effect upon men lost to every sense of humanity.

I am sorry to say, my Lord, that I have the same reason to lament the want of safe conveyances for my dispatches, which your Lordship regrets in your letter of the 6th January, having had several prepared for your Lordship ever since the beginning of that month, and I am even now obliged to trust them by the precarious conveyance of a merchant vessel, as I have in vain applied for a ship of war for these two months past for the purpose.

I request your Lordship's forgiveness for the omission I was guilty of in not answering the paragraph of your letter of the 30th June relative to Lt Governor Graham. As there are now

---

[17] *that*: the meaning may be 'as'. See p 9, note 4.

[18] Published with inconsequential differences in Stevens, op cit, i, 331.

[19] *your Lordship's dispatches*: of those of 18th November and 6th and 7th December, the Cornwallis Papers contain no copies.

no refugees in Georgia and of course no occasion for such an office as that to which he was appointed, and as he is now in full possession of his property and does not seem to wish for a continuance of the employment, it is very proper that it should cease, and but reasonable that Mr Graham should be reimbursed for the sums he has advanced as well as paid his salary of 20*s* per day for himself and clerk from the 3rd of March to the period he ceased to act.

It gives me very great pleasure to learn from your Lordship that the army under your command is now perfectly healthy and in good order.

I am sorry the oat ships met with an accident off Charlestown bar. It is a risk, in my opinion, which every fleet runs that anchors there. Surely it would have been better for them to have stood off and on, but of those sea matters I am of course not a competent judge.

I am glad to find that your Lordship intends to send the victuallers and all such transports to England as are unfit for service, their speedy return being most earnestly desired. I would wish to have all such invalids whose times of service do not entitle them to Chelsea, and [who,] tho' unfit for service in the field, may be able to do duty in garrison, sent here from time to time that they may be placed in the Garrison Battalion, which will finally insure to them His Majesty's royal bounty.

As I understand the *Chatham* has brought out £50,000 in specie to Charlestown, your Lordship's difficulties with regard to money will have been removed, but I cannot say so much for ours.

Lord George Germain having informed me, as Major Ross was of opinion that many of the prisoners in our hands in Carolina might be induced to serve on board the King's ships or in privateers or inlist in the regiments serving in the West Indies or go as volunteers upon expeditions in that quarter, he had recommended to your Lordship to get rid of all you could in those several ways or in any other your Lordship should think fit to be adopted, it is unnecessary for me to add any thing upon that subject but to say that I leave them entirely to your Lordship's disposal.

I wish it had been possible to have procured the horses for General Vaughan, as I fear the troops may suffer from the drudgeries they were intended to perform.

I know not at present how it is possible, my Lord, to avoid the expence of quartering the troops at Charlestown, consistent with the terms of the capitulation, but I will endeavor to find some means of doing it if it be practicable.

I am most exceedingly concerned, my Lord, at the unfortunate affair of the 17th January. From the account your Lordship gives me of it, I fear Morgan has been in very great force, that our first line has been too impetuous, and that the reserve has sustained the other too nearly and probably in too loose order, and that the enemy has moved against them in that critical situation. I confess I dread the consequences, but my hope is, as it ever will be, in your Lordship's abilities and exertions.

I shall always be happy in paying every attention to your recommendations in filling up the vacancies in the 33rd Regiment, as I shall be constantly guided by your Lordship's wishes with respect to the promotions of your own regiment. I have already had an opportunity of fulfilling my intentions respecting Colonel Webster, but this is too unsafe a conveyance to trust the commission by.

I have the honor to be
Your Lordship's most obedient and most humble servant

H CLINTON

Clinton to Cornwallis, 8th March 1781   5(107): LS

New York
March 8th 1781

Lt General Earl Cornwallis

My Lord

I beg leave to introduce to your Lordship Captain Amherst, aid de camp to General Dalling, who is so obliging to charge himself with my dispatches for your Lordship.

He goes to Charles Town with a view of inlisting some of the rebel prisoners at that place for the service of the Spanish Main in case your Lordship should be pleased to permit him.

I have the honor to be
Your Lordship's most obedient and most humble servant

H CLINTON

Cornwallis to Clinton, 20th May 1781[20]   74(7): C

Petersburgh
20th May 1781

His Excellency Sir Henry Clinton KB etc etc etc

Sir

You will easily conceive how sensible an affliction it was to me, on entering this province, to receive an account of the death of my friend General Phillips, whose loss I cannot sufficiently lament from personal or publick considerations.

The corps which I brought from North Carolina arrived here this morning. The information conveyed by your Excellency to General Arnold relative to the probable movements of the French armament restrains me at present from any material offensive

---

[20] Published in Stevens, op cit, i, 476. There are no differences.

operations, but as soon as I can hear any satisfactory account of the two fleets, I will endeavour to make the best use in my power of the troops under my command. General Arnold being of opinion that Portsmouth with its present garrison is secure against a coup de main, I would wish to avoid making a precipitate movement towards that place without absolute necessity, because it would lessen our reputation in this province, but I have sent to assure the commanding officer that I will do every thing I can to relieve him in case the French should attack the post. La Fayette is at Wiltown on the other side of James River, not far from Richmond. I have not heard that Wayne has yet joined him.

It is with infinite satisfaction that I inclose to your Excellency copies of two letters from Lord Rawdon[21], which have relieved me from the most cruel anxieties. His Lordship's great abilities, courage and firmness of mind cannot be sufficiently admired and applauded. There is now great reason to hope that we shall meet with no serious misfortune in that province. If, however, General Greene should persevere in carrying on offensive operations against it, we must, I think, abandon Camden, and probably Ninety Six, and limit our defence to the Congaree and the Santee. This will be only giving up two bad posts, which it is difficult to supply with provisions, and quitting a part of the country which for some months past we have not really possessed.

I have taken every means to inform Major Craig of my having passed the Roanoke, on which event it was previously concerted between us that he should fall down to Bald Head and from thence proceed to Charlestown as soon as transports arrive to carry him.

The Legion being in the utmost distress for want of arms, clothing, boots, and indeed appointments of all kinds, I must beg that your Excellency will be pleased to direct the Inspector General to forward a supply of every article with the greatest dispatch.

I have the honour to be with great respect, sir,
Your most obedient and most humble servant

CORNWALLIS

Cornwallis to Clinton, 26th May 1781[22]   74(13): C

Bird's Plantation north of James River
26th May 1781

Sir

The reinforcement is safely arrived in James River and I opened all your dispatches to poor Phillips marked *On His Majesty's Service*.

---

[21] *two letters..*: of 25th and 26th April, vol IV, pp 179-183.

[22] Published in Stevens, op cit, i, 487. There are no differences.

I hope that your Excellency has received my letters from Wilmington and one of the 20th from Petersburgh. As the latter went by an uncertain conveyance, I send a duplicate of it.

The arrival of the reinforcement has made me easy about Portsmouth for the present. I have sent General Leslie thither with the 17th Regiment and the two battalions of Anspach, keeping the 43rd Regiment with the army.

I shall now proceed to dislodge La Fayette from Richmond and with my light troops to destroy any magazines or stores in the neighbourhood which may have been collected either for his use or for General Greene's army. From thence I purpose to move to the neck at Williamsburgh, which is represented as healthy and where some subsistence may be procured, and keep myself unengaged from operations which might interfere with your plan for the campaign, untill I have the satisfaction of hearing from you. I hope I shall then have an opportunity to receive better information than has hitherto been in my power to procure relative to a proper harbour and place of arms. At present I am inclined to think well of York. The objections to Portsmouth are that it cannot be made strong without an army to defend it, that it is remarkably unhealthy and can give no protection to a ship of the line. Wayne has not yet joined La Fayette, nor can I positively learn where he is nor what is his force. Greene's cavalry are said to be coming this way, but I have no certain accounts of it.

Your Excellency desires Generals Phillips and Arnold to give you their opinion relative to *Mr Alexander's* proposal[23]. As General Arnold goes to New York by the first safe conveyance, you will have an opportunity of hearing his sentiments in person, Experience has made me less sanguine, and more arrangements seem to me necessary for so important an expedition than appear to occur to General Arnold.

Mr Alexander's conversations bear too strong a resemblance to those of the emissaries from North Carolina to give me much confidence, and from the experience I have had and the dangers I have undergone, one maxim appears to me to be absolutely necessary for the safe and honourable conduct of this war, which is that we should have as few posts as possible and that, wherever the King's troops are, they should be in respectable force. By the vigorous exertions of the present Governors of America large bodies of men are soon collected, and I have too often observed that, when a storm threatens, our friends disappear.

In regard to taking possession of Philadelphia by an incursion (even if practicable), without an intention of keeping or burning it (neither of which appear to be adviseable), I should apprehend it would do more harm than good to the cause of Britain.

I shall take the liberty of repeating that if offensive war is intended, Virginia appears to me to be the only province in which it can be carried on, and in which there is a stake, but to reduce the province and keep possession of the country a considerable army would be necessary, for with a small force the business would probably terminate unfavourably, tho' the beginning might be successfull. In case it is thought expedient and a proper army for the attempt can be formed, I hope your Excellency will do me the justice to believe that I neither

---

[23] *Mr Alexander's proposal*: 'Mr Alexander' was a pseudonym for Colonel William Rankin, whose proposals are set out on pp 61-2. See Stevens, op cit, ii, 34n & 55n.

wish nor expect to have the command of it, leaving you at New York on the defensive. Such sentiments are so far from my heart that I can with great truth assure you that few things could give me greater pleasure than being relieved by your presence from a situation of so much anxiety and responsibility.

By my letter of the 20th your Excellency will observe that instead of thinking it possible to do any thing in North Carolina I am of opinion that it is doubtfull whether we can keep the posts in the back part of South Carolina, and I believe I have stated in former letters[24] the infinite difficulty of protecting a frontier of three hundred miles against a persevering enemy in a country where we have no water communication and where few of the inhabitants are active or usefull friends.

In enumerating the corps employed in the Southern District your Excellency will recollect that they are all very weak and that some of the British as well as Provincial regiments retain nothing but the name. Our weakness at Guildford was not owing to any detachment, unless that with the baggage, but to our losses by action, sickness etc during the winter's campaign.

I saw with concern that you thought Lt Colonel Balfour had acted injudiciously in sending home some transports. That business has, I apprehend, been misrepresented by persons interested in retaining rotten vessels in the service of Government. The circumstances I do not now perfectly recollect, but I believe you will find that the ships sent home were either victuallers, which the Treasury desired in the strongest manner[25], or transports which were so exceedingly bad that they could never have gone out with safety after a stay of three months in Charlestown harbour. Whatever was done in it met with my approbation at the time, appearing evidently for the good of the service. I therefore think it my duty to exculpate Lt Colonel Balfour, whom I have found on all occasions a most zealous, intelligent and deserving officer.

Colonel Robinson's corps[26] is so weak and deserts so fast that at the recommendation of General Arnold I have consented that it shall return in the transports to New York.

I have the honour to be with great respect etc

[CORNWALLIS]

---

[24] *former letters*: Cornwallis to Clinton, 10th and 23rd April, vol IV, pp 109 and 112, and Cornwallis to Germain (copied to Clinton), 18th April, vol IV, pp 104-6.

[25] See vol III, p 29, note 25.

[26] *Robinson's corps*: the Loyal American Regiment.

Cornwallis to Clinton, 26th May 1781[27]

74(9): C

Byrd's Plantation, James River
May 26th 1781

His Excellency Sir Henry Clinton KB etc etc etc

Sir

I have consented to the request of Brigadier General Arnold to go to New York. He conceives that your Excellency wishes him to attend you there, and his present indisposition renders him unequal to the fatigue of service. He will represent the horrid enormities which are committed by our privateers in Chesapeak Bay, and I must join my earnest wish that some remedy may be applied to an evil which is so very prejudicial to His Majesty's Service.

I have the honour to be with great respect
Your most obedient and most humble servant

CORNWALLIS

Cornwallis to Clinton, 27th May 1781

6(117): C

Byrd's Plantation north of James River
27th May 1781

Sir Henry Clinton

Sir

The excessive burden of the prisoners of war at Charlestown made me extremely desirous of settling a cartel for their exchange. After several meetings the inclosed[28] was finally agreed to between General Greene and me.

I have etc

[CORNWALLIS]

---

[27] Published in Stevens, op cit, i, 487. There are no differences.

[28] *the inclosed*: see vol IV, p 88.

Clinton to Cornwallis, 30th April 1781[29]

5(299): LS

New York
April 30th 1781

Lt General Earl Cornwallis

My Lord

Captain Biggs of His Majesty's Ship *Amphitrite*, who arrived here the 22nd, has delivered to me your Lordship's two letters from Wilmington of the 10th instant[30] informing me of your having obtained a compleat victory over the rebel General Green near Guildford on the 15th ultimo, on which occasion I beg leave, my Lord, to offer your Lordship my most hearty congratulations and to request you will present my thanks to Major General Leslie, Brigadier General O'Hara and Lt Colonel Tarleton for the great assistance you received from them and to the officers and men under your command for their great exertions on the march thro' Carolina and their persevering intrepidity in action.

Brigade of Guards
23rd
33rd
71st, two battalions
Jagers
Regiment of Bose
Light infantry 71st
   and Legion
N Carolina Regt

The disparity of numbers between your Lordship's force and that of the enemy opposed to you appears to be very great, and I confess I am at some loss to guess how your Lordship came to be reduced before the action to 1,360 infantry, as by the distribution sent to me in your letter of the 6th of January I am to suppose it was your intention to take with you the regiments mentioned in the margin, which (notwithstanding the loss of the 71st and Legion in the unfortunate affair of Cowpens) I should imagine must have amounted to considerably above 3,000, exclusive of cavalry and militia.

Before I was favored with your Lordship's letter, the rebel account of the Battle of Guildford had led me indeed to hope that its consequences would have been more decisive and that Green would have repassed the Roanoke and left your Lordship at liberty to pursue the objects of your move into North Carolina. Under the persuasion therefore that you would soon be able to finish your arrangements for the security of the Carolinas I submitted to you in my letter of the 13th instant (a duplicate of which[31] I have the honor to inclose) the propriety in that case of your going in a frigate to Chesapeak and directing such corps to follow you thither as you judged could be best spared, but as it is now probable that your

---

[29] This dispatch and enclosure (published with no differences in Stevens, op cit, i, 405 and 441) were in the charge of Lord Chewton, who sailed from New York on 4th May. Having called at Wilmington and Charlestown, he eventually reached Cornwallis shortly before 24th June (see Leslie to Cornwallis of that date, pp 167-8).

[30] *two letters..*: see vol IV, pp 109-112, together with p 51, note 71 in this volume.

[31] *a duplicate..*: the original miscarried. See Craig to Cornwallis, 2nd May, vol IV, p 167.

Lordship's presence in Carolina cannot be so soon dispensed with, I make no doubt that you will think it right to communicate to Major General Phillips without delay the plan of your future operations in that quarter, together with your opinion how the Chesapeak army can best direct theirs to assist them. That general officer has already under his orders 3,500 men and I shall send him 1,700 more, which are now embarked and will sail whenever the Admiral is ready.

With these, my Lord, which are rank and file fit for duty, and great part of them taken from the elite of my army, General Phillips is directed by his instructions to act in favor of your Lordship to the best of his own judgement until he receives your orders, and afterwards in such manner as you may please to command him etc, but I shall be sorry to find your Lordship continue in the opinion that our hold of the Carolinas must be difficult, if not precarious, until Virginia is in a manner subdued, as that is an event which I fear would require a considerable space of time to accomplish and, as far as I can judge, it might be not quite so expedient at this advanced season of the year to enter into a long operation in that climate. This, however, will greatly depend upon circumstances, of which your Lordship and General Phillips may probably be better judges hereafter.

With regard to the operations of the summer, which your Lordship is anxious to receive my directions about, you cannot but be sensible that they must in great measure depend on your Lordship's successes in Carolina, the certainty and numbers of the expected reinforcement from Europe, and likewise on your Lordship's sending back to me the corps I had spared to you under Major General Leslie, which Lord Rawdon in his letter of the 31st October[32] told me you could return in the spring, for, until I am informed of the particulars of your Lordship's march thro' North Carolina, the effective strength of your moving army, your plan of operations for carrying those objects you had or may have in view into execution, as well by the corps acting under your own immediate orders as those acting in co-operation under Major General Phillips, it must be obviously impossible for me to determine finally upon a plan of operations for the campaign.

I was indeed in great hopes that your successes in North Carolina would have been such as to have put it in my power to avail myself of a large portion of your Lordship's army, the whole Chesapeak corps and the entire reinforcements from Europe for this campaign's operations to the northward of Carolina, but I observe with concern from your Lordship's letter that, so far from being in a condition to spare me any part of your present force, you are of opinion that part of the European reinforcement will be indispensably necessary to enable you to act offensively or even to maintain yourself in the upper parts of the country.

Had I known what your Lordship's further offensive measures were intended to be for the remaining part of the season, I might now have given an opinion upon them as well as upon the probable cooperation of the corps in the Chesapeak, without having which it will be scarce possible for me to form any, for, as I said before, I fear no solid operation can be carried on to the northward of Chesapeak before those to the southward of it are totally at an end either

---

[32] *his letter..*: see vol II, p 60.

from success or the season; and my letter to your Lordship of the 6th of November[33] will have informed you what were my ideas of the operations proper to be pursued in Chesapeak and my expectations from them had circumstances admitted of my pursuing the plan to its full extent. But I must now defer the fixing ultimately on a plan for the campaign until I am made acquainted with the final success of your Lordship's operations, your prospects and sentiments and I can judge what force I can collect for such measures as I can then determine upon.

I have the honor to be
Your Lordship's most obedient and most humble servant

H CLINTON

Enclosure
Clinton to Cornwallis, 13th April 1781   5(303): CS

New York
13th April 1781

Lt General the Earl Cornwallis

My Lord

As it appears, even from the rebel account of the action, that your Lordship has gained a victory over Green and it is probable he may in consequence have repassed the Roanoke, I beg leave to submit to your Lordship the propriety of your coming to Chesapeak Bay in a frigate as soon as you have finished your arrangements for the security of the Carolinas and you judge that affairs there are in such a train as no longer to require your presence, directing at the same time such troops to follow you thither as your Lordship is of opinion can be best spared.

By Lt Colonel Bruce's arrival I am made acquainted that six British regiments are intended as an immediate reinforcement to the army under my command. Should, therefore, any of these corps stop at Carolina, your Lordship may probably direct them either to replace such troops as follow you or to proceed immediately to the Chesapeak.

Agreeable to what I have already said to your Lordship in my letters of the 1st of June and 6th of November[34] it is my wish that you should continue to conduct operations as they advance northerly, for, except as a visitor, I shall not probably move to Chesapeak unless Washington goes thither in great force. The success which has hitherto attended your Lordship excites the fullest assurance of its continuance, and as it is my inclination to assist your operations to the utmost extent of my power, I am convinced from your disinterestedness that you will not ask from me a larger proportion of troops than I can possibly spare.

---

[33] *my letter..*: see vol III, p 21.

[34] *my letters..*: see vol I, p 60, and vol III, p 21.

As this goes by an unarmed vessel to Chesapeak, Major General Phillips will add what he thinks necessary to it and forward it to Cape Fear.

The Admiral has at last consented that the *Medea* shall sail for Cape Fear as soon as she is ready. Perhaps your Lordship may take that opportunity of returning in her, and if we can prevail upon the Admiral or commanding naval officer here to spare Captain Duncan to conduct the naval part of our business in the Chesapeak, I think we shall have gained a great point.

I have the honor to be
Your Lordship's most obedient and most humble servant

H CLINTON

Clinton to Cornwallis, 11th June 1781[35]   68(14): LS

New York
11th June 1781

Lt General Earl Cornwallis

My Lord

I am honored with your Lordship's letter of the 26th ultimo, and as I am unwilling to detain the convoy, I shall not have time to write so fully to your Lordship as I would wish.

Respecting my opinions of stations in James and York Rivers I shall beg leave only to refer your Lordship to my instructions to and correspondence with Generals Phillips and Arnold, together with the substance of my conversations with the former, which your Lordship will have found amongst General Phillips's papers and to which I referred you in my last dispatch[36]. I shall therefore of course approve of any alterations your Lordship may think proper to make in those stations.

The detachments I have made from this army into Chesapeak since General Leslie's expedition in October last, inclusive, have amounted to 7,724 effectives, and at the time your Lordship made the junction with the corps there, there were under Major General Phillips's orders 5,304, a force I should have hoped would be sufficient of itself to carry on operation in any of the southern provinces of America, where, as appears by the intercepted letters of

---

[35] Annotated: 'Received from Ensign Amiel 26th of June 1781', and published with inconsequential differences in Stevens, op cit, ii, 19.

[36] *my last dispatch*: not Clinton's last of 8th June, p 123, but his penultimate of 29th May and 1st June, p 118. For the other documents referred to, see vol III, p 55, and ch 50.

Washington and La Fayette[37], they are in no situation to stand against even a division of that army. I have no reason to suppose the Continentals under La Fayette can exceed 1,000, and I am told by Lt Colonel Hill[38] of the 9th Regiment that about a fortnight ago he met at Fredericktown the Pennsylvania line under Wayne of about the same number, who were so discontented that their officers were afraid to trust them with ammunition. This, however, may have since altered, and your Lordship may possibly have opposed to you from 1,500 to 2,000 Continentals, and (as La Fayette observes) a small body of ill armed peasantry – full as spiritless as the militia of the southern provinces and without any service.

Comparing therefore the force now under your Lordship in Chesapeak and that of the enemy opposed to you (and I think it clearly appears they have for the present no intention of sending thither reinforcement), I should have hoped you would have quite sufficient to carry on any operation in Virginia should that have been adviseable at this advanced season.

By the intercepted letters inclosed to your Lordship in my last dispatch[39] you will observe that I am threatened with a siege in this post. My present effective force is only 10,931. With respect to that the enemy may collect for such an object, it is probable they may amount to at least 20,000, besides reinforcement to the French (which from pretty good authority I have reason to expect), and the numerous militia of the five neighbouring provinces. Thus circumstanced, I am persuaded your Lordship will be of opinion that the sooner I concentrate my force the better. Therefore (unless your Lordship after the receipt of my letters of the 29th of May and 8th instant should incline to agree with me in opinion and judge it right to adopt my ideas respecting the move to Baltimore or the Delaware Neck etc) I beg leave to recommend it to you, as soon as you have finished the active operations you may be now engaged in, to take a defensive station in any healthy situation you chuse (be it at Williamsburg or York Town). And I would wish in that case that, after reserving to yourself such troops as you may judge necessary for an ample defensive and desultory movements by water for the purpose of annoying the enemy's communications, destroying magazines etc, the following corps may be sent to me in succession as you can spare them:

> Two battalions of light infantry
> 43rd Regiment
> 76th or 80th
> Two battalions of Anspach
> Queen's Rangers, cavalry and infantry
> Remains of the detachment of 17th Light Dragoons, and
> Such a proportion of artillery as can be spared, particularly men.

---

[37] *the intercepted letters..*: enclosed with Clinton's dispatch of 8th June, p 123.

[38] Having served with the 13th Regiment in Minorca, John Hill was promoted on 10th November 1775 to the lt colonelcy of the 9th Foot, a regiment whose catchment area lay in East Norfolk. In May 1776 he arrived with it at Quebec, and after seeing service on the Lakes, it took part in Burgoyne's offensive and was among the corps which capitulated at Saratoga in October 1777. Its presence among the Convention prisoners at Fredericktown, Maryland, accounts for Hill being there. (*Army Lists*)

[39] *my last dispatch*: that of 8th June. See note 37 above.

Until the arrival of the expected reinforcements from Europe it will be impossible for me to judge what future operations may be within my power under my present circumstances. I heartily wish I was able to spare a second army after leaving a sufficient defensive for this important post, but your Lordship will, I hope, excuse me if I dissent from your opinion of the manner in which that army should be employed, for experience ought to convince us that there is no possibility of reestablishing order in any rebellious province on this Continent without the hearty assistance of numerous friends. These, my Lord, are not I think to be found in Virginia, nor dare I positively assert that under our present circumstances they are to be found in great numbers any where else, or that their exertions when found will answer our expectations, but I believe there is a greater probability of finding them in Pennsylvania than in any except the southern provinces. In these your Lordship has already made the experiment. It has there failed. They are gone from us and I fear are not to be recovered. The only one therefore now remaining is this, and if I continue in the command, I am determined to give it a fair trial whenever it can be done with propriety. I am not, however, likely to have a choice of operation at least for some time to come. Nor can I altogether agree with your Lordship in thinking that a desultory move against Philadelphia would do more harm than good. There, my Lord, are collected their principal depots of stores for the campaign, an immense quantity of European and West India commodities, and no inconsiderable supply of money, which their uninterrupted trade and cruisers have lately procured them. And from these funds they are now forming a bank by subscription, which, if it succeeds, may give fresh vigor to their cause. Could we therefore at this moment seize those important magazines etc, overset their schemes and break up their public credit, the favorable consequences resulting from such success are too obvious to need explanation. And all this, my Lord, I have no doubt might have been effected, if our reinforcement had arrived in time and the enemy had no prospect of receiving any, without our either keeping or destroying Philadelphia, the latter of which is foreign from my inclination and the former is certainly at present inadviseable.

I have the honor to be
Your Lordship's most obedient and most humble servant

H CLINTON

Clinton to Cornwallis, 15th June 1781[40]

68(22): LS

New York
15th June 1781

Lt General Earl Cornwallis

My Lord

As the Admiral has thought proper to stop the sailing of the convoy with stores, horse accoutrements etc (which has been for some days ready to sail to the Chesapeak) without assigning to me any reason for so doing, I delay not a moment to dispatch a runner to your

---

[40] Annotated: 'Received from Ensign Amiel 26th June', and published with no differences in Stevens, op cit, ii, 24.

Lordship with a duplicate of my letter of the 11th instant, which was to go by that opportunity.

And as I am led to suppose (from your Lordship's letter of the 26th ultimo) that you may not think it expedient to adopt the operations I had recommended in the upper Chesapeak and will by this time probably have finished those you were engaged in, I request you will immediately embark a part of the troops stated in the letter inclosed (beginning with the light infantry etc) and send them to me with all possible dispatch, for which purpose Captain Hudson or officer commanding the King's ships will, I presume, upon your Lordship's application appoint a proper convoy.

I shall likewise in proper time solicit the Admiral to send some more transports to the Chesapeak, in which your Lordship will please to send hither the remaining troops you judge can be spared from the defence of the posts you may occupy, as I do not think it adviseable to leave more troops in that unhealthy climate at this season of the year than what are absolutely wanted for a defensive and desultory water excursions.

I have the honor to be
Your Lordship's most obedient and most humble servant

H CLINTON

Clinton to Cornwallis, 15th June 1781[41]

6(224): LS

New York
15th June 1781

Lt General Earl Cornwallis

My Lord

In answer to the part of your Lordship's letter of the 26th ultimo which relates to the transports sent home from Charlestown, I have the honor to inclose copies of some letters I have received from the principal agent, Captain Tomkins[42], and extracts of those which passed between Lt Colonel Balfour and me on this subject. By these it will appear to your Lordship that six of the transports sent home at that time were perfectly fit for service (as reported by the agent, Mr Walters[43]), notwithstanding Colonel Balfour has reported to me

---

[41] Annotated: 'Received from Ensign Amiel 26th June'.

[42] Commissioned a lieutenant in the Royal Navy on 6th April 1757, Thomas Tonken (?-1790) was promoted to commander on 25th December 1778 and to post-captain some seventeen months later. He was now serving as the principal agent for transports on the North American station. In December he would set sail with Cornwallis for England. (Syrett and DiNardo eds, *The Commissioned Sea Officers*, 440; *The Cornwallis Papers*)

[43] Commissioned a lieutenant in the Royal Navy on 4th November 1755, Richard Walter was serving as the agent for transports at Charlestown. On 10th May 1781 he was promoted to commander, but news had not yet reached America. He did not rise higher in the service. (Syrett and DiNardo eds, op cit, 456; *The Cornwallis Papers*)

that none were sent but such as were wholly unfit. Of their condition in this respect the agent is certainly the proper judge and ought immediately to report when he discovers any of them to be unserviceable. But with respect to there being surplus or unnecessary transports at any post of this army (which are the words made use of in the circular and Admiralty letters about sending them home) I can be the only proper judge, and none that were serviceable ought to have been sent home by any officer under that idea until he had first received my directions about them. I therefore cannot but disapprove of Lt Colonel Balfour's having done so, tho' I am happy that his conduct in other respects may have merited your Lordship's approbation.

With regard to this business having been misrepresented (as your Lordship apprehends) by persons interested in retaining rotten vessels in the service of Government, I am really ignorant whom your Lordship alludes to, as I hold no conference or correspondence on the subject of transports but with the principal agent, to whom I have thought proper to refer the investigation of your Lordship's suspicion. And (tho' I cannot suppose that any gentleman can be concerned in so great a delinquency), if it should appear that there is any foundation for it, I shall certainly insist upon the guilty persons being punished with the utmost severity.

I have the honor to be
Your Lordship's most obedient and most humble servant

H CLINTON

Enclosure (1)
Navy Board to Tonken, 17th November 1780   *6(234): C*

Navy Office
17th November 1780

Captain Tonken
New York

Sir

The great difficulty we find in procuring transports from the variety of services for which they are wanted obliging us to rely very much on the early return of those sent abroad, we direct you not to discharge any transport out of the service that shall not upon a proper survey be found unfit to be continued therein, and as the sending the provisions to the army is a particular and distinct service which makes it necessary to confine the ships hired for that purpose to the performance of it, you are not on any account to divert them from this or employ them on any other but keep every class of transports appropriated to the services for which they were fitted as far as it rests with you and to take care to send home all transports employed carrying out stores for the army and navy and all victualling transports with the first convoy that offers. In case of no convoy being intended when a sufficient number are unloaded, you are to apply in writing to the Commander in Chief to appoint one to return with them, the victuallers to Cork and the others to Spithead, and you are to give copies of these orders to the other agents for transports in America for their carrying them into execution so far as they may be concerned therein, instructing them also, when they are ordered to any port from which a convoy does not proceed to England, to apply to the commanding officer for a convoy as soon as possible to the nearest port from where the general convoy sails.

We are
Your affectionate friends

CHA^S MIDDLETON[44]
E WILLIAMS
GEO MARSH[45]

Enclosure (2)
Navy Board to Tonken, 7th December 1780   6(232): C

Navy Office
7th December 1780

Captain Tonkin
Agent to transports
New York

Sir

Intimation having been given to us that His Majesty's Secretaries of State and the Lords Commissioners of the Admiralty have given orders to the Commanders in Chief abroad not to detain the transports that proceed from hence under orders to return unloaded longer than is absolutely necessary, and that no surpluss transports be kept there, and the Lords Commissioners of the Treasury having given directions to their commissaries to cooperate in expediting their unloading, we think it necessary to inform you thereof and to repeat our desire you will use every means in your power for the speedy return of such transports, on which the regular supply of the army with provisions so much depends.

---

[44] Born at Leith, Charles Middleton (1726-1813) was a former post-captain who in August 1778 had been appointed Comptroller of the Navy, a key post in naval administration. The Navy Board, of which he became ex officio the leading member, was at that time responsible for dockyards, manning, and financial procedures and was supported by the Navy Office, which had a staff of about one hundred. A particular source of frustration was the uncoordinated and economically unrealistic bidding of four government departments – the Navy Board, Victualling Board, Ordnance Board, and Treasury – for the hire of transports to carry on the war in America. To reduce this competition Middleton proposed that the Navy Board should hire ships for all four departments, and in 1779, as a first step in that direction, it was agreed that the Navy Board should take over the hire of army victuallers from the Treasury. Middleton would continue in office until 1795 and serve as First Lord of the Admiralty between 1805 and 1806. A naval administrator of the first order, he made a pre-eminent contribution to maintaining and improving efficiency in the management of the navy, providing, in his recommendations for reform at the turn of the century, a platform on which the navy would operate for the next three decades. In 1805 he was rewarded with a peerage, becoming Baron Barham of Teston. (*ODNB*)

[45] Members of the Navy Board, Williams and Marsh were Principal Officers and Commissioners of HM Navy. They have not been otherwise identified. (*The Cornwallis Papers*)

We are
Your affectionate friends

CHARLES MIDDLETON
I WILLIAMS
GEO MARSH

Enclosure (3)
Walter to Tonken, 24th February 1781 6(230): C

Littledale
Charles Town
24th February 1781

Captain Tonken

Dear Sir

Since my last to you with the state, condition and employment of the transports on this station under my direction, the very pressing letters from the Ministry to the commanding officer of His Majesty's forces here has determined the Commandant with the senior officer of His Majesty's ships to send all the transports home from this place but the prison ships, Lt Colonel Balfour being satisfyed that the ships at present employed at Cape Fear and Savannah etc are sufficient to remain. I therefore in consequence have given orders that they may be all ready, the first division to sail with the *Galatea*, and the latter with the *Camilla* as soon as she is ready.

I am, dear sir,
Your most obedient humble servant

ROBERT WALTER

Enclosure (4)
Tonken to the Navy Board, 16th March 1781 6(228): C

New York
16th March 1781

Hon the Principal Officers and Commissioners
    of His Majesty's Navy

Honorable Gentlemen

I have the honor of your letter of the 17th November last by His Majesty's Ship *Chatham* and shall pay due obedience to the contents as much as in my power. I also received by the *Chatham* a letter from Lieutenant Walter, the agent at Charles Town, who informs me that, in consequence of orders from the Secretary of State to the officer commanding the troops there, that the senior officer of His Majesty's ships and him had come to a determination of sending all the transports then there (except the prison ships) to England, the first division under the convoy of the *Galatea*, and the second under the *Camilla*, for which I am very sorry, as among those ships are they that went with the troops under Major General Leslie. They were remarkably good and in excellent order. However, I hope that the ships that are now at Virginia will soon return here, as all the British and Hessian grenadiers, together with the 42nd Regiment, amounting to upwards of 3,000 men, are under orders for embarkation and you will perceive by my letter of the 4th instant that there are only two transports here.

I am, gentlemen, etc

THO[S] TONKEN

Enclosure (5)
Tonken to Clinton, 20th March 1781   6(226): C

New York
the 20th March 1781

His Excellency Sir Henry Clinton KB etc etc etc

Sir

By a return of transports from Lieutenant Walter, the agent at Charles Town, I find that the commanding officer of His Majesty's troops and senior officer of His Majesty's ships there had come to a determination (in consequence of letters from the Secretary of State) to send all the transports that were not then employed by the army to England, by which means six of the best ships that were intended to be kept in the country are sent home. I therefore think it necessary to acquaint your Excellency therewith.

I am with great respect, sir,
Your most obedient humble servant

THO[S] TONKEN
Agent for transports

Enclosure (6)
Extracts from correspondence between Balfour and Clinton,   6(236): C
13th February to 3rd May 1781

Charles Town
13th February 1781

Some few days since a packet from England arrived here. She left Falmouth the 14th of December and sailed in company with one for New York. By her the inclosed circular letter from Lord George Germain was received, and in consequence of it such unemployed transports as are here will be sent home with the *Galatea* convoy, which sails the end of this week.

New York
March 14th 1781

I am directed by the Commander [in Chief] to acquaint you that, as transports are very much wanted at this place, he is extremely sorry to find by your letter of the 13th ultimo you proposed sending all those that were unemployed at Charles Town to Europe with the *Galatea*'s convoy without waiting for his commands on that subject, in consequence of a circular letter received from Lord George Germain, which letter his Excellency apprehends you have not conceived in the light he does. If therefore any thing should have prevented their departure for Europe, he requests you will be pleased to order such of them as are fit for service to proceed hither with the very first convoy, there not being at this time a single transport in this port.

JOHN SMITH

Charles Town
April 7th 1781

About a week since the fleet for England sailed, and as only such transports as were wholly unfit for service went home with it, I am happy in this respect to have complied with your Excellency's intentions. Those that can be spared from this will be sent with the convoy to New York and only the prison ships remain here.

New York
May 3rd 1781

I was favored with your letter of the 7th ultimo, before the receipt of which Captain Tonken had reported to me that six of the transports sent home from Charlestown were the best and fitted for the service required and that Lieutenant Walter, the agent there, intended they should have been sent to this place. I am therefore sorry that Captain Barclay should have ordered these transports to Europe and have to request that the *Lyon* hospital ship and *Success Increase* transport may be sent here.

Cornwallis to Clinton, 30th June 1781[46]   *74(18A): ADf*

Williamsburgh
June 30th 1781

[His Excellency Sir Henry Clinton KB etc etc etc]

Sir

After passing James River at Westover, I moved to Hanover Court House and crossed the South Anna. The Marquis de la Fayette marched to his left, keeping above me at the distance of about 20 miles.

By pushing my light troops over the North Anna I alarmed the enemy for Fredericksburgh and for the junction with General Wayne, who was then marching through Maryland. From what I could learn of the present state of Hunter's Iron Manufactory it did not appear[47] of so much importance as the stores on the other side of the country and it was impossible to prevent the junction between the Marquis and Wayne. I therefore took advantage of the Marquis's passing the Rhappahannock and detached Lt Colonels Simcoe and Tarleton to disturb the Assembly then sitting at Charlotteville and to destroy the stores there, at Old Albemarle Court House and the Point of Fork, moving with the infantry to the mouth of Bird Creek near the Point of Fork to receive those detachments. Lt Colonel Tarleton took some members of the Assembly at Charlotteville and destroyed there and on his return 1,000 stand of good arms, some clothing and other stores, and between 4 and 500 barrels of powder, without opposition. Baron Steuben, who commanded about 800 twelve months' men and militia, retired with great precipitation from the Point of Fork. Lt Colonel Simcoe, after using every exertion to attack his rear guard, destroyed there and at places adjacent about 3,300 stand of arms, most of which unserviceable but then under repair, some salt, harness etc and about 150 barrels of powder.

I then moved by Richmond and arrived at Williamsburgh on the 25th instant, having, in addition to the articles already mentioned, destroyed on this expedition at different places above 2,000 hogsheads of tobacco and a great number of iron guns and brought off 4 brass 13 inch mortars, five brass 8 inch howitzers and four long brass nine pounders, all French. We found near Hanover Court House ten French brass 24 pounders, which we could not carry and had not time or means to destroy farther than spiking and throwing five or six of them into the Pamunky, and we found at Williamsburgh a considerable quantity of shot and shells, which are embarked. General Wayne joined the Marquis about the middle of the month, as did Baron Steuben soon after, and their army has generally kept about 20 miles from us without any material attempt by detachment, except in an attack on Lt Colonel Simcoe on the 26th as he was returning with his corps and the Yagers from the destruction of some boats

---

[46] Published without the enclosures in Stevens, op cit, ii, 31. Apart from the omission mentioned in note 49 below, there are no differences.

[47] After 'appear' the following words are deleted: 'a very material object and could be got at more conveniently by water'.

and stores on the Chickahominy. The enemy, tho' much superior in numbers, were repulsed with considerable loss. 3 officers and 28 private were made prisoners. The Rangers had 3 officers and 30 private killed and wounded. Lieutenant Jones[48], who was killed, behaved with great spirit and is much lamented by Lt Colonel Simcoe.

The morning after my arrival here I was honoured with your Excellency's dispatches of the 11th and 15th instant delivered by Ensign Amiel. By them I find that you think, if an offensive army could be spared, it would not be adviseable to employ it in this province. It is natural for every officer to turn his thoughts particularly to the part of the war in which he has been most employed, and as the security at least of South Carolina, if not the reduction of North Carolina, seemed to be generally expected from me both in this country and in England, I thought myself called upon, after the experiment I had made had failed, to point out the only mode in my opinion of effecting it and to declare that untill Virginia was to a degree subjected we could not reduce North Carolina or have any certain hold of the back country of South Carolina, the want of navigation rendering it impossible to maintain a sufficient army in either of those provinces at a considerable distance from the coast, and the men and riches of Virginia furnishing ample supplies to the rebel southern army. I will not say much in praise of the militia of the southern colonies, but the list of British officers and soldiers killed and wounded by them since last June proves but too fatally that they are not wholly contemptible.

Your Excellency being charged with the weight of the whole American war, your opinions of course are less partial and are directed to all its parts. To those opinions it is my duty implicitly to submit.

Being in the place of General Phillips, I thought myself called upon by you to give my opinion with all deference on Mr Alexander's proposals and the attempt upon Philadelphia. Having experienced much disappointment on that head, I own I would cautiously engage in measures depending materially for their success upon active assistance from the country. And I thought the attempt upon Philadelphia would do more harm than good to the cause of Britain because, supposing it practicable to get possession of the town (which, besides other obstacles, if the redoubts are kept up, would not be easy), we could not hope to arrive without their having had sufficient warning of our approach to enable them to secure specie and the greatest part of their valuable publick stores by means of their boats and shipping, which give them certain possession of the river from Mud Island upwards; the discriminating of the owners and destroying any considerable quantity of West India goods and other merchandize dispersed thro' a great town without burning the whole together would be a work of much time and labour; our appearance there without an intention to stay might give false hopes to many friends and occasion their ruin; and any unlucky accident on our retreat might furnish

---

[48] Born at Weston, Massachusetts, Charles Jones (1760-1781) was a son of Elisha Jones (?-1775), a member of the Massachusetts general assembly, and was attending Harvard College at the start of the revolutionary war. In August 1780 he entered the infantry of the Queen's Rangers as an ensign and in December transferred to its cavalry as a cornet in David Shank's troop. Mistakenly described as a lieutenant by Cornwallis, he was killed at Spencer's Ordinary on 26th June while leading part of the troop in the repulse of the attack now mentioned. The following day he was buried at Williamsburg with full military honours. (E Alfred Jones, *The Loyalists of Massachusetts: Their Memorials, Petitions and Claims* (Genealogical Publishing Co, 1969), 185; Simcoe, *The Queen's Rangers*, 233, 237; Donald J Gara, 'Biographical Sketches on Cavalry Officers of the Queen's American Rangers 1779-1783' (*The On-Line Institute for Advanced Loyalist Studies*, 8th April 2006); Raymond, 'British American Corps')

matter for great triumph to our enemies. However, my opinion on that subject is at present of no great importance, as it appears from your Excellency's dispatches that in the execution of those ideas a co-operation was intended from your side which now could not be depended upon from the uncertainty of the permanency of our naval superiority and your apprehensions of an intended serious attempt upon New York. I have therefore lost no time in taking measures for complying with the requisition contained in your dispatch of the 15th instant.

Upon viewing York I was clearly of opinion that it far exceeds our power consistent with your plans to make safe defensive posts there and at Gloucester, both of which would be necessary for the protection of shipping. The state of the transports has not yet been reported to me, but I have ordered the few that are at Portsmouth to be got ready, and as soon as I pass James River (for which purpose the boats are collecting) and can get a convoy, they shall be dispatched with as many troops as they will contain and shall be followed by others as fast as you send transports to receive them. When I see Portsmouth, I shall give my opinion of the number of men necessary for its defence or of any other post that may be thought more proper, but as magazines etc may be destroyed by occasional expeditions from New York and there is little chance of being able to establish a post capable of giving effectual protection to ships of war, I submit it to your Excellency's consideration whether it is worth while to hold a sickly defensive post in this bay which will always be exposed to a sudden French attack and which experience has now shewn makes no diversion in favour of the southern army.

Tarleton was lucky enough to intercept an express with letters from Greene and La Fayette, of which the inclosed are copies. By them you will see General Greene's intention of coming to the northward, and that part of the reinforcements destined for his army was stopped in consequence of my arrival here. As soon as it is evident that our plan is nearly defensive here,[49] there can be little doubt of his returning to the southward and of the reinforcements proceeding to join his army.

I still continue in the most painfull anxiety for the situation of South Carolina. Your Excellency will have received accounts of Lord Rawdon's proceedings previous to his arrival at Monk's Corner and of his intended operations. My last account from him is in a note to Lt Colonel Balfour dated the 9th instant at Four Hole Bridge[50], and he was then in great hopes of being in time to save Cruger. I have ordered Colonel Gould to proceed, as soon as convoy could be procured, with the 19th and 30th Regiments to New York, leaving the 3rd Regiment and the flank companies in South Carolina till your pleasure be known. I named the flank companies because they might be distant at the time of the arrival of the order and as a corps capable of exertion is much wanted on that service.

Your Excellency well knows my opinion of a defensive war on the frontiers of South Carolina. From the state of Lord Rawdon's health it is impossible that he can remain, for which reason, altho' the command in that quarter can only be attended with mortification and disappointment, yet, as I came to America with no other view than to endeavour to be usefull

---

[49] Stevens, op cit, omits the opening words of this sentence ending in 'here,'.

[50] *a note..*: see enclosure (1), p 281.

to my country and as I do not think it possible to render any service in a defensive situation here, I am willing to repair to Charlestown if you approve of it, and in the mean time I shall do every thing in my power to arrange matters here 'till I have your answer.

Major Craig represented so strongly to Lord Rawdon his regret at leaving the distressed loyalists in the neighbourhood of Wilmington and his hopes of a considerable insurrection in the lower part of North Carolina where the enemy have no force that his Lordship gave him a conditional permission to postpone the evacuation of Wilmington, but I have not yet learned whether he has availed himself of it.

La Fayette's Continentals I believe consist of about 17 or 1800 men, exclusive of some twelve months' men collected by Steuben. He has received considerable reinforcements of militia and about 800 mountain rifle men under Campbell. He keeps with his main body about 18 or 20 miles from us, his advanced corps about 10 or 12, probably with an intention of insulting our rear guard when we pass James River. I hope, however, to put that out of his power by crossing at James City Island, and if I can get a favourable opportunity of striking a blow at him without loss of time, I will certainly try it. I will likewise attempt water expeditions if proper objects present themselves after my arrival at Portsmouth.

I inclose a report made by Lieutenant Thomas Hagerty, who came with a Captain Fleming from Maryland to join us in North Carolina. I feel most sincerely for the sufferings of the unfortunate loyalists, but being of opinion that a detachment would not afford them substantial and permanent relief, I shall not venture such a step unless your Excellency should think proper to direct it.

[I have the honour to be with great respect, sir,
Your most obedient and most humble servant

CORNWALLIS]

Enclosure (1)
Greene to Steuben, 14th May 1781[51]

105(24): ALS

Camp at McCord's Ferry
May 14th 1781

Major General Baron Steuben

Dear Baron

Your favor of the 26th of April[52] came to hand the 7th instant.

I am happy you came to so judicious a determination as not to hazard a general action and yet not permit the enemy to advance without considerable opposition.

---

[51] Summarised in *The Greene Papers*, viii, 257.

[52] *Your favor..*: published in the above, viii, 147.

Your report of the conduct of General Mhulenberg and the troops under his command affords me great pleasure and claims my entire approbation. This spirited opposition will have a most happy effect on their future operations.

It affords me great satisfaction that I had so early and so warmly pressed the Marquis's return with his detachment as produced his timely arrival. Lord Cornwallis, contrary to my wishes, I find is moving northerly towards Hallifax. If the Marquis and you by any disposition of the troops now with you, or the Pennsylvania line if they have arrived, can make a disposition to prevent a junction of Lord Cornwallis and General Philips, I wish you to do it.

General Sumner of North Carolina has directions to collect and equip the drafts of that State for the regular service, in the neighbourhood of Hillsborough and Hallifax. This force and such militia as may be in arms in the northern parts of that State may join and cooperate in the plan. If you cannot prevent a junction, join all the force ordered to the southward (the Maryland troops excepted) and cooperate with the Marquis to prevent the enemy from penetrating the country. Should Lord Cornwallis march this way, the Pennsylvania line, the North Carolina regulars, and the detachment of Virginia regulars lately drafted are to follow him and form a junction with us to the southward, of which you will take the command. But as the season is getting very warm in this quarter, I am inclined to think his Lordship will confine his operations to the northward, and if he should, as soon as I have put things in a train here, I propose to set out to join that army and leave this to complete the reduction of the remaining posts and hold possession of the country, which will defeat at once what the enemy have been two campaigns in accomplishing at such an expence of blood and treasure.

For the state of our operations here, I must beg leave to refer you to the Marquis.

With great respect and esteem I am, dear Baron,
Your most obedient humble servant

NATH GREENE

Enclosure (2)
Lafayette to Steuben, 31st May 1781   105(42): LS

Davenport's Ford
31st May 1781

My dear Baron

It is with infinite satisfaction that I impart you the good news from the southward: Camden is evacuated; Fort Watson, Mott's, Granby, Orange Burg have surrendered; the army was marching against Ninety Six and Augusta; the number of prisoners — 50 officers, 380 privates, 375 Tories. The pleasure of overrunning Virginia will loose something to his Lordship. I ever am happy to hear that a judicious military manœvre has mett with success, but I feel much more so in an instance when the reputation of my intimate friend is so particularly concerned. Time will come, I hope, when Lord Cornwallis will see his expedition in this State amounts to nothing.

Inclosed you will find a letter from General Greene. In compliance with his directions we must gather every force we can gett in this State. I request you will give your orders to General Lawson[53] and others and gett the troops in readiness for a junction with us. When General Green speaks of preventing a junction, he does not know that the Pennsylvania line was still on the 23rd at York Town, that Carolina militia amount to 150, and their new levies hardly to the same number. The few militia I have you perfectly know. My regular force is little above 800. The enemy have 500 horse and we 40. It appears they mean to go towards Fredricksburg. To morrow I hope to form a junction with General Weedon, and shou'd have hoped to have formed one with General Wayne. He assures me he shall sett out the 23rd and come as fast as he can. Was he with us, matters wou'd be very different. The assurance that you will be near our stores gives me great satisfaction. You may defend them against a light party and I hope to reinforce you before their main army cou'd gett there. However, our intelligence is very bad. But shou'd they go to Fredricksburg, it is impossible (particularly if Wayne can be joined to us) that the works be destroyed without resistance.

I request you will give every order respecting the removal of stores and every other article that may occur. I wish these stores were in a place perfectly safe. The Governor has ordered rifflemen to rendesvous at Charlottesville, to whom you will give directions. I am to beg your pardon for opening your letter, but I was gone from the place where they arrived and Mr Constable, who had remained behind, hearing that Tarleton's horse were in his route to join me, unsealed every letter On Public Service that in case he shou'd destroy them he might know their contents. Some say that General Clinton is arrived at Portsmouth.

With the greatest regard I have the honor to be, dear Baron,
Your most obedient humble servant

LAFAYETTE

---

[53] Robert Lawson (?-1805) of Prince Edward County was a brigadier general in the Virginia revolutionary militia, a body of whom he had recently commanded at the Battle of Guilford. He would now lead a body of militia during the operations in Virginia. From February 1776 to December 1777 he had served as a field officer in a Virginia regiment of the Continental line. After the war he was awarded 10,000 acres. (Boatner, *Encyclopedia*, 601; Heitman, *Historical Register*, 343; *Appletons'*; Gwathmey, *Historical Register*, 462)

Enclosure (3)
Lafayette to Jefferson, 31st May 1781   105(46): *ALS*

Devenport's Ford
31st May 1781

His Excellency Governor Jefferson

Sir

I have received your Excellency's letter inclosing some resolves respecting the impress of horses and thought it was my best way to intrust General Nelson[54] with the care of carrying them into execution. Inclosed your Excellency will find the returns of General Mullenberg's brigade.

I have the pleasure to inform you that Camden is evacuated, that the posts of Fort Motte, Orange Burg, Fort Watson, Fort Granby have surrendered to General Greene's army. The General writes me the 16th and was then on his way to Ninety Six and Augusta. In these several places 50 officers, 380 privates, 375 Tories have been captured. The vast superiority the enemy have acquired in Virginia is not without some loss in other quarters. Over running a country is not to conquer it, and if it was construed into a right of possession, the French could claim the whole German Empire.

To my great satisfaction the Virginia recruits and the Virginia militia will remain in this State. I was guarding against motives of self interest, but am happy to see that the new levies, General Lawson's men, and the Pennsylvanians will cooperate with us against the same army.

In case the Baron was gone I request the inclosed may be immediately sent after him. It contains an order to remain in the State and cannot be forwarded too soon. I wish the stores may be collected very high up, as they will the less require our attention.

Lord Cornwallis was this day at Little Page's Bridge and it is said busy in repairing of it. We are marching on a parallel with him and keeping the upper part of the country. To morrow I form a junction with General Weedon at Mattopony Church, and should General

---

[54] Born at Yorktown, Virginia, Thomas Nelson Jr (1738-1789) was educated in England at Eton and Trinity College, Cambridge. In colonial days he was a member of the House of Burgesses, but as the rupture with Britain approached, he placed himself firmly in the revolutionary camp. A member of the Virginia revolutionary conventions of 1774-6, he also became a delegate to the Continental Congress and was a signer of the Declaration of Independence. Compelled by illness to resign his Congressional seat in May 1777, he was shortly after appointed brigadier general in command of the Virginia state forces. As such he played an important part in organising resistance to subsequent British incursions into Virginia. When Thomas Jefferson resigned in June 1781 after the Charlottesville raid, Nelson was elected Governor by the Virginia revolutionary assembly, which granted him emergency powers. During his short term of office, which lasted only six months, he ably struggled to support Lafayette and Washington with men and supplies. The victory at Yorktown, the culmination of his career, brought about the ruin of his personal fortune, for, unable to raise government loans, he had had to pledge his own security. He now had to sell off his vast estate to pay his public debts and never received compensation from government. Portly and asthmatic, he retired from public life in November 1781. Buried in an unmarked grave in the Grace Churchyard at Yorktown, he has been the subject of biographies by Emory Evans and Nell Moore Lee. (*DAB*; Boatner, *Encyclopedia*, 777-8; *Appletons'*)

Waine arrive, our inferiority will not be quite so alarming. My Lord is going from his friends and we are going to meet ours.

With the highest respect I have the honor to be, dear sir,
Your Excellency's most obedient humble servant

LAFAYETTE

[*Subscribed*:]

General Greene requests me to impart you the southern intelligence. He was engaged in very important services and requests you will excuse his not writing himself.

Enclosure (4)
Return of Muhlenberg's brigade, 1st June 1781   105(45): C

Ranks	Corps				Total
	Meriwether	Thorton	Edmunds	Vanmeter	
Field officers:					
Colonels		1			1
Lt Colonels	1	1	1		3
Majors	2	2	2	1	7
Commissioned officers:					
Captains	11	10	9	3	33
Lieutenants	11	15	9	3	38
Ensigns	11	6	8	3	28
Staff officers:					
Adjutants	2	1	1	1	5
Pay Masters					
Quarter Masters	1	1	1	1	4
Surgeons					
Surgeons' Mates					
Non commissioned officers:					
Serjeant Majors	2	1	1	1	5
Quarter Master Serjeants	1	1	1	1	4
Serjeants	44	30	46	10	130
Drum and Fife Majors					

Drummers and Fifers	1	4		2	7
Rank and file:					
Effectives	377	331	307	86	1,111[55]
Sick present	20	7	50	10	87
Sick absent	10	18	9	6	43
On command	60	78	50	41	229
On furlough	30	17	3		50
Total	494[56]	451	458[57]	170[58]	1,573[59]
Alterations since last joined:					
Dead					
Deserted	5			5	10
Discharged	7	7			14
Reduced					
Recruited					
Promoted					
Serjeants					
Drummers and Fifers					
Privates					

From what county	*At what date mustered*
Amelia	April 24th 1781
Chesterfield	May 18th 1781
Spotsylvania	May 18th 1781
Hanover	May 18th 1781
Charles City	May 18th 1781
Berkely	April 30th 1781
Fauquire	April 30th 1781
Fredrick	April 28th 1781
Orrange	May 15th 1781

---

[55] *1,111*: 1,101.

[56] *494*: 497.

[57] *458*: 419.

[58] *170*: 143.

[59] *1,573*: 1,510.

Shanadore	April 23rd 1781	
Hamshire	May 1st 1781	
Culpeper	May 21st 1781	
Cumberland	April 22nd 1781	

WILSON C NICHOLAS[60]
Brigade Major

Enclosure (5)
Thomas Hagerty's report, 29th June 1781   *6(270): D*

Williamsbourgh
June 29th 1781

That he left the shipping at Sherley's the 13th instant with an intent to return to the army under Lord Cornwallis's command, but falling in with 3 deserters from the Queen's Rangers who knew him and caus'd him to be pursued, he alter'd his course and went to the vicinity of Fredricks Town in Maryland, the place of his former residence, w[h]ere he arrived the 16th and was informed as followeth.

That a certain Christian Orendorff of Sharpsborough, a lieutenant in the rebel service and a prisoner on parole from New York, had professed friendship to the associated loyalists and, after taking the usual oath of secrecy, was entrusted with their combination and with the names of the officers and many privates of the associators, their intentions etc, and then went to Anapolis, discovered the whole affair to the Governor and seized the persons of many of them before they could have any notice of his perfidy, all of whom he conveyed under a strong guard to Fredericks Town and Hegers Town jails to the amount of upwards of 170, thirty of which were officers from different parts of Maryland and Pennsylvania. That Casper Frittzy, Peter Sueman and Hugh Kelly, captains, and George Poe, an ensign, all of Fredericks Town, were condemned to suffer death, as also ten others at Hegers Town. That they are still going on with the tryals of the remainder, seizing others, and do declare that they have discovered 1,500 of the associators in Maryland and a like number in Pennsylvania. That some of these unfortunate people are tryed by a court martial consisting of militia officers, and others by a court of oyer and terminer. That the loyalists are in great want of arms and ammunition, which keeps them from rising in arms and risking their imprisoned confederates. A small number armed with rifles are, however, determined to defend themselves and have already revenged the injuries of their friends on some of the rebels. And that the associators in Pennsylvania were also in great confussion, several of them confined, and that particularly one of the name of Rankin was mentioned to him to be a prisoner.

---

[60] Wilson Cary Nicholas (1761-1820) was an officer in the Virginia revolutionary militia or state forces. A member of a powerful Virginia family which contributed to Thomas Jefferson's political success, he would go on to serve in the Virginia legislature, the state convention which ratified the federal constitution, and Congress. In 1814 he was elected Governor of Virginia. He died at 'Tufton' near Charlottesville and was interred in the Jefferson burial ground at 'Monticello'. (*DAB*; *Appletons'*)

That the said Hagerty was desired by several of the principal loyalists of the vicinity of Fredericks Town to haste his return to the royal army, to represent their case to the Rt Hon the Earl of Cornwallis, and to entreat his Lordship to send a detachment of the King's forces to take post in some part of Maryland and to supply them with arms and ammunition that they may have it in their power to stop that horrid scene which is now opening.[61]

Clinton to Cornwallis, 28th June 1781[62]   68(28): CS

New York
28th June 1781

Lt General Earl Cornwallis

My Lord

2nd battalion, light infantry
43rd Regiment
76th or 80th
2 battalions of Anspach
Queen's Rangers, cavalry & infantry and such a proportion of artillery as can be spared, particularly men.

Having for very essential reasons come to a resolution of endeavoring by a rapid move to seize the stores etc collected at Philadelphia and afterwards to bring the troops employed on that service to reinforce this post, I am to request that, if your Lordship has not already embarked the reinforcement I called for in my letters of the 8th, 11th, 15th and 19th instant and should not be engaged in some very important move either of your own or in consequence of my ideas respecting operation in the upper Chesapeak, you will be pleased as soon as possible to order an embarkation of the troops specified in the margin and of the ordnance and other stores etc etc stated in the inclosed paper, or in as full a manner as your Lordship can with propriety comply, recollecting that whatever may have been taken too great a proportion of will be immediately returned to you the moment the expedition is over.

As it is possible that your Lordship may have sent Major General Leslie to Charles Town in consequence of what I said to you in my letter of the 29th ultimo[63], I have thought proper to appoint Lt General Robertson to the command of the troops on this service, which I should

---

[61] This document provides interesting supplementary information about the loyalist conspiracy and its discovery. Casper Frietschie and Peter Sueman were hanged on 17th August but the fate of Hugh Kelly and George Poe is unknown. For a brief and incomplete account of events, see Dorothy Mackay Quynn, 'The Loyalist Plot in Frederick', *Maryland Historical Magazine*, xl, N° 3 (September 1945), 201-210)

[62] Annotated: 'Received July 8th 1781', and published with the enclosure in Stevens, op cit, ii, 29. There are no material differences.

[63] *my letter..*: Cornwallis did not receive it until 12th July, when he also received those of 8th and 19th June referred to earlier. See pp 118 to 136.

not have judged necessary could I have been certain of his being named by your Lordship to accompany the troops coming hither. Should that, however, have been the case, your Lordship will be pleased nevertheless to direct him to proceed with the expedition.

I have the honor to be
Your Lordship's most obedient and most humble servant

H CLINTON

Enclosure
Ordnance and stores requested by Clinton   *68(30): D*

List of cannon, stores etc to be sent from Virginia

Artillery etc etc

      Two 8 inch howitzers, light
      Two 5½ inch ditto
      Two medium brass 12 pounders
      Four brass six pounders, field pieces
      12 waggons without the bodies for transporting boats etc etc
      A proportion of carcasses.

Vessels

      The sloop: *Formidable*
      Brigantines: *Spitfire*
                       Rambler
The prize ship *Tempest* if she can be unloaded and fitted without delaying the transports.

As many horses as are necessary for the artillery and waggons.

As many of the first 24 new boats as can be spared. Those with platforms to have cannon mounted in them and compleatly fitted if it can be done without delaying the embarkation. The cannon to be brought in the transports and the boats towed by them.

Lieutenant Sutherland of the Engineers with entrenching tools etc etc for 500 men.

Cornwallis to Clinton, 8th July 1781[64]

74(30): ADf

Cobham
July 8th 1781

His Excellency Sir Henry Clinton

Sir

I was this morning honoured with your dispatch of the 28th ultimo. The troops are perfectly ready and will proceed to Portsmouth to wait the arrival of the transports. I will give immediate orders about the artillery, stores etc.

The transports now at Portsmouth are sufficient to carry the light infantry. I had prepared them to receive that corps and should have sent them to you in a few days if your last order had not arrived. In your cyphered dispatch[65] the second battalion of light infantry only is mentioned, but I conclude that to be a mistake and shall keep both ready to embark. I take for granted that General Robertson will come with the transports to take the command of the expedition. General Leslie is still here, but as it was not my intention to have sent him with the troops to New York, and as he will be the properist person to command here[66] in case you should approve of my returning to Charlestown, I shall not send him on the expedition unless it shall then appear to be your Excellency's desire that he should accompany General Robertson.

I must again take the liberty of calling your Excellency's serious attention to the question of the utility of a defensive post in this country which cannot have the smallest influence on the war in Carolina and which only gives us some acres of an unhealthy swamp and is for ever liable to become a prey to a foreign enemy with a temporary superiority at sea. Desultory expeditions in the Chesapeak may be undertaken from New York with as much ease and more safety whenever there is reason to suppose that our naval force is likely to be superior for two or three months.

The boats and naval assistance having been sent to me by Captain Hudson, I marched on the 4th from Williamsburgh to a camp which covered a ford into the island of James Town. The Queen's Rangers passed the river that evening. On the 5th I sent over all the wheel carriages, and on the 6th the bat horses and baggage of every kind, intending to pass with the army on the 7th. About noon on the 6th information was brought to me of the approach of the enemy[67], and about four in the afternoon a large body attacked our out posts.

---

[64] Published, with the omission mentioned in note 66 below, in Stevens, op cit, ii, 56. There are no other differences.

[65] *your cyphered dispatch*: that of 28th June, the original of which (68(32)) is in cipher.

[66] Stevens, op cit, omits 'here'.

[67] The words from 'information' to 'enemy' are substituted for: 'I heard that small parties of the enemy appeared near our camp, and a Negroe who had been taken in a foraging party assured me that he had been carried to the French General, who was not above six miles from us. As the ford into James Island was only passable at low water and appeared to be but little known in the country, I concluded that the Marquis had not heard of it and

Concluding that the enemy would not bring a considerable force within our reach unless they supposed that nothing was left but a rear guard, I took every means to convince them of my weakness and suffered my piquets to be insulted and driven back. Nothing, however, appeared near us but riflemen and militia 'till near sunset, when a body[68] of Continentals with artillery began to form in the front of our camp. I then put the troops under arms and ordered the army to advance in two lines. The attack was begun by the 1st line with great spirit. There being nothing but militia opposed to the light infantry, the action was soon over on the right, but Lt Colonel Dundas's brigade, consisting of the 43rd, 76th and 80th Regiments, which formed the left wing, meeting the Pensylvania line and a detachment of the Marquis de Lafayette's Continentals with two six pounders, a smart action ensued for some minutes, when the enemy gave way and abandoned their canon. The cavalry were perfectly ready to pursue, but[69] the darkness of the evening prevented my being able to make use of them. I cannot sufficiently commend the spirit and good behaviour of the officers and soldiers of the whole army, but the 76th and 80th Regiments, on whom the brunt of the action fell, had an opportunity of distinguishing themselves particularly, and Lt Colonel Dundas's conduct and gallantry deserve the highest praise. The force of the enemy in the field was about two thousand, and their loss, I believe, between two and three hundred. Half an hour more of daylight would have probably given us the greatest part of the corps. I have inclosed a list of our killed and wounded[70]. We finished our passage yesterday, which has been an operation of great labour and difficulty as the river is three miles wide at this place. I have great obligations to Captain Aplin[71] and the officers of the navy and seamen for their great exertions and attention on this occasion.

I have not received the letters your Excellency alludes to of the 29th of May or 8th and 19th of June.

[I have the honour to be with great respect, sir,
Your most obedient and most humble servant

CORNWALLIS]

---

therefore intended an attack on our rear guard,'.

[68] Before 'body' is deleted 'considerable'.

[69] Before 'but' the following words are deleted: 'but as it began to grow dark and as the prisoners and deserters reported that the remainder of the rebel army was formed on some strong ground not far distant'.

[70] *a list..*: no copy.

[71] Having served as a captain's servant, able seaman and midshipman, Peter Aplin (1753-1817) passed his lieutenant's examination on 9th August 1775 and was assigned to the North American station. After service in the *Roebuck* he was promoted to commander on 23rd April 1778 and took charge, first of the fireship *Strombolo*, and then of the sloop *Swift*. On 23rd November 1780 he was promoted to post-captain and assumed command of the 24-gun frigate *Fowey*. An active officer, he had very recently been detached with five flat boats and a body of seamen to facilitate Cornwallis's crossing of the James River. Trapped at Yorktown, the *Fowey* would be destroyed by fire from the enemy's batteries on 10th October, but Aplin and his crew would survive and see service on shore. Between 1797 and 1799 he was captain of the 74-gun *Hector*, and although promoted to flag rank on 14th February 1799, he never again had an active command. He died an admiral of the white at Brickstone House, his home near Cheltenham. (*ODNB*; Syrett and DiNardo eds, *The Commissioned Sea Officers*, 9)

Clinton to Cornwallis, 29th May and 1st June 1781[72]

68(5): CS

New York
29th May 1781

Lt General Earl Cornwallis

My Lord

I had the honor of writing to your Lordship by Lord Chewton, who sailed from hence in the *Richmond* the 4th instant to join you at Wilmington, but your Lordship's departure from thence will have prevented his meeting you there and I hope he has since then joined you in the Chesapeak.

When I first heard of your Lordship's retreat from Cross Creek to Wilmington, I confess that I was in hopes you had reason to consider Green so totally *hors de combat* as to be perfectly at ease for Lord Rawdon's safety. And after your arrival at Wilmington I flattered myself that, if any change of circumstances should make it necessary, you could always have been able to march to the Walkamaw, where I imagined vessels might have passed you over to George Town. I cannot therefore conceal from your Lordship the apprehensions I felt on reading your letter to me of the 24th ultimo, wherein you inform me of the critical situation which you supposed the Carolinas to be in and that you should probably attempt to effect a junction with Major General Phillips. Lord Rawdon's officer like and spirited exertions in taking advantage of Greene's having detached from his army have indeed eased me of my apprehensions for the present, but in the disordered state of Carolina and Georgia, as represented to me by Lt Colonel Balfour, I shall dread what may be the consequence of your Lordship's move unless a reinforcement arrives very soon in South Carolina and such instructions are sent to the officer commanding there as may induce him to exert himself in restoring tranquillity to that province at least. These I make no doubt your Lordship has already sent to Lord Rawdon, and that every necessary measure for this purpose will be taken by his Lordship in consequence of them should he remain in the command, but as there are many officers in the regiments coming out who are older than Lord Rawdon, I have to lament the probability of his being superseded in it, as I can scarce flatter myself that any of them will be possessed of the knowledge requisite for conducting operations in Carolina without having ever served in that country or be so competent to the command there as officers of more local experience. I therefore beg leave to submit to your Lordship the propriety of sending either Major General Leslie or Brigadier General O'Hara to Charles Town to take the command of the troops in that district, which in the present critical situation of affairs in the southern colonies will certainly require an officer of experience and a perfect knowledge of the country. Had it been possible for your Lordship in your letter to me of the 10th ultimo to have intimated the probability of your intention to form a junction with General Phillips, I should certainly have endeavored to have stopped you, as I did then, as well as now, consider such a move as likely to be dangerous to our interests in the southern colonies. And this, my Lord, was not my only fear, for I will be free to own that I was apprehensive for the corps under your Lordship's immediate orders as well as for that under Lord Rawdon. And

---

[72] Annotated: 'Received from Lt Colonel McPherson, 71st, 12th July 1781', and published without the enclosures in Stevens, op cit, i, 493. Apart from the omission mentioned in note 74 below, there are no other differences.

I should not have thought even the one under Major General Phillips in safety at Petersburg, at least for so long a time, had I not fortunately, on hearing of your being at Wilmington, sent another detachment from this army to reinforce him.

I am persuaded your Lordship will have the goodness to excuse my saying thus much, but what is done cannot now be altered. And as your Lordship has thought proper to make this decision, I shall most gladly avail myself of your very able assistance in carrying on such operations as you shall judge best in Virginia untill we are compelled, as I fear we must be by the climate, to bring them more northward. Your Lordship will have been informed of my ideas respecting operations to the northward of the Carolinas by my instructions to the different general officers detached to the Chesapeak and the substance of some conversations with General Phillips on that subject, which I committed to writing and sent to him with my last dispatch with directions to communicate it to your Lordship.[73] By these your Lordship will observe that my first object has ever been a cooperation with your measures, but your Lordship's situation at different periods made it necessary for me occasionally to vary my instructions to those general officers according to circumstances. They were originally directed to assist your Lordship's operations in securing South, and recovering North, Carolina; their attention was afterwards pointed to the saving South Carolina; and now your Lordship may possibly think it necessary to employ your force in recovering both or either of those provinces by either a direct or indirect operation. With respect to the first, your Lordship must be the sole judge. With respect to the last, you have my opinions, which may, however, probably give way to yours should they differ from them, as they will have the advantage of being formed on the spot and upon circumstances which at this distance I cannot of course judge of. I shall therefore leave them totally to your Lordship to decide upon until you either hear from me or we meet.

I should be happy to be able to ascertain the time when our reinforcements may arrive, but as I have received no letters from the Minister of a later date than the 7th of February, I am at a loss to guess how soon we may expect them. As I had judged the force I sent to the Chesapeak fully sufficient for all operations there, even tho' we should extend them to the experiment (mentioned in the conversations referred to) at the western head of Chesapeak about Baltimore etc — and your Lordship will perceive that it was Generals Phillips' and Arnold's opinion they were sufficient for even that on the eastern (which, however, might certainly require a much greater force), it is possible that the additional corps your Lordship has brought with you may enable you to return something to me for this post, but I beg your Lordship will by no means consider this as a call, for I would rather content myself with ever so bare a defensive until there was an appearance of serious operation against me than cramp yours in the least. But (as I said in a former letter) I trust to your Lordship's disinterestedness that you will not require from me more troops than what are absolutely wanted and that you will recollect a circumstance which I am ever aware of in carrying on operations in the Chesapeak, which is that they can be no longer secure than whilst we are superior at sea. That we shall remain so, I most sincerely hope, nor have I any reason to suspect we shall not, but at all events I may at least expect timely information will be sent me of the contrary being likely to happen, in which case I hope your Lordship may be able to place your army in a

---

[73] For the several instructions, see p 7; vol II, p 50; and vol III, pp 23 and 55. For the substance of Clinton's conversations with Phillips, see p 55.

more[74] secure situation during such temporary inconvenience, for should it become permanent, I need not say what our prospects in this country are likely to be. The Admiral being now off the Hook gives me an opportunity of communicating with him by letter, and I have in the most pressing terms requested his attention to the Chesapeak, having repeatedly told him that, should the enemy possess it even for 48 hours, your Lordship's operations there may be exposed to most imminent danger. General Robertson has also endeavored to impress him with the same ideas, but until I have an answer in writing I cannot be sure that he will, as I do, consider the Chesapeak as the first object, for he at present seems rather inclined to lead his fleet to open the port of Rhode Island and to cruise to the northward of Nantucket for a fleet which he has heard is coming from Europe with a small reinforcement to the French armament and which I am of opinion is bound to Rhode Island. I have, however, taken every occasion to represent to him the necessity of hearty cooperation and communication. If they fail, I am determined it shall not be on my side.

The requisitions your Lordship has made in your letter to me of the 20th instant for horse accoutrements etc shall be supplied to the utmost extent of our abilities; and the inclosed extracts of letters from Lt Colonel Innes to his deputy at Charles Town etc will explain to your Lordship why they are not more ample.

June 1st

I have this moment received the Admiral's answer to my letter and I am to suppose from it that he will do every thing in his power to guard the Chesapeak. The copy is inclosed for your Lordship's information. I heartily wish he may continue in this disposition, the necessity of which I shall not fail to urge by every opportunity he may give me of communicating with him.

As I shall frequently send one of my advice boats to your Lordship with any information which may deserve your attention, I hope to hear often from you by the same conveyance. Lord Chewton has a cypher which was given him for that purpose, but should he not have joined you, we may make use of Colonel Dundas's until he does.

I shall spare your Lordship and myself the pain of saying much to you on the loss of our valuable friend. I feel it too sensibly for expression.

I have the honor to be
Your Lordship's most obedient and most humble servant

H CLINTON

---

[74] Stevens, op cit, omits 'more'.

Enclosure (1)
Innes to Clinton, 30th May 1781 6(162): CS

*The Inspector General of Provincial Forces' Report
to His Excellency the Commander in Chief*

New York
30th May 1781

The Inspector in consequence of your Excellency's commands presents a return of cloathing for 300 men, exclusive of serjeants and drummers, and such articles of camp equipage as he conceives will be useful for the Legion. All these can be embarked at an hour's notice. The like number of saddles and bridles may also be delivered immediately, but a few days will be necessary to compleat them with holsters, pads etc, as they were sent from England deficient in many articles absolutely wanted for a dragoon. 100 saddles compleat shall be ready on Saturday, and 100 more the Wednesday after, and the utmost diligence used to compleat the rest. 67 swords are now in store. 50 more are at the cutler's. He can finish 25 per week and shall go on compleating swords. Pistols we have none.

The Inspector takes the liberty of presenting with this extracts of his letters to the Under Secretary of State and his deputy at Charles Town, which he hopes will convince your Excellency it is not owing to any neglect or inattention of his office that larger supplies cannot be immediately forwarded.

ALEX INNES
Inspector General, Provincial Forces

Enclosure (2)
Extract, Innes to Thompson[75], 14th May 1781 6(67): C

Our distress for want of cavalry appointments both here and to the southward is beyond conception and obliges us to purchase at an immense expence a number of articles that are at best a wretched temporary expedient yet swells our Provincial contingent account to an enormous sum... I am therefore most earnestly to entreat his Lordship will use his influence that our supplies for cavalry may be expedited and that nothing if possible may be sent to this country unmade as the expence of labour is immense... I hope his Lordship will have the goodness to excuse my very great earnestness on this subject, as the publick money for that service is intrusted to me by the General and for which I am accountable to the *publick*... Had all the appointments intended for Brigadier General Ruggles[76] come out compleat, it

---

[75] Benjamin Thompson, Under Secretary of State for the Northern Department.

[76] A native of Massachusetts, Timothy Ruggles (1711-1795) had been authorised in 1780 to raise the King's American Dragoons, a British American regiment of six troops of horse. Having graduated in law from Harvard in 1732, he established himself as a lawyer in Massachusetts and was appointed a Judge of the Court of Common Pleas in 1756. Six years later he became Chief Justice of the Court, an office which he held until the revolution. During

would have afforded us a small temporary supply, but unfortunately there is a great deficiency there in horse appointments.

I take the liberty of inclosing the deficiency in the appointments and the estimate I got from the tradesman of the expence that will attend supplying it... I have delayed from time to time compleating those saddles in hopes our appointments would arrive, but must now be under a necessity, as the demands from the southward are become too pressing not to be attended to, and after this is done, the helmet, carbine and sword are still wanting.

Enclosure (3)
Extract, Innes to Prevost[77], 26th May 1781 6(119): C

I am perfectly sensible of your distress as to cavalry appointments and have repeatedly represented it to the Commander in Chief, who laments it as much as we do without having it in his power to relieve us. His requisition for 1,000 cavalry sets of appointments of all kinds went home early last year. Major Cochrane was exceedingly industrious in fixing upon proper ones. He laid the pattern with the price before the Treasury, and by Lord George's influence the patterns given in were approved and ordered, but they are not yet arrived and by Major Cochrane's information I have reason to fear they are not in the forwardness we could wish.

I shall send you every saddle I can get here by the first convoy, but the repeated applications made by the General to the Admiral for a convoy both to Charles Town and Halifax have not as yet been complied with.

I send you an extract of a letter I lately wrote to Mr Thompson, the Under Secretary of State. I can do no more, and I am so truly sick of my situation that nothing but the General's positive commands would make me remain in it.

The prices of things are high, and altho' you and I know it is unavoidable, it is not a little distressing to be put to such shifts and such expence when such ample supplies are ordered at home.

---

the Seven Years' War he served as a Provincial officer and in that capacity rose to be a brigadier general under Amherst. In recognition of his military services he was appointed Deputy Surveyor General of the King's Forests in Massachusetts and awarded a farm at Princeton. For many years a member of the lower house of the Massachusetts legislature, he was chosen one of its delegates to the Stamp Act Congress in 1765, of which he became President, but refused to sign the addresses to Great Britain. On his return home he was censured by the house for his refusal. A commanding figure and forcible orator, he became in 1774 a member of His Majesty's Council in the province, a body which acted partly as the upper house of the legislature and partly as a privy council advising the Governor in the exercise of his functions. As a leader of the King's party in Massachusetts, he accompanied the British troops to Nova Scotia when Boston was evacuated at the beginning of the revolutionary war. In 1779 he was granted 10,000 acres at Wilmot, having had his property in Massachusetts confiscated by the revolutionary authorites there. (PRO 30/55/28(12) (National Archives, Kew); Rossiter Johnson ed, *The Twentieth Century Biographical Dictionary of Notable Americans* (Gales Research Co reprint, 1968); *Appletons'*; Nan Cole and Todd Braisted, 'The King's American Dragoons' (*The On-Line Institute for Advanced Loyalist Studies*, 17th April 2006))

[77] Major Augustine Prevost was Deputy Inspector General of Provincial Forces at Charlestown.

I shall only repeat that the General is to make another effort to get a convoy and every thing I can muster shall be sent you, let the expence be what it will.

Enclosure (4)
Arbuthnot to Clinton, 30th May 1781

6(160): C

Royal Oak off Sandy Hook
30th May 1781

His Excellency General Sir Henry Clinton etc etc etc

Sir

I am this morning honored with your Excellency's letter by Captain Keppel[78], previous to whose arrival I had wrote the Commodore to desire the *Roebuck*, which will be ready in three days, to perform that service the *Charon* was before intended for in case the *Charon* should not arrive in time.

I am persuaded your Excellency will believe that every measure will be taken to protect and cover your Excellency's operations in the Chesapeak and every other quarter.

I have the honor to be
Your Excellency's most obedient and most humble servant

M^T ARBUTHNOT

Clinton to Cornwallis, 8th June 1781[79]

68(11): CS

New York
June 8th 1781

Lt General the Earl Cornwallis

My Lord

I inclose to your Lordship copies of some intercepted letters. By these your Lordship will see that we are threatned with a siege. The enemy have had bad information respecting my force. It is not, however, as your Lordship knows, what it ought to be. Your Lordship will see by Fayette's letter that you have little more opposed to you than his corps and an unarmed

---

[78] Either George Keppel, a post-captain, or George Augustus Keppel, a commander, whose rank carried the courtesy title of captain. (Syrett and DiNardo eds, *Commissioned Sea Officers*, 255)

[79] Annotated: 'Received from Lt Colonel McPherson, 71st, 12th July 1781', and published with no differences in Stevens, op cit, ii, 14.

militia, for we are told here that the Pensylvania troops have revolted a second time at York Town. Your Lordship can therefore certainly spare 2,000, and the sooner they come the better, without it should be your intention to adopt my ideas of a move to Baltimore or the Delaware Neck and put yourself in nearer cooperation with us, but even in that case you can spare us something, I suppose.

I am naturally to expect reinforcement from Europe, but not having heard from thence since February, I can say nothing positive as to when it sailed. It is rumored here (from what authority I cannot learn) that the three battalions from Corke are arrived at Charlestown and that your Lordship has ordered them to Chesapeak. Should that have been the case, I have by this opportunity directed them not to disembark but to join me here as soon as a convoy can be obtained for them, in the first place because I want them, and in the next because it would be death to them to act in Chesapeak in July.

From all the letters I have seen I am of opinion, if circumstances of provisions, stores etc turn out as they wish, that the enemy will *certainly* attack this post. As for men for such an object as this (circumstanced as they suppose it to be), it cannot be doubted that they can raise a sufficient number. By a commissary of provisions' intercepted letter, he now feeds (at West Point only) 8,000, and they are coming in very fast. My dispatches for your Lordship and the stores etc you sent for have been waiting for a convoy — these ten days. I hope it will sail immediately, but I dispatch this runner in the meantime, referring your Lordship to the bearer, Lieutenant Nairne, for particulars.

I request that the officer commanding at Portsmouth may have positive orders to dispatch a runner once a week while they last, whether he has any thing material to say or not. Every circumstance in the present situation of the corps of this army is of consequence to know. As your Lordship is now so near, it will be unnecessary for you to send your dispatches immediately to the Minister. You will therefore be so good to send them to me in future.

I am much in want of howitzers etc. I think your Lordship can spare some. If so, I request they may be sent, and a good proportion of artillery men with them. Captain Fage[80] of the Artillery and Lieutenant Sutherland of the Engineers are to return here, as I particularly want them, and Lieutenant Fiers if your Lordship can possibly spare him. I likewise request that your Lordship will send General Arnold to me.

I send by Lt Colonel Macpherson[81] a commission for Colonel Abercrombie to act as

---

[80] Edward Fage (*c.* 1740-1809) entered the Royal Regiment of Artillery as a cadet on 1st November 1755 and was commissioned a 2nd lieutenant five years later. He was promoted to 1st lieutenant on 17th June 1772 and to captain lieutenant on 7th July 1779. As a colonel he would serve from 1803 to 1805 as Inspector of the Royal Carriage Factory, a manufacturing department of Woolwich Arsenal. In 1808 he became a major general and Colonel Commandant of the Royal Artillery, dying a few months later at Greenwich. (*Royal Regiment of Artillery*, 11, 170; *Army Lists*)

[81] Duncan MacPherson (1748-1817) was the son of Ewan MacPherson, whose involvement in the Jacobite rebellion led to his estate of Cluny near Ben Alder being confiscated. Now a lt colonel in the British Army, Duncan had latterly served in the 63rd and 42nd Regiments before being assigned to the 71st (Highland) Regiment on 31st December 1780. He was now arriving in Virginia to take command of the 2nd Battalion, which had lately been commanded by Captain Robert Hutcheson. He would be taken prisoner with it at Yorktown. In 1784 the estate

brigadier general until further orders, but I fear it will not be in my power to establish him in that rank as I understand there are six older than him coming out. The commission will therefore be delivered to your Lordship to use or not as you may see expedient, but at all events I imagine your Lordship will not think it necessary to give the commission to Colonel Abercrombie whilst Major General Leslie or Brigadier General Arnold remain with you.

I am persuaded that I need not say to your Lordship how necessary it is that I should be informed without delay of every change of position in your Lordship's army, and I am sure you will excuse me for observing that, had it been possible upon the arrival of the last reinforcement from hence (which I am told joined you the day after the date of your letter of the 20th ultimo) for your Lordship to have let me know your views and intentions, I should not now be at a loss to judge of the force you might want for your operations. Ignorant, therefore, as I am of them, I can only trust that, as your Lordship will see by the inclosed letters my call for a reinforcement is not a wanton one, you will send me what you can spare as soon as it may be expedient, for should your Lordship be engaged in a move of such importance as to require the employment of your whole force, I would by no means wish to starve or obstruct it but in that case would rather endeavor to wait a little longer until my occasions grow more urgent or your situation can admit of your detaching, of which, however, I request to be informed with all possible dispatch. But with respect to the European reinforcement I must request that, should it arrive in the Chesapeak, it may be sent to me without delay, agreable to the orders I have sent to the officer commanding at Portsmouth and the requisition I make by this opportunity to Captain Hudson or officer commanding the King's ships.

Should your Lordship not propose to send Major General Leslie to command in South Carolina, I beg leave to mention that his assistance may probably be wanted here if he can be spared from your army.

I have the honor to be
Your Lordship's most obedient and most humble servant

H CLINTON

---

of Cluny was restored to him and fourteen years later he retired from the army to marry his second cousin, Catherine Cameron, with whom he had eight children. One of his daughters married Robert Fitzroy, captain of HMS *Beagle* when Charles Darwin made his voyage of discovery. (William Lowrie, 'Edinburgh to Inverness via Ladybank' (Internet, 24th August 2006); *Army Lists*)

Enclosure (1)
Lafayette to Washington, 18th May 1781 6(79): C

Wilton
North side of James River
May 18th 1781

His Excellency General Washington

Dear General

Having been directed by General Greene to take command of the troops in Virginia, I have also received orders from him that every account from this quarter be immediately transmitted to Congress and to your Excellency, in obedience to which I shall have the honor to relate our movements and those of the combined armies of the enemy.

When General Phillips retreated from Richmond, his project was to stop at Williamsburgh, there to collect contributions he had imposed. This induced me to take a position between Pamunky and Chickahomany Rivers, which equally covered Richmond and some other interesting parts of the State, and from where I detached General Nelson with some militia towards Williamsburgh.

Having got as low down as that place, General Phillips seemed to discover an intention to make a landing, but upon advices received by a vessel from Portsmouth the enemy weighed anchor and, with all the sail they could croud, hastened up the river. This intelligence made me apprehensive that the enemy intended to manœuvre me out of Richmond, where I returned immediately and again collected our small force. Intelligence was the same day received that Lord Cornwallis (who I had been assured to have embarked at Wilmington) was marching thro' North Carolina. This was confirmed by the landing of General Phillips at Brandon, south side of James River. Apprehending that both armies would move to meet at a central point, I marched towards Petersburgh and intended to have established a communication over Appamatox and James River, but on the 9th General Phillips took possession of Petersburgh, a place where (his right flank being covered by James River, his front by Appamatox, on which the bridges had been destroyed in the first of the invasion, and his left not being attackable but by a long circuit through fords that at this season are very uncertain) I could not (even with an equal force) have got any chance of fighting him unless I had given up this side of James River and the country from which reinforcements are expected.

It being at the enemy's choice to force us to an action while their own position insured them against our enterprises, I thought it proper to shift this situation and marched the greater part of our troops to this place, about ten miles below Richmond. Letters from General Nash, General Sumner and General Jones are positive as to the arrival of Colonel Tarleton and announce that of Lord Cornwallis at Halifax.

Having received a request from North Carolina for ammunition, I made a detachment of 500 men under General Muhlenburg to escort 20,000 cartridges over Appamatox, and to divert the enemy's attention Colonel Gimat[82] with his battalion and 4 field pieces cannonaded their position from this side the river. I hope our ammunition will arrive safe, as, before General Muhlenberg returned, he put it in a safe road with proper directions.

On the 13th General Phillips died and the command devolved on General Arnold.

General Wayne's detachment has not yet been heard of. Before he arrives it becomes very dangerous to risk any engagement where (either of the British armies being vastly superior to us) we shall certainly be beaten, and by the loss of arms, the dispersion of militia, and the difficulty of a junction with General Wayne we may lose a less dangerous chance of resistance.

These considerations have induced me to think that, with our so very great inferiority and with the advantage the enemy have by their cavalry and naval superiority, there would be much rashness in fighting them on any but our ground and this side of the river, and that an engagement which I fear will be soon necessary ought if possible to be deferred 'till the Pennsylvanians arrive, whom I have by several letters requested to hasten to our assistance.

No report has lately come from near Halifax, tho' a very active officer has been sent for that purpose, but every intelligence confirms that Lord Cornwallis is hourly expected at Petersburgh. It is true there never was such difficulty in getting tolerable intelligence as there is in this country, and the immense superiority of the enemy's horse renders it very precarious to hazard our small parties.

Arnold has received a small reinforcement from Portsmouth.

Dear General, your most obedient humble servant

LA FAYETTE

PS

In justice to Major Mitchel[83] and Captain Muir[84], who were taken at Petersburgh, I have

---

[82] Jean-Joseph Sourbader de Gimat (c. 1745-?) was born in Gascony, the son of a military officer. In 1761 he entered the Regiment de Guyenne as an ensign, but though well liked and respected by his superiors, he attained the rank of 1st lieutenant only in June 1776. One year later he arrived with Lafayette at Philadelphia, was commissioned a major on the Continental establishment, and became Lafayette's aide-de-camp. Promoted to lt colonel shortly afterwards, he continued to serve Lafayette as an aide-de-camp until February 1781, when he was assigned to the command of a light infantry battalion. With it he accompanied Lafayette to Virginia, where he took part in operations until the capitulation of Yorktown. Taking passage for France in January 1782, he was promoted seven months later to colonel of the colonial regiment at Martinique. Between June 1789 and June 1792 he was Governor of St Lucia. (Boatner, *Encyclopedia*, 433-4; Heitman, *Historical Register*, 249)

[83] Born near Laurel in Sussex County, Delaware, Nathaniel Mitchell (1753-1814) had served as major in both Grayson's and Gist's Additional Continental Regiments before transferring to the staff of Peter Muhlenberg in Virginia. He was captured at Petersburg on 10th May, having been sent forward with Francis Muir (see below) to reconnoitre Arnold's post there and to obtain intelligence of Cornwallis's advance. After the war he would represent Delaware for a term in the Continental Congress, serve as the Protonotary of Sussex County, become Governor of Delaware, and go on to serve in the state legislature. He died at 'Rosemont', his home in Laurel, and

the honor to inform your Excellency that they had been sent to that place on public service. I have requested General Lauson to collect and take command of the militia south of Appamatox. Local impediments was thrown in the road from Halifax to Petersburgh and precautions taken to remove the horses from the enemy's reach. Should it be possible to get arms, some more militia might be brought into the field, but General Greene and myself labour under the same disadvantage: the few militia we can with great pains collect arrive unarmed and we have not a sufficiency of weapons to put into their hands.

Enclosure (2)
Barras to Luzerne, 27th May 1781   6(115): C

a Newport
le 27 May 1781

Je viens de recevoir, Monsieur, la lettre que vous m'avez fait l'honneur de m'ecrire en date du 20 May ainsi que la memoire qui y etoit joint. Par ma lettre du 19 je vous ay mandé le parti que j'avois pris, ce qui m'empechoit d'aller a la conference qu'il ya eu du General Wasseintong avec Monsieur de Rochambeaud. Ce dernier m'a prevenu qu'il vous faisoit part de ce qui y a eté decidé. J'avois repondu a deux propositions que Monsieur de Rochambeaud avoit prevu que le general americain fairoit et il paroit qu'il les approuvées. Je desirerois pouvoir suivre pour les operations le memoire que vous m'avez envoyé. Vous verrés par ce que vous mande Monsieur de Rochambeaud mes reponses, ainsi que mes observations. Je desire qu'elles ayent votre approbation. L'escadre angloise n'a pas paru depuis le 23. Comme il est decidé que l'escadre va a Boston, je me presseray de m'y rendre pour ne pas retarder le depart des troupes qu'on est obligé de me fournir au nombre de 900 hommes pour completter les equipages. Vous imaginés bien que, ces troupes renvoyées, l'escadre est en partie desarmée.

Je n'ecris pas a Monsieur de la Touche. S'il est encor a la Delaware ainsy que l'*Ariel* et que vous destiniez pour la partie du nord ils ont besoin de naviguer avec la plus grande precaution et de venir a Boston.

Je suis avec un respectueux attachement, monsieur, etc

BARRAS

PS: A mon arrivée a Boston j'expedieray la *Concorde* pour porter les paquets et l'état de la Virginie au Comte de Grasse.

---

was buried in Broad Creek Episcopal Cemetery nearby. (Andrew R Dodge ed, *Biographical Directory of the United States Congress 1774-2005* (US Government Printing Office, 2006); *Wikipedia*, 7th October 2006)

[84] A Virginian, Francis Muir (?-c. 1810) had served as a captain in Gist's Additional Continental Regiment before transferring, like Nathaniel Mitchell, to the staff of Peter Muhlenberg. He had now been captured with Mitchell while on the mission to which the preceding note refers. After the war he would be awarded 4,000 acres in recognition of his revolutionary service and in his final years was living in Dinwiddie County. (Heitman, *Historical Register*, 406; Gwathmey, *Historical Register*, 571)

TRANSLATION

Newport
27th May 1781

Sir

I have just received the letter of 20th May which you did me the honor of writing to me, together with the attached memorandum. In my letter of the 19th I advised you of the decision I had made preventing me from attending the conference which has taken place between General Washington and Monsieur de Rochambeau. The latter has informed me that he was imparting to you what was decided. I had responded to two proposals which Monsieur de Rochambeau had foreseen the American general would make and he apparently approved of them. Operationally, I would wish to be able to follow the memorandum you have sent me. You will see my reactions and observations from what Monsieur de Rochambeau reports to you. I hope they may meet with your approbation. The British squadron has not put in an appearance since the 23rd. As it is decided to dispatch the squadron[85] to Boston, I shall make haste to go there so as not to delay the departure of the troops who are ordered to accompany me to the number of 900 men for completing the crews. You may well imagine that, with the return of these troops, the squadron will be in part disarmed.

I do not write to Monsieur de la Touche[86]. If he and the *Ariel*[87] are still in the Delaware and you intend them for northern parts, they will need to navigate with the greatest care and come to Boston.

I am, sir, with respectful attachment etc

BARRAS[88]

PS: On arriving at Boston I shall expedite the *Concorde* for conveying the dispatches and state of Virginia to the Comte de Grasse.

---

[85] *the squadron*: the French one at Newport.

[86] The Chevalier de la Touche was captain of the frigate *l'Hermione*, on which, while at Philadelphia, he had entertained the President of Congress in early May. During the month he had been involved with the Chevalier de la Luzerne in an attempt to gain the support of the Pennsylvania authorities for rounding up French sailors to man French ships under his command. (*Pennsylvania Packet*, 8th May 1781; *Minutes of the Provincial Council of Pennsylvania...* (Philadelphia/Harrisburg, 1853), xii, 723)

[87] The *Ariel* was a French vessel loaned to John Paul Jones for the conveyance of military supplies. He had set sail with it from Lorient in December and arrived at Philadelphia on 18th February. (Boatner, *Encyclopedia*, 567)

[88] Admiral Jacques-Melchior Saint-Laurent, Comte de Barras (?-*c*. 1800) had succeeded Admiral Destouches in May as commander of the French squadron at Newport. On 10th September he would arrive in the Chesapeake to reinforce de Grasse, bringing siege artillery and provisions. After distinguishing himself in 1782 by the capture of Montserrat, he retired from active service. (Boatner, op cit, 58; *Appletons'*)

Enclosure (3)
Washington to Sullivan, 29th May 1781[89]

6(135): C

Head Quarters
New Windsor
May 29th 1781

Hon General Sullivan[90]

Dear Sir

I have been favoured with your two letters of the 2nd and 17th of May. The former reached me at Weathersfield after I had met the Count de Rochambeau at that place, from which time to the present moment my whole attention has been so occupied by a variety of concerns that I have been hitherto involuntarily prevented from doing myself the pleasure of writing to you.

No arguments were necessary to convince me of the great public utility which would result from the success of the plan you proposed laying before Congress. Had I been unapprised of the advantages which might be derived to our cause from a successful attempt or even a powerful diversion in that quarter, the reasons you have offered would have carried irrefragable demonstration with them and induced me to be of your opinion; but the perplexed, distressed and embarrassed state of our affairs on account of supplies (with which you are well acquainted), the languid efforts of the States to procure men, and the insuperable difficulties in the way of transportation would, I apprehend, have rendered the scheme (however devoutly to be wished and desired) abortive in the first instance, and I must inform you there is yet another obstacle, which makes the attempt you have suggested *absolutely impracticable* with the means you propose, but which I dare not commit to paper for fear of the same misfortune which has already happened to some of my letters.

You will have seen before the receipt of this, by my public letter to Congress of the 27th instant, the result of the deliberations of the Count de Rochambeau and myself at Weathersfield. That plan, upon the maturest consideration and after combining all the present circumstances and future prospects, appeared (though precarious) far the most eligible of any we could possibly devise while we are inferior at sea. The object was considered to be of greater magnitude and more within our reach than any other. The weakness of the garrison of New York, the centrical position for drawing together men and supplies, and the spur which an attempt against that place would give to every exertion were among the reasons

---

[89] Published in Stevens, op cit, i, 500. There are no differences.

[90] John Sullivan (1740-1795) had retired in November 1779 from being a major general in the Continental line. He was now serving as a delegate from New Hampshire to the Continental Congress, where he was involved in the reorganisation of the army and the establishment of the public finances and credit. He would resign in August. After the war he became, at one time or another, Attorney General and President (now Governor) of New Hampshire besides being chosen as Speaker in the state legislature. He is buried in the Sullivan family cemetery at Durham. (*DAB*; Boatner, *Encyclopedia*, 1070-2; *Appletons*'; Joel D Treese and Dorthy J Countryman, *Biographical Directory of the United States Congress 1774-1996* (Cq Pr, 1996))

which prompted to that undertaking and which promised the fairest prospect of success unless the enemy should recall a considerable part of their force from the southward, and even in this case the same measure which might produce disappointment in one quarter would certainly in the event afford the greatest relief in another.

While an opportunity presents itself of striking the enemy a fatal blow, I will persuade myself the concurring exertions of Congress, of the several States immediately concerned, and of every individual in them who is well affected to our cause will be united in yielding every possible aid on the occasion. At this crisis, while I rejoice at the appointment of the Minister of Finance, I have sincerely to regret that the Ministers of the other departments have not also been appointed, especially a Minister of War. At the same time I am happy to learn the mode of promotion is on the point of being finally established.

With the highest sentiments of regard and esteem I am, dear sir,
Your obedient servant

Gº WASHINGTON

Enclosure (4)
Washington to Huntington, 30th May 1781   *6(3): C*

Head Quarters
New Windsor
30th May 1781

His Excellency Sam Huntington Esq[91]

Sir

I am honored with your Excellency's favors of the 23rd and 24th. I am sorry that you took the trouble to transcribe the dispatches from General Greene, as I had received them immediately from him. It is to be regretted that so small an accident shou'd have turned the fortune of the day before Campden. The General's conduct, however, in the action and the perseverance with which he pursues his plan, notwithstanding his disaster, do him infinite honor.

There have been various reports for several days past that a further embarkation was taking place at New York and some have even gone so far as to suppose a total evacuation of the place was in contemplation. I have an account through a pretty good channel, as late as the 27th instant, in which nothing of the kind is mentioned. There had been some very

---

[91] In January 1776 the Hon Samuel Huntington (1731-1796) had taken his seat in the Continental Congress as a delegate from Connecticut, in July he had signed the Declaration of Independence, and in September 1779 he had been chosen the Congress's President, an office he would hold until July 1781, when he was compelled to resign from ill health. Among other things a lawyer and Judge of the Superior Court in Connecticut, he would be elected Governor of the state in 1786 and serve until his death. He is buried in the Old Norwichtown Cemetery, Connecticut. (Boatner, *Encyclopedia*, 535)

uncommon movements among the troops upon Long Island which may have given rise to the conjectures I have spoken of. My informant says that Pensacola is taken and that General Robertson goes to Virginia to succeed General Phillips.

G° WASHINGTON

Enclosure (5)
Washington to Lafayette, 31st May 1781[92]

6(164): C

Head Quarters
New Windsor
31st May 1781

Major General Marquis de la Fayette

My dear Marquis

I have received your favors of the 4th, 8th, 17th and 18th instant. Your conduct upon every occasion meets my approbation, but in none more than your refusal to hold a correspondence with Arnold. By an account which I have just received from New York General Robinson[93] goes to succeed General Phillips. You may have something to apprehend from his age and experience, but not much from his activity.

In a letter which I wrote to Baron Steuben on the 16th instant I desired him to inform you, as I did not know at that time where you might be, that I had good reason to believe a detachment of between 1,500 and 2,000 men had sailed from New York a few days before. I now have it confirmed and I think you may either look for them in Chesapeak or further southward.

Your determination to avoid an engagement with your present force is certainly judicious. I hope the Pensylvanians have began their march before this, but I have no information of it. General Wayne has been pressed both by Congress and the Board of War to make as much expedition as possible, and extraordinary powers are given him to enable him to procure provision.

Upon your intimation that Colonel Vose[94] wished to return to the northward I ordered

---

[92] Published in Stevens, op cit, i, 503. There are no material differences.

[93] *Robinson*: Robertson. See enclosure (4) above.

[94] The Vose brothers, Elijah (*c.* 1740-1822) and Joseph (1738-1816), were respectively Lt Colonel and Colonel of the 1st Massachusetts Continental Regiment. In February one of them – but which one is uncertain – had been assigned to the command of a light infantry battalion composed of the light companies of the 1st to 8th Regiments of the Massachusetts Continental line and had come south with it to Virginia as part of Lafayette's corps. According to Wright Jr, it was Elijah; according to Boatner (citing William Heath), it was Joseph. (Heitman, *Historical Register*, 561; Robert K Wright Jr, *The Continental Army* (Center of Military History, US Army, 1983),

Colonel Tupper[95] to relieve him, and he had set out before your letter of the 4th reached me.

I am with very sincere regard, my dear Marquis,
Your most obedient and humble servant

G⁰ WASHINGTON

Enclosure (6)
Washington to Lafayette, 31st May 1781[96]

6(5): C

Private

New Windsor
May 31st 1781

Major General the Marquis de la Fayette

My dear Marquis

I have just returned from Weathersfield, at which I expected to have met the Count de Rochambeau and Count de Barras, but the British fleet having made its appearance off Block Island, the Admiral did not think it prudent to leave Newport. Count Rochambeau was only attended by Chevalier Chattellux[97]. Generals Knox[98] and Duportail were with me.

Upon a full consideration of our affairs in every point of view, an attempt upon New York with its present garrison (which by estimation is reduced to 4,500 regular troops and about 3,000 irregulars) was deemed preferable to a southern operation as we had not the command of the water. The reasons which induced this determination were the danger to be apprehended from the approaching heats, the inevitable dissipation and loss of men by so long a march, and the difficulty of transportation, but above all it was thought that we had a

---

167; Boatner, *Encyclopedia*, 1157)

[95] Since 1st January Benjamin Tupper (1738-1792) had been serving as Colonel of the 10th Massachusetts Continental Regiment. Among other things, he had previously been involved in the siege of Boston, the Battle of Long Island, the Saratoga campaign, and the Battle of Monmouth. In 1783 he would retire from the army with the brevet rank of brigadier general. The last nine years of his life were identified with the westward movement to what soon became the Northwest Territory. (*DAB*; Boatner, *Encyclopedia*, 1129; *Appletons'*; Heitman, op cit, 551)

[96] Published in Stevens, op cit, i, 505. There are no differences.

[97] A man of many parts, François Jean de Beauvoir, Chevalier de Chastellux (1734-1788) was a French major general who had arrived with Rochambeau at Newport in July 1780. Described as the diplomat of Rochambeau's expeditionary force, he is said to have been equally at ease in staff conferences, in the drawing rooms of Boston and Philadelphia, and in roadside taverns. In his *Travels in North America in the Years 1780, 1781 and 1782* (Chapel Hill, 1963) he has left an interesting account of people, places and events of the period. (Boatner, op cit, 218-9)

[98] Born in Massachusetts to Scotch-Irish parents, Henry Knox (1750-1806) was a brigadier general in command of the Continental artillery. He was one of Washington's closest friends and advisers, a sanguine and resourceful officer who had seen much active and distinguished service. (*DAB*)

tolerable prospect of expelling the enemy or obliging them to withdraw part of their force from the southward, which last would give the most effectual relief to those States. The French troops are to march this way as soon as certain circumstances will admit, leaving about 200 men at Providence with the heavy stores and 500 militia upon Rhode Island to secure the works.

I am endeavouring to prevail upon the States to fill up their battalions for the campaign, if they cannot do it upon better terms, and to send in ample and regular supplies of provision. Thus you perceive it will be some time before our plan can be ripe for execution and that a failure on our part in men and supplies may defeat it, but I am in hopes that the States in this quarter will exert themselves to attain what has long been a favourite and is an important object to them.

We have rumours, but I cannot say they are well founded, that the enemy are about to quit New York altogether. Should they do this, we must follow them of necessity, as they can have no other view than endeavouring to seize and secure the southern States, if not to hold them finally, to make them the means of an advantageous negociation of peace.

I take it for granted that your last dispatches inform you fully of European affairs and that you can judge from them of the probability of such an event as I have mentioned taking place. As you have no cypher by which I can write to you in safety and my letters have been frequently intercepted of late, I restrain myself from mentioning many matters I wish to communicate to you.

I shall advise you every now and then of the progress of our preparations. It would be unnecessary for you to be here at present, and I am sure you would not wish to leave your charge while you are so near an enemy or untill you could deliver them up to General Greene or to another officer capable of exercising the command which you are in. You will always remember, my dear Marquis, that your return to this army depends upon your own choice, and that I am with every sentiment of esteem, regard and affection

Your most obedient servant

G° WASHINGTON

PS

My public letter contains an answer to your several favors. We have just heard from New York that General Robinson[99] is going to supply the place of Philips.

---

[99] *Robinson*: see p 132, note 93.

Clinton to Cornwallis, 19th June 1781[100]

68(24): CS

New York
19th June 1781

Lt General Earl Cornwallis

My Lord

The intercepted letters which I had the honor to transmit to your Lordship with my dispatch of the 8th instant will have informed you that the French Admiral meant to escape with his fleet to Boston from Rhode Island (from whence it is probable they sailed on the 15th instant, the wind being then fair) and that it was proposed the French army should afterwards join such troops as Mr Washington could assemble for the purpose of making an attempt on this post.

I have often given it as my opinion to your Lordship that for such an object as this they certainly could raise numbers, but I very much doubt their being able to feed them. I am, however, persuaded they will attempt the investiture of the place. I therefore heartily wish I was more in force that I might be able to take advantage of any false movement they may make in forming it.

Should your Lordship have any solid operation in the Chesapeake to propose or have approved of the one I mentioned in my former letters, I shall not, as I have already told you, press you for the corps I wished to have sent me — at least for the present, but if in the approaching inclement season your Lordship should not think it prudent to undertake operation with the troops you have (and you may easily conceive I cannot possibly spare more), I cannot but wish for their sake, if I had no other motive, that you would send me as soon as possible what you can spare from a respectable defensive. And that your Lordship may better judge what I mean by a *respectable* defensive, it is necessary to inform you that other intelligence besides Monsieur Barras' letter makes it highly probable that Monsieur le Grasse will visit this coast in the hurricane season and bring with him troops as well as ships. But when he hears that your Lordship has taken possession of York River before him, I think it most likely he will come to Rhode Island and in that case that their first efforts will be in this quarter. I am, however, under no great apprehensions, as Sir George Rodney seems to have the same suspicions of le Grasse's intention that we have and will of course follow him hither, for I think our situation cannot become very critical unless the enemy by having the command of the sound should possess themselves of Long Island, which can never be the case whilst we are superior at sea.

What I said to your Lordship in my letter of the 8th instant respecting reinforcement from England was only occasioned by a report prevailing here that you had ordered them from Charles Town to the Chesapeak, but as it is now probable there is no real foundation for the report, it is unnecessary to trouble your Lordship again on the subject, as they will of course

---

[100] Annotated: 'Received from Lt Colonel McPherson, 71st, 12th July 1781', and published with inconsequential differences in Stevens, op cit, ii, 26.

remain in South Carolina should they arrive there. In the hope that your Lordship will be able to spare me 3,000 men I have sent 2,000 ton of transports from hence, and what is wanting may be made up from those in Chesapeak. The corps I named in my letter of the 11th will, I imagine, amount to nearly that number, but should your Lordship not be able to spare the whole, it is necessary to mention that I expect the detachment of the 17th Dragoons, as they happened to be placed last in the list. I likewise request your Lordship will at the same time send me the 24 boats built by General Arnold if you should have no particular call for them, as they will be usefull here and it is probable the ten (which I understand are now building in Chesapeak) will be sufficient for your Lordship's purposes; but as your Lordship will be the best judge of this, you will send them or not as you please.

I have at last had a personal conference with the Vice Admiral, and he has agreed, if he does not intercept the French fleet, to take his station between the Nantucket Shoals and Delaware, where his fleet is to cruise for the protection of this harbour and our communication with the Chesapeak.

I have the honor to be
Your Lordship's most obedient and most humble servant

H CLINTON

Clinton to Cornwallis, 1st July 1781[101]   *68(36): LS*

New York
July 1st 1781

Lt General Earl Cornwallis etc etc etc

My Lord

For reasons which I think it unnecessary to mention to you by this opportunity I request that whatever troops etc your Lordship may have embarked for this place may sail 48 hours after the departure from the Chesapeak of the frigate which carries this letter and which has orders to return whenever your Lordship signifies to the captain of her that the troops etc are all on board and ready to proceed on the intended service.

I have the honor to be
Your Lordship's most obedient and most humble servant

H CLINTON

---

[101] Annotated: 'Received 12th July 1781 by the *Orpheus*', and published in Stevens, op cit, ii, 41. There are no differences.

Cornwallis to Clinton, 12th July 1781[102]

74(37): ADfS

Suffolk
July 12th 1781

His Excellency Sir Henry Clinton KB etc etc etc

Sir

I acknowledged in my letter of the 8th the receipt of your Excellency's dispatch of the 28th June. I have since been honoured with that of the 1st instant by the *Orpheus*, and of the duplicates of those of the 29th of May, 8th and 19th of June by the *Charon*, the originals of which have miscarried.

I have only now to inform your Excellency that every exertion shall be made to fit out the expedition in the compleatest manner without loss of time, and as by your letter to General Leslie[103] you seem to wish that he should accompany it, I have sent him directions for that purpose.

I have the honour to be with great respect
Your Excellency's most obedient and most humble servant

CORNWALLIS

Cornwallis to Clinton, 17th July 1781[104]

74(41): C

Suffolk
17th July 1781

His Excellency Sir Henry Clinton KB etc etc etc

Sir

I am glad to hear from Portsmouth that the expedition is almost ready to sail, and having given General Leslie full powers relating to the equipment of it, I hope it will be to your satisfaction. I have detained six infantry boats and four horse boats for the service here and have directed all the others to go if they can be carried. The 23rd light company has done duty for some time past with the Legion, which is not yet returned from an excursion to the upper part of the country. I have therefore in place of the 23rd sent the light company of the 80th.

---

[102] Published in Stevens, op cit, ii, 66. There are no differences.

[103] *your letter..*: that of 23rd June, 26th June or 1st July. See pp 147-8.

[104] Published in Stevens, op cit, ii, 79. There are no material differences.

The enemy's army having come so low down the country, and we having by the destruction of their craft rendered it difficult for them to pass James River below Tuckahoe, and the militia of the upper counties of this side of the river being with them, I thought it a good opportunity to endeavour to destroy the magazines between James River and the Dan that are destined for the use of their southern army. I accordingly detached Lt Colonel Tarleton with the Legion cavalry and something upwards of 100 mounted infantry on the 9th instant from Cobham with orders to call among other places at Prince Edward and Bedford Court Houses, where I was informed their principal military stores had been collected. This will be a fatiguing expedition, but I shall be able to give them rest upon their return as I see little appearance of cavalry being much wanted in this quarter for some time to come. In the mean time I shall remain at or near this place till he comes back, which I hope will be in a few days. I have detached Lt Colonel Dundas with part of the 80th to destroy the shipping and stores at South Quay, and if possible I shall send a detachment to Edenton for the same purpose before I fall back to Portsmouth.

Colonel Gould has not received my order for sending two of the late arrived regiments to New York, the express vessel with my dispatches having been taken by a rebel privateer. And as it appears by your Excellency's dispatch to me of the 19th of June that you approve of the three regiments remaining in South Carolina, I have notified this to Colonel Gould by the *Amphitrite*, which retook the express vessel and called here two days ago in her way to Charlestown.

The variety of fatiguing services for which pioneers are constantly wanted obliged me to augment the detachment with this army to a company of 50 men, and I appointed Lieutenant Brown[105] of that corps captain and Mr Jackson[106], a North Carolina refugee, lieutenant. Mr Brown is an old officer of pioneers and in his own line a man of uncommon merit.

The officers of the Guards having repeatedly represented the very superior merit of Mr Rush[107], their surgeon, and his unwearied and skilfull attention to their numerous sick and wounded, I think it right to mention him to your Excellency as a man highly worthy of a mark of favour.

---

[105] Ebenezer Brown (1736-?) was an American who had been commissioned into the Royal Guides and Pioneers when the corps was raised on the Provincial establishment in December 1776. He had recently taken part in the winter campaign. His promotion by Cornwallis to captain, effective from 26th June, would be confirmed. At the close of the war he was placed on the Provincial half-pay list. (Treasury 64/23(20), WO 65/164(38), and WO 65/165(13) (National Archives, Kew))

[106] As Cornwallis says, Basil Jackson was a North Carolinian. His commission as a lieutenant in the Royal Guides and Pioneers would not be confirmed but be downgraded to an ensigncy. He would later become a 2nd lieutenant in the corps. At the close of the war he was placed on the Provincial half-pay list. (Treasury 64/23(20), WO 65/164(38), and WO 65/165(13) (National Archives, Kew); Raymond, 'British American Corps')

[107] While remaining attached to the Guards, John Rush (?-1801) would be promoted in July 1782 to an apothecary on the staff of the General Hospital in North America, the department responsible for hospitals other than small regimental ones. From 1788 to 1798 he drew pay as a reduced officer but was then appointed Inspector of Regimental Hospitals, becoming also a member of the newly constituted Army Medical Board. (Johnston, *Commissioned Officers in the Medical Service*, 59)

I received your Excellency's letter with the inclosures relating to the transports intended to be sent home by the agent and Lt Colonel Balfour. The resolution of sending all had been adopted after I left South Carolina in consequence of the Minister's circular letter, and which if executed I should no doubt have disapproved of, being entirely of opinion with your Excellency that it is with you to decide whether serviceable transports can be spared. But I am happy to find that Lt Colonel Balfour returned to his first resolution, which I approved of, only dispatching victuallers and unserviceable transports, and which I hope before now has been explained to your Excellency's satisfaction.

It gave me great pleasure to learn from a Charlestown paper lately brought in here that General Greene had raised the siege of Ninety Six after having been repulsed in an attempt to carry it by assault, and that Lord Rawdon had arrived there on the 20th ultimo. I have likewise been informed in this country that Greene was on his march on the 24th ultimo towards Broad River.

[I have the honour to be etc

CORNWALLIS]

Clinton to Cornwallis, 11th July 1781[108]   68(50): LS

Head Quarters
New York
July 11th 1781

Earl Cornwallis

My Lord

I have received your Lordship's letter of the 30th June and the *Admiral has dispatched* a *frigate with his* and *my opinions* in *answer to it*. I cannot be more explicit by this opportunity than to desire that, *if you have not already passed the James River*, you will *continue on* the *Williamsburg Neck* until *she arrives with my dispatches by* Captain Stapleton. If you *have passed it* and find it expedient to *recover that station*, you will please to do it and *keep possession* until you hear further from me. *Whatever troops may have been embarked by you for this place* are likewise *to remain untill further orders*. And if they should have been *sailed* and within *your call, you will be pleased to stop them*. It is the *Admiral's* and *my wish at all events to hold Old Point Comfort*, which *secures Hampton Road*.

HC

[*Subscribed*:]

This cypher brought by Colonel Watson from Lord Rawdon.

---

[108] Annotated: 'Received from Brigade Major Bowes at 1 am, 20th July', and published without the subscription in Stevens, op cit, ii, 61. There are no other material differences.

Clinton to Cornwallis, 8th July 1781[109]

68(38): LS

Head Quarters
New York
July 8th 1781

Lt General Earl Cornwallis

My Lord

I am this moment honored with your Lordship's letter by Ensign Amiel of the 30th ultimo and am very happy to be informed you have had an opportunity of destroying such a quantity of arms and public stores, the loss of which must be very heavily felt by the enemy.

By your Lordship's answer to my letters of the 11th and 15th ultimo (which are the only ones you acknowledge the receipt of and in which I made a requisition for some of the corps serving in the Chesapeak *if you could spare them*) I am to understand that your Lordship does not think that with the remainder (which would have amounted to at least 4,000, supposing even that you sent me 3,000) you could maintain the posts I had proposed to be occupied at York Town etc, so necessary in every respect to cover our fleet and give us entire command over the entrance of that bay. I therefore think proper to mention to your Lordship that whatever my ideas may have been of the force sufficient to maintain that station and the corresponding one on the Gloucester side, your Lordship was left the sole judge of that sufficiency to the whole amount of the corps under your immediate orders in Virginia, nor did I mean to draw a single man from you until you had provided for a respectable defensive and retained a small corps for desultory water expeditions, for my requisition was made after the receipt of your Lordship's letter of the 26th of May, from which I apprehended that you had no immediate operation of your own to propose and did not think it expedient to adopt the one I had recommended to General Phillips. But I confess I could not conceive you would require above 4,000 in a station wherein General Arnold had represented to me (upon report of Colonel Simcoe) that 2,000 men would be amply sufficient; and being strongly impressed with the necessity of our holding a naval station for large ships as well as small, and judging that York Town was of importance for securing such a one, I cannot but be concerned that your Lordship should so suddenly lose sight of it, pass James River, and retire with your army to the sickly post of Portsmouth, where your horses will, I fear, be starved and a hundred other inconveniences will attend you – and this, my Lord, as you are pleased to say, because you were of opinion that it exceeded your power, consistent with my plans, to make safe defensive posts there and at Gloucester. My plans, my Lord, were to draw from Chesapeak, as well for the sake of their health as for a necessary defensive in this important post, such troops as your Lordship could spare from a respectable defensive of York, Gloucester or such other station as was proper to cover line of battle ships and all the other services I had recommended, but I could not possibly mean that your Lordship should for this give up the hold of a station so important for the purposes I designed, and which I think La Fayette will immediately seize and fortify the moment he hears you have repassed James River, for tho' I am to suppose the enemy will be as little able to defend it with 5,000 men

---

[109] Annotated: 'Received from Captain Stapleton 21st July 1781', and published with inconsequential differences in Stevens, op cit, ii, 49.

as your Lordship judges yourself to be, and of course may be for the same reason dispossessed, I should be sorry to begin with a siege the operations I am determined to carry on in Chesapeak whenever the season will admit of it. I will therefore consult Rear Admiral Graves on this subject and let your Lordship have our joint opinion in consequence.

With regard to Portsmouth your Lordship will have seen by my former letters and the papers in your possession that when I sent General Leslie to the Chesapeak, I only wished for a station to cover our cruizing frigates and other small ships. That general officer thought proper to make choice of Portsmouth and had, I doubt not, good reasons for so doing, but it has ever been my opinion that if a better could be found, especially for covering line of battle ships, it ought to have the preference, and I think, if Old Point Comfort will secure Hampton Road, that is the station we ought to choose, for if Elizabeth River is at all kept, a small post for about 300 men at Mill Point would in my opinion answer. But as to quitting the Chesapeak entirely, I cannot entertain a thought of such a measure but shall most probably on the contrary send there, as soon as the season returns for acting in that climate, all the troops which can possibly be spared from the different posts under my command. I therefore flatter myself that, even altho' your Lordship may have quitted York and detached troops to me, that you will have a sufficiency to reoccupy it or that you will at least hold Old Point Comfort if it is possible to do it without York.

I find by the intercepted letters you sent me that La Fayette's Continentals, when joined by Stuben and Wayne, do not altogether exceed 1,800, and that even if he could collect a numerous militia, he had but few arms to put into their hands, and those your Lordship I see has effectually destroyed. It likewise appears that altho' Green may himself come to the northward, his corps is to remain in South Carolina. I therefore suppose your Lordship has recollected this when you sent orders to Brigadier General Gould to bring the 19th and 30th Regiments to this place, especially as you tell me you still continue in the most painfull anxiety for the situation of that province.

I am sorry Lord Rawdon's health should oblige him to return to Europe. I think it is highly proper that either your Lordship, General Leslie, or General O'Hara should go to Charlestown, but I can by no means consent to your Lordship going thither, before you hear further from me, for very essential reasons, which I shall not now trouble your Lordship with.

I was very unhappy to hear of the unfortunate move of our friends and its consequences, as related by Lieutenant Haggarty. Those under the influence of Mr Alexander[110] were desired by me not to rise and they seemed contented to remain quiet until operation came to them, but as it is probable they have no arms to defend themselves, I should imagine that if a station could be found in their neighbourhood which was safe and tenable and arms could be given them, it might be the means of saving many of them. Your Lordship will, however, as being upon the spot, be the best judge how far this may be proper or practicable, for as I know nothing of the district where this is supposed to have happened, or what their numbers, I cannot say how far it may be expedient to give them assistance. Your Lordship has, I believe, many spare arms in Chesapeak and there are likewise a considerable number at Charlestown, but if any should be wanted from hence, I will spare as many as I can.

---

[110] *Mr Alexander*: see p 89, note 23.

As your Lordship must be sensible how necessary it is I should have frequent and accurate returns of the state of the troops under my command, I am persuaded you will pardon me for requesting you to order that returns are prepared, and if possible sent to me every fortnight, of the troops under your Lordship's immediate orders in the Chesapeak, and as accurate ones as can be procured of those in Carolina and the other southern posts.

By the letters brought to me from the Minister by the last packet I understand that three battalions originally destined for this army are to accompany Sir George Rodney in case le Grasse comes on this coast, from whence I am to conclude he will be certainly followed by that admiral. I am likewise told that nearly 2,200 German recruits and auxiliary troops may be hourly expected to arrive here.

I have the honor to be
Your Lordship's most obedient and most humble servant

H CLINTON

Clinton to Cornwallis, 11th July 1781[111]   *68(43): LS*

Head Quarters
New York
July 11th 1781

Lt General Earl Cornwallis

My Lord

I am just returned from having a conference with Rear Admiral Graves in consequence of your Lordship's letter of the 30th ultimo, and we are both clearly of opinion that it is absolutely necessary we should hold a station in Chesapeak for ships of the line as well as frigates. And the Admiral seems to think that should the enemy possess themselves of Old Point Comfort, Elizabeth River would no longer be of any use to us as a station for the frigates, therefore judges that Hampton Road is the fittest station for all ships, in which your Lordship will see, by the papers in your possession, I likewise agree with him. It was moreover my opinion that the possession of York Town, even tho' we did not possess Gloucester, might give security to the works we might have at Old Point Comfort, which I understand secures Hampton Road.

I had flattered myself that after giving me as nearly 3,000 men as you could spare, your Lordship might have had a sufficiency not only to maintain them but to spare for desultory expeditions, for I had no other plans in view than to draw, for the defence of this post and operation in its neighbourhood, such troops as could be spared from your army after leaving an ample defensive to such stations as your Lordship might judge proper to occupy and a

---

[111] Annotated: 'Received from Captain Stapleton 21st July 1781', and published in Stevens, op cit, ii, 62. There are no differences.

small moving corps for desultory water expeditions during the summer months, in which no other might be proper in that unhealthy climate. But as your Lordship seems to think that you can in no degree comply with my requisition for troops and at the same time establish a post capable of giving protection to ships of war and it is probable from what you write me that you may have repassed James River and retired to Portsmouth, I beg leave to request that you will without loss of time examine Old Point Comfort and fortify it, detaining such troops as you may think necessary for that purpose and garrisoning it afterwards. But if it should be your Lordship's opinion that Old Point Comfort cannot be held without having possession of York, for in this case Gloucester may perhaps be not so material, and that the whole cannot be done with less than 7,000 men, you are at full liberty to detain all the troops now in Chesapeak, which I believe amount to somewhat more than that number – which very liberal concession will, I am persuaded, convince your Lordship of the high estimation in which I hold a naval station in Chesapeak, especially when you consider that my whole force in this very extensive and important post is not quite eleven thousand effectives. And how far I may be justifiable in leaving it to so reduced a garrison time will shew.

I am as much mortified as your Lordship can possibly be at the necessity there is at present for leaving you upon the defensive in Chesapeak, and your Lordship will do me the justice to observe that I have for some months past been myself content with a starved defensive from the desire I had to give your Lordship as large an army for offensive operations as I could. Therefore, until the season for recommencing operations in the Chesapeak shall return, your Lordship or whoever remains in the command there must, I fear, be content with a strict defensive, and I must desire that you will be pleased to consider this as a positive requisition to you not to detain a greater proportion of the troops now with you than what may be absolutely necessary for defensive operations etc as before mentioned. When, therefore, your Lordship has finally determined upon the force you think sufficient for such works as you shall erect at Old Point Comfort and the number you judge requisite to cover them at York Town and for the other services of the Chesapeak during the unhealthy season, you will be pleased to send me the remainder. Your Lordship will observe by this that I do not see any great necessity for holding Portsmouth while you have Old Point Comfort, for should a station on Elizabeth River be judged necessary, I think Mill Point will answer every necessary purpose of covering frigates etc.

I have the honor to be
Your Lordship's most obedient and most humble servant

H CLINTON

§ - §

2 - From Arbuthnot or Graves to Cornwallis

Arbuthnot to Cornwallis, 2nd May 1781　　　　　　　　　　　　　　　　　　*70(10): ALS*

Royal Oak
New York
May the 2nd 1781

My dear Lord

The various reports that have been propagated by rebels and others have kept your friends in constant hot water concerning your safety, but the letter which you have so very obligingly honored me with[112] has more than paid me for all my solicitude in your behalf. It is impossible for me to give your Lordship an idea how sincerely I shall enjoy the moment in which you may reap the fruits of that magnanimity that you have lately produced for your country's good and your own honour. I hope to be among the first of your friends with my congratulations.

In the mean time my good wishes can only attend your Lordship, because I am hourly in expectation to be *relieved*, having received an answer to my request on that head.

Sir Henry Clinton will inform you that forces are embarqued and ready to proceed to the Chessapeake, but as he has very obligingly honored me with intelligence that he says may be relyed on that the whole of the French fleet were ready to put to sea from Rhode Island and would certainly sail the 29th past if possible, their force being so nearly proportioned, I shall certainly postpone taking charge of these transports untill this business is decided by blocking them up if they get into the Chessapeak before me or otherwise, unless his Excellency will be pleased to inform me the instantly conducting the troops to their destination is of more consequence to the general cause than any other consideration, in which case I will protect them with my whole force, less not being sufficient to secure their safety. I did not think to take up so much of your Lordship's time, but if you come to the Chessapeake in the *Richmond*, I shall have the heartfelt pleasure to say in person how sincerely I am

Your Lordship's most faithfull, most obedient and most humble servant

M[T] ARBUTHNOT

---

[112] *the letter..*: no extant copy.

Arbuthnot to Cornwallis, 20th June 1781

6(245): ALS

Bedford
New York
June the 20th 1781

My dear Lord

I sailed on the last day of May from this place towards Boston Bay in quest of a French convoy destined for Boston, but was disapointed by incessant fags[113] and easterly winds, which obliged me to return to this place, where I arrived on the 13th instant.

I have it not in my power to describe the pleasure I felt when it was anounc'd that your Lordship was arrived in perfect health after all your fatigue at Petersburgh, where I presume any further exertions will cease untill a more favorable season. In the mean time I sincerely lament that I shall not have it in my power to embrace your Lordship before I leave this country, because I expect every moment to be relieved, which I am waiting for with much impatience, and therefore I fear that I must postpone the aforesaid pleasure till we meet in England, which honor I will pursue with much solicitude. We have no news that can be depended on. A report is propagated that our fleet have had an engagement with the Spaniards and come off victorious and thereby relieved Gibraltar. I hope it is true. Another report prevails that things are hastening to a general peace by the mediation of the Courts of Viena and Petersburgh. This is the whole of the rumours, which you will credit or not, but I earnestly entreat that you will believe that

I am very faithfully, my Lord,
Your most obliged, most obedient and most humble servant

M^T ARBUTHNOT

Graves to Cornwallis, 12th July 1781[114]

88(51): ALS

London off Sandy Hook
12th July 1781

Rt Hon Lt General Earl Cornwallis

My Lord

I have the honor to acquaint your Lordship that the *Solebay*, Captain Everett, carries Captain Stapleton charged with his Excellency Sir Henry Clinton's dispatches to your

---

[113] *fags*: slang for 'fatigues'.

[114] Annotated: 'Received from Captain Stapleton 21st July 1781', and published with inconsequential differences in Stevens, op cit, ii, 67.

Lordship and with my orders to the captain of the King's ships to return with the troops under his convoy to the Cheasapeak and, if not sailed, for them to remain and to conform to your Lordship's requisition in the disposal of them.

I need only say to your Lordship that there is no place for the great ships during the freezing months on this side the Cheasapeak where the great ships will be in security and at the same time capable of acting, and in my opinion they had better go to the West Indies than be laid up in Hallifax during the winter. If the squadron is necessary to the operations of the army, Hampton Road appears to be the place where they can be anchored with the greatest security and at the same time be capable of acting with the most effect against any attempt of the enemy. To this end Old Point Comfort seems necessary to be occupied by us as comanding the entrance to the road, and if York can be secured, it will give the command of the lower or Elizabeth county and deprive the rebels of the use of the two best settled rivers of the Cheasapeak and deter an enemy from entering the Cheasapeak whilst we command the access to it, for we shou'd have all his convoys and detachments exposed to our attempts.

I have the honor to be
Your Lordship's most obedient and most humble servant

THO^S GRAVES[115]

§ - §

---

[115] After some forty years' service in the Royal Navy, Thomas Graves (1725-1802) was promoted to rear admiral of the blue on 19th March 1779. One year later he was ordered to prepare a squadron for reinforcing the North American station and arrived at New York to join Arbuthnot on 13th July 1780. Having taken part with Arbuthnot in the action off the Capes of Virginia on 16th March 1781, he succeeded him as naval Commander-in-Chief at the beginning of July. Outnumbered by the French fleet in the Chesapeake, he would fail to defeat it in September and, accompanied by Clinton and 7,000 troops, would arrive too late in October to relieve Cornwallis. His role in these events has proved controversial, with much of the criticism perhaps misplaced. After the war he continued in active service and was created an Irish peer. He died an admiral of the white at his family seat in Thankes, Cornwall, where he was buried. (*ODNB*; Syrett and DiNardo eds, *The Commissioned Sea Officers*, 185)

3 - From Clinton or Graves to Leslie

Clinton to Leslie, 23rd June 1781[116] *97(2): LS*

New York
23rd June 1781

Hon Major General Leslie

Sir

I am honored with your letter[117].

As I think it probable that the season may have put an end to all operation in Chesapeak except by water and that Lord Cornwallis will have embarked a considerable part of his army to join me, I have desired that you may come here with such troops as his Lordship shall send if he has not already named you for the command at Charles Town and he can spare you. You will of course bring *Mr Alexander*[118] with you.

I have the honor to be, sir,
Your most obedient and most humble servant

H CLINTON

Clinton to Leslie, 26th June 1781 *97(4): LS*

New York
26th June 1781

Hon Major General Leslie

Sir

It is now three weeks since I wrote to Lord Cornwallis to request that if his Lordship had not determined upon sending you to command in South Carolina, you might be sent hither with the troops I had called for to reinforce this post, but not having since heard from his

---

[116] This and the following three letters were conveyed by the *Orpheus* and received by Leslie on 8th July under cover of one of the 7th from Hudson (p 214). Leslie wrote to Cornwallis on the 8th (p 179), apparently forwarding all five, though he mentions only two.

[117] *your letter*: no copy.

[118] *Mr Alexander*: annotated in Leslie's hand, 'I don't know who his Excellency means.' See p 89, note 23.

Lordship or indeed from Chesapeak, I am ignorant of the numbers he proposes to send me or who is to command them. Therefore, having since my last letter to his Lordship determined upon an expedition against Philadelphia to endeavour to seize the public stores etc collected there if it can be done without destroying the town, I have appointed Lt General Robertson for that service, which I most probably should not have thought necessary could I have been certain of your being embarked with the troops or remaining in Virginia, but as I was totally ignorant how that was, I judged it right to name General Robertson for the command and I have in consequence settled the plan of the expedition with him. Should you, however, have been destined to join this part of the army, it will make no alteration, as I shall be glad to have the assistance of your services not only on this but such other operations as may be undertaken to the northward in the progress of the campaign.

I have the honor to be, sir,
Your most obedient and most humble servant

H CLINTON

Clinton to Leslie etc, 1st July 1781

97(6): LS

New York
July 1st 1781

Hon Major General Leslie or officer commanding
the troops embarked in the Chesapeak for New York

Sir

Whenever the troops which Lord Cornwallis shall have embarked under your orders are ready to sail, it is the Admiral's and my wishes that the frigate which carries this should return to us and that forty eight hours after she leaves the Chesapeak you will if possible put to sea and proceed to the River Delaware, off which you will hover out of sight until joined by the Admiral, when you will receive further orders.

I have the honor to be, sir,
Your most obedient and most humble servant

H CLINTON

PS

If this meets you at sea, you will of course proceed as above mentioned off Delaware, waiting for the Admiral.

Graves to Leslie, 2nd July 1781   97(8): ALS

London off Sandy Hook
July 2nd 1781

Hon Major General Leslie

Sir

I have the honor to acquaint you that the *Orpheus*, Captain Colpoys[119], has my orders to carry his Excellency General Clinton's dispatches for Lord Cornwallis and yourself and is to return here the moment you can form a judgement upon what day the detachment will be ready to sail, which I understand is not intended to move forward for eight and forty hours afterward, the better to enable us to join you as nearly in point of time as possible off the Delaware. You will have the *Richmond, Charon, Loyalist* and *Bonetta* sloop to accompany you, and Captain Hudson, who alone knows the place you are to stop at, will consult and act in concert with you in case of any unforeseen intelligence. The captain of the *Orpheus* knows no more than is necessary for finding you out and returning with your dispatches in the line proper for either of us to take in case of a moval before the concerted time.

I have the honor to be, sir,
Your most obedient humble servant

THO[S] GRAVES

Clinton to the officer commanding the embarked troops, 11th July 1781[120]   97(12): LS

Head Quarters
New York
July 11th 1781

To the officer commanding the troops
    embarked from the Chesapeak etc etc

Sir

You will be pleased, wherever this letter may meet you, to return to the Chesapeak with the troops under your command and wait there for further orders from Earl Cornwallis, which will be given you in consequence of instructions I have sent to his Lordship by Captain

---

[119] Commissioned a lieutenant in the Royal Navy in 1762, John Colpoys (1742-1821) was promoted to commander in 1770 and to post-captain three years later. He was now commanding the *Orpheus*, a new 32-gun frigate launched at Deptford in 1780. As a vice admiral of the blue he would hoist his flag aboard the 98-gun man of war *London* and command a squadron blockading Brest in late 1796. He went on to become a Lord Commissioner of the Admiralty and Governor of Greenwich Hospital. Knighted in 1798 and awarded a GCB in 1815, he died an admiral of the red. (Syrett and DiNardo, *The Commissioned Sea Officers*, 93; Michael Phillips, 'Ships of the Old Navy' (Internet, 25th September 2006))

[120] Probably received by Cornwallis from Leslie on 20th July.

Stapleton.

I have the honor to be, sir,
Your most obedient and most humble servant

H CLINTON

§ - §

4 - From Germain to Cornwallis

Germain to Cornwallis, 7th March 1781[121]   65(19): LS

(N° 2)   Whitehall
7th March 1781

Earl Cornwallis

My Lord

I have had the honor to receive and lay before the King your Lordship's dispatch of the 18th of December from Weymesborough[122] transmitting copies of your own and Lord Rawdon's letters to Sir Henry Clinton and Brigadier General Leslie, and His Majesty observed with particular satisfaction that you were in perfect health when the former were written, and I beg leave to add my own congratulations upon your Lordship's recovery.

The reasons which you assign for calling General Leslie from Virginia are founded in wisdom and could not fail being approved by the King, and as I have had the pleasure to learn from Colonel Balfour that General Leslie had joined you and you were in motion on the 11th of January, I make no doubt but your Lordship will by this time have had the honor to recover the province of North Carolina to His Majesty, and I am even sanguine enough to hope from your Lordship's distinguished abilities and zeal for the King's Service that the recovery of a part of Virginia will crown your successes before the season becomes too intemperate for land operations, as Sir Henry Clinton has informed me that he has sent a force under Brigadier General Arnold to replace General Leslie's at Portsmouth and cooperate with your Lordship.

I am, my Lord,
Your Lordship's most obedient humble servant

GEO GERMAIN

---

[121] This and the following dispatch arrived at Portmouth, Virginia, on 7th July. See Hudson to Leslie of that date, p 214, and Leslie to Cornwallis of 8th July, p 179. Only the first is published in Stevens. Others written on the same dates from Germain to Clinton were received by Clinton on or by 27th June. (Stevens, op cit, i, 334, 337 and 379)

[122] *your Lordship's dispatch..*: see vol III, p 43.

Germain to Cornwallis, 4th April 1781   65(23): LS

(N° 3)

Whitehall
4th April 1781

Earl Cornwallis

My Lord

I had the honor to receive and lay before the King on the 31st of last month your Lordship's dispatch of the 18th January[123] inclosing copy of your letter of the same date to Sir Henry Clinton containing an account of the severe check Colonel Tarleton had received near Broad River, but it was a great satisfaction to His Majesty to find by Colonel Balfour's letters, which were received at the same time but dated so late as the 25th of February, that your Lordship had by your own able conduct and rapid movements soon deprived the enemy of all cause of triumph by defeating them at the passage of the Cataba River and in another place on the 1st of February, and that in the last action Colonel Tarleton's corps had an opportunity of again distinguishing itself, and that meritorious officer of renewing the dread his former intrepidity and success had impressed upon the rebels.

The great advances your Lordship had made towards James River when the packet sailed, the success of Major Craig's detachment, and the happy effects of General Arnold's exertions, supported, as I understand he will be, by a considerable body of troops which Sir Henry Clinton was preparing to send into the Chesapeak when the last accounts came away from New York, confirm me in the hopes I expressed in my last letter to your Lordship that you would have the honor to recover to His Majesty great part of Virginia and all the country south of it before the season became too intemperate for active service.

The long continuance of contrary winds has delayed the three regiments and the recruits intended for Charles Town beyond all expectation, but I have reason to believe they sailed from Corke the 26th of last month.

I am, my Lord,
Your Lordship's most obedient humble servant

GEO GERMAIN

§ - §

---

[123] *your Lordship's dispatch..*: see vol III, p 47.

5 - From Robertson to Cornwallis

***Robertson to Cornwallis, 4th March 1781*[124]**   *69(5): LS*

New York
4th March 1781

Earl Cornwallis

My Lord

When the Spanish war broke out, it occurred to me that if some enterprises from North America were made against wealthy and weak parts of the islands belonging to Spain and the undertakers returned with money, many of the rebel army tired of a fruitless rebellion might be encouraged to engage in adventures that promised wealth, especially as they might save the point of honor and avoid engaging against their countrymen and fellow soldiers. Unluckily, the attempt we have made is far from giving us a prospect of raising such a wish among the rebels.

Officers have arrived here from Governor Dalling to raise men for the service at Jamaica. The bait was thrown out to the rebels, but as no money appeared nor even a prospect of success, none of them bitt. As the rebels overbalanced us in the number of prisoners, General Dalling's officers could not be permitted to enlist rebel soldiers who were prisoners, as for every such man we should have continued a British soldier in captivity.

The navy prison ships, from whence we could get no men to be trusted in this country, seemed a scanty but the only resource open for the South Sea service. A Major Odell has been very active and persevering and has got about three hundred men who are sailed for Jamaica.

I have letters from the Secretary of State signifying the King's wish that I would encourage rebel prisoners to enlist for the southern service. As Washington has declined exchanging any prisoners till his demands for his Convention bill are satisfyed, it is probable that no more exchanges will take place. In that case our poor soldiers will lose nothing by the rebel prisoners being enlisted. We have no prisoners here, and therefore these gentlemen who General Dalling has employed in this service go to solicit your Lordship's permission to engage rebels whether they be prisoners or such men as you may not judge worthy of being trusted with arms in any of the corps under your command.

Captain Amherst, one of these, is General Dalling's aid de camp and is vastly zealous to accomplish his general's views. I have a good opinion of him and a great desire to serve him.

---

[124] This letter formed part of the bundle to which p 71, note 1 refers.

I wish this may be sufficient to justify the liberty I presume to take of recommending him to your favorable notice and protection.

I have the honor to be, my Lord,
Your Lordship's most obedient and obliged servant

JAMES ROBERTSON

§ - §

CHAPTER 52

Letters to or from Portsmouth

1 - From von Fuchs or Rochfort to Cornwallis

von Fuchs to Cornwallis, 23rd May 1781   *6(102): LS*

Portsmouth
23rd May 1781

Lt General Rt Hon Earl Cornwallis

My Lord

As the late Major General Philips has appointed me Commandant of this garrison, I thought it my duty to inform your Excellency of the state of it at present.

The works are in general but slender, and the soil being sandy, they want daily repair, especially the redoubts.

The late and continued desertions are, I think, owing to the severity of the duty in this garrison, which requires above four hundred men daily including the fatigue parties. In the inclosed report[1] your Excellency will see the total number fit for duty exclusive of the Royal Artillery. I beg your Excellency will be pleased if possible to let me have a reinforcement for this post. The late Major General Philips has been pleased to order an embargo on all vessels here. Would wish to know whether your Excellency will continue it in force or permit those for New York to proceed.

---

[1] *the inclosed report*: not extant.

I, as a German, and not being sufficiently master of the English language to explain myself upon the many subjects, perticularly those alluding to the laws of the British Constitution, humbly request that your Excellency will be pleased if possible to releave me with the Regiment Prince Hereditary of my present command in order to join the army that I may have the satisfaction to partake of the honors the troops are reaping under your Excellency's command.

With the utmost respect I have the honor to be, my Lord,
Your Lordship's most obedient and most humble servant

DE FUCHS[2]
Lt Collonel

Rochfort to Cornwallis, 24th May 1781

6(113): ALS

Portsmouth
24th May 1781

Earl Cornwallis

My Lord

I think it my duty to transmit your Lordship a return of the ordnance and stores, together with a state of the detachment of Royal Artillery[3], in the garrison of Portsmouth.

I hope to receive your Lordship's pardon for making it a request that should the artillery serving with the army now at Petersbourg be augmented by any draught from this post, your Lordship will be pleased to allow me to join with it and have the honor to serve immediately under your own orders, a wish that I have much at heart and have more than once been disappointed in.

I have the honor to be
Your Lordship's most faithful and humble servant

G ROCHFORT

---

[2] On 19th September 1779 Matthias von Fuchs had been appointed Lt Colonel of the Hessian Erb Prinz Regiment, commonly called the Regiment du Prince Héréditaire. (Ewald, *Diary*, 296; WO 65/164(19) (National Archives, Kew))

[3] *a state..*: not extant.

Enclosure
Return of ordnance etc at Portsmouth, 24th May 1781   103(32): DS

> RETURN of Ordnance, Ammunition and Stores in His Majesty's Garrison at Portsmouth in Virginia and its Dependencies, 24th May 1781

Ordnance:

    Iron, heavy:

	24 pounders		1
	18		4
	12		18
	6		5
	4		4

    Brass:

	Medium:	12 pounders	4
	Light:	6	4
	Howitzers:	8 inch	3
		5½	4
	Mortars:	5½	8
		42/5	10

Aprons of lead, of sorts	65
Burning stores: Fire rings	30
Faggots	24
Curtains	7
Carcasses, oblong for 42/5 mortars	84

Cartridges:
- Fill'd:
  - Musquet — 200,000
  - Carbine — 26,000
- Flannel:
  - Fill'd:
    - 24 pounder — 400
    - 12 — 1,000
    - 6 — Nil
    - 3 — 80
    - 8 inch howitzer — 244
    - 5½ ditto — 646
  - Empty:
    - 24 pounder — 100
    - 12 — 750
    - 6 — 200
    - 8 inch howitzer — 300
    - 5½ — 250
- Paper:
  - Empty:
    - 24 pounder — 245
    - 18 — 800
    - 12 — 3,250
    - 9 — 350
    - 4 — Nil
    - ½ — 2,000
  - Fill'd:
    - 18 pounder — 170

	4			200
Chests laboratory with proportions compleat for howitzers and mortars				10
Flints:				
Musquet				22,820
Carbine				5,700
Match, slow, cwt				30
Musquets, short land				600
Portfires, dozens				56
		Cannon cartridge		1
		Musquet ditto		20
Rockets, signal, 1 lb				15
Shot:				
Fix'd to powder:		(Round		30
	6 pounder	(		
		(Case		206
	4 pounder	Case		38
To wood bottoms:		(Round		304
		(		
	24	(Case		206
		(		
		(Grape		102
	18	Case		111
		(Round		732
	12	(		
		(Case		610
		(Round		290
	6	(		
		(Case		188
		(Round		115
	3	(		
		(Case		64

Round loose:	24 pounder		198
	18		680
	12		3,180
	9		160
	6		200
	4		300
	½		2,000
Shells:			
Fix'd:	8 inch		102
	5½		300
	Handgrenadoes		202
Empty:	8 inch		300
	5½		1,600
	4 2/5		2,000
Waggons, pole:			
Light			4
Heavy			1
Harness, sets:			
	(Thill		30
Horse:	(Trace		159
	(Pole waggon		28
Men's:			60

159

Powder:		
Corn'd:	Whole barrels	247
	Half ditto	24
Glazed:	Ditto ditto	5
Thread, lbs		20

G ROCHFORT
Captain, Royal Artillery

2 - Between Cornwallis and Leslie

Cornwallis to Leslie, 24th May 1781　　　　　　　86(47): C

Byrd's Plantation
24th May 1781, 11 pm

Major General Leslie

Dear Sir

After considering the many extraordinary events of this war and the clouds of militia which sometimes pour down upon us, I am much inclined to retain the 43rd Regiment. I must therefore beg that you will proceed with the other troops to Portsmouth and order the 43rd, with some armed vessels to cover the transports, to come to this place with all possible expedition.

The empty transports which brought the reinforcement will proceed immediately to New York according to the desire of the Commander in Chief. I shall be much obliged to you if you will send the new constructed boats as soon as possible. Our passage here will be very troublesome.

Etc etc

[CORNWALLIS]

Leslie to Cornwallis, 25th May 1781 — 6(112): ALS

Favorite transport
25th May 1781
9 o'clock

Earl Cornwallis

My Lord

At six this morning I had the honor of yours. Sorry it was not a recall for the whole.

It blew too hard for any thing to come up last night. Two ships in sight. The ship the recovered men are in is not arrived. I shall forward them in a horse sloop.

I've landed the horses of the 43rd and sent them round with an escort of 40 men.

If your Lordship means the transports of the 43rd to go to New York, please order them doun imediately. You said nothing of an ordnance vessell. I have ordered the agent to take her up to the army. The boats shall be forwarded as soon as possible from Portsmouth.

I expect to get under sail by 10 o'clock. The horse sloops being below with the 17th, who are aground, has pusled me[4] about our horses. I can't inform you if the ships are off or not.

Very sincerely yours

A LESLIE

Leslie to Cornwallis, 27th May 1781 — 6(121): ALS

Portsmouth
Sunday morning
11 o'clock

My Lord

I am just arrived with most of the transports. The whole will be here in a few hours.

There's nothing new here, nor no arrivals.

I have ordered the 76th to New Town, the 80th to Camp's[5] Landing, 1st Anspack to Norfolk, the 2nd Anspacks and 17th infantry quartered in town.

---

[4] *pusled me*: an archaic form of 'puzzled', with the now obsolete meaning of 'made me at a loss what to do'.

[5] *Camp's*: Kemp's.

Red hot bar between the navy and army. If it will amuse your Lordship, you shall have the particulars when I am more master of the subject.

A legion of staff officers here. I had never such a suite before.

Captain Ewald[6] of the Yagers will deliver your Lordship this scrawl. He wishes much to have those at Wilmington sent for and to be under his orders. Without orders to the contrary, I shall send off all the horse vessells to New York.

I have the honor to be, my Lord,
Your most faithfull servant

A LESLIE

[*Subscribed*:]

Excuse my hurry.

Leslie to Cornwallis, 30th May 1781

6(137): ALS

Portsmouth
30th May 1781

Earl Cornwallis

My Lord

I had the honor of yours, an old date, of the 26th[7]. A victualler in consequence is now sent. The duplicates for Charles Town and Cape Fear[8] also go off today. The boats are not yet finished. As soon as four are fit for the water they shall be sent. I fear they are too long and will soon get out of repair from the extreme lenth.

---

[6] A captain in the Hessian Jäger Corps, Johann Ewald (1744-1813) was commanding a detachment of jägers with whom he had arrived in Virginia at the beginning of the year. Born in Cassel, he entered military service at the age of sixteen and took part in the last campaigns of the Seven Years' War. After losing an eye in a duel in 1770, he studied military engineering at the Collegium Carolinium in Cassel. In 1774 he published a treatise on military tactics and was promoted to captain in the Leibjäger Corps. In October 1776 he arrived at New York in command of a company of jägers and was from then onwards heavily involved in military operations. The élite of the Hessian troops, the jägers were employed to great advantage in leading the van of an army, covering a withdrawal, reconnoitring, and partisan warfare, particularly ambuscades. Courageous, humane, and possessing a rare combination of daring, self-reliance and outstanding military abilities, Ewald was commended for his services by Howe, Clinton, Cornwallis and Knyphausen. After the war he published further treatises on military tactics, entered the Danish service, and became a lt general. In 1979 Yale University Press published his *Diary of the American War*, translated and edited by Joseph P Tustin. A fascinating account of his exploits and opinions, it is especially notable for its relation of his experiences of 1781 in Virginia.

[7] *yours..*: no extant copy.

[8] *The duplicates..*: see pp 274, 286 and 300.

I've sent Colonel Johnson[9] with 300 men to Halls Mills on the Suffolk Road, an old post of mine. Before he went, I am informed a few rascally militia insulted our pickets near town.

General Arnold goes off tomorrow. He tells me you bid him take his own Legion and Robinson's corps to New York. They are gone. The plague of the officers was more than the use of the few men they had.

Johnson wishes much for his people from South Carolina. Suppose you was to send Hamilton's light company and bring Cubbidge[10]. Their numbers are near the same.

I long to hear from your Lordship. All we know is you marched from Bird's Sunday afternoon.

I am with the utmost respect, my Lord,
Your most obedient humble servant

A LESLIE

Leslie to Cornwallis, 3rd June 1781　　　　　　　　　　6(172): ALS

Portsmouth
3rd June 1781

Earl Cornwallis

My Lord

Comodore Hudson very cheerfully went into sending an armed schooner to Cape Fear and Charles Town. She also took, besides your Lordship's duplicates, Bryand and all those miserable people and Negroes to the amount of 21 persons. I hope we shan't quarrel so much as other people have done. Fortunately for the public, I have no tobacco.

Nothing from sea. I fancy the fleet for New York is gone this morning, for it's a fine wind to get an offing. General Arnold was very ill. Had the gout in both feet and hands. He wished much to take a new horse and other boat to show at Head Quarters and assured

---

[9] Henry Johnson (1748-1835) had spent most of his military service in the 28th Regiment, entering it as an ensign on 19th February 1761 and rising to be major by 1773, the year in which he accompanied the regiment to North America. On 8th October 1778 he was promoted to the lt colonelcy of the 17th Foot but nine months later, while commanding at Stony Point on the Hudson, he had the misfortune to be taken prisoner with the regiment when the fort was carried by Anthony Wayne in a *coup de main*. Exchanged, he and the bulk of the 17th were now serving in Virginia as part of the garrison at Portsmouth, while a detachment was under Rawdon's command in South Carolina. In October, for his part in the defence of Yorktown, Johnson would be mentioned by Cornwallis in dispatches. In later life he would see distinguished service during the Irish rebellion, become a full general, and be made a baronet. (*DNB*; *Army Lists*; *The Cornwallis Papers*)

[10] George Cuppiage had been serving as a captain lieutenant in the 17th Foot since 16th July 1779. He presumably commanded the detachment in South Carolina. (WO 65/164(7) (National Archives, Kew))

me he had your Lordship's permission for it, which I beg to know. At all events it was overruled and not gone. They shall be sent as soon as possible. 54 prisoners come down without any account what they are or for what. I have found a number here, mostly sea men, and sent all that chose to go on board ship as sea men. I see, by the return sent[11], McAlister is Comissary for Prisoners. If he can't be spared, I shall be under the necessity of appointing one, for the business can't be done by an ignorent sergeant provost martiall.

I have got £15,000 by the *Richmond*. The foreigners as usual made a demand for their June pay.

The regiments lately arrived have the York compliment of waggons and keep them still. I beg to know if your Lordship would wish them get your orders in regard to bat horses etc.

I fancy the public expences have been great here, the new boats the dearest I fancy ever England paid for, and all departments full and have contrived to get wonderfully snug and comfortable from what I can learn. Trafick was not unfationable here, and the fleet gone this morning will show it. Public and private ships have all been plundering up the bay and on the eastern shore. Some stop must be put to it, for our friends there complain bitterly of it. If your Lordship would write Hudson to forbid all those rascally privateers from going up the river or up the bay, for there are no prizes now on the water and they of course should not go on shore. Now that the works are almost finished, I shall diminish the black regiment. There are near 500 of them. Frazer seems to be a clever young man and has them in good order.

I have the honor to be, my Lord,
Your most faithfull humble servant

A LESLIE

[*Subscribed*:]

Next opportunity a secrecy[12] of the harbour and works of this place will reach your Lordship.

Leslie to Cornwallis, 10th June 1781   6(220): ALS

Portsmouth
10th June 1781

My Lord

I have not heard of your Lordship since you left Mrs Bird's. We have various reports of you but no certainty.

---

[11] *the return..*: no extant copy.

[12] *a secrecy*: used in the now archaic sense of 'a secret state'.

Lord Chewton is here. He could not get to the army from Westover, so returned back for a few days.

Six of the new boats are sent up the river. I hope they may answer. I doubt it much myself. If ever they ground, they must get out of order. The expence of building them is very great.

General Robertson sailed in the *Amphitrite* the 28th ultimo from New York. It was not told where he was gone to. Nothing come in here since I came doun, only a privateer from York — left it the 30th.

I have the honor to be, my Lord,
Your most obedient humble servant

A LESLIE

Cornwallis to Leslie, 19th June 1781   *87(9): ADfS*

Richmond
June 19th 1781

Hon Major General Leslie etc etc etc

Dear Sir

Having in vain endeavoured to bring the Marquiss to action and having destroyed all the stores within my reach, *I shall now proceed to Williamsburgh* and set seriously to work on the very important business of *establishing a proper place of arms and withdrawing our post from Portsmouth*. *I mean at the same time to send an expedition to Fredericksburgh and, as I shall weaken my corps by it*, must desire that you *will send immediately to Williamsburgh* the Regiment de *Prince Hereditaire* and the remainder of the 80th and 76th and convalescents belonging to the army and take every measure *for the speedy evacuation of Portsmouth* consistent with the strictest secresy. You may depend on my losing no time in delivering you from your present very disagreeable situation.

Please to send some warrants for holding courts martial.

I would not have my intention *of attacking Fredericksburgh* communicated to any body, but as *the boats* must have some distant *protection from the navy*, I should wish that Captain Hudson would be kind enough to keep a frigate or two near the mouth of James River, *without explaining to him the reason of my request*. The Quarter Master General's *armed vessels will be the proper convoy to attend the boats up the Patowmac*. If an opportunity should offer of writing to the Commander in Chief, you will please to communicate to him my present situation and designs. I propose moving from hence on the 21st.

I am, my dear General, with great regard
Most sincerely yours

CORNWALLIS

[*Subscribed:*]

I would not have the horse sloops sent away yet nor the company of Negroes diminished, as the latter will be very usefull in carrying on our works.

I have heard of the arrival of the reinforcement, which does not alter my plan. If the gentlemen of the navy approve, I would have the transports move up and anchor *opposite to Williamsburgh*. You will be pleased to detain Lieutenant Sutherland of the Engineers untill you hear further from me.

Leslie to Cornwallis, 20th June 1781   6(247): ALS

Portsmouth
20th June 1781

Earl Cornwallis

My Lord

The bearer, Lieutenant Amiel of the 9th Regiment[13], is just arrived from New York with dispatches from Sir Henry[14] to your Lordship. I sent him off without loss of time.

No accounts of Lieutenant Nairn of the 71st[15], sent from New York some days before Mr Amiel sailed.

Nothing new here.

I have the honor to be, my Lord,
Your very faithfull humble servant

A LESLIE

---

[13] In fact Amiel was either Otho Amiel, an ensign commissioned into the 17th Foot on 12th November 1778, or Henry Amiel, an ensign commissioned into the army on 1st January 1781. (*Army Lists*; WO 65/164(7) (National Archives, Kew))

[14] *dispatches..*: of 11th and 15th June. See pp 95 to 103.

[15] Nairne was charged with the original of Clinton's dispatch of 8th June, p 123. It miscarried.

Leslie to Cornwallis, 24th June 1781   6(261): LS

Portsmouth
24th June 1781

My Lord

I have the honour of your Lordship's in cypher the 19th from Richmond. I received it yesterday and complied with your Lordship's orders.

Instead of the 76th I send an equal number of the Guards. I hope you got a letter from Sir Henry[16]. *I understand he requires some troops from you. One of his letters*[17] *was taken at sea. The French from Rhode Island have joined Washington. They are also superior to us in the West Indies. There is a report that six ships of the line with troops have left the West Indies for this coast*.

I am, my Lord,
Your most faithfull humble servant

A LESLIE

Leslie to Cornwallis, 24th June 1781   6(263): ALS

Portsmouth
24th June 1781

My Lord

I refer your Lordship to mine in cypher as an answer to yours of the 19th.

I don't send Sutherland to you, as he had a letter from Haldane himself and not ordered. I can spare him with his suite and 150 Negroes at any time.

I have wrote the Comodore what you desired.

As I expect the express vessell doun the river that came from York[18], I shall send nothing there.

The fleet sailed only 3 days ago for New York.

---

[16] *a letter..*: of either 30th April or 11th June. See pp 92 and 95.

[17] *One of his letters*: of 13th April, 29th May, or 8th or 19th June. See ch 51.

[18] *the express vessell..*: the one from New York conveying Ensign Amiel with Clinton's dispatches.

I hope you will let me keep the 76th, as I am weak of British troops, to keep the country open.

I hope Lord Chewton is with your Lordship.

I have the honor to be, my Lord,
Your most faithfull humble servant

A LESLIE

Cornwallis to Leslie, 27th June 1781[19]

87(13): C

Williamsburgh
June 27th 1781

Hon Major General Leslie

Dear Leslie

My orders from New York make it necessary for me to give up all thoughts of a post on this side of James River. I mean therefore to pass it as soon as possible, I believe at James Town or Hog Island. If this letter reaches you in time, you will stop all the detachment that I ordered up except the part of the 80th under Major Maxwell[20]. You will send up all the boats that you think can be usefull. I have written to Captain Hudson[21] to desire a reinforcement of seamen to man them on this occasion, with a good officer.

I shall probably have occasion to send letters to Charlestown in a day or two. You will be kind enough to order the vessel which arrived from thence to be ready to return thither at the shortest notice. I hope to be with you soon. In the mean time try to conceal our real design and give out that we are going on a secret expedition.

Yours sincerely

[CORNWALLIS]

---

[19] A brief extract is published in Ross ed, *Cornwallis Correspondence*, i, 101.

[20] Commissioned an ensign in the 20th Regiment on 27th September 1762, William Maxwell was promoted there to lieutenant on 26th December 1770 and to captain on 2nd August 1775. He transferred to the 80th Regiment (Royal Edinburgh Volunteers) on 23rd May 1778 as the second of two majors. He had now been serving in Virginia since the beginning of 1781, having accompanied his regiment as part of Arnold's expedition. (*Army Lists*)

[21] *I have written..*: on 27th June, p 211.

Leslie to Cornwallis, 27th June 1781
6(276): ALS

Portsmouth
27th June 1781

My Lord

I do myself the honor of writing these few lines by the Hessian Regiment Prince Hereditaire. The Guards and 80th detachments will follow very soon. The reason of their not going now is owing to their having been in the country to surprise a rebell post, which they have carryed. The particulars have not yet reached me. Their loss I hear is triffling.

I should be glad to know if the hospital should be moved up the river – this place begins to get sickly – and if I should begin to send on board any of the heavy ordnance.

I am in haste, my Lord,
Your most obedient humble servant

ALEX^R LESLIE

[*Subscribed*:]

Please order the seamen and boats back if not wanted. The seamen belong to the [few?] transports here.

Cornwallis to Leslie, 28th June 1781[22]
87(27): C

Williamsburgh
28th June 1781

Hon Major General Leslie

Dear Leslie

I am very unwilling to give up the idea of fixing the place of arms at York if it is possible to effect it consistent with the arrangement of the force in this country. I shall therefore go tomorrow to York to examine that place before I take my final resolution. As the war in Virginia is to be only defensive, except some desultory expeditions, all idea of diversion in favour of the Carolinas must cease, and consequently the war in South Carolina will be kept up by the enemy as long as we attempt to hold any part of the province. In that case I think that either you or I should go thither. Perhaps you may go for a time and I may relieve you. I don't think at this season the voyage would be hurtful to your health and I believe the climate of Charlestown is full as good as the lower part of Virginia. If Lord Rawdon goes home, every thing must fall into the greatest confusion, nor can Balfour, however able, do any

---

[22] The bulk of this letter is published in Ross ed, op cit, i, 101-2.

good without support. I mention this to prepare you for going if it should be necessary. When we meet we will talk it over. You will please to send off the letters to Charlestown[23] with the utmost dispatch.

I am with great regard etc

CORNWALLIS

Leslie to Cornwallis, 28th June 1781

6(259): ALS

Portsmouth
28th June 1781

Earl Cornwallis

My Lord

The Hessian regiment is returned and brings me your Lordship's of yesterday.

I have sent three of the large boats to Captain Hudson to be filled with seamen, and Captain Vallancy informs me this will complete your number to 15.

As the 80th detachment are still at Camp's[24] Landing, I shall not send them untill I hear from your Lordship. Their baggage, as also that of the Guards, Queen's Rangers and 43rd Regiment, is all on board but shall be detained here untill further orders.

Nobody shall know your Lordship's intentions.

There are two very fine armed boats almost fit for sea, the one at Smithfield, the other within 2 miles of McKay's house. I intended landing the 80th to have brought them off or destroyed them. McKay[25] is here, and a friend. His house ought to be protected.

---

[23] *the letters..*: Cornwallis's to Barkley and Gould, 28th June, pp 213 and 298.

[24] *Camp's*: Kemp's.

[25] Andrew and Richard Mackie were brothers, the former living in Isle of Wight County and the latter in Nansemond. The one to whom Leslie is referring has not been ascertained. Whereas Andrew may have been a closet loyalist, surviving the war seemingly without injury or loss, Richard openly supported the Crown. A seafarer, he had conveyed over one hundred Scottish merchants to New York when they were banished from Virginia in 1776, an act which led to his being fined on his return and to his ship being impounded. In 1779 he was imprisoned on suspicion of providing intelligence to the British, but escaping, he joined Mathew and Collier at Portsmouth and returned with them to New York. He was subsequently employed by the Corps of Engineers during the Charlestown campaign before accompanying either Arnold or Phillips to Virginia and acting as a pilot as far as Westover. Soon, in mid to late August, he would take passage in the *Richmond* for New York, where he remained until late September 1783. Then 'he returned to Virginia in hope of trading but was seized by a mob, beaten, and threatened with tarring and feathering before being given twelve hours' notice to leave or be hanged from the nearest tree'. His ill luck continued. Making his way to Nova Scotia, he was one year later aboard a trading vessel at anchor below Shelburne when it was boarded at night by pirates, who beat him, left him for dead, and carried

If your Lordship thinks it worth your notice, Simcoe and Dundas knows both places.

A vessell is ordered to be ready for Charles Town.

Comissary Butler goes in a day or two for York in a fast sailing schooner. No opportunity of writing there since the fleet sailed.

Major Maxwell lossed no men on his scout. If the refugees had not fired, General Gregory would have been taken. Maxwell showed great judgment in this expedition.

I am with great truth
Your Lordship's most faithfull humble servant

A LESLIE

[*Subscribed*:]

2 more boats on second thoughts are ordered, in all 17.

Cornwallis to Leslie, 29th June 1781   87(35): C

Williamsburgh
29th June 1781

Hon Major General Leslie etc etc etc

Dear Leslie

You will be kind enough to order the transports now at Portsmouth to be prepared to receive troops immediately and let me know by the first opportunity what number they can contain.

Yours most sincerely

CORNWALLIS

---

off his papers, including his deeds to property in Virginia. By 1787 he had repaired to England, where he pursued a claim to the royal commission in respect of his extensive property confiscated by the revolutionaries. (Coldham, *Loyalist Claims*, 22, 318-9)

Cornwallis to Leslie, 29th June 1781   *87(33): C*

Head Quarters
Williamsburgh
29th June 1781

Hon Major General Leslie

Dear Leslie

It is just possible that we may be able to strike a blow before we pass James River, in which you may have an important share. Be so good therefore as to draw in your posts. Keep the Hessian regiment and all the British fit for marching ready to embark at the shortest notice, leaving de Voit[26] with the command at Portsmouth.

Yours most sincerely

CORNWALLIS

Cornwallis to Leslie, 30th June 1781   *87(37): ADf*

[30th] June 1781

Dear Leslie

As I think it just possible that I may do something, I wish you to bring up in the boats which I send from 800 to 1,000 men beginning with Guards and Hessian regiment and then as many of the British as you think proper to make up nearly that number. You will bring them to James Town unless you see our vessels still at Burrell's Landing.

Yours very sincerely

[CORNWALLIS]

[*Subscribed*:]

Bring very little baggage and four days' provisions with you and as many boats besides those that I send as you think will be usefull.

---

[26] On 28th January 1777 Freiherr August von Voit von Salzburg had been appointed Colonel of the 1st Battalion, Ansbach-Bayreuth Regiment. (WO 65/164(28) (National Archives, Kew))

Leslie to Cornwallis, 30th June 1781   6(266): ALS

Portsmouth
30th June 1781
11 morning

Earl Cornwallis

My Lord

I am honored by both your Lordship's letters[27] this morning. I sent off the dispatches for Charles Town instantly.

As to myself, I am always at your Lordship's disposal and ready to go to sea on the shortest notice.

Three of the transports returned fit for sea have still the stores and baggage of the Hessians, Guards, Rangers, and 80th Regiment and 43rd on board. When you have fixed your plan, please inform me that I may unload those ships, for every thing they have is on board in consequence of your letter in cypher[28].

I have above 150 prisoners here, many of them taken on the water, and many sent doun from your army without any crime. Otherwise, I should have paroled the most innocent, but only those of this neighbourhood are known to the people here. A partie of refugees have killed a great rascal of this country who commanded a banditti, named Knot[29]. Another partie were very usefull to Major Maxwell in his excurtion. The 80th are still here and ready to go on the shortest notice.

I have the honor to be, my Lord,
Your very faithfull humble servant

A LESLIE

[*Subscribed:*]

Inclos'd is the return of transports etc.

---

[27] *both your Lordship's letters*: that of the 28th and the first of the 29th.

[28] *your letter..*: of 19th June, p 165.

[29] Perhaps Elvinton Knott, who had begun to serve as an officer in the Nansemond County revolutionary militia by March 1776. (*Va Military Records*, 482-3, 609; Gwathmey, *Historical Register*, 451)

Enclosure
State of transports in Virginia, 30th June 1781

6(269): DS

A State of the Transports in His Majesty's Service under the direction of Lieutenant G Robertson on the Virginia station					
Ships' names	Tonage	Masters' names	N° of Men	Guns	State and condition
Houston	258	Robt McLish	16	6	Loaded with the bagage of the Guards and 80th Regiment
Harpinton	235	Chris^t Johnston	16	6	Ditto with the Hesian bagage
Racehorse	231	Chris^t Cheesman	14	6	Ditto with the 43rd Regiment and Queen's Rangers' bagage
Ship Wright	301	Thos Kay	20	6	Fitt for service
Andrew	259	Franc^s Todrige	17	6	Ditto
Present Succession	286⅔	Willm Chapman	17	6	Ditto
Selina	221	John Croskill	14	6	Ditto
Robert	235	Jon^n Moore	14	6	In James River with provisions for the army commanded by Earl Cornwallis
Army victualers: *Diana* *Ocean* *Providence Increase* *Mercury*	2,026⅔	— in coasting service will cary 1,351 men				

Portsmouth in Virginia
30th June 1781

G ROBERTSON[30]
Agent

---

[30] Commissioned a lieutenant in the Royal Navy on 5th March 1762, George Robertson (?-1799) was serving as the agent for transports in Virginia. He would not rise higher in the service. According to Leslie, he was 'a good man, but slow and stupid and not fit for much exertion'. (Syrett and DiNardo eds, *The Commissioned Sea Officers*, 381; *The Cornwallis Papers*)

Leslie to Cornwallis, 30th June 1781　　　　　　　　　6(278): ALS

Portsmouth
Saturday, 4 afternoon

Earl Cornwallis

My Lord

About an hour ago your Lordship's[31] reached me. The British troops from Kemp's and the 17th Regiment I expect will be here by tomorrow morning by 6 o'clock.

The Anspac corps are at Great Bridge. I am loath to call them in, having a work and two 12 pounders and two sixes, without a certainty of moving, as it will open the country to the insolence of the enemy.

I am, my Lord,
Your most faithfull humble servant

A LESLIE

Cornwallis to Leslie, 2nd July 1781　　　　　　　　　88(1): C

Williamsburgh
2nd July 1781

Hon Major General Leslie

Dear Leslie

I shall begin passing the river as soon as the boats arrive, and as I find there are transports at Portsmouth sufficient to carry the light infantry to New York, I should be obliged if you would order them to be prepared for the voyage immediately and direct that the baggage of the other corps should be taken out of them. You will likewise acquaint Captain Hudson that as Sir Henry seems very desirous to get the light infantry to New York as soon as possible, I must beg his assistance for a convoy as soon as the seamen can be spared from the boats if no ships of war arrive in the mean time from New York. I should apprehend that two frigates would be sufficient convoy. La Fayette certainly marched back with the Continentals yesterday morning. The militia still keep in our neighbourhood.

I am, dear sir,
Your most obedient and faithfull servant

[CORNWALLIS]

---

[31] *your Lordship's*: the second letter of the 29th.

[*Subscribed*:]

Mr Amiel will return immediately in the dispatch vessell to New York with my letter to Sir Henry[32].

Leslie to Cornwallis, 2nd July 1781   6(158): ALS

Hampton Road
Monday morning
8 o'clock

My Lord

I had the honor of yours[33] yesterday at 3 o'clock, and at 8 I had 1,000 men on board and would have been with your Lordship in a few hours. I am sorry La Fayette is gone. I should have liked to have had a stump[34] with him.

As you don't order me to forward you any troops, I carry them all back, their baggage being all left.

I wrote you of several boats and craft building at and near Smithfield. I once thought of landing now some troops there, but it will retard the boats, and I fancy it will fall into the range of the troops when they cross the river.

There are five sloops or schooners lately arrived from the West Indies at South Key full of goods. If I knew the troops that are to remain here, I would make a push there.

Your Lordship must recollect from a former letter and the return sent you from the agent that three of the transports are full of baggage. I should like to know if I am to land it. I hope also to know a few hours before your Lordship arrives at Portsmouth that I may have a house prepared for you and one for your family.

I have the honor to be, my Lord,
Your most obedient humble servant

A LESLIE

---

[32] *my letter..*: of 30th June, p 104.

[33] *yours*: of 30th June. Cornwallis later countermanded his orders either orally or in a letter no longer extant.

[34] *stump*: 'dance', used figuratively to mean 'engagement'.

[*Subscribed:*]

Comodore Hudson wants the *Bonetta* back in order to send her to the eastern shore[35], where the enemy are troublesome. A couple of the gun boats will also be wanted for that service.

Leslie to Cornwallis, 4th July 1781　　　　　　　　　　　　　　　　6(290): ALS

Portsmouth
4th July 1781

My Lord

Ensign Amiel delivered me your Lordship's letter yesterday. The transports will be victualled and empty'd fit to take in the light infantry in a few houres.

I have informed the Comodore with your request and make no doubt of his doing his utmost, but he has not two frigates fit for sea besides his own ship.

Something must be done on the eastern shore. The rebel armed craft are distressing the people there wonderfully. They have carryed off Parson Lyon[36] lately and some others called violent Torys.

I should not have been so idle here, but your Lordship had most of the boats and all those with guns.

Something must be sent to Albemarle Sound. They have five galleys there, and a smart trade carryed on.

Excuse my hurry.

I am, my Lord,
Your most faithfull humble servant

A LESLIE

---

[35] The eastern shore lies across the Chesapeake from mainland Virginia and is a narrow peninsular running southward from the Maryland boundary to Cape Charles. It comprises Accomack and Northampton Counties.

[36] The Reverend John Lyon was a Rhode Island man who had been Rector of St George's Parish, Accomack County, since 1774. Of the loyalist persuasion, he had now been arrested by the revolutionary authorities and charged with trading with the enemy, giving them aid and comfort, and dissuading the militia from serving the revolutionary State. Influential as he was in his community (many of whom were loyalists) and connected by marriage to a prominent Accomack family, few would give evidence against him and the court would recommend to higher authority that he be treated leniently. By the time of his transportation to the mainland at the end of September, he would have recanted his loyalism and expressed the desire 'to spend the remains of his life with people of known attachment to the independency of America'. Accompanying him was a petition in his favour by the leading citizens of his county. (Bishop Meade, *Old Churches, Ministers and Families of Virginia* (Philadelphia, 1857), i, 266; Barton Haxall Wise, *Memoir of General John Cropper of Accomack County, Virginia* (Eastern Press Printers, Onanock VA, 1974))

Leslie to Cornwallis, 6th July 1781

6(288): ALS

Portsmouth
6th July 1781
½ after 6 afternoon

The Earl Cornwallis etc etc etc

My Lord

The inclosed[37] is this instant arrived from New York in a whale boat sent off very sudenly after the arrival of two packets from Falmouth. They came in together, the one 6 and the other 9 weeks from England. He does not bring any news, not a Rivington, nor did he know where he was going untill he left the wharf at New York.

The French army and fleet still at Rhode Island.

Nothing new here.

I have the honor to be, my Lord,
Your most faithfull humble servant

A LESLIE

[*Subscribed*:]

Transports ready for embarkation, but I shall detain any troops that may arrive to embark untill I hear from you in consequence of this from New York.

Cornwallis to Leslie, 8th July 1781[38]

88(5): ADf

Cobham
July 8th 1781

Dear Leslie

I inclose a copy of the General's dispatch, which was written in cypher[39]. You will please to make the necessary arrangements for the embarkation of the stores and artillery etc and prepare as many horse vessels as possible, observing the strictest secrecy as to the object of the expedition.

---

[37] *The inclosed*: Clinton to Cornwallis, 28th June, p 114.

[38] An extract is published in Ross ed, op cit, i, 105. It contains no differences.

[39] *the General's dispatch..*: see p 116, note 65.

I shall march tomorrow for Suffolk, where I shall arrive in four or five days, and from thence send the troops destined for embarkation to Portsmouth.

The Marquis intended to attack our rear guard and luckily stumbled on our army. It was near dark, but the 76th and 80th gave the Pensylvania line a trimming and took two six pounders, all they had with them. One of them is marked *taken at Bennington*. A little more daylight would have given us the whole corps. All the vessels, craft and boats are ordered down except four boats which are going with Dundas to destroy shipping in Lyons Creek etc and will then meet us to facilitate the passage of the Nansemund. You will please to send off my dispatch[40] immediately to Sir Henry in the properest vessel, taking care to see it loaded and sending a trusty person to sink it in case of danger of being taken, as I had not time to put it into cypher.

[CORNWALLIS]

Leslie to Cornwallis, 8th July 1781

6(286): ALS

Portsmouth
8th July 1781

Earl Cornwallis

My Lord

The *Orpheus* frigate is just arrived in six days from New York with dispatches from England and the Commander in Chief for your Lordship[41].

I inclose your Lordship two letters I have from his Excellency[42]. I see he intended me for the northward if you had not disposed of me otherwise.

I am willing to go any where your Lordship thinks I may be usefull.

I understand there's the *Charon* with a fleet of small craft sailed for this 13 days ago. Inclosed is Comodore Hudson's letter to me[43]. He and the *Bonetta* are ordered from here.

A cartel just arrived in 11 days from Charles Town with 150 prisoners, and one other ship sailed at the same time with 200 on board — not yet arrived. And 4 more were to sail imediately, the whole above 1,000 men, and are to proceed to James Town. No letters from

---

[40] *my dispatch*: of 8th July, p 116.

[41] *dispatches..*: Germain's of 7th March and 4th April, pp 150-1, and Clinton's of 1st July, p 136.

[42] *two letters I have from his Excellency*: Leslie apparently enclosed three (pp 147-8).

[43] *Hudson's letter to me..*: see p 214. Leslie also forwarded one to him from Graves (p 149).

Carolina. Augusta is taken and the master of the vessell tells me the prisoners are exchanged. A packet from England in 7 weeks. He met her passing the bar as he sailed from Charles Town. He also met a ship 13 days from Antigua but had not time to ask for news.

Skelley[44] will deliver you this. Colonel Grandfield[45] wished to join his corps and attends him.

The advice boat still here that arrived two days ago.

The transports all ready for sea.

I have the honor to be, my Lord,
Your most faithfull humble servant

A LESLIE

[*Subscribed*:]

Excuse my scraul.

I send the cartels, as they arrive, to James Town.

Leslie to Cornwallis, 12th July 1781

6(284): ALS

Portsmouth
12th July 1781

My Lord

The *Charon*[46] and her convoy all arrived. Only a horse vessel that has the baggage of the Regiment de Bose on board and 100 sadles for the Legion. Colonel McPherson will explain to your Lordship all particulars.

Arrived 8 transports equall to 1,500 men, 4 horse vessells equal to 150 horses.

---

[44] Having entered the 25th Regiment as an ensign on 16th September 1767, Francis Skelly saw service with it at Minorca, being promoted to lieutenant on 26th December 1770. On 28th October 1775 he transferred to the 71st (Highland) Regiment as a captain in the 1st Battalion. He was now acting as an aide-de-camp to Leslie, a post he would occupy for the rest of the war. (*Army Lists*; WO 65/164(1) (National Archives, Kew))

[45] Grandfield has not been identified. No officer with his name appears in the *Army Lists* or in Raymond's 'British American Corps'.

[46] *The Charon*: conveying MacPherson with duplicates of Clinton's dispatches of 29th May, 8th and 19th June, pp 118-136. The originals miscarried.

The row boat is still here, sent with a single letter from Sir Henry for you[47]. She wishes much to get back but will be detained untill I know your Lordship's directions.

I hope Albemarle Sound will be attended to, as also the eastern shore. Petitions come from thence dayly for protection.

I have the honor to be, my Lord,
Your most obedient humble servant

A LESLIE

Cornwallis to Leslie, 12th July 1781   88(10): ADfS

Suffolk
July 12th 1781

Hon Major General Leslie etc etc etc

Dear Leslie

I was much surprized to find by your letter of this day's date that you had not received mine of the 8th inclosing one to Sir Henry Clinton. I must beg that you will forward it as soon as it arrives, as well as the inclosed[48].

As it appears by the General's letter to you[49] that he wishes you to go on this expedition, and as I have offered to go myself to Charlestown, I must desire that you will take the command of the detachment and forward every thing without loss of time. Please to order forage etc to be prepared and put on board. Leave me five of the new infantry boats and three of the new horse boats and take all the rest with you if you can. All the troops from hence destined for the embarkation will be at Portsmouth on the 15th.

As the success of this armament depends much on the expedition with which it is sent out, I am sure I need say nothing to quicken your zeal and exertions.

I am, dear Leslie,
Most sincerely yours

CORNWALLIS

---

[47] *A row boat..*: see Leslie's letter of 6th July, p 178.

[48] *the inclosed*: Cornwallis to Clinton, 12th July, p 137.

[49] *the General's letter..*: of 23rd or 26th June, pp 147-8.

Leslie to Cornwallis, 13th July 1781
6(280): ALS

Portsmouth
13th July 1781

My Lord

Skelly arrived at 5 this morning. Sorry I did not explain myself more fully to your Lordship. I received yours of the 8th instant and a single letter for Sir Henry Clinton, which I sent off without delay in the *Maria* sloop that belonged to New York, for I did not think the row boat a safe conveience. This had led you to think I had not got it. If you wish me to send the duplicate in the row boat, please inform me.

Every thing is in forwardness in regard to the embarkation. There are horse vessels in all fit to take in 300 horses including a schooner belonging to the artillery. And transports equal to 2,800 men.

The comissary is anxious to land all his provisions, as they complain of the expence of keeping the transports in port. A good deall is already on shore but I prevent'd any more or[50] I heared from you.

The *Tempest*, the ship your Lordship mentioned to be bought on Government's service, was sold the day before I got your letter[51] and will, I am informed, take above 14 days to be put in trim for sailing. Her bottom is very open. She was sold for under £300 and, from the hands she is got into, might be still bought for the public. It's a Mr Hoksley[52] of the northern army who returned from Alexandria in the flag with the things sent for that army. A person named Geddes[53] was left by General Hamilton to receive the money. There's a Colonel Conelly come from York, intends waiting on your Lordship. I fancy his corps is somewhat like Governor Martin's[54].

Your Lordship's things on board the navey victuallers I sent for yesterday. Those belonging to Major Ross shall be attended to.

I beg your Lordship to inform me if the guns and mortars lately taken are to be put on board or to remain here, for the artillery are anxious to know for arrangements.

---

[50] *or*: obsolete for 'until'.

[51] *your letter*: no extant copy.

[52] Hoksley is probably a misspelling of Hawksley. He has not been otherwise identified.

[53] Alexander Giddes was an ensign in the 31st Regiment, which was part of the Convention army that capitulated at Saratoga. (*Army Lists*)

[54] John Connolly (see p 200, note 74) was Lt Colonel of the Loyal Forresters, a corps which, like Martin's North Carolina Highland Regiment, had yet to be embodied.

Captain Hudson very anxious to get his and the *Bonetta*'s men from the boats. I suppose he meanse those up Nansemond.

Sutlers are ordered round. If I knew where you fix the Regiment de Bose I would send O'Reilly[55] and 90 men, for I am push'd quartering so many stragling officers.

Lieutenant Alston[56] of the 80th dyed on his way here.

Above 700 Negroes are come doun the river in the small pox. It will ruin our market, which was bad enough before.

I shall distribute them about the rebell plantations.

I have the honor to be, my Lord,
Your very faithfull humble servant

A LESLIE

[*Subscribed:*]

All the cartel ships gone up to James Town. No letters for your Lordship. Lord Rawdon remained at 96. He did not follow Green far.

It is reported that one 50 gun ship, three frigates, seventeen transports had arrived at Boston some time ago, and of the *Warwick* having taken a twenty gun ship (a rebell) going to New York, and the *Assurance* had taken a 50 gun ship, her lower deck guns out, bound to Boston with naval stores. The morning packet.

Leslie to Cornwallis, 13th July 1781   6(305): ALS

Portsmouth
13th July 1781

My Lord

I had the honor to write you this morning by two dragoons. Since then all the boats but two are arrived.

---

[55] O'Reilly had been appointed a major in the Regiment von Bose with effect from 3rd November 1780. (WO 65/164(23) (National Archives, Kew))

[56] Commissioned a lieutenant in the newly forming 80th Regiment (Royal Edinburgh Volunteers) on 24th January 1778, Andrew Alston had been severely wounded on 6th July while commanding the picket-guard of Dundas's brigade at Green Spring. (*Army Lists*; Colonel James John Graham ed, *Memoir of General Graham...* (Edinburgh, 1862), 53)

The morning news I sent in the cover of your letter[57] I can't confirm, for I don't know how it came.

Major O'Reilly now here at dinner. Wishes to join his corps. Allow me to recommend Colonel de Fucx of the Prince Hereditaire to your Lordship. You will find him a good, discreet, zealous officer, and may be trusted with any post and is not at all interested.

The master of the row boat is anxious to go off. He is not in the public service, only taken occasionally.

I am, my Lord,
Your most faithfull humble servant

A LESLIE

[*Subscribed*:]

Several people are here for some days from the eastern shore and anxious to know if they are to be protected.

Cornwallis to Leslie, 14th July 1781   88(12): C

Suffolk
14th July 1781

Hon Major General Leslie

Dear Leslie

I received your letter of yesterday afternoon. You will have ample information from Damer, England etc. I wish you would assure the people of the eastern shore of every protection which may be in my power to give them, and take any steps you think proper at present. I would not, however, encourage them to make any open declaration.

Indian corn is what we most want from that quarter. I shall be obliged to you if you will direct the commissary to agree with them for a very considerable quantity. You know the Legion have good stomachs.

Yours very sincerely

CORNWALLIS

---

[57] *The morning news..*: see preceding subscription.

Leslie to Cornwallis, 14th July 1781

6(303): ALS

Portsmouth
14th July 1781

My Lord

Major Damer and Simcoe are arrived. I find by a letter from England to Captain Vallancy that your Lordship intends to return all the Quarter Master General's horses of the New York department.

The Regiments of Anspac brought artillery and waggon horses to the amount of:	64
The 43rd also brought waggon horses:	14
Simcoe returns:	180
Suppose the light infantry troop, including the 76th:	50
	308

I had the honor to write your Lordship of horse vessels being equal to 300, including an artillery sloop. From the above your Lordship will see there is not room for the half of the horses that are intended to be sent. Fortunately the Anspac officers have not many, but there's the officers' horses of the light infantry, Anspac, 43rd and 76th, besides the staff, unprovid'd for, as also those of the Quarter Master General's, I fancy near 40.

I imagine your Lordship's intentions are first to attend to the artillery and cavalry, taking care there's no abuse. In that event most of the officers' and all the Quarter Master General's horses must be sent by some other opportunity.

The row boat is going off, as Major Damer will inform you. The Regiment Prince Hereditaire marches tomorrow morning, as also the Guards from Kemp's. Only the baggage goes by water for want of seamen.

I beg your Lordship's answer about the horses.

I am, my Lord,
Your very faithfull humble servant

A LESLIE

Cornwallis to Leslie, 14th July 1781   88(14): C

Suffolk
14th July 1781

Hon Major General Leslie

Dear Leslie

The cavalry, mounted light infantry and artillery are to be first embarked, but you must even with them take care that only officers' horses and troop horses are to go, for there can be no reason for indulging an officer of cavalry with more baggage horses than an officer of infantry. The general officers will be taken care of, then the horses for the 12 waggons required by the General in his letter[58], and the field officers and staff of the infantry, allowing two to the former if possible. None besides can be allowed on any account, and if any officer should have bought a horse who is not permitted to carry him away, he shall be allowed the money that he paid. If the horse vessels should be insufficient for what I have mentioned, you will please to strike off from the part which you think can be diminished with the least hurt to the service. If there should be more vessels than are required for this plan, I beg they may be left at Portsmouth as I shall have great occasion for them.

I understand that my orders were disobeyed by the regiments that marched from hence, who were directed positively to take only the officers' riding horses and to put their baggage into the Quarter Master General's waggons. I beg that you will please to make enquiry into this business and, if the fact is true, that you will report it to me and send back the horses. You will please to observe that the 76th were directed to leave the horses and appointments of their mounted men. I shall be happy to hear that you are on board.

Yours very sincerely

CORNWALLIS

Leslie to Cornwallis, 15th July 1781   6(299): ALS

Portsmouth
15th July 1781

Earl Cornwallis

My Lord

I am this morning honored with yours of yesterday. There is no intercourse at all with the eastern shore. The rebell armed boats have put an entire stop to it, and nothing but armed vessels and some troops will open that county.

---

[58] *his letter..*: of 28th June, pp 114-5, which enclosed a list requiring the waggons.

The baggage of de Bose's Regiment and the sadles of the Legion are fortunately arrived.

Should I take a victualler with me? I wrote your Lordship I had detained two victuallers of the last fleet equall to provisions for 8,000 men for two months, and there was here for three months for that number.

I shall get the Anspacs and infantry of Simcoe on board some time this day.

I expect to get all on board and under sail sometime the day after tomorrow, and the *Orpheus* may proceed tomorrow.

I am, my Lord,
Your most obedient humble servant

A LESLIE

[*Subscribed*:]

Hessians marched this morning and will be at Couper's Mills tomorrow night.

Leslie to Cornwallis, 15th July 1781   6(301): ALS

Portsmouth
15th July 1781

My Lord

After getting in the embarkation returns we find, allowing only 1¼ ton per man, we fall short of room for above 300 men. There's an armed ship here called the *Cockrane*, the *Argo* (another empty ship belonging to some merchants), and an empty ordnance ship called the *Tartar*. These three are equall to take the above men if your Lordship thinks proper to have them chartered for 3 months.

Or if you chuse to have the 43rd Regiment, their number being nearest to the defitiency of tonnage. I shall wait your Lordship's directions in regard to them.

I am, my Lord,
Your very faithfull humble servant

A LESLIE

[*Subscribed*:]

Only two of the 3 to be chartered.

Cornwallis to Leslie, 15th July 1781   88(18): Df

Suffolk
15th July 1781

Dear Leslie

I am just favoured with both your letters of this date. Being very desirous to send off the expedition to the extent of the General's wishes, I shall approve of your engaging any vessels willing to be chartered that are necessary to carry the number of troops required, but if the whole cannot be embarked, the remainder may be of the corps that you think can be best spared from the service on which you are going. I am happy to hear that you are in so great forwardness, but, before dispatching the *Orpheus*, I think it will be right that you should be perfectly ready, even in Hampton Road, for fear of unforeseen accidental delays. And be so kind as let me know before she sails in case I should have occasion to write to the Commander in Chief. Tho' I have not mentioned artilery men in former letters, not knowing the number at Portsmouth, you will of course take a full proportion for manning the guns going on the expedition.

I am etc

[CORNWALLIS]

[*Subscribed*:]

Upon further reflexion I wish you to leave me six infantry boats and four horse boats.

Cornwallis to Leslie, 16th July 1781   88(24): Df

Suffolk
16th July 1781

Hon Major General Leslie

Dear Leslie

Inclosed are my letters to South Carolina[59], which you will be so kind as request the captain of the *Carysfort* to take charge of.

Two or three of our flats having been carelessly left in the river, it is just possible that the rebels may be inclined to make use of them in passing small parties to teize us, and which at present I wish to prevent. If the *Defiance* belonging to the Quarter Master General's Department is in proper order, be pleased to direct her to go up immediately as far as James City Island and to cruize six days about six or eight miles above and below it to deter the

---

[59] *my letters..*: see pp 284 and 299.

rebels from venturing in boats upon the river, after which she may return to Portsmouth. But if she is not fit for that service, be kind enough to request that the *Guadaloupe* or *Fowey* may undertake it.

I ever am with great regard, dear Leslie,
Your very faithfull servant

[CORNWALLIS]

Leslie to Cornwallis, 17th July 1781　　　　　　　　　　　　　　　　　*6(309): ALS*

Portsmouth
17th July 1781

My Lord

If your Lordship intends to write by the *Orpheus*, you have not much time to spare. Major Damer intends going doun this afternoon and I think they will certainly get away tomorrow. The transports begin to fall doun this tide, and by tomorrow at noon every thing must be doun. The only delay at present is the victuallers for the 43rd getting them wattered etc, but our agent is a good man, but slow and stupide and not fit for much exertion.

I send you a Lieutenant Mckensie[60], 71st, that went to York Town with the prisoners.

The Comodore yesterday informed me he learnt from the lieutenant of the *Carysford* that a French fleet had sailed from Europe for this bay or Charles Town and that Admiral Digby[61] was following them. As to troops being on board he could not say, but that he expected Captain Peacock on board of the *Richmond* when he returned, and promised to send me up a boat if he knew any thing of moment. No boat arrived. Your letters went doun last night.

The Comodore thinks if we meet with bad weather the boats will be lossed. Kind providence I hope will take care of them. Sorry to hear your Lordship had not been well.

---

[60] Perhaps Roderick MacKenzie.

[61] After serving as a post-captain during the Seven Years' War, Robert Digby (1732-1814) returned to active service in 1778 and was promoted to rear admiral of the blue in March 1779. He had since been second in command of the Channel fleet and second in command of the fleets which had twice relieved Gibraltar. Now a rear admiral of the red, he would be sent out in August 1781 as naval Commander-in-Chief on the North American station. He arrived at New York just as his predecessor, Thomas Graves, was preparing to set sail with Clinton in a vain attempt to relieve Cornwallis. Courteously refusing to take on himself the command at this critical juncture, he did not accompany the fleet. Afterwards, when he had assumed the command, he allowed several of his ships to accompany Sir Samuel Hood to the West Indies. With the tide of war rolling away from North America, his period in command was uneventful. Returning home at the peace, he was never again on active service. He died an admiral of the red. (*ODNB*; Syrett and DiNardo eds, *The Commissioned Sea Officers*, 124)

I regret I had not the honor of seeing you for several reasons, but I am constantly teised here by some one or other. I shall put a few remarks on paper and put 'secret' over the seal.

The only vessell armed of ours here is under repair except those going to sea. This I explained to Mr Hudson, who will send either the *Guardaloupe* or *Fowey* up James River as directed.

I have the honor to be, my Lord,
Your most faithfull humble servant

A LESLIE

Cornwallis to Leslie, 17th July 1781   88(30): Df

Suffolk
17th July 1781

Hon Major General Leslie

Dear Leslie

I have received your letter of this date and am exceedingly glad to hear that your embarkation is in so great forwardness.

Inclosed is my letter to the Commander in Chief[62], so that the *Orpheus* need not be detained on my account; and I likewise trouble you with a letter to Captain Peacock inclosing one to Major Craig[63], which you will be so kind as forward to the *Carysfort* if she is not sailed.

As we have no person here proper for a provost, Needham[64] must spare us his man for a little while, and we shall send him after the regiment by the first good opportunity. As the Portsmouth garrison is rather slight, be so good as tell Colonel Johnson that in a day or two I will send him a reinforcement of a hundred men.

---

[62] *my letter..*: of 17th July, p 137.

[63] *a letter..*: see pp 217 and 301.

[64] The younger of two surviving sons of Viscount Kilmorey, the Hon Francis Needham (1748-1832) had served as a captain in the 17th Light Dragoons at Bunker Hill and during the New York, Philadelphia and Charlestown campaigns. On 10th August 1780 he became the second of two majors in the 76th (Highland) Regiment and accompanied it to Virginia as part of Arnold's expedition. Recently, on 6th July, he had led the regiment as part of Dundas's brigade in the action at Green Spring. Soon he would be among the troops who capitulated at Yorktown. However, he is remembered not so much for his service during the revolutionary war as for his part in commanding a brigade at the decisive victory of Arklow during the 1798 Irish rebellion. A general officer, he succeeded to the viscountcy in 1818 on the death of his childless elder brother Robert and in 1822 was created the Earl of Kilmorey. His country seat was at Mourne Park, County Down. (John Phillipart, *Royal Military Calendar 1820...* (Savannah Publications reprint, 1985); Colonel James John Graham ed, *Memoir of General Graham...* (Edinburgh, 1862), 33, 54; *Army Lists*)

It would have given me very particular pleasure to have seen you, but I am afraid, circumstanced as we both are, it will not be possible. You will oblige me by giving me as much information about the place, persons etc etc as you can. And I dare say you have no doubt of my invariable good wishes for your health and happiness, being with the greatest esteem and regard, dear Leslie,

Etc

[CORNWALLIS]

Cornwallis to Leslie, 18th July 1781　　　　　　　　　　　　　　88(36): C

Suffolk
July 18th 1781

Hon Major General Leslie

Dear Leslie

I am very glad to find you received my letter by Captain Aplin, as things will be in the greater forwardness.

The guns and mortars will go if they occasion no delay or inconvenience to the expedition, otherwise you will please to land them.

I should not wish to have any more provisions landed untill I come to Portsmouth.

I refer you to Major Damer about my dispatches and the whale boat.

Provisions are ordered up. The commissary has received the order for the quantity. You will please to send them by water and all the men fit for duty in the Brigade of Guards. If you can, man the boats without the assistance of the ships ordered to sea, otherwise they must come by land. The Regiment of Prince Hereditaire will send fifty or sixty, as you think proper, of its worst marchers to the Great Bridge, and Lt Colonel Fucks will with the regiment exclusive of that detachment join the army by land as soon as possible. Maxwell with the detachment of the 80th will take post at Kemp's Landing, and the 17th Regiment with O'Reilly and the 90 men of the Regiment of Bose will take care of Portsmouth till I come.

England will give you every assistance in his power.

The news from 96 gives me great pleasure.

I am etc

CORNWALLIS

Cornwallis to Leslie, 18th July 1781

88(34): C

Suffolk
18th July 1781

Hon Major General Leslie

Dear Leslie

As the only armed Quarter Master General's vessell intended to be left here is not at present fit for service, I beg that you will be so good as leave with us the *Rambler* or *Formidable* (which you think proper), as circumstances may arise in which such assistance might be of great importance.

I ever am etc

[CORNWALLIS]

Leslie to Cornwallis, 19th July 1781

6(325): ALS

Portsmouth
19th July 1781

My Lord

All will be doun this morning's tide. By a letter from Major Damer last evening I find the *Carysford* won't sail yet for 24 houres. The cause of it I can't say. Your letters[65] went doun the evening of the 17th, and I am just sending doun the letter for Captain Peacock containing one for Major Craig[66].

I imagine the *Orpheus* will sail this morning.

One Weeks[67] etc I find has got a large boat and threatens coming into Princes Ann from North Carolina with 200 or 300 men.

If your Lordship chuses to write to Charles Town, I am confident you will have time from what Major Damer writes me. I shall let you know the time we sail. I have left papers and letters with the Town Major. They in general relate to the town and departments.

I have the honor to be, my Lord,
Your very faithfull humble servant

A LESLIE

---

[65] *Your letters*: see pp 284 and 299.

[66] *the letter..*: see pp 217 and 301.

[67] Perhaps Amos Weeks. See Weeks to the commanding officer of Gloucester, 30th August, vol VI, ch 62.

[*Subscribed*:]

The *Spitfire* detained in consequence of your letter yesterday.

There is rather too weak a garison here and they are not strong enough to support Princes Ann if any push is made that way.

Leslie to Cornwallis, 19th July 1781   *6(327): ALS*

Portsmouth
19th July 1781
8 o'clock at night

My Lord

On my way to get on board the *Richmond* I met a sloop from New York with the inclos'd letter from the Commander in Chief to your Lordship[68]. I took the liberty to open it.

As it is in cypher I did not examine it.

Every thing is going doun the river at this instant (I mean the 43rd and some horse sloops), the other transports being already doun to Hampton Road.

I shall stay on shore untill Brigade Major Bowes returns, taking care to have every thing ready to go to sea without delay.

I inclose you a New York paper. There's a Captain Hall[69] of this country belonging to Arnold's corps come from New York, who I have forward'd along with Bowes.

Another express vessel left York at the same time which is not yet arrived.

I have the honor to be with the utmost respect, my Lord,
Your very faithfull humble servant

A LESLIE

---

[68] *the inclos'd letter..*: of 11th July, p 139.

[69] Thomas Hall had been commissioned a captain in Benedict Arnold's newly raised American Legion in February 1781. Partly composed of infantry and partly of cavalry, it would be disbanded on 24th August 1782 when it was found impracticable to fulfil the terms of the warrant for its establishment. One company of infantry and two troops of cavalry were assigned to other corps, with a number of its officers being reduced and placed on half pay. By that date Hall had ceased to be an officer in the Legion. (Raymond, 'British American Corps'; Treasury 64/23(18), (34) and WO 65/165(12), (16) (National Archives, Kew))

[*Subscribed*:]

I have ordered the sloop doun to the Comodore without permitting any one to come on shore.

Cornwallis to Leslie, 20th July 1781[70]

88(40): Df

Suffolk
20th July 1781

Dear Leslie

By a letter I have received this instant from the Commander in Chief it is necessary to stop the sailing of the expedition, which you will be pleased to do and remain with the transports in Hampton Road untill you hear further from me. You will be pleased to communicate this to the Commodore and make an apology to him for my not writing.

[CORNWALLIS]

PS

You will remain at Portsmouth and transmit this to the commanding officer of the troops with an order to have the boats in readiness to land.

Leslie to Cornwallis, 20th July 1781

6(319): ALS

Portsmouth
20th July 1781

Earl Cornwallis

My Lord

I am honored with your Lordship's this morning at 7 o'clock by Brigade Major Bowes.

I have sent Captain Skelly to Captain Hudson with a letter informing him of the fleet not going untill I hear further from your Lordship, and told him some alterations may take place in consequence of your letter from New York. The boats are all doun with the transports, so are ready to land at any time.

I told Captain Hudson, if the *Carysfort* was not gone, to detain her for 24 houres as your Lordship might wish to write by her.

---

[70] Published without the postscript in Ross ed, op cit, i, 106. There are no other differences.

I beg you will inform me if you write by her. How she came not to sail on receiving your letters I know not.

I am ready here to obey your orders when they arrive. Every body now is in the dark.

I am, my Lord,
Your most obedient humble servant

A LESLIE

Cornwallis to Leslie, 20th July 1781 — 88(42): DfS

Suffolk
20th July 1781

Hon Lt General Leslie

Dear Leslie

Inclosed is a copy of Sir Henry Clinton's letter[71]. Nothing can be done untill the arrival of the frigate with the dispatches, nor indeed can I conveniently move from hence till Tarleton joins, which I am now in hourly expectation of. In the mean time I wish you to remain in Hampton Road with the troops that they may be ready to act without loss of time as occasion may require; and be so kind as send Sutherland, protected by a detachment, on shore on Point Comfort to examine the ground as minutely as he can in one or two days, and desire that he will report to me the nature of that spot of ground, how far it is practicable to construct a work there strong in itself and capable of commanding the entrance and anchorage of Hampton Road. And that our communication may be frequent and certain, be so good as send me two of the new boats well manned to carry my expresses. You will please to present my compliments and communicate with the Commodore, whose dispatches from the Admiral will no doubt be in the same frigate that brings mine. I heartily wish you joy of your promotion and ever am with great regard, dear Leslie,

Your affectionate faithfull servant

CORNWALLIS

---

[71] The following is deleted: 'countermanding the expedition'.

Cornwallis to Leslie, 20th July 1781   88(38): C

Suffolk
20th July 1781

The Hon Lt General Leslie etc etc etc

Dear Leslie

The letter I received from New York does not occasion the least alteration to be made in those I have already written to South Carolina. Therefore I wish you would be pleased to communicate to Captain Hudson that I do not wish the *Carysfort* to be detained on that account but that she may proceed as soon as it is convenient.

Etc

[CORNWALLIS]

Cornwallis to Leslie, 21st July 1781   88(45): Df

Suffolk
21st July 1781

Dear Leslie

As I am informed that the *Carysfort* cannot sail today and as I shall be at Portsmouth tomorrow, I should much obliged to you if you would request of the Commodore or of Captain Peacocke to allow her to remain until I see you.

[CORNWALLIS]

§ - §

3 - Between Haldane and Major England

Haldane to England, 20th June 1781   87(11): ACS

Head Quarters
Richmond
20th June 1781

Major England
Deputy Quarter Master General

Dear Sir

It appears by the abstract of warrants for extraordinaries granted by Major General Phillips that a warrant for £2,000 was granted to Captain Vallancey to defray the contingencies of the

Quarter Master General's Department, and as there is also a requisition from Captain Vallancey for a warrant for 451 guineas to defray the further expences of the said department, Lord Cornwallis desires you will be pleased to order Captain Vallancey to transmit to you an abstract of the expenditure of the £2,000 before any further warrants will be granted.

I have the honour to be, dear sir, etc

H HALDANE

England to Cornwallis, 15th July 1781 6(295): ALS

Portsmouth
July 15th 1781

Lt General Earl Cornwallis

My Lord

General Leslie desires me inclose your Lordship a letter he this moment received from Captain Hudson[72]. He will write to him to request the *Carysfort* may be detained here untill your Lordship's dispatches reach him. No letters from Charles Town are yet come ashore, nor any account from thence. Shou'd I hear any in the morning, I will do myself the honor of forwarding them to you.

Two victuallers are this evening taken up to convey three hundred men. They are taking in water and wood and will be shortly ready for the troops.

I have the honor to be
Your Lordship's very obedient humble servant

R^D ENGLAND

England to Haldane, 15th July 1781 6(313): ALS

Portsmouth
July 15th 1781

Lieutenant Haldane etc

Dear Haldane

I inclose you Captain Vallancy's letter to me with his request for two warrants to be granted him by Lord Cornwallis. The different sums and the use they were appropriated to are mentioned by him. This express goes on purpose to receive my Lord's approbation as Captain Vallancy intends to embark with the troops.

---

[72] *a letter..*: of 15th July, p 215.

The embarkation has already taken place and the Anspach battalions will be on board before this reaches you. I fear our number of transports, even only allowing a ton and quarter per man, will be so short as to occasion the 43rd Regiment to wait untill another opportunity.

The vessel with Tarleton's saddles and the Hessian baggage arrived here yesterday. She complains loudly of her convoy neglecting her.

General Leslie has demanded payment for three horses lost last November on their way to Charlestown. I propose paying him fifteen guineas for each horse provided there is no objection at Head Quarters. He has ordered me to pay all the officers whatever they paid for their horses in this country by a return to be given in *upon honor* certified by the officer commanding each corps.

Captain Vallancy wishes the money under his care shou'd be immediately taken from him. Be so good as to let me hear from you on that subject, but don't encumber me with it if you can otherwise conveniently dispose of it.

I am with regard
Your very obedient humble servant

R^D ENGLAND

Enclosure
Vallancey to England, 15th July 1781   *6(315): ALS*

Portsmouth
15th July 1781

Major England

Sir

When the late Major General Phillips left this post to go up the James River upon an expidition, he desired that I would pay to the Hessian regiment quartered here a sum of money for their subsistence for the month of May amounting to £299 8s 10⅔d sterling (dollars at 4s 8d) as also the sum of £491 1s 9½d sterling (dollars 4s 8d) to myself in order to pay the expences of the department in building etc etc as money was not then to be had, which sums I accordingly paid and have charged myself with that sum in my accounts. I do myself the honor to enclose you two warrants for the above sums, requesting you will have the goodness to obtain his Excellency Lord Cornwallis's signing them. I beg leave also to acquaint you for the information of his Lordship that there is a sum of money in my hands (as I and Captain Campbell[73] officiated as Deputy Pay Master General by order of General

---

[73] Of various Campbells with the rank of captain in the regular and Provincial forces, William Campbell of Caithness (1758-1834) is most likely the officer mentioned here. A captain in the 76th (Highland) Regiment, he had accompanied it to Virginia as part of Arnold's expedition and begun to serve on secondment as a deputy paymaster general. By mid August he would have transferred as a deputy to the Quartermaster General's Department. Among the troops who capitulated at Yorktown, he retired on half pay at the close of the war and settled in Nova Scotia, becoming a lawyer, Justice of the Peace, militia captain, and member of the lower house of the legislature.

Phillips) of about £10,000 or near that after paying several warrants granted by General Leslie. I request you will be so good as to take his Lordship's orders to whom I shall pay this money to.

I have the honor to be, sir,
Your most obedient humble servant

GEO VALLANCEY
Assistant Deputy Quarter Master General

Haldane to England, 15th July 1781 — 88(16): ACS

Head Quarters
Suffolk
15th July 1781

Dear Sir

I received your letter inclosing one from Captain Vallancey with a requisition for two warrants, which I immediately laid before Lord Cornwallis. As there is a great ballance at present in his possession, his Lordship desires he will remain at Portsmouth untill he arrives, at which time he will see the accounts of the Quarter Master General and Paymaster General and appoint some person to receive the ballance.

I am, dear sir, etc

HENRY HALDANE

[*Subscribed:*]

Lord Cornwallis consents to the payment of General Leslie's horses.

Let Despard have any money he may want on his receipt.

Yours etc

HENRY H

§ - §

At the turn of the century he moved on to Cape Breton, where he served for a time as Attorney General, member of HM Council, and superintendent of the coal mines. After falling out with the Lt Governor in 1808, he was dismissed from these offices and took passage for London, where three years later he was appointed a Judge of the Court of King's Bench in Upper Canada. In 1825 he became Chief Justice and a member of HM Council. Retiring due to ill health in 1829, he was awarded an annual pension of £1,200 and knighted the same year. He died at York (Toronto). (*DCB*; The Cornwallis Papers; *Army Lists*)

4 - From Connolly[74] to Cornwallis

Connolly to Cornwallis, undated[75]   *5(11): ALS*

The Rt Hon Earl Cornwallis, Lt General etc etc etc

My Lord

The importance of the western settlements in their present state as well as their increasing consequence, together with its influence on the operations in this unhappy war, are subjects with which I am satisfied your Lordship is well acquainted.

If I presume to lay before your Lordship my opinion of the expediency of securing the transmontane territory of Virginia and should be unhappy enough to entertain sentiments upon that matter repugnant to your Lordship's, my zeal to serve my King and perfect knowledge of that country must plead my apology.

The jealousy with which France viewed the growing strength of the British colonies occasioned that administration to take advantage of the communication afforded by the lakes and rivers from Canada with the western frontier of this Government and to establish a post at the Forks of the Ohio.

By this measure our trade and influence with the Western Indians were immediately annihilated; and notwithstanding the great inconvenience arising from the transportation of provision from Canada and the Illinois, the expence of blood and treasure to dislodge those intruders from that quarter is too well known to your Lordship to require a repetition. The objection just mentioned is now obviated, as that district is tolerably well settled, at least so far as to furnish the necessary supplies for any body of troops that might be requisite for its conquest and security. When your Lordship casts an eye upon the map of the middle colonies and considers that great chain of mountains that separates the western emigrants from the antient settlers, at the same time viewing the Ohio River with the easy access that it affords to Louisiana, it must certainly suggest to your Lordship striking considerations.

---

[74] Born in Lancaster County, Pennsylvania, John Connolly (*c.* 1750-?) was a doctor of medicine who had acted before the revolution as the agent of Lord Dunmore, the royal Governor, at Fort Pitt in transmontane Virginia. After being involved in Dunmore's War in 1774 against native Americans, he came in August 1775 to meet the deposed Governor off Portsmouth, whose dispatches he delivered to Gage, the Commander-in-Chief, at Boston. There he obtained Gage's approval to a plan whose intended effect was akin to the one now proposed, and when he rejoined Dunmore, he was commissioned Lt Colonel of the Loyal Forresters, a regiment to be raised in the west on the British American establishment. While on his way to implement the plan, he was taken prisoner at Hagerstown, Maryland, and was not exchanged until October 1780. Now, he would fare no better with his current proposals and would soon be recaptured. In March 1782 he was released on undertaking to take passage for England and at the close of the war was placed on the Provincial half-pay list. (Boatner, *Encyclopedia*, 261-2; *Appletons'*; Treasury 64/23(36) and WO 65/165(16) (National Archives, Kew))

[75] This letter was written on or around 13th July, when Leslie records Connolly's arrival at Portsmouth. See p 182.

The route observed by Monsieur Contrecœur[76] in seizing upon His Majesty's western dominion of this colony, by Presq'Isle, French Creek and the Alleganey, puts in the power of administration to pursue the same plan but with prospects of advantage infinitely superior. The rebels now occupy three posts in those parts (viz, Fort Pitt, Fort Armstrong (the Kittanning) and Fort McIntosh (the mouth of Great Beaver Creek)). These places are garrisoned by about three hundred Continental troops under the command of Colonel Brodhead[77]. Your Lordship from Evan's Map of the middle colonies will observe the position of these forts with respect to each other, from whence it will appear that there is a great probability of their being separately carried without much effusion of blood. Should the enemy be apprized of an intended invasion by the communication intimated and in such case concentrate their force, Fort Pitt most probably would be the place of rendezvous. Commanded as it is by Grant's Hill on the east, the Coal Hill on the south, and the heights on the north side of the Allegany, it would only tend to collect so many prisoners at discretion. The road opened by General Forbes[78] leads from Pennsylvania and traverses near sixty miles of a very mountainous country intersected by rivers and full of dangerous defiles. Another from Virginia, undertaken by General Braddock[79], crossing the mountains, is liable

---

[76] Born at Contrecœur, Quebec, Claude-Pierre Pécaudy, Seigneur de Contrecœur (1705-1775) began his military career in 1722 as a cadet in the colonial regular troops. Newly promoted to captain, he served in 1749 as second to de Blainville in an expedition down the Ohio valley and immediately afterwards was appointed Commandant at Fort Niagara (near present-day Youngstown NY). It was a post strategically situated for maintaining liaison between the settlements on the St Lawrence and the vast and sparsely occupied regions of the west and the Ohio valley on the line of passage to Louisiana. In December 1753 he was given the command of 2,000 men, who, having been dispatched earlier in the year to establish France's hold on the Ohio valley, had already opened a route as far as the Ohio watershed and built Fort de la Rivière au Bœuf (now Waterford PA). He proceeded to achieve the objective by displacing a body of Virginia troops at the Forks of Ohio and constructing there Fort Duquesne. He remained in command at the fort till sometime after Braddock's defeat, which occurred three leagues away, but he did not take part in it. Retiring on half pay, he remained in Canada after the Seven Years' War and was finally able to attend to his personal affairs and his seigneury. In 1768 he was called the third most influential Canadian by the Governor, Guy Carleton, and in August 1775 he was sworn in as a member of the Legislative Council. He died four months later. (*DCB*; Fred Anderson, *Crucible of War* (Faber & Faber Ltd, 2000), *passim*)

[77] Daniel Brodhead (1736-1809) was a colonel commanding Pennsylvanian troops in the Continental line. Commissioned in March 1776, he had previously farmed, run a grist mill, and served as a deputy surveyor for Pennsylvania. Ordered west in early 1778, he one year later succeeded Lachlan McIntosh at Fort Pitt as commanding officer of the Western Department. By some accounts a martinet with an irascible, jealous temperament, he is said to have been unable to cooperate with other commanders. Whether these accounts are true or not, he would lose his command at Fort Pitt in September 1781 over allegations of mishandling supplies and money. Acquitted by court martial of all charges except spending recruiting money on supplies, he ended the war as a brigadier general and went on to serve for eleven years as Surveyor General of Pennsylvania. He died at Milford, Pike County, and was buried there. (*Wikipedia*, 1st July 2006; Boatner, *Encyclopedia*, 115-6)

[78] Born in Edinburgh, John Forbes (1707-1759) was a brigadier general in the British Army when he commanded the expedition which captured Fort Duquesne (renamed Fort Pitt) in 1758. He decided not to follow Braddock's route but to cut a fresh road through western Pennsylvania across the Alleghenies. Forbes's road, as it came to be known, provided a highway for western expansion and permanent conquest. After the success of the expedition Forbes returned in a prostrate condition to Philadelphia, having suffered much from the flux. He soon died there and was buried in the chancel of Christ Church. (*ODNB*)

[79] Major General Edward Braddock (1695-1755) commanded the unsuccessful expedition to take Fort Duquesne in 1755 and was killed in the attempt. His route over mountainous, heavily wooded terrain proceeded from Fort Cumberland on the northern branch of the Potomac River. Crossing the Allegheny divide into the Youghiogheny drainage and the Monongahela Valley, it ended at Fort Duquesne, where he met disaster. (Boatner, *Encyclopedia*, 103; Fred Anderson, op cit, 89)

to the same objections. Once possessed of Fort Pitt, and taking the necessary precaution for the security of those passes, there would be nothing to fear from all the force of the middle colonies, and it is to be supposed that General Washington would be constantly too well engaged nearer home to give him any opportunity of making detachments sufficiently respectable to regain a lost footing in a country so unfavorably situated. The flame of rebellion that for some time had been checked by the intervention of the Apalachian Mountains and the legal authority which I had the honor to maintain, soon after my recall from that country by his Excellency Lord Dunmore[80] raged with all imaginable violence, and Congress were enabled to draw from that quarter upwards of sixteen hundred men, the most hardy and enterprizing of the distracted league. The bad œconomy of the rebel army and that train of disgrace which tarnished their arms in 1776 either cut them off by camp disorders or extinguished the ill timed ardor at first so conspicuous in their conduct. They soon saw the fugitive dreams of liberty pass away and a tyranny real and oppressive substituted in its place. To add to their calamity they were harrassed by His Majesty's Indian allies and knew that these hostilities were the effects of their rebellion and not a local quarrel. After the war had assumed a form and the penal laws of republickanism were began to be executed, numbers of the well disposed inhabitants, unwilling to arrange themselves under an unconstitutional standard, emigrated into the western country, preferring inconveniencies of an infant establishment and the danger of an Indian enemy to the crime of disloyalty, and, I can assure your Lordship, now constitute the most respectable part of those detached settlements. Having been formerly honored with the confidence of Lord Dunmore and favored with the good opinion of His Majesty's Council, I was entrusted with very ample authority in those parts, being charged with the recommendation of all magistrates and the appointment of all militia officers. By this means it may be supposed that I gained a considerable influence, which I have reason to think is yet far from being extinguished. Colonel Croghan[81], formerly Deputy Superintendant of Indian Affairs under Sir William Johnston, with whom I correspond and to whom I have remitted money for secret services by order of the Commander in Chief, and Mr McKee[82], now in the same employment, are both connected with me by ties of

---

[80] John Murray (1732-1809), Earl of Dunmore, was the royal Governor of Virginia from 1771 till the revolution. On returning to England he sat in Parliament as a Scottish peer before serving as Governor of the Bahamas from 1787 to 1796. (Boatner, *Encyclopedia*, 340-1; *DAB*)

[81] Born in Dublin, Ireland, George Croghan (*c*. 1720-1782) migrated to North America in 1741 and within eight years had been involved in establishing the richest trading post west of the Appalachians, the site of which lay on the upper Great Miami River in what is now western Ohio. In June 1752 it was totally destroyed by a combined force of French and native Americans. Three years later Croghan was appointed Deputy Superintendent of Indian affairs in the Northern District — an office he would occupy until 1772 — and took part in the ill-fated Braddock expedition, leading a small party of native American scouts. Flamboyent and tenacious, he acted throughout his term of office as an able deputy to Sir William Johnson while always on the lookout for opportunities to promote his own interests as a private trader and land speculator. By 1781 he was an old man who had fallen on hard times and was largely a spent force. It has been asserted that in the present conflict he was of the revolutionary persuasion, but as Connolly's letter now makes clear, he was a loyalist at heart, if only a quiescent one. (Albert T Volwiler, *George Croghan and the Western Movement, 1741-1782* (Cleveland, 1926); Nicholas B Wainwright, *George Croghan — Wilderness Diplomat* (University of NC Press, 1959); Fred Anderson, op cit, *passim*)

[82] Born in the western part of Pennsylvania, Alexander McKee (*c*. 1735-1799) served as a lieutenant in the province's forces during the early part of the Seven Years' War. In 1760 he became Assistant Deputy Superintendent of Indian affairs under George Croghan and served in the Indian department of the Northern District until the outbreak of the revolutionary war. During the Pontiac War in 1763 he was involved in presenting two Delaware chiefs with a couple of blankets and a handkerchief taken out of the smallpox hospital at Fort Pitt in the hope that the disease

consanguinity, friendship and political sentiments, and I can with truth declare that they are capable to assemble any number of Indian auxiliaries to meet me whenever judged necessary. A proper management of this force regulated by French and American partizans co-operating with Provincial troops raised in that country could not fail to occupy the attention of all the superior counties on the east side of the Allegeny down to the Kittatinny Mountains and consequently allow your Lordship's good intentions to be more successfully carried into execution. I presume it is allmost unnecessary for me to observe that, unless some real and permanent regard is paid to the state of the frontier country, the re-establishment of constitutional authority in the middle colonies must be yet far distant.

During my residence on parole at Germantown in Pennsylvania I had frequent and pressing solicitations from the western settlers to lay their request before his Excellency the Commander in Chief that some troops might be sent to their assistance barely sufficient to expel the Continental forces, and that they would be ready to support their professions of loyalty by a vigorous conduct on behalf of Government.

In consequence of my representations Sir Henry Clinton was disposed to send me into Canada with the necessary force and authority, but the refusal of Admiral Arbuthnot to grant a convoy for that purpose and the advanced season of the year dashed my hopes and put it out of the power of his Excellency to act in conformity to his inclination.

I have yet to flatter myself that your Lordship will find it expedient to penetrate the interior part of this government and that I may be authorized to sound the opinion of the principal persons on the west side of the mountain, to correspond with Mr McKee at Detroit in order to prepare the minds of the Indians, and to do every thing possible to favor a sudden excursion into the western country. In such case, should part of the army under your Lordship's command move up as far as Fort Cumberland, I could be there join'd by a body of Indians and by rapid marches would immediately cross the mountain and seize possession of Fort Pitt, which, by the assistance of the well disposed and the contiguity of the Indian tribes, I could easily maintain and reduce the settlements to His Majesty's obedience. These crude hints that I thus venture to lay before your Lordship may appear extraordinary at first view and may indicate an inclination only of accomplishing undertakings of a magnitude too considerable for my abilities. I must, however, beg leave to insinuate to your Lordship that my enemies have supposed me adequate to the task and that I feel myself perfectly convinced of its practicability. Permit me to subjoin that, as the operations suggested must be yet distant and collaterally depend upon your Lordship's movements and opinion, I should be happy in the mean time to render any services in my power either civil or military that your Lordship might judge necessary for the promotion of His Majesty's interest during your Lordship's continuance at this post.

---

might spread among the disaffected Delawares. A loyalist, McKee fled from Fort Pitt in March 1778 and made his way to Detroit, where he re-entered the Indian department as a captain and interpreter. For the rest of the war he helped in directing the operations of native Americans in the Ohio valley against the revolutionaries. At the close of hostilities he continued in the Indian department as deputy agent at Detroit and used his influence in the following years to encourage native American resistance to American settlement beyond the Ohio River. When the British withdrew from Detroit in 1796, he moved to Upper Canada, dying three years later by the Thames River. (*DCB*; Erhard Geissler and John Ellis van Courtland Moon eds, *Biological and Toxin Weapons: Research, Development and Use from the Middle Ages to 1945* (Oxford University Press, 1999), 14-17)

I have the honor to be with the greatest respect
Your Lordship's most obedient and faithfull humble servant

JN⁰ CONNOLLY

§ - §

CHAPTER 53

Correspondence etc with naval officers in Virginia and South Carolina

1 - With naval officers

Cornwallis to Robinson etc, 20th May 1781 *86(43): ADfS*

Petersburgh
May 20th 1781

Captain Robinson or officer commanding His Majesty's ships
  in Chesapeak Bay

Sir

I must request that you will please to direct one of His Majesty's ships to proceed with all possible dispatch to Cape Fear and to Charlestown to carry my letter to Major Craig at the former place and to Lt Colonel Balfour at the latter[1]. As it is of very great importance to His Majesty's Service that these letters should be conveyed as speedily as possible, and as the winds at this time of the year make the passage to the southward very tedious, I trust that you will be kind enough to send a ship that sails well and give directions that the letters may be destroyed in case of danger. I must likewise beg leave to recommend that the ship may not go over the bar at Cape Fear as it may be the cause of her being long detained in that port.

---

[1] *my letter..*: see pp 300 and 274.

I am, sir,
Your most obedient and most humble servant

CORNWALLIS

Cornwallis to Pattison, 22nd May 1781　　　　　　　　　　　　86(45): C

Petersburgh
22nd May 1781

Lieutenant Paterson commanding at City Point

Sir

The troops will cross the Appomatox to morrow morning and I have to request that you will move the boats some time in the forenoon up to Bermuda Hundred, where I will send a detachment with an officer to communicate our future plan of operations. He is directed to pull off his hat three times when he hails you, by which you will know him to be sent by me.

I have the honour to be etc

[CORNWALLIS]

Robertson to Cornwallis, 22nd May 1781　　　　　　　　　　　　6(100): ALS

Selina transport off Brandham, James River
22nd May 1781

The Rt Hon Earl Cornwallis etc etc etc

My Lord

Understanding that your Lordship now commands His Majesty's forces in this province, I take the liberty to inform you that a reinforcement is now arrived here from New York, which a collonel of one of the Anspach battalions commands, who has the late Major General Philips' orders to land here and march to Petersburgh and chuses to follow that order when all the transports are got up here, two of which, the *Charming Nancy* and *Providence*, are yet missing, supposed to be aground in this river.

I told him, as the wind was now fair, I would cary him up with the ships that are arrived or, if he chose, I should land him here and procure a guide for Petersburgh. All this he declined and now remains here untill the two missing ships arrives. Then he is to follow his former orders provided that he has no new instructions from your Lordship.

My Lord, I am order'd to return all the transports from New York the instant that the troops are landed provided that your Lordship has no objections. If you have, I herewith send you a copy of the state which I received of them[2] and I shall comply with your Lordship's orders.

With the greatest respect I am, my Lord,
Your Lordship's most obedient humble servant

G ROBERTSON
Agent

Hudson to Cornwallis, 29th May 1781   6(123): LS

Richmond
Hampton Road
29th May 1781

His Excellency Lt General Earl Cornwallis etc etc etc

My Lord

Notwithstanding my utmost endeavours for this month past to have a communication with your Lordship, your movements has been so rapid as to prevent it. My Lord Chewton, to whom I refer your Lordship, can and will inform you of my anxiety for that purpose, but now that I know where you are, I have the honor of inclosing your Lordship a copy of the orders that I am at present under, and if it is in the compass of my power in any respect with the King's ships at present under my command to be of any assistance to you, I beg that your Lordship would regard me as a person totally devouted for that purpose.

I have the honor to be, my Lord,
Your Lordship's most obedient and very faithful humble servant

CHARLES HUDSON[3]

---

[2] *a copy of the state..*: not extant.

[3] Commissioned a lieutenant in the Royal Navy on 27th June 1757, Charles Hudson (?-1803) had been promoted to commander on 24th August 1762 and to post-captain some three years later. In 1775, having taken command of the 32-gun frigate *Orpheus*, he was assigned to the North American station. In early August 1778, when bottled up by d'Estaing at Newport, Rhode Island, he was constrained to destroy his ship during a French naval attack on the port rather than risk her falling into enemy hands. On his return to England he was eventually appointed to the 32-gun frigate *Richmond* and again came out to North America in December 1779. He proceeded to take part in the Charlestown expedition, commanding 500 seamen on shore who took possession of Mount Pleasant and Fort Moultrie. Now, with the temporary rank of commodore, he was the naval officer commanding in Virginia, a post he would occupy till the latter part of August, when he was replaced by Thomas Symonds. On 6th September, when he was part of Graves' fleet opposed to de Grasse, he would be ordered with the *Richmond* to stand into the Chesapeake for the purpose of cutting away the buoys from the French anchors, the enemy having slipped their cables and left them behind. Accompanied by the *Iris*, he was hemmed in on attempting to emerge from the bay

Enclosure
Arbuthnot's instructions to Hudson, 2nd May 1781   6(125): C

By Mariot Arbuthnot Esq,
Vice Admiral of the White and
Commander in Chief etc etc etc

To Captain Hudson, Commander of His Majesty's Ship the *Richmond*

You are hereby required and directed to proceed with His Majesty's ship under your command to Lynhaven Bay, and having forwarded the dispatches you will receive from General Sir Henry Clinton to Major General Phillips, you are to proceed with those for Lt General Earl Cornwallis to Cape Fear in North Carolina, and having forwarded these, you are to wait his Lordship's answer, and should he determine to take the command of the army in Virginia, you are to convey his Lordship and his suit there with all possible dispatch, otherwise you are to convey his Lordship's instructions to Major General Phillips, who at present commands His Majesty's forces in that colony, and upon your return to the Chesapeake you are to take the command of all His Majesty's ships and vessels employed in that bay and to do your utmost to promote (in conjunction with the army) His Majesty's Service.

You are to order the *Delight* to Charles Town with the enclos'd letter for Captain Barkley of the *Blonde* or the commanding officer of His Majesty's ships there.

For which this shall be your order.

Given on board His Majesty's Ship *Royal Oak* off New York
the 2nd May 1781

M^T ARBUTHNOT

Pattison to Cornwallis, 16th June 1781   6(242): ALS

Rambler off Shirley Hundred
16th June 1781

Earl Cornwallis

My Lord

I have the honor to inform you that the fleet under my command are moved up to Shirley Hundred agreable to your Lordship's directions, and I flatter myself they are anchored in such

---

and both ships were captured on the 11th. After the war he commanded the frigate *Venus* for three years before eventually becoming a superannuated rear admiral. (Charnock, *Biographia Navalis*, vi, 565-6; Syrett and DiNardo eds, *The Commissioned Sea Officers*, 232; Boatner, *Encyclopedia*, 226; *The Cornwallis Papers*)

a possission as to prevent a surprize shou'd molestation take place. Nothing material happened on our passage more than recovering the lost horse boat, which I towed from the shore and have now with me. I have taken the liberty to enclose for your Lordship's perusal a copy of my summons for fresh beef for the use of the fleet. It had its desired effect and fiveteen head were immediately drove in for us. I hope that this mode of proceeding will meet with your Lordship's approbation, as it inevitably prevents the seamen strageling or doing mischief to those who perhaps deserve protection.

I have the honor to be, my Lord,
Your Lordship's most obedient and very humble servant

GEORGE PATTISON[4]
Lieutenant, Royal Navy, commanding the fleet off Shirley Hundred

PS

I hope, my Lord, that the fireing of Bermuda Hundred will meet your Lordship's approbation, especially as it afforded cover to some rebel militia under a Colonel Goode[5] who shewed themselves. I have all the reason to believe they wou'd have been of much diservice to the fleet as we lay within pistol shot of the shore. The guns of the vessels, who all have springs upon their cables, now wholly command it.

Enclosure
Summons, 29th May 1781   6(244): ACS

Rambler brigg
29th May 1781

To all whom it may concern

His Britanic Majesty's fleet under my command being in want of fresh provisions, you are hereby summoned to cause the same to be drove in and delivered for their use. My reason for thus addressing you is to prevent the mischief which may arise to individuals by landing my people and perhaps distressing those who are not at this time in actual rebellion. I further expect and demand that the flagg will be treated according to the customs used among civilized nations. If otherways, you must stand to the consequences which will ensue, as I shall certainly make use of that force which my King has honor'd me with.

---

[4] George Pattison (?-1803) had been commissioned a lieutenant in the Royal Navy on 11th April 1778. He would rise no higher in the service. (Syrett and DiNardo eds, *The Commissioned Sea Officers*, 350)

[5] Robert Goode III (1744-1809) was a colonel in the revolutionary militia of Chesterfield County, where he was later recorded as being head of a household of 10 whites and 104 slaves. From 1783 he would serve in the Virginia House of Delegates until elected to the Council in 1788. (*Va Military Records*, 290; Gwathmey, *Historical Register*, 315; *Heads of Families at the First Census of the United States Taken in the Year 1790: Virginia* (Genealogicial Publishing Co, 1966); Cynthia M Leonard, *The General Assembly of Virginia...* (Library of Virginia, 1978); G Brown Goode, *Virginia Cousins...* (Clearfield Publishing Co, 1987), 54-8; *The Visitor* (Richmond VA), 6th May 1809)

GEORGE PATTISON
Lieutenant, Royal Navy, commanding the fleet off Shirley Hundred

[*Subscribed*:]

Mr Austin[6], commander, brigg *Rambler*, and 2 men to pass with this flagg.

Cornwallis to Hudson, 19th June 1781   *87(7): C*

Richmond
19th June 1781

Captain Hudson commanding His Majesty's ships
   in Chesapeake Bay

Sir

I have received your very obliging letter of the 29th ultimo and beg leave to assure you that it gives me the greatest satisfaction to find that we are to serve together. It will always give me the greatest pleasure to have opportunities of shewing my regard for the navy and in joining heartily in any operations that may tend to the service of our country. I hope soon to be in a situation of more immediate communication with you. In the mean time you will oblige me in complying with any request made by Major General Leslie.

I have the honour to be, sir, etc

CORNWALLIS

Ross to Pattison, 20th June 1781   *87(15): ACS*

Head Quarters
Richmond
20th June 1781

Lieutenant Paterson commanding the fleet at City Point

Sir

Your boats, which arrived safe and have been exceedingly usefull to us, are dispatched again to you this day. The army will march to morrow towards Williamsburgh, and Lord Cornwallis begs that you will be pleased to detach without loss of time to Portsmouth as much craft with a proper escort as will be sufficient to transport about seven hundred men with their baggage from thence to Williamsburgh, and that you will remain with the rest of

---

[6] Austin is not recorded by Syrett and DiNardo. He may not have been a commissioned officer.

the vessells at City Point 'till the 24th instant and then proceed with them and those below to the mouth of the creek that runs from Williamsburgh into James River, where his Lordship hopes to be soon in communication with you. The craft found here and all suttling vessells you will be so good as keep with you, as well as the brass artillery, which you will dispose of among the most proper vessells for carrying it down.

I was favoured with your letter relative to the demand of Negroes[7]. Our rule with the army on that subject will perhaps suit you. It is to give up those that are willing to return and can be conveniently spared from the publick service.

You will be pleased to give Lord Cornwallis's letter to General Leslie[8] in charge to the officer commanding the craft detached to Portsmouth.

I have the honour to be with great respect, sir,
Your most obedient and most humble servant

A ROSS
Aide de camp

Cornwallis to Hudson, 27th June 1781   87(17): C

Williamsburgh
June 27th 1781

Captain Hudson commanding His Majesty's ships
    in Chesapeak Bay

Sir

As I propose passing the James River at Hog Island Ferry with all convenient expedition, and as it will be a troublesome operation and require some arrangement, I should be much obliged to you if you will be so kind as to send an active officer with as many seamen as you can conveniently spare to Burrell's to assist in managing the boats.

I am, sir, with great esteem
Your most obedient and most humble servant

[CORNWALLIS]

---

[7] *your letter..*: not extant.

[8] *Lord Cornwallis's letter..*: of 19th June, p 165.

Hudson to Cornwallis, 28th June 1781　　　　　　　　　　*6(274): ALS*

Richmond
Hampton Road
the 28th June 1781
at 10 o'clock in the morning

His Excellency Earl Cornwallis etc etc etc

My Lord

   I am just now honored with your Lordship's letter making a requisition for an active officer and seamen from the King's ships here. I send on that service Captain Aplin of the *Fowey* with such seamen as possibley can be spared, a great number being already from them up the river attending the King's troops. Every requisition of your Lordship's to me shall be paid due attention to, and I hope, when this service is over, that your Lordship will have the goodness to order them to be returned to their duty on board their respective ships.

I have the honor to be
Your Lordship's most obedient very faithfull humble servant

CHARLES HUDSON

Hudson to Cornwallis, 28th June 1781　　　　　　　　　　*6(272): ALS*

Richmond
Hampton Road
the 28th June 1781

The Rt Hon Earl Cornwallis etc etc etc

My Lord

   I did myself the honor of writing to your Lordship this morning by Captain Aplin, who I detach'd with three flat boats and all the seamen I could spare to attend the army. Since that, Major General Leslie has sent me two other flat boats, which I now forward with the utmost expedition to your Lordship, and

I have the honor to be, my Lord,
Your Lordship's most obedient very humble servant

CHARLES HUDSON

Cornwallis to Barkley, 28th June 1781[9]   *87(21): C*

Williamsburgh
June 28th 1781

Captain Barklay commanding His Majesty's ships
  on the Southern Station

Dear Sir

As I am convinced that it is the earnest desire of Sir Henry Clinton that part of the troops lately arrived from Europe should proceed to New York with the utmost dispatch, I have sent directions accordingly to Colonel Gould[10]. I must therefore beg that you will be kind enough to provide as soon as possible a suitable convoy. I will take the first opportunity of informing the Admiral of the requisition I have made and can have no doubt of its meeting with his approbation.

I am, sir, with great esteem
Your most obedient and most humble servant

[CORNWALLIS]

Haldane to Pattison, 28th June 1781   *87(31): ACS*

Head Quarters
Williamsburgh
28th June 1781

Lieutenant Paterson
Navy

Sir

Lord Cornwallis desires you will be pleased to order the inclosed letters[11] to be carried to Portsmouth with the greatest dispatch and safety possible. You will be kind enough to acknowledge the receipt of them from the corporal of dragoons.

I am, sir, etc

H HALDANE

---

[9]   This letter miscarried. See Hudson to Leslie, 15th July, p 215, and enclosure.

[10]   *directions..*: of 28th June, p 298. They miscarried.

[11]   *the inclosed letters*: the above to Barkley and Cornwallis's to Leslie and Gould, pp 169 and 298.

[*Subscribed*:]

Lord Cornwallis desires you will give particular directions to destroy them in case of danger.

Hudson to Leslie, 7th July 1781   97(10): ALS

Richmond
Hampton Road
the 7th July 1781

Hon Major General Leslie etc etc etc

Sir

I am just now honored with dispatches from Rear Admiral Graves, which are of consequence, and I dare say that you will receive some to morrow morning by the same conveyance, as Captain Colpoys is still in Lynhaven Bay. He only sent his boat here to know whether we were friends or not and would not risque your dispatches till that was ascertained. It would be necessary that I should have the officers and seamen belonging to this ship, now up James River in the flatt boats, returned to their duty on board, and the *Bonetta* sloop to join me, as she as well as this ship is ordered on service. If it is necessary that she should be relieved their by another, I will order the *Swift* on that service as soon as she is refitted.

I have the honor to be, sir,
Your most obedient very faithfull humble servant

CHARLES HUDSON

PS

Since I wrote the above, the 1st lieutenant of the *Orpheus* has come on board here with dispatches for Earl Cornwallis as well as yourself[12], which he will have the honor of delivering to you.

---

[12] *dispatches..*: Clinton's to Cornwallis of 1st July, p 136; Germain's to Cornwallis of 7th March and 4th April, pp 150-1; and those to Leslie, pp 147-9.

Hudson to Leslie, 15th July 1781[13]

6(297): ALS

Richmond
Hampton Road
the 15th July 1781

Hon Major General Leslie etc etc etc

Sir

His Majesty's Ship *Carysfort*, who is just now arrived in Lynhaven Bay, has brought in with her the convert[14] packet boat that you dispatched from this to Charles Town. She was taken by a rebel privateer and retaken by the above ship. The dispatches were destroyed before she was boarded by the enemy, as they probably were of importance. I shall detain the *Carysfort* here for twenty four hours in order to wait your commands for Charles Town, where she is going. I shall, if the weather will permitt, do myself the honor of seeing you early to morrow morning.

I have the honor to be, sir,
Your most obedient very faithfull humble servant

CHARLES HUDSON

Enclosure
Peacock to Hudson, 15th July 1781

6(317): ALS

Carysfort
Lynhaven Bay
July 15th 1781

To Captain Hudson of His Majesty's Ship *Richmond*

Sir

On the 5th instant I sailed from off Charles Town in company with His Majesty's Ship *Blonde* (and the pacquet bound to Europe). Captain Barkley's intention was to see the pacquet 40 or 50 leagues to the NE. The only particular orders which I received from him were that in case of parting company the place of rendezvous was to be from 5 to 15 leagues east of Charles Town.

At four am of the 9th I made a signal for a sail in the SW and chaced by signal. At ½ past 9 lost sight of the *Blonde*. ½ past 11, light airs. Found the chace had got her oars out

---

[13] This and the enclosure accompanied England's first letter of the same date to Cornwallis, p 197.

[14] *convert*: 'converted', now a rare usage.

and left us fast. Hauled to a vessel we saw in the SW and, employing every thing, bro't her too at 7 pm. Found her to be a prize to the rebel letter of marque *Porpoise*, which had taken her a few days before.

Her papers are all destroyed, but from the intelligence of her mate and the American prize master I was concerned to find that she was from Portsmouth in Virginia to Charles Town with Government dispatches.

I endeavoured to join the *Blonde* but without success, and finding a strong NE current and the wind southly, I thought it wou'd best answer the good of the service to repair to this place with an account of the dispatches being destroyed. I have been more particular in that respect than perhaps I might have been, did I not know from the best authority to the southward that the evacuation of Cape Fear or the prosecuting the war in that quarter immediately rests on the advices which were daily expected from Lord Cornwallis.

The situation of a ship here will be, I am assured, a sufficient apology for my not waiting on you.

And the officer who delivers this letter is desired to request your advice and immediate assistance in procuring the sloop's salvage, for altho it is not a matter of the smallest consideration to the officers, it will convince the seamen that their interests are not neglected, which I must think a very material point. I wish to know your commands as soon as possible, and have the honor to be, sir,

Your most obedient servant

W PEACOCK[15]

[*Subscribed:*]

A fleet is daily expected of[16] Charles Town commanded by Admiral Digby. A French fleet is likewise expected. 4 or 5 vessels are on their passage from the Havannah, bound to the Chesapeak or Baltimore with very valuable cargoes. The *Porpoise*, which captured the sloop I send, had 30,000 dollars on board.

---

[15] Now commanding the *Carysfort*, a 28-gun frigate launched at Sheerness in 1766, William Peacock had been commissioned a lieutenant in the Royal Navy on 12th June 1776, rising to commander in 1778 and to post-captain on 27th January 1780. As these Papers later reveal, he was an accommodating officer who was prepared to cooperate heartily with the army in forwarding the King's service. (Michael Phillips, 'Ships of the Old Navy 2' (Internet, 27th July 2006); Syrett and DiNardo eds, *The Commissioned Sea Officers*, 351)

[16] *of*: off.

Aplin to Cornwallis, 16th July 1781

6(311): ALS

Fowey
Hampton Road
July 16th 81

My Lord

It is with the highest pleasure that I had the honour of receiving your Lordship's letter[17] and warm expression for my conduct and officers and seamen under my command during my service with your Lordship. Give me leave to add nothing could afford me more satisfaction than meeting with the approbation of so great an officer.

I shall with pleasure communicate your Lordship's wishes to the officers and seamen.

My Lord, I have the honour to be with the greatest esteem
Your Lordship's most obedient and very humble servant

PETER APLIN

Cornwallis to Peacock, 17th July 1781

88(32): C

Suffolk
17th July 1781

Captain Peacock
His Majesty's Ship *Carysfort*

Sir

I beg leave to offer my best thanks for your attention to the good of the service and to myself in particular by the early information you have given of the loss of the express vessell carrying dispatches to Charlestown. I take the liberty of troubling you with dispatches[18] in place of those lost, and with a letter to Major Craig[19], which I wish to be forwarded to him by the earliest opportunity in case it is not convenient for you to touch at Cape Fear Bar.

I have the honour to be etc

[CORNWALLIS]

---

[17] *your Lordship's letter*: no extant copy.

[18] *dispatches*: see pp 284 and 299-300.

[19] *a letter..*: see p 301.

Hudson to Cornwallis, 20th July 1781
6(335): ALS

Richmond
Hampton Road
20th July 1781

Rt Hon Lt General Earl Cornwallis etc etc etc

My Lord

As I am ordered by Rear Admiral Graves, Commander in Chief etc, to take the command of the King's ships that accompany the embarkation from Portsmouth, I of course will sail with them and will leave the command of the ships that are to remain at this anchorage, viz, *Guadaloupe, Fowey, Swift* sloop and *Vulcan* fire ship, with Captain Robinson, who I am sure will be happy in cooperating with and giving your Lordship assurances how much he has the interest of the service at heart. I am sorry that I have not had the honor of paying my personal respects to your Lordship since I have been here.

I have the honor to be, my Lord,
Your Lordship's most obedient and very faithfull humble servant

CHARLES HUDSON

Hudson to Leslie, 20th July 1781
6(329): ALS

Richmond
Hampton Road
the 20th July 1781

Hon Major General Leslie etc etc etc

Sir

I have this moment received orders from Rear Admiral Graves, Commander in Chief etc etc etc, informing me that the expedition that Sir Henry Clinton had plan'd, and to be executed by the troops from Portsmouth under your command, is countermanded, and at the same time desiring that I may see them returned to that garrison. I am likewise directed by the Admiral that, if the Earl Cornwallis has any troops or transports to send immediately to New York, that a convoy will be appointed for them, viz, the *Charon* and *Loyalist*, but I beg leave to inform you, sir, that this convoy cannot be detained long here. I presume that you have received dispatches relative to this business[20] and I am thougherly convinced that you will not only give directions for the troops' speedy disembarkation but to facilitate the departure of any thing destined for New York. Captain Everate of the *Solebay*, who brot these dispatches, informs me that he has eighty prisoners on board that ship, very short of

---

[20] *dispatches..*: Clinton's of 11th July, pp 139, 142 and 149-150.

complement, and sickly, and requesting that they may be put to prison, which I am sure you will very readily contribute to and order a reception for them. I must beg leave to observe that I have strict directions from the Admiral not to detain the *Solebay*, and I hope that the Earl's and your dispatches will be speedily expedited that I may forward her.

I have the honor to be, sir,
Your most obedient very humble servant

CHARLES HUDSON

§ - §

2 - Desultory water operations

Note of operations from 13th to 16th July 1781 5(1): D

Friday at 2 o'clock in the morning we left Suffolk.

At eight arriv'd in James River. At 12 ditto landed on the southern shore and destroy'd one large boat and three small cannoes at Carrol's Plantation near Pagan Creek.

Saturday morning at five o'clock saw about thirty horsemen about three miles below Cobham. At six arriv'd at James's Island, where we found one of the large horse boats, which we burnt. Saw three ships lying above the island with flags of truce, which we supposed were landing rebel prisoners. At eight o'clock row'd over to Cobham and was informed by Mr Sinclair[21] that Colonel Brown[22] in conversation with him yesterday said that the Marquis's army lay at Chickahomeny Church last Tuesday, and that since we crossed the river there had been a strong guard of horse on the main near James Island, which was withdrawn the day before yesterday. He also says that one Laurie, a deserter from the British Army, told him yesterday that the Marquis's army left the church on his way to Richmond on Wednesday last, that he saw one of Colonel Tarleton's guides yesterday, who said he left him last Tuesday at Bland's Ordinary, and that he saw another last night, who left Colonel Tarleton nineteen miles beyond Petersburg on Wednesday (NB: both these guides live in the neighbourhood). He also says that an officer of Colonel Parker's corps was at his house

---

[21] Arthur Sinclair of Surry County had begun trading in tobacco and other local products by March 1773, at which time he purchased property in Cobham. Apparently a covert loyalist, he would pay no price for his sin. (Information from Sally Spangler, 29th July 2000)

[22] William Browne (1739-1786) was the owner of 'Four Mile Tree', a plantation of some 2,200 acres which had been patented in 1635 by Henry Browne, the father-in-law of his paternal grandfather. It lay in Surry County, abutting James River and present-day Eastover. Apparently a colonel in the Surry County revolutionary militia, he had been a member of the county's committee of safety in 1776 before going on to serve in the lower house of the Virginia revolutionary legislature. (Tyler, *Encyclopedia*, i, 197)

yesterday, who said that their head quarters was at Black Water, and he thinks that the horsemen we saw this morning were some of Parker's. At ½ past three landed on Charles City shore, about six miles below Sandy Point, where we burnt another of the horse boats. At five pm sail'd up the river within four miles of Hood's Battery. The wind came so fresh ahead, and the tide so strong against us, we were obliged to come to an anchor for the night. On our way up we were dodged[23] by a number of light horse on the same shore.

Sunday morning, the wind continuing the same, we sail'd down the river, having left several boats below, which we had not destroy'd. About eight o'clock am we landed at Lightfoot's at Sandy Point, where we destroy'd five large cannoes. Mr Fitzwilliams, the stewart[24], told us that the Marquis marched for the forge about 25 miles from Chickahomeny Church on Wednesday and that yesterday he march'd from the Long Bridge on his way to Richmond. He says likewise that it was about forty volunteer cavalry that followed us yesterday. A Negroe man at the same plantation mentioned the same circumstances to Watt[25]. Yesterday afternoon we took a canoe with two Negroes from the south shore, who told us that the Baron Steuben had been pressing men, horses and Negroes for some days before. From Sandy Point we sail'd down the river to Mowcock's, where we burnt another of the horse boats and destroy'd two canoes. We then sail'd over to the southern shore, where we brought off two Negroes, who said that Colonel Tarleton passed by Cabin Points Tuesday last on his way to Petersburg. We then proceeded up the river within a few miles of Hood's Battery, still dodged by the horsemen on shore, and at nine at night got under way to come down.

Monday morning on our way down we went ashore opposite to Chickahomeny Creek, destroyed a large canoe, and brought off two Negroes who came from Brunswick County but could gain no intelligence from them. At nine o'clock am landed at Colonel Brown's, where we destroy'd a long boat and a canoe. Being informed by a Negroe who came off from the shore last night that Colonel Brown and his three sons were at home, we went with a party of men to the house, but finding they had left it some hours before, we made a patrole of about half a mile and saw only one horseman. We then return'd and halted the party at the house 'till the boats were destroy'd, when a small party of horse drove in our advance centrys, with whom they exchanged a few shot, but on seeing our party they retir'd immediately. A Negroe woman belonging to Colonel Brown was wounded by one of their own shots. From Colonel Brown's we proceeded with all possible expedition for Suffolk. Number of boats destroy'd:

Horse boats	3
Long boats	2
Cannoes	12
Total	17.

---

[23] *dodged*: followed stealthily, with shifts to avoid discovery.

[24] *stewart*: an archaic form of 'steward'.

[25] Watt was probably a non-commissioned officer and is therefore not recorded by Syrett and DiNardo.

Note of operations from 18th to 22nd July 1781　　　　　　　　6(321): D

Wednesday, 18th July. Left Suffolk at nine o'clock in the evening and came to an anchor about three in the morning at the entrance of the Nansimund.

Thursday, 19th. Got under way about five in the morning but, the wind blowing very fresh ahead, cou'd not reach farther than Hog Island.

Friday, 20th. Weigh'd anchor about six o'clock, saw a boat with three hogsheads in her on Hog Island, sent the cannoe for her, and landed our men to get wood. Sir Peyton Skipwith[26] came down to us, who mention'd he was at Williamsburg yesterday, that the report there was of the Marquis's being at Holt's Forge and it was supposed he intended to cross the river at Four Mile Creek, that he beleiv'd Baron Steuben and Morgan were with the Marquis, that Tarleton, he was inform'd, lay about eight miles from his house, that Colonel Parker's people were about sixteen miles from there, and that Colonel Brown was to assemble the militia of the county at Surry Court House this day. On passing James's Island we were hail'd from one of the ships, who told us that a boat had been up the river the day before yesterday with a flag, that the rebels had some pieces of cannon on the shore near Sandy Point, and that the Marquis's army lay about twelve miles up the river on Charles City side. We proceeded up the river and a little above Sandy Point saw about thirty horsemen and fifty infantry, who followed us till we came to an anchor about three o'clock in the afternoon close to the ship yard, the tide coming against us. About four o'clock saw a boat ahead on the southern shore. Sent the small boat to reconnoitre her. They reported her to be a new yawl, which we brought off. The tide being slacken'd and the wind almost fair, got under way again and came to an anchor off Bird's House about ½ past ten. At eleven we landed with thirty men, but on seeing a number of fires in the rear of the house with men round them, we halted the party and sent Watt with six men to the house to endeavour to bring Jack[27] off undiscover'd, but they fell in with a patrole of two dragoons coming towards them, one of whom they kill'd. We, on finding ourselves discover'd, retreated to our boats, not being able to procure any intelligence, and lay off at an anchor all night. Before we landed and during the night we observ'd a number of signals made by fire balls in the air.

Saturday. At five o'clock saw a canoe in shore, brought her too, and found a Negroe on board, who left Petersburg yesterday. He inform'd us that Wayne was at Chesterfield Court but was hourly expected at Petersburg, that the Marquis was somewhere about Richmond but

---

[26] Sir Peyton Skipwith Bt (1740-1805) was the sixth successor to a baronetcy which had been created in 1622. The 3rd baronet, Sir Grey, had migrated to Virginia during the Cromwellian era. A planter, mainly of tobacco, Sir Peyton was now residing in Surry County, having moved there from Mecklenburg in 1778. A covert loyalist, as evinced by his present conduct, he sailed close to the wind and during the war was charged with carrying on a clandestine and treasonable correspondence with the Crown. He was acquitted. In 1782 he moved back to Mecklenburg County, where in the 1790s he built Prestwould, a Georgian mansion high above a bank of the Roanoke River. It is still standing. (The Skipwith Family Papers, Earl Gregg Swem Library, College of William and Mary; Mecklenburg County Court Records, Order Book 5, pp 96-7)

[27] Perhaps Jack White, who had been the personal slave of William Byrd III (1728-1777) until his master committed suicide on New Year's Day 1777. (Terri L Snyder, *Stories of Suicide in Eighteenth-Century Virginia: Masters, Slaves, and Print Culture during the Imperial Crisis* (presented to the Ohio Seminar in Early American History and Culture, 14th October 2005), 5, 8)

was expected to follow Wayne. At ten o'clock we brought off a Negroe from Mr Hardimand's, who inform'd us that he saw a party of cavalry and infantry pass the road on Thursday going to take post at Westhover, that they came from the Marquis's army, who lay at Richmond, and that part of the army lay at Four Mile Creek, that a sloop pass'd up the river with a number of men in her about three days ago, that he heard drums beat this morning about Shirley's Mill. Brought too another canoe with a black boy in her near Epse's Island[28]. He told us that a party of the Marquis's army was sent down to Westhover to anoy the boats coming up, that one of Mr Epse's Negroes was over at Barclay's this morning, who heard that there was six boats of ours coming up, and that the men sent to Mrs Bird's were meant to anoy them. The boy further added that a large skow[29] passed up the river about dusk last night full of men. Sent Watt ashore on Epse's Island, who was inform'd by some intelligent Negroes that the best part of the Marquis's army lay at Cox's on Mawble Hills about three miles and a half from Four Mile Creek, that a part of them had cross'd over the river at Four Mile Creek to Chesterfield some days ago, that the skow that was seen last night went up James's River, and that two more were expected up this evening. A black was sent by Watt to Mr Hardiman[30] to request he wou'd come on the island, who, on sending our boat on shore, came off with Mr Epse[31]. They inform'd us that General Wayne had lain at Chesterfield Court with 600 Continentals for some days, that he cross'd at Four Mile Creek, that the Marquis, Steuben and Lawson with about 1,200 Continentals lay at Cox's near Shirly Mills, that owing to the small pox his army was very sickly, particularly his militia, whose numbers cou'd not be ascertain'd, tho' they beleiv'd they did not exceed two thousand, that the troops at Westhover consisted of about two hundred Continentals and militia with a small detatchment of cavalry, that Mulinburg went up the Back Country four days ago, that it was reported the Marquis was going to the northward and that Wayne was going to join Green, who was marching this way, that Tarleton had pass'd down. They likewise said that Mr W[m] Hopper[32], on seeing our boats, went instantly express to the Marquis. At three got under way to come down the river, when we observed on Hardiman's Bluff a number of men coming down, from whom we receiv'd a volly of small arms and for a quarter of an hour were very severely cannonaded by four field pieces which the Marquis had sent down. Our foremast was shot away, another shot thro' our foresail, and one struck the boat astern. The *St Patrick* escaped without any damage. On passing Mrs Bird's we observ'd them coming down again in great haste with the cannon, but we fortunately had passed the Point before they cou'd bring them to bear on us. We also saw a large body of cavalry and infantry

---

[28] Eppes Island lies in Charles City County.

[29] *skow*: an obsolete spelling of 'scow', a large flat-bottomed lighter or punt.

[30] Hardiman was no doubt a descendant of John Hardiman (?-*c.* 1710), who had settled in Charles City County in the 17th century. He left five sons, one of whom, perhaps Francis, appears to have been the father of the Hardiman here. (Tyler, *Encyclopedia*, i, 251)

[31] The Eppeses, who were related to the Hardimans, were an extended family of planters, whose ancestor, Francis, had settled in Virginia in the early 17th century. The Eppes referred to here is probably Richard (?-1792), though he may have been Francis (1747-1808). (Tyler, op cit, i, 230-1; Marie Tyler-McGraw, *Slavery and the Underground Railroad at the Eppes Plantations...* (NE Region National Parks Service, 2005), 19)

[32] William Hopper was a captain in the Virginia revolutionary militia. (Heitman, *Historical Register*, 301)

paraded nigh the house. We proceeded down the river without further opposition and came to an anchor off Sandy Point at 9 o'clock.

Sunday, 22nd. At three in the morning got under way, passed seven ships with flags off James's Island. At seven brought too a sloop who left Chickahomeny Creek yesterday. She had on board a Mr Calvert[33] and his family, who were proceeding down to Norfolk, having a pass from Major England. At nine came to an anchor off Hog Island.

§ - §

---

[33] The Calverts were an extended family descended from Cornelius Calvert (?-1747), a sea captain of Lancashire, England, who settled in Norfolk, Virginia, sometime before mid 1719 and established himself as a merchant. Of his nine sons and their offspring, William (1734-?), Cornelius's seventh child, was of the loyalist persuasion and may therefore be the Calvert mentioned here. (Information from Sally Moore Koestler, 17th May 2006)

CHAPTER 54

Miscellaneous correspondence etc relating to Virginia or Maryland

1 - Between Cornwallis and Simcoe or Tarleton

Simcoe to Cornwallis, 2nd June 1781 *6(156): ALS*

Price's Mill
June 2nd 1781

Rt Hon Lt General Earl Cornwallis

My Lord

I have not the least doubt but that Jonathan Webster and Lewis Trepan, private dragoons in Captain Cooke's troop of the Queen's Rangers, were guilty of a rape on Jane Dickinson yesterday.

I have the honor to be, my Lord, with great respect
Your most obedient and most humble servant

J GRAVES SIMCOE
Lt Colonel commanding Queen's Rangers

Cornwallis to Simcoe, 5th June 1781[1]   *87(1): C*

5th June 1781

To Lt Colonel Simcoe

I can subsist a few days between Goochland Court House and the Fork. If you can strike a blow without risque to your corps, do it.

[CORNWALLIS]

Parole of Robert Nelson, 4th June 1781[2]   *93(13): DS*

June 4th 1781

I, Robert Nelson of Virginia, hereby bind myself not to act in a civil or military capacity against His Britannick Majesty untill discharg'd from this obligation.

BAN TARLETON
Lt Colonel Commandant, British Legion

ROB[T] NELSON[3]

Cornwallis to Tarleton, 11th June 1781[4]   *87(5): C*

Camp at Jefferson's
11th June 1781

Lt Colonel Tarleton

Dear Tarleton

You will proceed with the detachment of cavalry and mounted infantry under your command before day break tomorrow morning to Old Albermarle Court House, where you

---

[1] Annotated: 'This letter was not delivered. The express returned.'

[2] This parole was taken during the Charlottesville raid. Others extant (93(12) and (14) to (17)) are signed by Dudley Digges, William Nelson, Peter Lyons, Albridgton Jones, James Hayes and John Syme (misidentified by various writers as Simms). William was a brother of Thomas Nelson Jr (see p 110, note 54).

[3] Robert Nelson (1743-1818) was a younger brother of Thomas Nelson Jr. In 1769 he graduated from William and Mary College and was professor of law there from 1813 till his death. (*Appletons'*)

[4] Annotated: 'This was counter ordered in the evening.'

will destroy any stores you may find. If you then hear of no other stores of any consequence on this side of the Fluvanna, and that[5] Baron Steuben should be still on the other side, you will cross the river and make it your principal object to strike a blow at Baron Steuben. As the corps under his command consists of part of the new levies and is the foundation on which the body of eighteen months' men lately voted by the province of Virginia will be formed, it will be of the utmost importance to defeat and disperse it. I should therefore wish you to take every means in your power of effecting this service if you should see a probability of success.[6] I likewise recommend it to you to destroy all the enemy's stores and tobacco between James River and the Dan, and if there should be a quantity of provisions or corn collected at a private house, I would have you destroy it, even although there should be no proof of its being intended for the publick service, leaving enough for the support of the family, as there is the greatest reason to apprehend that such provisions will be ultimately appropriated by the enemy to the use of General Greene's army, which from the present state of the Carolinas must depend on this province for its supplies.

I shall proceed by easy marches to Richmond, and it will probably be a business of eight or nine days from this date before I can get up my boats to that place to receive you, so that you may very well employ that time on your expedition.[7]

As it is very probable that some of the light troops of General Greene's army may be on their return to this country, you will do all you can to procure intelligence of their route. I need not tell you of what importance it will be to intercept them or any prisoners of ours from South Carolina. I would have all persons of consequence, either civil or military, brought to me before they are paroled.

Most sincerely wishing you success and placing the greatest confidence in your zeal and abilities, I am with great truth and regard, dear Tarleton,
Most faithfully yours

[CORNWALLIS]

[*Subscribed in Cornwallis's hand:*]

I will leave a detachment at Suffolk to receive you on your return. Three light waggons with good horses and a puncheon of rum will be delivered to you on application to the Quarter Master General.

---

[5] *that*: the meaning is 'if'. See p 9, note 4.

[6] A line is struck through the passage from 'Old Albermarle Court House' to ' probability of success' inclusive.

[7] This paragraph is struck through.

Syme to Tarleton, 15th June 1781   93(18): ALS

Louisa County
15th June 1781

Colonel Tarleton
Commandant, Brittish Legion

Sir

After returning you my sincere thanks for your polite treatment to me on the 4th instant, I am to ask your indulgence in a matter which I very strangley omitted on that occasion. It is to be permitted to go to the Sweet Springs for the confirmation of my health; and moreover, as I presume it was not mean'd to lay me under particular restriction, my wish is to have the limits of my parole in the same style as the other gentlemen of that day, viz, America.

When I inform you, sir, with the greatest truth, to these salubrious waters the last season I owe my existence here at present and always intended (as many know) to visit there again this summer, I hope to be oblig'd to your humanity for complying [with] or using your influence for granting this most important and favorite plan of mine, at same time not contrary in any one point to the principles of the parole.

I have the honor to be, sir,
Your most obedient and humble servant

J SYME[8]

Haldane to Syme, 28th June 1781   93(20): ACS

Head Quarters
28th June 1781

J Syme Esq

Sir

Lord Cornwallis has directed me to acquaint you that he extends the limits of your parole in the same style as the other gentlemen of that day: not acting either in a military or civil

---

[8] Born in Hanover County, Virginia, John Syme III (1729-1785) was a half-brother of Patrick Henry and for many years represented the county in the colonial House of Burgesses. Of the revolutionary persuasion, he became a member of the Virginia conventions of 1774-6 before going on to serve in the Virginia revolutionary legislature. He also served in the military line. From December 1776 to January 1778 he was a captain in the 10th Virginia Continental Regiment, and when captured by Tarleton at Charlottesville, he was the County Lieutenant of Hanover and had been serving as a colonel in the Virginia revolutionary militia. Now the subject of his letter, his parole had been limited to Hanover, Louisa, Goochland, King William and Albemarle Counties. He died at Studley, Hanover County. (Tyler, *Encyclopedia*, i, 334-5; Heitman, *Historical Register*, 530; Josephine Lindsay Bass and Becky Bonner, 'My Southern Family — John Syme III of "Rocky Mills"' (Internet, 6th June 2006); Gwathmey, *Historical Register*, 754)

capacity against the interest of Britain untill you are released from your parole or regularly exchanged.

I am, sir,
Your most obedient and most humble servant

HENRY HALDANE
Aide de camp

Cornwallis to Tarleton, 8th July 1781[9]   88(7): ADf

Cobham
July 8th 1781

Lt Colonel Tarleton

Dear Tarleton

I would have you begin your march tomorrow with the corps of cavalry and mounted infantry under your command to Prince Edward Court House, and from thence to New London in Bedford County, making the strictest enquiry in every part of the country through which you pass for amunition, clothing or stores of any kind intended for the use of the publick[10], and as there is no pressing service for your corps in this province, I must desire that you will be in no haste to return but do every thing in your power to destroy the supplies destined for the rebel army[11]. All public stores of corn and provisions are to be burnt[12].

You will publish that you are the advanced guard of my army and order under pain of military execution the people of the country to furnish waggons etc to expedite the movements of my army.[13]

[CORNWALLIS]

§ - §

---

[9] The letter as sent is published in Tarleton, *Campaigns*, 402. It includes parts of the letter of 11th June, p 225, viz, the first paragraph in so far as it relates to the provisions or corn collected at private houses, the final paragraph, and the subscription.

[10] 'the use of the publick' is substituted for 'General Greene's army in Carolina'.

[11] 'rebel' is substituted for 'southern'.

[12] After 'burnt', the following is deleted: ', and if any private person seems to have a much greater quantity than the subsistence of his family can require, I would have it destroyed if it can be done without any great inconvenience or delay to you or occasioning the burning of the owner's plantation.'

[13] This paragraph is substituted for: 'You will publish everywhere that you form the advanced guard of my army and order a magazine of provisions to be formed for me at Prince Edward Court House under pain of military execution.'

2 - Between Cornwallis and Lafayette, Heth or Steuben[14]

Lafayette to Cornwallis, 21st May 1781   *92(1): LS*

American camp
21st May 1781

Lt General Earl of Cornwallis

My Lord

The inclosed extract[15] had been directed by his Excellency Governor Jefferson to Major General Phillips but from several circumstances cou'd not reach him so soon as was expected. Your arrival at Petersburg makes me happy in a correspondance with the British General and I hasten to send papers that are so interesting to the Convention troops.

With due respect I have the honor to be, my Lord,
Your most obedient humble servant

LAFAYETTE

Lafayette to Cornwallis, 25th May 1781   *92(3): LS*

American camp
25th May 1781

Lt General Earl of Cornwallis

My Lord

At the request of Captain Miller of your army I have the honor to send you the inclosed letter[16] by a flag. Mr Murray[17], a gentleman of this State, has my permission to wait upon your Lordship respecting a flag vessell.

---

[14] For completeness these papers extend to 25th July.

[15] *inclosed extract*: not extant, but its purpose is explained in Cornwallis's reply.

[16] *inclosed letter*: not extant.

[17] James Maury Jr (1746-1840) was a grandson of Matthew Maury, a French Huguenot who had migrated to Virginia in 1718. From 1790 he would serve for forty-five years as the US Consul at Liverpool, England. His portrait is in the collection of the Virginia Historical Society (Accession N° IMGO6349). (Sue C West-Teague, *The Maury Family Tree: Descendants of Mary Anne Fontaine (1690-1755) and Matthew Maury (1686-1752)* (pp Birmingham AL, 2004, and available through the Fontaine-Maury Society, Arlington VA); Virginius Cornick Hall, *Portraits in the Collection of the Virginia Historical Society* (University Press of Virginia, 1981), 165)

With due respect I have the honor to be
Your Lordship's most obedient humble servant

LAFAYETTE

Cornwallis to Lafayette, 26th May 1781 92(5): Df

Head Quarters
26th May 1781

Major General Marquis de la Fayette etc etc etc

Sir

I have been honoured with your letters of the [21st] and [25th] instant, the first inclosing a passport for a flag vessel to carry necessaries for the Convention army, for which I am much obliged to you.

I have now the honour to inclose to you a copy of a cartel settled between General Greene and me for the exchange of prisoners that have been or may be taken in the Southern District[18], and it will give me great pleasure to see it operate for the relief of the unfortunate people of both sides.

Some Virginia militia having fallen into our hands, I shall be happy to make an immediate exchange of them for any of ours belonging to the Carolinas that may be in your possession, to save the former the distress of being sent to Charlestown.

I have the honour to be, sir,
Your most obedient and most humble servant

[CORNWALLIS]

Lafayette to Cornwallis, 27th May 1781 92(7): LS

Head Quarters
27th May 1781

Lt General Earl Cornwallis etc etc etc

My Lord

I have been honored with your letter of yesterday and am happy to find that a cartel has been settled between your Lordship and Major General Greene. The copy you are pleased to send shall in future regulate every transaction in this army to which it may relate.

---

[18] *a cartel..*: see vol IV, p 88.

Your proposition respecting some Virginia militia is perfectly agreeable but on account of distances cannot immediately take place. It shall be complied with as soon as possible and I intend having the honor of writing you in a few days on this and other matters of the same nature. It seems Captain Miller of the British Legion has business which makes it important for him to have his rout altered. I will offer him the opportunity of the first flag, as at his own request he has gone some miles into the country.

I have the honor to be
Your most obedient humble servant

LAFAYETTE

Lafayette to Cornwallis, 2nd June 1781 — 92(9): LS

Head Quarters
2nd June 1781

Lt General Earl Cornwallis

My Lord

By a letter from his Excellency the Governor of this State I am requested to apply to your Lordship and gett a passport for nine hundred hogsheads of tobacco we wish to send to our officers in Charles Town. I shall ever be happy to do any thing that may relieve British prisoners and personally oblige your Lordship. Upon the same principle I make no difficulty in sending in Mr Mauray, whom the Governor has appointed to accompany the flag vessels. His presence at your head quarters may more speedily arrange matters, and the situation of our officers in Carolina makes me very anxious that a supply be immediately forwarded.

I have the honor to be, my Lord,
Your most obedient humble servant

LAFAYETTE

Cornwallis to Lafayette, 4th June 1781 — 92(11): C

Head Quarters
4th June 1781

Marquis de la Fayette

Sir

I had the honour to receive your letter of the 2nd instant.

I shall always with great pleasure and readiness grant every indulgence to prisoners that I think consistent with my publick duty and shall be happy to embrace any opportunity of showing personal civility to you.

The present request of Governor Jefferson of a passport to export nine hundred hogsheads of tobacco to Charlestown for the use of the prisoners in confinement there is a commercial privilege of great magnitude and can only be founded upon some negociation with the Commandant of that town with which I am unacquainted.

A request from me to be permitted to open warehouses of British goods in Philadelphia to supply from the produce of their sales the wants of our prisoners in possession of the Congress would be nearly similar to this. However, I have so much respect for the humanity of the Commandant of Charlestown, who may have been influenced by uncommon distresses among your officers, that I will grant a passport under proper restrictions for the quantity that he may have agreed to receive at that place, and I shall desire to know from him by the first opportunity the extent and conditions of his consent.

The passport being delayed rendered Mr Maury's admission unnecessary, but it would not then have been convenient for me to have received any person from your side. As similar circumstances may frequently occur, I take the liberty of proposing that it may be agreed that no person in future shall expect to be admitted at either of our outposts without having previously obtained permission. And I likewise propose, if agreeable to you, that our publick correspondence may be carried on in the manner practised between General Greene and me, which was by a single dragoon, accountable for the propriety of his conduct under a flag of truce, and without being reconducted to either army.

I have the honour to be, sir, etc

[CORNWALLIS]

Heth to Phillips, 23rd May 1781   90(13): ALS

Wales
23rd May 1781

Major General Philips
Commander in Chief of the British army in Virginia

Per flag

Notwithstanding I am inform'd General Philips has refus'd a passport to Governour Jefferson to send a quantity of tobacco to Charles Town as pay for the Virginia troops who are prisoners of war there, I am fully persuaded that his feelings as a soldier and sentiments as a private gentleman will induce him to listen with attention and to favor *my* request.

As the Commandant of Charles Town was pleas'd to grant General Scott permission to receive any quantity of tobacco at that port for the purpose of supplying the *real* wants of the prisoners of war belonging to Virginia, the General and a number of other officers, upon my being indulg'd with an extension of my parole for the recovery of my health, authoris'd me to charter a vessel to send as a flag with such partial supplies as they had drawn upon their friends for, upon the faith and expectation of which some British merchants in Charles Town have advanc'd to them a very considerable sum. Now, as the whole amount of those private orders will not exceed 130 hogsheads and are to be furnished by gentlemen who very probably have not as yet sent their tobacco to the warehouses, I hope that General Philips will, in pity to what those officers have already suffer'd in an unhealthy climate and from a wish to give assistance to their future wants, grant me permission to send as soon as convenient a flag of truce for that purpose. And if he will not consent that any tobacco's now on float or in the warehouses on James River shall be ship'd as part, therefore his farther permission to hoist a flag on board such vessel as I may charter for the reception of the tobacco will be consider'd and acknowledg'd as a very great favor and indulgence.

I have the honour to be, sir,
Your most obedient servant

WILL HETH
Colonel, 3rd Virginia Regiment[19]

Cornwallis to Heth, 4th June 1781   90(15): Df

Head Quarters
4th June 1781

Colonel Heth
3rd Virginia Regiment

Sir

I received your letter of the 23rd of May addressed to the late General Phillips.

I have by this opportunity acquainted the Marquis de la Fayette that I will grant passports under proper restrictions for the quantity of tobacco that the Commandant of Charlestown has agreed to receive at that place for the use of the prisoners in confinement there, as soon as I can receive information from him of the extent and conditions of such consent. These passports will, I hope, answer the purposes mentioned and wished for by you.

I am, sir,
Your most obedient and most humble servant

[CORNWALLIS]

---

[19] As a captain under Daniel Morgan, William Heth (1750-1807) had taken part in Arnold's expedition against Canada. On 31st December 1775 he was wounded and captured during the assault on the town of Quebec. Paroled in the summer of 1776, he was shortly afterwards exchanged and became a field officer in the Virginia Continental line. Again taken prisoner in the capitulation of Charlestowm, he would remain on parole till the close of the war. He later served as a State Councillor before being appointed to the office of Collector of the Ports of Richmond, Petersburg and Bermuda Hundred, an office from which he was dismissed in 1802 due to certain infelicitous remarks about Jefferson. He died suddenly of apoplexy. A stout man of medium height, he had lost an eye in the revolutionary war. (*Wikipedia*; Heitman, *Historical Register*, 287)

Steuben to Cornwallis, 8th June 1781   *92(13): LS*

Camp in Prince Edward
June 8th 1781

Lt General Earl Cornwallis

My Lord

Lieutenant Fairlie[20], one of my aids, was unfortunate enough to be taken prisoner a few days since by Colonel Simcoe. I have wrote to Major General the Marquis de la Fayette to procure his exchange so soon as possible, and till this can be effected I shall be exceedingly obliged to your Lordship to permit him to come out on parole.

With all due respect I am, my Lord,
Your Lordship's most obedient humble servant

STEUBEN
Major General

Lafayette to Cornwallis, 20th June 1781   *92(14): LS*

Head Quarters
20th June 1781

Lt General Earl Cornwallis

My Lord

As soon as I received your Lordship's letter of the 4th June I endeavoured to obtain a perfect knowledge of the permission given to our officers by the British Commandant in Charles Town. It luckily happened that Brigadier General Scott had settled this business, and the inclosed letter from him will I hope remove every difficulty. I am convinced that your professions are sincere, and as I wish every transaction between you and me to be marked by a soldier like frankness, I have no doubt but that you will admit Mr Mauray to a conference with a person from your side and immediately grant the necessary passport. Should General Scott's proposition be agreeable, I wou'd beg leave to propose a meeting between him and General O'Hara, as upon the Commandant's permission engagements have been entered into which we are obliged to comply with in a given time. I will not examine in its extent your Lordship's objection to the sending tobacco to Charles Town for the relief of the American prisoners. It may, however, be observed that the Convention officers dispose of bills of

---

[20] James Fairlie (c. 1757-1830) was a Continental officer who had been serving as an aide-de-camp to Steuben since July 1778. Why Steuben should refer to his rank as lieutenant is uncertain, given that in a letter of 8th January 1781 to Greene he refers to it as captain. By the close of the war Fairlie would be promoted to major. (Heitman, *Historical Register*, 221; *The Greene Papers*, vii, 76)

exchange, which is a British commodity, and receive gold from American purchasers in return. I will not say that these bills are converted into English goods, but the supposition is reasonable. We sell tobacco, which is an American commodity, in Charles Town, for which we receive gold and apply it among the people from whom it is received. I shou'd think it inhuman were we to prevent the British prisoners in our hands from negotiating British bills of exchange. Your Lordship, I am persuaded, will consider the sale of American tobacco in a similar point of view. If I spoke in my private capacity, I wou'd add that there cou'd be no good argument against admitting certain British commodities to be disposed of at Philadelphia for the discharge of any debts incurred by British troops in the possession of the Congress.

Inclosed are some letters[21] which the Convention officers have requested might be sent to your Lordship. The flag vessel must by this time have arrived at George Town.

I have the honor to return several letters[22] which fell into our hands. They are of a private nature and can have no interference with public measures.

I readily agree, my Lord, to the regulations you have proposed respecting flags. By a dragoon's being accountable for the propriety of his conduct under a flag I suppose, however, your Lordship means that all punishment upon a proper representation is to come from those who send him.

I have the honor to be, my Lord,
Your most obedient servant

LAFAYETTE

Enclosure (1)
Scott to Lafayette, 19th June 1781   *92(19): ALS*

June the 19th 1781

Major General the Marquis Lafayette

I am honour'd, my dear Marquis, with your obliging favour of the 15th instant respecting the permission for sending tobacco to the prisoners at Haddril's Point. I am happy that I have it in my power to inclose you the original permission, together with the extract of my letter to the Commandant of Charles Town relative thereto. I make no doubt that the inclos'd papers will remove every obstruction, but should his Lordship wish an explanation of the whole or any part of this business, I am at no great distance from you and will on the shortest notice with much pleasure meet any gentleman from Lord Cornwallis's army in order to remove every possible doubt that may arise with respect to this business.

---

[21] *some letters*: see pp 241-3.

[22] *several letters*: not extant.

As this is a matter in which my honour is in some degree at risk, I could wish to hear from you as soon as circumstances will admit.

I have the honor to be, dear Marquis,
Your obedient servant

CH^S SCOTT

Enclosure (2)
Extract, Scott to Balfour, 30th January 1781　　　　　　　　　　*92(16): C*

January 30th 1781

I murst therfore beg your permission that tobacco be sent to this port in such quantity as may be thought necessary to pay the debts already contracted and make the prisoners comfortable during captivity.

Enclosure (3)
Fraser to Scott, 30th January 1781　　　　　　　　　　*92(17): LS*

Charlestown
January 30th 1781

Brigadier General Scott

Sir

I am directed by the Commandant to acquaint you that he has no kind of objection to the requests you make respecting tobacco being sent here for the purpose you mention and General Woodford's and Lt Colonel Ball's baggage etc being sent by the flag.

I have the honor to be, sir,
Your most obedient humble servant

C FRASER[23]
Town Major

---

[23] Charles Fraser was a brother of Thomas Fraser (see vol I, p 243, note 11). As Town Major of Charlestown, he was responsible to the Commandant for policing the town, whereas the Board of Police, despite its name, acted essentially as a judicial tribunal. Naturally resented by townsfolk of the revolutionary persuasion, who in consequence had few good words to say about him, he has received a bad press. He nevertheless deserves a more balanced, less embittered assessment of his conduct in carrying out what was inevitably a thankless task. (Johnson, *Traditions*, 271-2, 362; Garden, *Anecdotes* (1st series), 228; McCowen Jr, *Charleston, 1780-82*, ch II)

Lafayette to Cornwallis, 25th June 1781

92(22): LS

Head Quarters
25th June 1781

Lt General Earl Cornwallis

My Lord

As the time for the first delivery of British prisoners, agreeable to the 11th article of the cartel establish'd between your Lordship and General Greene, is not very remote, I have to request that the American commissary, Mr Ewell[24], may have permission to go into your lines for the purpose of conferring with your commissary on several official matters which it is necessary they shou'd arrange as soon as possible.

I have the honor to be
Your Lordship's most obedient humble servant

LAFAYETTE

Cornwallis to Lafayette, 28th June 1781

92(24): Df

Head Quarters
28th June 1781

Major General Marquis de la Fayette etc etc etc

Sir

I have had the honour to receive your letters of the 20th and 25th instant by two separate flags of truce.

I have no doubt remaining that the Commandant of Charlestown has agreed to receive a certain quantity of tobacco for the purpose of discharging the debts of the prisoners in confinement there, and to prove my desire of seconding his intentions for relieving the distresses of those prisoners and of acting in a frank and open manner with you I will in the mean time, without giving you further trouble, grant a passport for four hundred hogsheads of tobacco upon your notifying to me that the vessell (with its name) in which it is shipped is ready to sail, objecting only to its going from James or York Rivers, and provided the vessell and tobacco is not within the immediate reach of the British troops at the time of this notification, which I hope will not appear to you to be unreasonable restrictions.

---

[24] Either Charles Ewell (?-1830) or Thomas Winder Ewell (?-1784), both of whom were captains in a Virginia State regiment. One had been seconded to the commissariat of prisoners, whereas the other, contrary to Heitman's assertion, was continuing to serve in the field. (Heitman, *Historical Register*, 220; Revolutionary pension application of Henry Whiteman of Randolph County, Virginia, 23rd October 1832)

This quantity of tobacco will be worth a considerable sum of money at Charlestown. However, if I learn from the Commandant that it is insufficient to answer the purposes intended by this indulgence, I shall readily grant another passport to the extent that appears to him to be necessary.

This point being reduced to so simple a state renders it unnecessary to give Generals Scott and O'Hara the trouble of a conference, but if Mr Mauray wishes to come within our posts, I have no sort of objection to receive him at the time the passport is applied for.

Being extremely desirous to make the situation of prisoners as little distressing and their exchanges as expeditious as circumstances will admit of, I can have no objection to your proposal of a meeting of the commissaries. Your commissary will therefore be received when he presents himself at our outposts.

My meaning with respect to the footing on which dragoons are who carry flags of truce entirely coincides with yours.

I have the honour to be, sir, etc

[CORNWALLIS]

Cornwallis to Lafayette, 18th July 1781

92(28): C

Head Quarters
18th July 1781

Major General Marquis de la Fayette

Sir

A number of your prisoners have arrived from Charlestown agreeable to the cartel settled for the Southern Department. Part of them have already been landed, and the officers in whose charge they came have directions to deliver the remainder to persons appointed by you to receive them for receipts upon an assurance from you that an equal number of our prisoners shall be sent with as much dispatch as possible to James City Island, where the flag vessels will remain to receive them. And trusting that your prisoners will remain in a state of inactivity untill a reasonable interval elapses to enable us to put our prisoners on military duty, I have etc

CORNWALLIS

Lafayette to Cornwallis, 19th July 1781

92(30): LS

Head Quarters
19th July 1781

Lt General Earl Cornwallis

My Lord

I find by a representation from my commissary of prisoners that he could not get yours to agree upon an exchange of the volunteer militia dragoons of the American army taken by your Lordship's troops. It seems he considered them as superior to common privates and grounded his refusal on this. These men, my Lord, are of the same character as the other militia, perform the same tours of duty, are subject to the same laws, and have the distinction only of volunteer dragoons from their consenting to the horse service in preference to the infantry. I flatter myself with your orders for their relief, but should any thing remain which may be thought to require further explanation, perhaps it could be obtained best by an interview between an officer of your army and one from this. In this case I leave it to your Lordship to fix the time and place of meeting.

I have the honor to be, my Lord,
Your Lordship's most obedient servant

LAFAYETTE

Cornwallis to Lafayette, 24th July 1781

92(32): Df

Head Quarters
24th July 1781

Major General Marquis de la Fayette

Sir

I have been honoured with your letter relative to the objections made by our commissary of prisoners to the exchange of your volunteers, and to put an end to farther altercation between the commissaries on that subject I have given directions that in future the volunteers shall be considered and exchanged as privates.

I have the honour to be, sir, etc

[CORNWALLIS]

Lafayette to the British officer   *92(34): LS*
   having charge of the American prisoners, 25th July 1781

Head Quarters
25th July 1781

To the British officer
   having charge of the American prisoners

Sir

Lt General the Earl Cornwallis writes me on the 18th of this month: 'A number of your prisoners have arrived from Charlestown agreeable to the cartel settled for the Southern Department. Part of them have already been landed, and the officers in whose charge they came have directions to deliver the remainder to persons appointed by you to receive them for receipts upon an assurance from you that an equal number of our prisoners shall be sent with as much dispatch as possible to James City Island, where the flag vessels will remain to receive them.'

I have appointed Captain Ewell, the American commissary, to receive and receipt for our prisoners upon the above conditions, which shall be observed strictly, as well as their remaining inactive 'till exchanged by an equal number of British which are on their way from General Greene's army to James Town.

As our prisoners will remain in the vicinity of James Town or Williamsburg till fully exchanged, I shall of course consider them as under your flag, altho' removed from your officers.

I have the honor to be, sir,
Your most obedient servant

LAFAYETTE

§ - §

3 - With or concerning the Troops of Convention

Nutt to Cornwallis, 27th May 1781   6(133): ALS

Frederick Town
Maryland
May 27th 1781

My Lord

I beg leave to address your Lordship on the subject of an exchange, as the cause assign'd by Major General Phillips for detaining me does not any longer exist, the Convention officers being separated from their men by a resolve of the American Congress.

I had the strongest reasons to suppose without further application to have had the honor of serving under your Lordship's command before this time, but hitherto every means that I cou'd devise to so desirable an end have been frustrated.

From repeated experience of friendship and kindness I am sensible your Lordship will commiserate my situation and view the life of idleness I have led for almost four years (so repugnant to the character and principles of my profession) in the light it deserves, when I cannot in the least doubt of your extricating me out of my present difficulties.

I have the honor to be, my Lord,
Your Lordship's most obedient and very humble servant

G NUTT[25]
Lieutenant, 33rd Infantry

Hamilton to Cornwallis, 30th May 1781   6(166): ALS

Frederick's Town
30th May 1781

Earl Cornwallis

My Lord

From disagreeable reports[26] spread here for some days past and for which I hope there is no foundation, I think it my duty to send your Lordship extracts of two letters wrote Major General Phillips. Those extracts contain a request made by Lieutenant Nutt of your

---

[25] George Anson Nutt had spent his entire service in the 33rd Regiment. Commissioned an ensign there on 28th August 1771, he was promoted to lieutenant on 26th October 1775. (*Army Lists*)

[26] *disagreeable reports*: of Phillips' death.

Lordship's regiment, who I shall think myself happy in contributing to serve and gratify in what he now wishes, which with power granted me I make no doubt of obtaining.

The other two extracts relate to Mr Weir[27], Surgeon General, whose case in being detained, tho' long since exchanged, I am persuaded your Lordship will look on as singularly hard. The cause of his detention I have given as I received it, and it is your Lordship alone that can judge if the fact is properly stated and what mode of relief can be administer'd.

I have the honor to be, my Lord,
Your Lordship's most obedient and most humble servant

JAS HAMILTON[28]

Enclosure (1)
Extract, Hamilton to Phillips, 23rd April 1781

6(168): C

Frederick's Town
Maryland
23rd April 1781

I have now to inform you that orders are come here for Colonel Wood to detain Mr Surgeon General Weir on account of Doctor Oliphant's being so to the southward after having been exchanged and the officer of the British, for whom he was, having done his duty in the corps he belonged to near two months.

Colonel Wood is directed to acquaint General Green of this immediately, and I hope, sir, that you will take the necessary steps that Mr Weir may have that liberty he is intitled to by being so long exchang'd, and who on account of the troops here has sacrafised both interest and pleasure.

---

[27] John Weir (?-1819) had been acting as Surgeon General to the Convention army. Although exchanged, he was now detained by the revolutionary authorities on account of the detention of Dr David Oliphant at Charlestown (see vol II, p 112, note 106). Both would soon be freed. After the war he served for several years in Jamaica before eventually retiring on half pay in 1798. He returned to active service in 1810 as the first Director General of the Army Medical Department and retired again in 1815 on an annual allowance of £1,500. (Johnston, *Commissioned Officers in the Medical Service*, 46)

[28] Laird of Murdostoun, James Hamilton (?-1803) was Lt Colonel of the 21st Regiment (the Scots Fusiliers) when he was promoted in 1777 to the local rank of brigadier general in America. As such, he took part in Burgoyne's offensive, commanding the British 2nd brigade. Part of the so-called Convention army which capitulated at Saratoga, he was now the senior British officer with the Convention prisoners at Fredericktown, Maryland. In later life he would see action as a major general in the West Indies. He died at his estate of Murdostoun. (*Army Lists*)

Enclosure (2)
Extract, Hamilton to Phillips, 21st May 1781 6(168): C

Frederick's Town
Maryland
21st May 1781

Lieutenant Nutt of the 33rd Regiment, from his commanding a detachment of it, has many accompts to settle and wishes to be allowed to join his regiment to the southward for this purpose, and which I believe may be obtained if permitted, likewise that for many of the officers were I indulged with the power.

Mr Weir's cruel situation I wrote fully to you on in my last and hope no time will be lost in explaining it to Earl Cornwallis, from whose orders in detaining Doctor Oliphant of the Americans this has proceeded, and whose orders, tho' no doubt well founded, strikes hard on this gentleman.

Hamilton to Phillips, 3rd June 1781 6(170): ALS

Fredericks Town
3rd June 1781

Major General Phillips

Sir

The officers of the Troops of Convention being order'd to Hartford in Conecticut and the flag of truce not proceeding to George Town as requested, I am under the necessity of applying for two thousand pounds in specie, which I beg you will order for the relief of the officers, it being impossible for them to move without it.

I expect that leave will be granted to Mr Giddes and Mr Mutzell[29] of the Germans to go from this to the Marquis de Fayette's head quarters, there to receive it, in the event of the flag's having sailed or received orders not to proceed to George Town.

I have the honor to be, sir,
Your most obedient and most humble servant

JA^S HAMILTON
Brigadier General

---

[29] Mutzell was no doubt paymaster to the German troops of Convention. He has not been otherwise identified.

Riedesel to Cornwallis, 3rd June 1781[30]

6(139): LS

Brooklyn
3rd June 1781

The Rt Hon Earl of Cornwallis etc etc etc

My Lord

Permit me to report to your Lordship the situation of a flag of truce sent with the Commander in Chief's permission by the late General Phillips in the spring of the year to Chesapeak with money, cloathing, stores and refreshments for the Troops of Convention under the care of my Deputy Quarter Master General, Captain Gerlach[31], provided with a proper passport from General Washington and orders for the vessel to go into Chesapeak and there receive farther directions from Mr Jefferson, the rebel Governor of Virginia.

The copies of letters which I beg leave to inclose under cover with this contains every transaction that has passed respecting our flag of truce, which is now laying in Hampton Road, that I can obtain for your Lordship's farther information. I am informed there is an unopened letter from Mr Jefferson to General Phillips left among his papers in which there is scarce a doubt is inclosed a passport for the ship's proceeding to Alexandria, from whence the money, stores etc are to be conveyed by land to the Troops of Convention: for the English to York Town and Frederick Town, and for the Germans to Winchester.

I should now take the liberty of beging your Lordship to have the letter before mentioned, addressed to General Phillips, opened and to give the farther requisite orders for the flag vessel's proceeding to its destination at Alexandria as the distressed Troops of Convention are in the greatest want of every article in it, had not Lieutenant Noble, aid-de-camp to the late General Phillips, mentioned an accident that happened to an American flag which, as the Americans are ever disposed to seize any pretence of retaliating, might endanger ours meeting a proper reception. The circumstances of this affair, as I understand, were briefly as follows. A rebel vessel came down the bay and, one of ours coming up with her, she (the rebel vessel) fired several shot and afterwards, perhaps seeing she could not escape, hoisted a white flag and said she was going under a flag of truce to Charles Town. In consequence of this very improper conduct it was thought proper to stop the vessel and she is now, as I am informed, at or near Portsmouth.

After having detailed all these particulars, I only presume to request your Lordship to act and give such orders as your Lordship may think most proper in this affair for forwarding the vessel to the Troops of Convention; but as I find myself left (by the very melancholy loss of

---

[30] Probably received from Ensign Amiel on 26th June.

[31] Gerlach had been serving as deputy QMG to the Brunswick troops for some time, having taken part as such in Burgoyne's offensive.

my much esteemed friend[32]) the senior officer of the unfortunate Troops of Convention in this country, I think it a duty to represent to your Lordship that those troops are destitute of every comfort and almost every necessary of life and that the money, cloathing etc reaching them with the least possible delay through your Lordship's kind assistance can alone alleviate their very painful situation.

I have the honor to be with all respect and regard, my Lord,
Your Lordship's most obedient and very humble servant

RIEDESEL

Enclosure (1)
Jefferson to Gerlach, 31st March 1781   *6(141): C*

Richmond
March 31st 1781

Captain Gerlach

Sir

The departure of the German as well as British Troops of Convention from this State is a circumstance probably unknown to you before your arrival here. I am not informed to what place they were destined but believe it was to York Town and Lancaster in Pensylvania, the nearest navigation to which is the head of Chesapeak Bay. I have, however, dispatched the letters transmitted me, by express to Congress for their determination on the several articles of your application and expect an answer within about a fortnight from this date, which shall be certainly transmitted you the moment I receive it.

I have the honor to be with much respect, sir,
Your most obedient servant

TH JEFFERSON

---

[32] *friend*: Phillips.

Enclosure (2)
Phillips to Gerlach, 6th April 1781   6(145): C

Portsmouth, Virginia
April 6th 1781

Captain Gerlach

Sir

I have received a letter from Governor Jefferson, an extract of which concerning you I inclose you, and make no doubt but you will be at liberty to go with your flag up the Chesapeak, from whence it will not be difficult to convey the cloathing, necessarys and refreshments to the Troops of Convention should they be, as Governor Jefferson imagines, in Pensylvania.

I take for granted you will be extreamly careful not to suffer any of the people on board with you to violate the flag of truce, but that they will act with all becoming caution and propriety.

You will inform me as soon as possible of the resolution of the Congress upon your subject.

I am, sir,
Your most humble servant

W PHILLIPS

Enclosure (3)
Extract, Jefferson to Phillips, 31st March 1781   6(147): C

Richmond
March 31st 1781

I have duly received your favour dated New York, March 8th. The removal of the German Troops of Convention also from this State was a circumstance probably not known to you at that date. I am as yet uninformed of the post at which they have been stationed but believe at York Town and Lancaster in Pensylvania, the nearest navigation to which is the head of Chesapeak Bay. The permissions desired for facilitating the delivery of stores on board the flag are consequently no longer within our gift, but I have forwarded the applications to Congress and shall hope shortly to communicate their consent to the gentleman conducting the flag.

Enclosure (4)
Gerlach to Jefferson, 29th April 1781   6(149): C

On board the flag of truce *General de Riedesel*
Hampton Road
the 29th April 1781

Sir

I have been waiting with great anxiety to receive your Excellency's answer to my letter of the 27th March last, which your Excellency was pleased to inform me you had forwarded to Congress for their determination.

I beg leave to inform your Excellency I am very desirous to get the business of the flag of truce settled as soon as possible and to propose, if it can be done without any trouble to your Excellency or the executive power of Virginia, permission to go from this place with the flag of truce to the head of Chesapeak Bay or to the nearest place which your Excellency thinks proper and wait there the determination of Congress, and that your Excellency will be pleased to give directions to render me every proper assistance and to prevent all possible delays.

I have the honor to be, sir,
Your Excellency's most obedient and most humble servant

H GERLACH
Captain

Enclosure (5)
Jefferson to Gerlach, 3rd May 1781   6(143): C

Richmond
May 3rd 1781

Sir

I am very sorry for the delay which has happened in sending the passport. I received it the 20th of April and sent it the same day to Major General Baron Steuben to be forwarded. He immediately delivered my letter covering it to an officer with orders to proceed. The papers being directed to General Phillips, the officer was uncertain whether he was at Portsmouth or with the British army then coming up the river, and the movements here since prevented his going on with the letter... He will set out, I am in hopes, this day... A letter from General Phillips to me with a very improper address came to hand since the 20th of April, obliged me on seeing the officer to day to recall my letter of that date, which was written in the stile I had always used towards him, and to put the passport under an address adapted to that which he had been pleased to use towards me...

I shall be sorry if this shall prevent your being availed of the passport, as it will produce an eternal bar to the passage of any thing through this State to the Convention Troops...

I have had yet no reason to repent the services I have endeavoured to render the *German* part of the Convention officers and soldiers, and for them only feel concern should they be cut off from supplies by that want of temper and decency which seems to be introducing on the part of our enemies in this State. To yourself personally I wish to give every assurance of regard, and that

I am with much respect, sir,
Your most obedient and most humble servant

TH JEFFERSON

PS

The German Convention Troops are stationed at Winchester in this State, which has occasioned the passport to be made out for Alexandria, that being equally convenient to both the German and British troops.

Cornwallis to Hamilton, 6th July 1781 88(3): C

Head Quarters
6th July 1781

Brigadier General Hamilton commanding the Convention Troops

Sir

I have received your letter addressed to the late General Phillips desiring a supply of two thousand pounds for the use of the officers of the Convention Troops in the event of the flag vessell not being permitted to proceed to George Town.

Having dispatched that vessell some time ago with a passport, I hope your necessities are before now relieved. If they are not, be pleased to apply for permission for the two officers to go to Portsmouth and to return with the money, as I cannot spare so much from my stock in the field. I have given directions to the commanding officer there to comply with your requisition.

I have likewise been honoured with your letter relating to Lieutenant Nutt and to Surgeon General Wier.

I shall entirely approve of any steps that you may think proper to take for effecting Mr Nutt's exchange or, failing that, in procuring leave for him to come to the regiment to settle his accounts. I have desired to know from the Commandant of Charlestown the particulars of the cause of Doctor Oliphant's detention, which I trust will appear to furnish no good ground for retaliation upon Mr Wier.

I have the honour to be, sir,
Your most obedient and most humble servant

[CORNWALLIS]

§ - §

4 - Intelligence

Intelligence, 4th May 1781   6(45): C

Friday night
4th May 1781

Intelligence —— Washington may have 2,500 effective men. Philadelphia is in a very unguarded state. It is the opinion of the most judicious men there that now, before guards are fixed at Mud Fort etc, one barge of 50 good men would easily destroy the 2 magazines in town of powder etc etc. Provision they have trifling to mention, there being great abundance, particularly of flower, in the hands of trading people. They have a grand arsenal 70 miles distant at Carlisle in Cumberland. Here 200 artificers were lately sent. General Wayne is under marching orders with 1,200 men to join General Green with all expedition but has been labouring some weeks to collect his men — not yet effected. La Fayette doubtless must be with Green before now with such of his 1,500 men as have not deserted him (I fear of desparate principle) that will give little quarter to such as the fate of war may put in their power.

Baltimore makes the appearance of defence, has little public provision in town except a very considerable quantity of flower and tobacco in Smith's & Co Stores on the County Wharfe. Some powder etc etc in the Market House. Their chief magazine 8 miles out on Little York Road[33]. In Talbot County (eastern shore) at their court house about two or 3 miles from good water on Miles River they have one 18lb cannon, four 6lb ditto, two of which are brass, and 1,000 stand of arms. Those are divided among their own and the neighbouring militia.

I would now beg leave to observe that, in order to the earliest and best intelligence being expeditiously and safely conveyed from the northward to you, I have presumed to form a scheme with two men in Philadelphia, gentlemen of property and of the first characters, to collect every matter of consequence and forward it to a person I have provided at [*blank*], who on any emergency agrees to ride to Mr [*blank*] or myself. In order effectually to establish this plan I enter'd on the scheme of procuring suitable stages etc etc where proper

---

[33] After 'Little York Road' there is the following interlineation: 'at one Towson's. Anapolis magazine at the head of Severn is 10 miles out on Baltimore Road.'

confidents would give every necessary aid to the above bearer. In this work I found difficulties too great to surmount within the time I had allowed for my return home. Particularly, I found some whose principles and conduct had always been as my own, however finding the promiscuous ruin done by your bargemen, where determined in future never more to expose themselves to the resentment and ravages of their country by striving to assist Britain. To have every thing to fear from their country, while numbers of them experienced the severest depredations by the servants of Britain, was and is a trial to them too great. One instance of this kind I think deserves mentioning, viz: one [blank] on [blank]'s Island, who had been forced to pay treble taxes and suffered many other real evils by his country, was by Stephen Myster[34] and his company plundered of every thing portable. Alas, these efforts discourage most of your friends, nay really turn numbers from you. They encourage and strengthen your enemies — in fact of late have been the efficient cause of a great variety of guards being fixed, the militia called out, to save themselves from indiscriminate ruin, which the great laws of self preservation influence to prevent. Here I am constrain'd to observe that in my neighbourhood are a number of guards forming, which I had every reason to believe would no more be the case in this part, nor could it ever have been the case but from the real danger the friends of Britain find themselves in. I am convinced I could prevail that an arm should scarcely by an individual be lifted against Britain in my neighbourhood, or even in the county, could a final period be put to such indiscriminate ravages, for your friends would then be neither afraid nor ashamed to appear and your enemies, however clothed with power, would find every of their efforts fail, their best concerted schemes die in the execution. However, in these matters I presume not to dictate, yet ardently pray the Father of all Wisdom to inspire and influence you to the truly wise and great conduct of so conquering as to save, *particularly your friends*. May Phillips, may Arnold, may every officer of the British line in America lead their brave soldiery to the effectual ruin of every limb of rebellion, terminating in a glorious conquest and real freedom by the restoration of good and salutary laws. This ejaculation among others is the daily employ of

[blank]

Chaney to Noel, May 1781   2(64): DS

Intelligence

Baltimore, 9th May. There is a battery of 20 guns, mostly 18 pounders; a large magazine of powder and ball in Market Street; about 500 stands of arms in the Market House; a large quantity of powder at Townsend's Tavern 8 miles from Baltimore; quarter[35] gun powder, Forrest Road; a large quantity of bar iron and flour in the different stores and 500 hogsheads of tobacco; 15 arm'd vessels, mostly smal and badly manned.

---

[34] A son of Abraham Mister of Dorchester County, Maryland, Stephen Mister was one of the most notorious picaroons infesting Chesapeake Bay. Sailing in and from the guts and creeks of the islands and those of the mainland, he indiscriminately plundered homes and vessels. Despite a high price on his head, he was never caught. (Donald G Shomette, *Pirates of the Chesapeake: Being a True History of Pirates, Picaroons, and Raiders on Chesapeake Bay, 1610-1807* (Tidewater Publishers MD, 1985))

[35] *quarter*: of a hundredweight.

Head of Elk. 2,000 barrels flour, some tobacco and bar iron, no fortification, but numbers of militia.

Annapolis. Horn Point Fort — 12 eighteen and twelve pounders — 20 soldiers doing duty — 250 militia of the town — 2 field pieces, one on each side of the State House door — 7 or 8 more on the west side of the town — magazines of provision on the dock where Joseph Williams lives — 4 arm'd vessels — the brigg *Nesbit* of 14 guns and 20 men — the sloop *Porpus* of 10 guns and 2 look-out boats sailed the 11th instant for the eastern shore to get the Dorcester and Worcester militia to burn the buildings of the loyal inhabitants on the Tanjier and other islands to prevent their trading with the British.

Frederick Town. 20 waggon loads of powder on the west side of the town leading to Hagars Town and a large quantity of small arms with some field pieces. About five hundred of the Convention Troops imprisoned on the east side of the town in the barracks. On the road to George Town, about a mile and a half from the barracks, there is a magazine of powder and arms. Privates letters may be conveyed to the officer commanding the Convention Troops with safty.

JACOB CHANEY[36]

Wm Noel[37]

? to Leslie, 5th June 1781[38]   *2(62): L*

Tuesday morning

To General Leslie

Sir

From the best information there are about seven thousand barrels of flour and seventy or eighty thousand weight of bread in Baltimore.

A hundred barrels of powder in town and a considerable quantity in a magazine about six miles distant.

---

[36] Jacob Chaney (1715-1801) was born in South River, Anne Arundel County, Maryland, to which place his grandfather, Richard, had migrated from England. By 1748 Jacob had moved to what became Pittsylvania County, Virginia, where he would end his days at Laurel Grove. The intelligence now provided by him may have resulted from a visit to family or friends in Maryland. (Information from Bill Hyatt and Preston Glenn Humphrey, 17th May 2006)

[37] Perhaps William Nowell, a lieutenant in the Royal Navy, who may have been in command of a gunboat blockading Baltimore, in which case he would have had the opportunity of conveying Chaney's intelligence down the Chesapeake to Portsmouth. (Syrett and DiNardo eds, *The Commissioned Sea Officers*, 334)

[38] Leslie assumed the command at Portsmouth on 27th May. From this and internal evidence the date can be deduced.

The French and American armies are principally supplied with bread from Baltimore.

They are building a galley that will carry four eighteen pounders to defend the bay, and the planters on the River Patuxent have a schooner of ten or twelve guns for its protection. Five schooners and one sloop are loading with tobacco in that river. The schooners, being all outward bound, will carry near four hundred hogsheads. [torn] vessels from Baltimore are loading [torn] [Patowmack?] River. A gentleman at Port Tobacco wrote to his friend in the Patuxent that there was an embarkation of troops taking place at Portsmouth and their destination suppos'd to be against Baltimore. The fall of Continental money has made great impression on the people in general, and the rapid depreciation of their State money convinces them that it must soon expire. It is the opinion of Mr [erased] and Mr [erased] that nine out of ten in the province wish to be under British government and that three thousand men would in a short time subdue it. General Wayne with ten or twelve hundred Continental troops was near Frederick Town on his way to the southern army, and about the 12th or 14th of May was order'd back. In Prince Charles County the people in general are arm'd and refuse to pay taxes. One such people, who have a settlement back of Frederic, are prepared to take the earliest opportunity to join the King's forces and will bring in a number of the best horses in the province. [torn], who lives about thirty [miles] [torn], assured me he would have it in his power to capture all the principal officers who (if the British troops mov'd towards Baltimore) would retreat into the country. There are eight or ten guns mounted in the fort and about a hundred Continental soldiers etc etc.

[torn]

St George to Leslie, 30th June 1781   6(265): L

June 30th 1781

Sir

I beg leave to inform you that on Thursday night last two boats with armed men robed Mr Lowry[39] and Colonel Celden[40] of their most valuable goods and slaves. The bearer, a poor man, was also robed by them of his all. He can describe both boats and people to you. The boats were repaired that day in Harrises Creek, a south branch of Back River. I escaped the same fate of my neighbours by my living a few miles higher up the river. They threaten me with death. This evil is owing to some people that is easy removed from hence, which I think would be an advantage, and a great one too, to His Majesty's Service, as every one of them are violent rebels and great corrupters of His Majesty's subjects. I give you an account of their names, title and place of abode, and humbly submit to you, sir, what is to be done.

---

[39] John Lowry was a loyalist living on Back River in Elizabeth City County. (*The Cornwallis Papers*)

[40] Colonel Richard Selden (*pre*-1725-1789) was the grandson of a lawyer who had come to Virginia in 1699 and settled in Elizabeth City County. Appointed Deputy King's Attorney for the county in 1752, Richard soon moved on to Lancaster County, where, besides serving as a Justice of the Peace and for two years as a Burgess, he was apparently commissioned a colonel in the militia. Of the loyalist persuasion, he had removed by 1781 to Back River, rejoining the extended family of Seldens in Elizabeth City County near to his younger brother William, who was rector of the church at Hampton. (Tyler, *Encyclopedia*, i, 321)

Commodore Ja^s Barron[41])
) lives in Warwick County, about three miles from Frank Jones
Colonel Ro Cooper[42]   )

upon James River, where a boat ought to land to bring them two off. Jones is about seven miles from Newport News up the north side of the river. A very small party of men will be sufficient for the purpose. Captain Willm Davis[43] and Miss^r Armestead[44] of Hampton - a small party will do for them as for the others before mention'd. Two boats are a-fiting out upon Harrises Creek to obstruct the trade to Portsmouth, which are easily destroy'd, and at the same time and from the same place to bring off Captain Ned Mallery[45] and Williams, a ship carpenter. I believe it would be proper to take Mallery and Williams before the destruction of the boats for fear of an alarm. I have a deserving wife and five small children that are dear to me and has no other dependance but me for their support. Notwithstanding this or any other cause, I shall be happy to receive your commands and I promise you, sir, upon the faith of a loyal subject that I will be ready to obey and to the utmost of my power execute them, as the commands of any other British general during the war. I received the inclos'd from a real friend to Government.

I have the honour to be with the most profound respect, sir,
Your most obedient and very humble servant

[H U St GEORGE][46]

---

[41] James Barron (1740-1787) was a commodore in the Virginia Navy who would be awarded 12,127 acres in recognition of his revolutionary service. He was the son of Samuel Barron, who some forty years earlier had commanded at Fort George on Point Comfort, and the father of James Jr (1769-1851), who would later have an undistinguished career in the US Navy. (Gwathmey, *Historical Register*, 43; Tyler, *Encyclopedia*, i, 181; *Appletons*'; information from Hope Stanley of Hertford NC, 5th March 2002)

[42] Commissioned a major in the Elizabeth City revolutionary militia in 1775, Roe Cooper was still serving in this capacity in May 1777. By mid 1781 he had apparently been promoted to lt colonel or colonel, but whether he was still active has not been ascertained. (Gwathmey, *Historical Register*, 178; *Va Military Records*, 454)

[43] Of the various William Davises or Davieses listed in Gwathmey's *Historical Register* and in the *Va Military Records*, none has been identified as the person mentioned here.

[44] Of the Armisteads listed in the enclosure, the one referred to here may be Moss, who would later be seized and confined in a prison ship at Yorktown. Moss was a descendant of William Armistead (*c*. 1660-*c*. 1715), a High Sheriff of Elizabeth City County, a Burgess and a major of militia, and of his last wife Rebecca, née Moss. Of their sons, one was named Moss, who may have been the person named here or his father. (Tyler, *Encyclopedia*, i, 173; Josephine Lindsay Bass and Becky Bonner, 'My Southern Family – Maj. William Armistead I' (Internet, 10th June 2006))

[45] The context suggests that Edward ('Ned') Mallory may have been a sea captain, perhaps master of the *William*, which was permitted to set sail for Martinique in October 1776. Like others of his surname in Elizabeth City County, he was descended from Roger Mallory, who came to Virginia before 1660. (Gwathmey, *Historical Register*, 496; Tyler, *Encyclopedia*, i, 283)

[46] Hamilton Usher St George, whose erased signature may be deduced from his next letter, raised crops and livestock at various localities: on Hog Island (1,750 acres); in Surry County adjoining James River (2,500 acres); at another locality adjoining the same river (900 acres); on Back River in Elizabeth City County (1,050 acres); and elsewhere

PS

I am told the pirates' place of rendevous is Nancock up the bay. I am told also that their force consists of three boats and fifty or sixty men.

Be pleased to remove my name from its place.

Enclosure
List of disaffected persons and others   *3(18):* **D**

People who have corn to spare in Elizabeth Citiy County

Those marked 'B' are very bad men, in other words damned rebels

B.   Captain John Tabb, a majestrate

       Augustine Moore

       William Moore

B.   John Cary, a captain and senator, has corn and oats. A rebel indeed.

       Thos Parsons

B.   John Amistead

B.   Thos Allen

B.   Ja^s Bray Armistead, comisary, has country corn.

B.   Ned Allen

---

in the same county (700 acres). In 1776 he ran foul of the revolutionaries when he supplied cattle and provisions from Hog Island to the British Army at Boston. His action caused much resentment among the local populace, who burned down his house, drove off his cattle, and locked him up with his overseer and slaves. He also got into hot water when he was charged by the revolutionaries with holding a treasonable correspondence with the deposed royal Governor, Lord Dunmore, and put on trial for his life. Now, in 1781, he would soon begin supplying the army at Yorktown, an act which would lead to his house being ransacked on the night of 22nd September by the crews of four whaleboats in the revolutonary service and to his property being eventually confiscated. Destitute, he and his family sought shelter at New York after the capitulation, presumably spirited away in one of the flag vessels to save him from the halter. By 1783 he had taken passage for England while his wife, a native of Virginia, returned to her friends and relatives there, eventually dying of a broken heart. In the meantime he entrusted others with interim relief, including an award of £1,043, provided for the family on Cornwallis's recommendation (see Memorandum for Clinton (74(139)), vol VI, ch 65) but was defrauded of it. Throughout the rest of the 1780s he resided in Knightsbridge, London, pursuing a claim for compensation with the royal commission. In daily fear of imprisonment for debt, he indicated his intention to settle eventually with his sons in Nova Scotia. (Coldham, *Loyalist Claims*, 430-1)

B.   W R W Curle, Lieutenant of the County, has corn at Scones Dam and Hampton.

—— Ganey

B.   Commodore Ja^s Barron

B.   Captain Richd Barron

B.   Moss Armistead, comisary, a persecuteing villain

B.   John Rogers, pirate

B.   —— Gibson. As bad as can be.

B.   David Davis has a vessel in Deep Creek, Warwick County, and several hogsheads of rum at Colonel Richd Cary's in S^{d47} County or there abouts.

B.   Colonel Roe Cowper

B.   Captain Edwd Malery

B.   Captain David Mossom

B.   Ned Rud   )
) French pilots
B.   Wm Ballard)

B.   Captain Bayley, ditto

York County

B.   John Robinson has much arms, some of which belongs to the King.

B.   Starky Roinson, commissioner

B.   John Kirby, comisary, has some country cattle. A villain par^{d48}.

B.   John Turner, commissioner

B.   Thos Wild

---

[47] S^d: Stafford?

[48] par^d: paroled or pardoned?

B.   Colonel Rich Cary, Judge of the Courts of Appeals and Admiralty

B.   Colonel Edw[d] Harwood, County Lieutenant

Ought not the pirates' boats in Harris's Creek to be destroyed?

St George to Leslie, 2nd July 1781   6(294): ALS

Hampton
July 2nd 1781

Sir

Since writeing my letter of the 30th ultimo, Commodore Ja[s] Barron of Warwick County and Captain Rogers[49] of Hampton have taken the boats that were then fiting out upon Harris's Creek and are gone to Gloucester. The other three pirate boats are gone (as I am informed) to Nancock and Nanticock on the eastern shore with their cargo's. They took six Negroes from Colonel Celden and nine from Mr Loury. Rogers and Barron spent the day preceeding the robbery with the pirates, and also one Gipson[50] of this town was with them. Gipson is a very active fellow indeed and, if he can be got, deserves good care to be taken of him. I am wiling [to] pledge my life for the loyalty of Colonel Celden and Mr Loury. I am and ever will be unchangable, and happy while I have the honour of being, sir,

Your most respectful, humble and obedient servant

H U St GEORGE

PS

The pirates have promised to return in ten days to Harris's Creek. You may think propper or have occation to shew my letters. I beseech you to take my name from them, sir, as I know not how soon I mightn't be obliged to fly from my family. It is my happiness as well as my duty to be with you, sir, and pray you to command me in all thing you please.

H U St G

§ - §

---

[49] John Rogers was a captain in the Virginia revolutionary navy. For his service during the war he would be awarded 5,333 acres. (*Va Military Records*, 778; Gwathmey, *Historical Register*, 675)

[50] Perhaps James or John Gibson, both of whom were gunners in the Virginia revolutionary navy. For service during the war each would be awarded 2,666 acres. (*Va Military Records*, 782; Gwathmey, *Historical Register*, 305)

5 - Intercepted letters

Jones to Muhlenberg, 11th May 1781   *105(7): ALS*

Mrs Bolling's Quarter on Namazeen
March 11th 1781[51]

Brigadier General Mulenburg
Camp

Dear General

The enemy had a party of light horse within four miles of this and took several horses from the people of this neighbourhood. There went another party up to Colonel Banister's Quarter on Hatcher's Run and took every Negro, except a few old and little ones, and all his good horses.[52] My dear General, I think, if we had a party sent over here in the lower edge of Amelia, it would be a means of all the militia on the south side of Appomattox turning out; otherwise I fear not at present, as I would wish to keep them from coming out in small parties. Lord Cornwallis from every account will be in Petersburg to night. They have never been higher up the river than about 15 miles from Petersburg. I beg that you would urge to the Marquis to have men sent over here. As soon as I understand there's a party sent over, I shall join them and lend my feeble aid.

I am, dear General,
Your most obedient humble servant

JOS JONES[53], Dinwiddie

---

[51] The letter is misdated. It relates to events in May.

[52] John Banister's family seat was Hatcher's Run, which lay not far from Petersburg in Bristol Parish, Dinwiddie County. Born there in 1734, he was educated in Wakefield, England, from where he moved on to London and was admitted as a barrister to the Middle Temple in 1753. Returning to Virginia, he began practising law at Petersburg and proceeded to represent Dinwiddie for several years in the colonial House of Burgesses. Of the revolutionary persuasion, he took part in the Virginia conventions of 1775-6, and when a revolutionary constitution for Virginia was adopted, he became a member of the House of Delegates in 1776-8. He went on to serve as a delegate to the Continental Congress from March 1778 to September 1779. Now, in 1781, he was a colonel in the Dinwiddie revolutionary militia and again a member of the House of Delegates, where he would sit for the next three years. In 1785 he became the first Mayor of Petersburg, where he died three years later at his town house, Battersea. He was buried in the family plot at Hatcher's Run. (Joel D Treese and Dorthy J Countryman, *Biographical Directory of the United States Congress 1774-1996* (Cq Pr, 1996); 'Colonel John Banister' (http://www.coljohnbanister.org, 15th June 2006); Gwathmey, *Historical Register*, 37)

[53] Joseph Jones (1749-1824), who lived very near Petersburg at Cedar Grove plantation in Dinwiddie County, is not to be confused with his namesake who was presently serving in Philadelphia as a Virginia delegate to Congress. A prominent figure in his community, he had been a vestryman of Bristol Parish since 1773, a member of his committee of safety in 1775, and a delegate from Dinwiddie to the Virginia revolutionary assembly in 1778-9. Commissioned a captain in the Dinwiddie revolutionary militia in 1776, he had by now been promoted to a

Mason to Mason, 13th May 1781 *105(23): ALS*

At Mr Daniel Mason's
Sunday morning
13th May 81

Mr Littleberry Mason[54]
At Hicks's Ford, Greensville

Per favour of Mr John Butts

My dear Littleberry

I received Mr Richard Ions' letter last night and observe what he says with respect to yourself. I am induced to think, my dear, that unless you do take charge of a company in this quarter, you will meet with censure if not with blame by General Mughlenburg for not returning agreable to your furlough. I wou'd therefore wish you, if you can make out a company, to join Captain Boling[55] or whoever commands a party now going out on the scouting business. I wish I had my sword and pistols for you, but I don't know how to get them. Colonel Richard Elliott[56] has them. If you cou'd send for them you might get them and let him know it is my wish that you have them. Should you not join this corps of light horse, I wou'd advise you to come in immediately to me to go to head quarters. I will go with you if possible. I hope our army will in a few days be at Petersburg and drive the enemy away before Lord Cornwallis reinforces them. I wou'd wish you to get a certificate

---

colonelcy there, but in keeping with the tenor of his present letter he has left no record of military achievement. After the war he served four years (1784-8) in the House of Delegates and two (1788-9) in the Senate. In 1802 he became a major general in the militia. For the last three years of his life he was Postmaster of Petersburg and Collector of the port. A wealthy property and slave owner at his death, he was buried at Cedar Grove. In 1937 the DAR erected a memorial to him in Blandford Cemetery, Petersburg. (Churchill Gibson Chamberlayne, *The Vestry Book and Register of Bristol Parish, Virginia, 1720-1789* (Southern Historical Press, 1994), 239, 242, 250, 252, 260, 272; Cynthia M Leonard, *The General Assembly of Virginia, July 30, 1619–January 11, 1978: A Bicentennial Register of Members* (Library of Virginia, 1978); Memorial to General Joseph Jones, Blandford Cemetery, Petersburg; *Death Notices from Richmond, Virginia Newspapers, 1821-1840* (Virginia Genealogical Society, 1987), 164; *Va Military Records*, 479, 480; Gwathmey, *Historical Register*, 427)

[54] Like his father David, who was the writer of this letter, Littleberry Mason came from Sussex County, Virginia. He was paymaster to the 15th Virginia Continental Regiment from 12th March 1777 to 14th September 1778, the date on which the Virginia Continental regiments were reduced. Heitman has him retiring on that date, but it is clear from this letter that he continued in service, probably as a paymaster. (Heitman, *Historical Register*, 383; *Va Military Records*, 488)

[55] Captain Robert Bolling IV (1759-1839) was a cavalry officer who came from Petersburg, where he is buried at Blandford Cemetery. For an account of his revolutionary services, see Nora F M Davidson, 'Revolutionary Services of Robert Bolling of Petersburg, Virginia', *Virginia Magazine of History and Biography*, xii (October 1904), 154-6. For wider information about the Bollings, see Alexander R Bolling Jr, *The Bolling Family: Eight Centuries of Growth* (Gateway Press Inc, 1990).

[56] Richard Elliott was a colonel in the revolutionary militia of Brunswick County. (*Va MilitaryRecords*, 74, 77, 742)

from Colonel Gee[57] that you have been on duty from the day you went into service to satisfie the General of your conduct, or if you take a command with the light horse, you should get from Colonel Gee a brevett commission, or if you should be taken prisoner you wou'd be treated as a common soldier. I imagine you have seen those kind of commissions. If not, they are made as follows: a certificate from the commanding officer of corps, county or other ways that such a one is an officer of such rank and kind of service. This, if taken prisoner, intitles him to be treated as a gentleman and officer, and also he sits in courts martial and takes rank agreable to the date of his commission. I was yesterday at home. I have moved most of my people to this place but am at a loss what to do further. Sometimes I think I had better return home and shall do so if our army moves over to Petersburg as I have hopes they will in a few days again. I dread Cornwallis's party more than Phillips's, as we have too many proofs of their cruelty and inhumanity. Phillips is expected to dye at Mrs Bolling's in Petersburg.[58] I wish to see you, but unless you come this way to go to head quarters, I don't know when I can ride over. Poor Tommy I hear nothing of. I wish I cou'd. My concern for all of you is great, as I really fear the enemy will march thro your way. I think of waiting a day or two longer here. Circumstances will determine what I had best to do. I must then either go home or give it out altogether and move up the country and join the army. I beg to hear from or to see you. Beg of poor Tommy to let me see or hear from him and to advise me of his intentions. I wou'd not wish any of you to move unless the southern enemy comes on. If they do not in a few days, I shall either go home or come out to you. Give my best respects to Colonel Gee, Colonel Judkin[59] and other friends. Tell poor Mr Godwin[60] I wou'd advise him to get away if Cornwallis's party comes on, or I fear a rascal wou'd treat him in a manner too cruel to bear. If you can with your waggon assist your brothers, I beg you wou'd so as not to injure yourself. God bless and protect you and all of my dear children.

---

[57] Henry Gee was a colonel in the revolutionary militia of Sussex County, where he had lived for many years. He was captured and confined at Portsmouth. (Gwathmey, *Historical Register*, 301; W J Fletcher, *The Gee Family, Descendants of Charles Gee (d. 1709) and Hannah Gee (d. 1728) of Virginia, with a Chapter on the English Background* (1937), 37)

[58] Phillips died on 14th May at 'Bollingbrook', the Petersburg home of Mary Bolling (née Tabb), and was buried in Blandford Cemetery. Mary (1737-1814) was the widow of Robert Bolling III (1730-1775) and the mother of Robert Bolling IV (see above). 'Bollingbrook' was built about 1725 and consisted of two separate buildings, the larger of which was burned in 1855 and the smaller demolished in 1915. Its location lay at East Hill on a knoll between North Jefferson Street and the Atlantic Coast Line tracks.

[59] In mid 1779 Judkin was serving as a colonel in the revolutionary militia of Brunswick County. Whether he was still active has not been ascertained. (Revolutionary pension application S2661 of William Johnson of Anson County, North Carolina, dated 14th October 1832)

[60] Of the Goodwyns of Greensville County, the one to whom Mason is referring has not been positively identified. He may, for example, have been John, who would go on to become a Judge of Richland County Court, or his father. Peterson Goodwyn (1745-1818) of Dinwiddie, an adjoining county, who would later serve as a US representative, may have been related. (Greensville County Court, Deed Book 2, 520; Joel D Treese and Dorthy J Countryman, *Biographical Directory of the United States Congress 1774-1996* (Cq Pr, 1996))

With my love to yourself and my other children, your Mamma's sisters and brothers included, I am your affectionate father

DAVID MASON[61]

PS

The bearer, Mr John Butts[62], will tell you of the enemy's committing depredations on Colonel Banister and others near Petersburg. Numbers of Negros go to them.

Langborn to Claiborne, 31st May 1781   105(40): LS

Devenport's Ford
May 31st 1781

Major Richard Claiborne[63]
Deputy Quarter Master at Carter's Ferry

Dear Sir

Our army at present is a few miles from Devenport's Ford. The British army from the best accounts is near Hanover Court House. It's impossible to conjecture what's their object. It must be our stores at the Point of Fork or Hunter's Iron Works at Fredericksburg. We keep as near as possible between the two supposed objects. Wayne will, I hope, join us in three or four days, at what place is uncertain, as our movements are intirely governed by the motions of the enemy. I have advised the quarter master at Goochland Courthouse to have all the stores removed from that place to Albemarle Old Courthouse. Indeed I think the stores

---

[61] David Mason (?-1785) had represented Sussex County, Virginia, in the colonial House of Burgesses from 1758 to 1775. He became a member of the Virginia revolutionary conventions in 1774-6 and Colonel of the 15th Virginia Continental Regiment from November 1776 to July 1778. He was then appointed a colonel in the Sussex County revolutionary militia and saw action at Stono Ferry in South Carolina, but by now he had apparently been superseded in the colonelcy by Henry Gee. (*Va Military Records*, 267n, 274, 278; Tyler, *Encyclopedia*, i, 285; Heitman, *Historical Register*, 383; Gwathmey, *Historical Register*, 504)

[62] John Butts, who served in Robert Bolling IV's troop of horse, was captured while carrying this letter. He was confined at Portsmouth, where he died of smallpox. Because he was heading into Greensville County when captured and was perhaps familiar with the terrain, he may have been related to Jesse and Peter Butts, who served respectively as a lieutenant and an ensign in the Greensville revolutionary militia. (*Virginia Magazine of History and Biography*, xii (October 1904), 155-6; Gwathmey, *Historical Register*, 118; *Va Military Records*, 160, 167, 646)

[63] One of numerous descendants of William Claiborne, who migrated from Westmoreland to Virginia in 1621, Richard Claiborne had been appointed to the Continental post of Deputy Quartermaster General for Virginia on 1st January 1781. He had previously served as a lieutenant in the 1st Continental Artillery, as an adjutant in the 2nd Virginia Continental Regiment, and as a brigade major under George Weedon. After the war he would be awarded 3,555 acres in recognition of his services. (Erna Risch, *Supplying Washington's Army* (Center of Military History, US Army, 1981), ch 2; Heitman, *Historical Register*, 155-6; *Va Military Records*, 646-7; Gwathmey, *Historical Register*, 152)

at the Point of Fork are not quite secure, but as you have been making preparations for their transportation, I hope you may be able at the shortest notice to baffle their scheme.

I have waited as patiently as possible for the wagons harness, paper, saddles, paper ink, brown linnen, duck, rope, bridles, tents etc etc, all of which we are destitute off, and permit me to assure you, unless we receive a supply of all matters requisite to the army in the Quarter Master's Department, it will be impracticable to get in motion, especially when Wayne arrives. The Marquis requests that all the brown linnen and every kind of duck may be without delay sent to this place. Captain Young[64] has a large quantity which he will spare the public. We have not yet a single artificer or iron to shoe our horses. I would make out an invoice, did I conceive you did not know better than myself what is necessary to this army. What you have I desire may be sent on without a moment's delay. The stores at the Point of Fork ought to be kept ready to move. The British army is evidently greatly superior to ours. By our rapid movements towards the mountains our intelligence, as usual, therefore can not be particular.

I have not the least objection to correspond with you. Your request gives me pleasure, and if you will accompany every other letter with a cargo of stores, you will make me superbly happy.

Adieu

W^M LANGBORN[65]
Deputy Quarter Master General

---

[64] A Virginian, Captain Henry Young had until recently been serving as a deputy quartermaster general in the Continental Army and had been sent south with a reinforcement of troops in December 1779. About March 1781 he was appointed to head the Virginia state quartermaster department while retaining his Continental commission. (Greene to Charles Pettit, and Henry Young to Greene, Nathanael Greene Papers 1777-1780, Series I: Correspondence M-Z, B G83, American Philosophical Society; *The Greene Papers*, viii, 27)

[65] William Langborn came from King William County, Virginia, where his parents had migrated from London, England. He was now employed as the deputy quartermaster general attached to Lafayette's corps. In recognition of his services he would in October 1783 be granted a brevet commission of lt colonel on the Continental establishment. Later he would be awarded 6,224 acres. His surname is frequently misspelt by historians. (Tyler, *Encyclopedia*, i, 274; Heitman, *Historical Register*, 339; Gwathmey, *Historical Register*, 457)

Ross to Nicolson, 2nd June 1781   *105(48): ALS*

Point of Fork
2nd June 1781

Mr George Nicolson[66]
Philadelphia

Care of Mr Chas Logan

Sir

I wrote to you the 28th ultimo, which would be forwarded to you by Mr Pleasants[67].

This letter goes by three waggoners, Leonard March, James Rue and John Chesnut, loaded with cordage belonging to the State, which was saved from the Public Rope Walk at Warwick before it was burnt by the British.

You'll please to dispose of this cordage for the best price you can obtain and pay the waggoners the balances due to them, which you'll see by their respective accounts, and the rest you'll be pleased to appropriate to the use of the State in the purchase of necessaries for the army. In a few days seven more waggons will be loaded and sent on to Philadelphia with cordage and rope yarns for the same purpose. The articles mentioned to you in my former letters are much wanted, viz, Russia sheeting[68] or Rains duck[69], good strong oznaburgs, saddles and other accoutrements for dragoons, cartridge paper, writing paper, tools, arms, including horsemen's swords and pistols. The accoutrements for dragoons are exceedingly wanted, and a large supply of them. The enemy have a great superiority in horse, which will enable them to ravage the country at pleasure. You'll therefor neglect no opportunity of representing this in the strongest terms to our delegates in Congress. I have not heard from Mr Mathies[70] since I wrote to you last. I hope he will soon be able to forward the hemp that I then mentioned, but I am sorry to inform you there are disturbances in that back country which may retard the business a little. The Marquis and the army are at and above Scotstown in Hanover. The main body of the British by last accounts were at Bottom's Bridge and Tarlton's Legion has been at New Castle, Hanover Town and Hanover Courthouse. This State will be greatly distressed this campaign without assistance from the northward.

---

[66] George Nicolson was an assistant of David Ross, the writer of this letter. On 30th April he arrived in Philadelphia, having been sent there to purchase military supplies for the Virginia state troops. (Paul Hubert Smith et al, eds, *Letters of Delegates to Congress, 1774-1789* (US Government Printing, 1990), xvii, *passim*)

[67] Like Nicolson (see above), Thomas Pleasants was an assistant of David Ross in Philadelphia. (William T Hutchinson and William M E Rachal eds, *Papers of James Madison* (University of Chicago Press, 1962-91), iii, 87n) He may have been related to Robert Pleasants (see p 266, note 78).

[68] *Russia sheeting*: stout cloth of linen or cotton chiefly imported from Russia.

[69] *Rains duck*: strong untwilled linen or cotton fabric for outer clothing imported from Rennes in Britanny.

[70] No one with the name Mathies or a variant of it has been identified.

I shall write to you again in a few days by the other waggons, and in the mean time am, sir,

Your very humble servant

DAVID ROSS[71]
Contracting Agent

[*Subscribed*:]

The waggoners are to be [paid] in State paper money or other money at 75 for 1, but as an alteration has taken place in the Continental money, I think they ought to be paid agreable to their expectations when they took on the loads.

They have each of them a state of their accounts as noted below and are to be paid for the load they now carry at the same rate with their former load, viz, 90 pounds sterling in State money.

	Dr		*Cr*
	Hard money	*State money*	
James Rue	£3.15.0	£37.0.0	£113.0.0
Leonard Martz	£3.15.0	£36.9.10	£113.0.0
John Chesnut	£3.15.0	£37.9.10	£113.0.0

---

[71] David Ross (?-1817) had been appointed commercial agent for Virginia in early 1781, a responsibility which he was discharging ably and indefatigably. He was an enterprising Scot who had prospered on migrating to Virginia, becoming an affluent businessman and an extensive landowner in six counties. One of his holdings lay at the Point of Fork, near where he owned a home (still standing) in Columbia. Surprisingly, and for unknown reasons, he was to be recompensed, as promised by Cornwallis, for the provisions appropriated from his different plantations for the use of the British troops. By 1807 he had overextended his business empire and it came to a catastrophic end, leaving him bankrupt. At his death his affairs were in such a disorderly state that it took the administrator of his estate seventeen years to untangle them. (Herman E Melton, 'David Ross: Pittsylvania's Unsung Hero of the Revolution', *The PittsylvaniaPacket* (Pittsylvania Historical Society, Chatham VA), Fall 1992, 3-4; *The Cornwallis Papers*)

Constable to Drew, 4th June 1781

105(51): ALS

Wilderness
4th June 1781

Captain Thomas Drew[72]

Dear Tom

I was very happy to hear from you — rely upon it, my honest fellow. I lived with old Peter[73] about 2 months. From some unaccountable whim the Baron[74] wished to have me in his family but I liked one old friend too well to quit him. The Marquis did me the honor to request me to join him, which I refused, but he applied to General Muhlenberg to spare me, which the old fellow consented to and turned me off.

You'll hear of the enemy's being up at Charlottesville before this reaches you. They stole a march upon us by means of the horses they have collected. Colonel Davis[75], notwithstanding the Marquis's orders to remove the stores to Albemarle Court House, chose to have them at Charlottesville, where all our amunition with 1,000 stand of good arms are. This will be a cripling stroke. Wayne not yett to [be] heard of certainly, but at Newland's Ferry the 31st. We will cross at Ely's Ford today to join Wayne. We shall then have 2,000 Contis, I hope, but the enemy's horse so outflank us they we [*sic*] can do nothing.

By God, I shall lose my breakfast if I write any more, and we are to march.

Your friend

W CONSTABLE[76]

§ - §

---

[72] Thomas Haynes Drew of Caroline County, Virginia, had served as a lieutenant in the Continental line from February 1777 to July 1779. He resigned his commission in return for a captaincy in Charles Porterfield's Virginia State Regiment and took part with it in the Battle of Camden. He fled from the battlefield with the remains of the regiment to Hillsborough, from where they returned to Virginia and continued in service. After the war he was granted 4,000 acres. (Heitman, *Historical Register*, 204; Revolutionary pension application of Bernard Reynolds of Russell County, Virginia, 7th August 1832; *Va Military Records*, 418; Gwathmey, *Historical Register*, 236)

[73] *old Peter*: Muhlenberg.

[74] *the Baron*: Steuben.

[75] A Princeton graduate and lawyer, William Davies (?-1805) had for a few years been a Continental field officer and had lately served as colonel in command of the Continental depot at Chesterfield Court House, Virginia. His administrative ability led in March 1781 to his being appointed Virginia's Commissioner of War, an office partly involved in procuring, storing and furnishing military supplies. He retained his Continental commission. (*The Greene Papers*, vi, 483n, viii, *passim*; Heitman, *Historical Register*, 187)

[76] William Constable was an officer in the 9th Virginia Continental Regiment. This letter explains how he came to be an aide-de-camp to Lafayette. (Gwathmey, *Historical Register*, 175)

6 - Other letters

Pleasants to Phillips, 14th May 1781   *90(10): ALS*

Curles
14th of 5th month 1781

Major General Philips

General Philips

From a full persuasion that LIBERTY is the natural right of all men and an apprehention of duty as trustee of my father and brother, John and Jonathan Pleasants deceased, respecting the rights and previledges of the Negroes which by the law were accounted a part of their estates, but from a consciousness of their undoubted title to freedom, did order and direct by their last wills and testaments that they should enjoy that enestimable previledge as they came to the age of thirty years, nearly in the following words, viz: 'Believing that all mankind have an undoubted right to freedom and commiserating the situation of the Negroes which by the law I am invested with the property of, and being willing and desirous that they may in a good degree partake and enjoy that enestimable blessing, do order and direct, as the most likely means to fit them for freedom, that they be instructed to read, at least the young ones as they come of sutable age, and that each individual of them which now are or hereafter may arive to the age of thirty years may enjoy the full benifit of their labour in a manner the most likely to answer the intention of relieving them from bondage, and whenever the law of the country will admit absolute freedom to them, it is my will and desire that all the slaves I am now possesed of, together with their increase, shall emediately, on their coming to the age of thirty years as aforesaid, become free, at least all such as will accept thereof or that my trustees hereafter to be named or a majority of them may think so fitted for freedom, as that the enjoyment thereof may conduce to their happiness, which I desire they may enjoy in as full and ample a manner as if they never had been in bondage.'

Now, as sundry of these people were given to a maiden sister of mine on those expres conditions, who is since married to Charles Logan[77] of the City of Philadelphia and who jointly with her husband hath also executed a manumition (as I am informed) for them to take place, the males at the age of twenty one and the females at eighteen, and as divers of them are lately gone of with thy army with an expectation, I suppose, more fully to enjoy the liberty intended them, I conceive it to be my duty to inform thee of their peculiar circumstance and to request, if they should choose to continue where they are, that thou would give such direction concerning them as may prevent privatears or designing men from converting them into property. For that purpose I herewith subjoin the names of them, at least such as are grown.

---

[77] Charles Logan (1754-1794) married Mary Pleasants on 8th July 1779 at the Friends' Meeting House, High Street, Philadelphia. In due course they took up residence in Powhatan County, Virginia. (Josephine Lindsay Bass and Becky Bonner, 'My Southern Family – Charles Logan' (Internet, 15th August 2006))

I have also to represent the peculiar situation of a Negro man named Charles White, who was directed by my father's will to be free and hath enjoy'd it for several years with as much reputation and respect in the neighbourhood as most men in a low station and hath acquired some property, but what makes it peculearly hard on him is that it is said he and his family were forced away, and it is evident he has left most of his property behind, which he need not have done had he been desirous of going away. If that should be the case, I hope thou will give direction for his discharge. There is also another case in respect to two Negroes of mine who went away with the army under General Arnold in the month of January last: one, a man call'd Carter Jack aged between thirty and forty years, and the other, a boy named London about fifteen, concerning whom I wrote some time ago to General Arnold but have never been informed whether or not it got to hand. These Negroes were manumitted under hand and seal, Jack on the 14th of 5th month 1777 and London on the 21st of 7th month following, the latter to be free on the 1st of 12th month 1787, who I should be glad to reclaim, as also a horse which was taken at the same time and from his gentle good qualities to a person of my years was very valuable, but as to the Negro man, I don't wish his return except with his own choice.

I wished to have waited on thee in person had it been convenient, but as that is not the case at present, and being desirous to give thee the earliest inteligence of the above matters, I hope thou wilt excuse it.

Thy compliance with the above request will greatly oblige one who is a friend to peace, to liberty, and to mankind in general.

ROBERT PLEASANTS[78]

[NAMES SUBJOINED]

Negro Jacob, a carpenter, Amy, his wife, and three children	5
Suky and four ditto	5
Frank and Nelly	2
Fanny and one child	2
Jessie, a boy, and Dycy, a girl	2

---

[78] Robert Pleasants was a Quaker and an exceedingly wealthy tobacco merchant of Curles, Henrico County. Unusually for Quakers, both he and his father John, who died in 1771, owned slaves. Under Virginia's manumission law of 1782 Robert would emancipate seventy-eight of his own slaves and would attempt to get all of the family to honour the request in John's will that all John's slaves be freed. Eventually he brought a case before the Virginia High Court of Chancery, where he was represented by John Marshall, a future Chief Justice of the United States, and by John Warden. In 1799 the Court decided in favour of emancipating the slaves, some of whom settled on Robert's land and formed the Gravely Hill community. For more information about Robert, see, *inter alia*: 'Letters of Robert Pleasants', *William and Mary Quarterly*, 2nd series, i & ii (1921-2); Kenneth L Carroll ed, 'Robert Pleasants on Quakerism: "Some Account of the First Settlement of Friends in Virginia..."', *Virginia Magazine of History and Biography*, lxxxvi (1978), 3-16; Robert Pleasants of Curles, Henrico County, Letterbook, Library of Virginia)

Charles White and Sarah, his wife, and their two daughters   4

Jack and London   2

Statement of damages, June 1781   *5(9): DS*

Damages done at Mr Ross's plantations exclusive of provisions taken away

At the Point of Fork:

126 gallons wine	£126
3 saddle horses and saddles	£160
1 waggon and team	£120
2 houses pull'd down and destroy'd	£50
The fences destroyed	£40
The growing crop of corn, wheat, oats and tobacco destroyed	£350
	£846

At the plantation on the North Run at the ferry landing:

2 large draft horses	£40
The growing crop of wheat and corn and the fences destroyed	£200
	£240

At Harrison's:

2 fine mares	£100
3 draught horses	£60

4 young horses	£120
A vast deal of fencing destroyed and the growing crop on near 400 acres of land destroyed, wheat, oats, hemp etc	£850
	£1,130

5 draft horses	£125
The fencing destroyed and the whole crop of every kind	£300
	£425
	£2,641

Exclusive of the above, 18 Negros carried off and not recovered and a vast deal of other damages not included in the above. A large quantity of coarse cloathing also carried off.

DAVID ROSS

Margaret Money to Cornwallis, 5th March 1781[79]   71(19): ALS

East Bergholt
March 5th 1781

My Lord

Unequal as I am to the task, I think my self in duty bound to return your Lordship many thanks for your goodness to one who, had it pleased the Almighty to spare, would, I am very sure, ever have retain'd with gratitude a due sense of the many obligations he was under to your Lordship.

As to your kindness to me in wishing to have the fatal news[80] convey'd with tenderness, was such an instance of humanity as must ever reflect the highest honor, and was what I could not have expected, that one in your exalted station should have bestow'd a thought of sharing in the grief of an afflicted mother who is robb'd of every comfort but that of knowing her child died gloriously. I am sensible it is not in my power to do justice to your Lordship for the favors I am indebted to you, but I hope you will give me leave to do all I can, which is to offer up my prayers to almighty God to preserve the life of *Lord Broom* that your Lordship *may* in the decline of life receive that comfort from him which I should have had from my beloved son.

---

[79] This letter probably arrived at Portsmouth, Virginia, on 8th July.

[80] *the fatal news*: of the death of her son, Lieutenant John Money.

I flatter my self you will not think I intrude too much upon your goodness when I beg that, whatever letters come from England, you will order them to be burnt, as I know many for my son besides what I wrote went off in the last packet. I beg pardon if I have made an improper request. It proceeds from ignorance, having been inform'd the packet is always sent to your Lordship.

I am much surprized that I have received no account from any officer of the 63rd, nor do I know to whom to apply. I am certain by my son's last letter of October 5th that, if he was sensible of his death, he has a *will*, which it is my desire to have fullfill'd, and I have a wish that all his papers should be sent over to me. He mention'd having left some at Charlestown, but as I cannot learn with certainty who commands the troops there, I did not know who to write to. Therefore hope your Lordship will excuse the liberty I now take in intreating you will order any person whom you think proper to be intrusted with his affairs to transmit an account to me and I will with great pleasure pay any demand whatever, any compliments your Lordship thinks proper to be paid to any officer of the 63rd or any part of your household. 'Tis my earnest request that every respect that is due to the memory of so worthy a child may be paid. I have made all the inquiry I can in hopes of finding Captain Mallom, but in vain. Had he arrived in England, I should only have return'd your Lordship thanks. If I have offended in the requests I have made, it will add one affliction more to the many heavy ones I am sinking under, my husband deprived of his faculties, my only child having embark'd with his regiment last November, but his destination is not yet known. If these melancholly circumstances will not plead my excuse, I must lay under your Lordship's displeasure, as I have nothing else to offer.

I pray God preserve your health and send you safe to England. You have already immortalized your name, but the happiness of your friends cannot be compleat till your return. No one will share with them with more gratitude than her who, tho' oppress'd with misery, has the honor to be, my Lord,

Your Lordship's most obedient servant

MARGARET MONEY

Haldane to persons on parole, 17th July 1781   *101(32): ACS*

Head Quarters
17th July 1781

Persons on parole are authorized and desired to seize and bring to head quarters all stragglers from the British Army, particularly those whom they may detect in committing depredations and robberies in the country, that they may be punished.

By order of Earl Cornwallis

HENRY HALDANE
Aide-de-camp

Hutcheson to Cornwallis, 20th July 1781   6(331): ALS

Camp
July 20th 1781

My Lord

Having now compleated twenty one years of military service, and being compell'd by the exigency of my own private affairs, together with increasing infirmities arising from a constitution much hurt by long service in a southern climate, to the necessity of retiring from the army, I have humbly to request your Lordship's permission to apply to the Commander in Chief for leave to sell out. And as during the time I have had the honor to serve under your Lordship I have endeavour'd to promote not only the letter but the spirit of your Lordship's military wishes as far as I understood them, I hope your Lordship will not refuse your fiat to the inclos'd memorial[81] to prevent delay and trouble.

I have the honor to be
Your Lordship's most humble servant

R^T HUTCHESON[82]
Captain, 71st Regiment

Cornwallis to Hutcheson, undated   88(56): Df

Sir

I am sorry that the exigency of your private affairs and your bad state of health should render it necessary for you to think of retiring from the army. You will be pleased to make your application to the Commander in Chief and I beg that you will accept my thanks for the zeal and attention with which you have served under my command.

[CORNWALLIS]

§ - §

---

[81] *the inclos'd memorial*: no copy.

[82] Robert Hutcheson had been commanding the 2nd Battalion, 71st (Highland) Regiment. His wish to sell out may have been partly prompted by the very recent arrival of Lt Colonel Duncan MacPherson to assume the command.

CHAPTER 55

Correspondence relating to the Carolinas

---

1 - Between Cornwallis and Balfour

Noble to Cornwallis, 18th May 1781 *6(72): ALS*

Off Chickahominy
May 18th 1781

Earl Cornwallis

My Lord

By an express boat this moment arrived from Portsmouth I have received the inclosed letters from Lt Colonel Balfour to Major General Phillips, as also your Lordship's dispatches[1]. I have taken copys of the letters from Charlestown for the satisfaction of the Commander in Chief. Not thinking it proper to open your Lordship's dispatches, I have sent them. I hope my conduct on this occasion will meet your Lordship's approbation.

I take the liberty of sending your Lordship an extract of a private letter to me from Captain Vallancey dated Portsmouth, May 16th 1781:

---

[1] *your Lordship's dispatches*: as evinced by the following enclosure, the reference is to dispatches written by Cornwallis, possibly copies of those to Germain, vol IV, pp 104-9.

'Numbers of the inhabitants are flocking in to us and offering their services. 10 this day, one a French officer, and several of the others have been in the rebel service. New Kent County have absolutely laid down their arms and the enemy have disarmed them. Paul Jones with 4 frigates and 2 twenty gun ships is said to have sail'd for this place.'

Wishing your Lordship success, I have the honor to be
Your Lordship's most obedient humble servant

M NOBLE[2]

Enclosure (1)
Balfour to Phillips, 1st May 1781 6(75): C

Charles Town
May the 1st 1781

Major General Phillips etc etc etc

Sir

By the extract which I have the honor to enclose you of my letter of this date to Lord George Germain you will see the alarming situation of this province at present and the very honorable efforts which have been made by Lord Rawdon to relieve it.

Lord Cornwallis's views on this head are communicated in his dispatches sent by this occasion, and if I can further either them or yours by every exertion in my power (as his Lordship has left with me a counterpart of the cypher transmitted to you) in any way I am honored with your commands, I shall esteem myself happy in obeying them.

I have the honor to be, sir,
Your obedient humble servant

[N BALFOUR]

---

[2] Mungo Noble had been commissioned a lieutenant in the 21st Regiment (Scots Fusiliers) on 20th September 1777, too late to be with it at Saratoga. On 9th June 1781 he would be promoted to captain lieutenant in the 3rd Battalion, 60th (Royal American) Regiment, and on 28th April 1782 would transfer to a captain lieutenantcy in the 7th (Royal Fusiliers), a regiment which had been taken prisoner at the Cowpens. In 1783 he was acting as aide-de-camp to Major General James Paterson. (*Army Lists*; WO 65/164(1) and (6) (National Archives, Kew))

Enclosure (2)
Extract, Balfour to Germain, 1st May 1781[3] 6(77): C

Charles Town
May the 1st 1781

By Lord Cornwallis's dispatches[4] which are herewith transmitted your Lordship will be informed that after the action of Guildford General Green, being obliged to retreat from before the King's army, turned his views towards this province as the more vulnerable point in the absence of Lord Cornwallis.

With this idea, on the 19th ultimo he came before Camden, having with him near fifteen hundred Continentals and several corps of militia, Lord Rawdon having charge of that post and about eight hundred British and Provincial troops to sustain it.

For some days General Greene kept varying his position, waiting, as is supposed, to be reinforced by the corps under Brigadier Marrian and Colonel Lee, which were on their way, being ordered to join him.

Judging it necessary to strike a blow before this junction could take place and learning that General Greene had detached to bring up his baggage and provisions, Lord Rawdon, with the most marked decision, on the morning of the 25th marched out the greater part of his force to meet him and about 10 o'clock attacked the rebels in their camp at Hobkirk's Hill with that spirit which, prevailing over superior numbers and an obstinate resistance, compeled them to give way, and the pursuit was continued for three miles. To accident only they were indebted for saving their guns, which, being drawn into a hollow out of the road, were overlooked by our troops in the flush of victory and pursuit, so that their cavalry, in which they greatly exceeded us, had an opportunity of taking them off.

My Lord Rawdon states the loss of the enemy on this occasion as upwards of an hundred made prisoners and four hundred killed and wounded, his own not exceeding an hundred, in which is included one officer killed and eleven wounded.

After this defeat General Greene retired to Rugeley's Mills (12 miles from Camden) in order to collect his troops and receive the reinforcements, but as Lt Colonel Watson of the Guards, who had for some time been detached by Lord Rawdon with a corps of 500 men to cover the eastern frontiers of the province, is directed by me to join his Lordship, I am in hopes he will be able speedily to accomplish this and Lord Rawdon be placed in such a situation as will empower him either to make head against the enemy, should they attempt any thing further, or retire with security on this side the Santee, as circumstances may require.

---

[3] The extract omits a final paragraph about the situation at Pensacola. The entire letter containing no other material differences is published in Davies ed, *Docs of the Am Rev*, xx, 130-1.

[4] *Lord Cornwallis's dispatches*: see vol IV, pp 104-9.

It is to the several letters which (notwithstanding the enemy having well nigh overrun the province) Lord Rawdon has been so good to transmit to me that I am indebted for the detail I have now the honor to present your Lordship, and which I trust his Lordship will hereafter conclude in the most satisfactory manner.

Cornwallis to Balfour, 20th May 1781

86(37): C

Petersburgh
May 20th 1781

Lt Colonel Balfour
Commandant of Charlestown

Dear Balfour

My letter to Lord Rawdon[5] will explain my situation here and my sentiments relative to South Carolina. I have only to add my warmest acknowledgements for your able and zealous exertions. You will lose no time in withdrawing Craig and in sending to the Chesapeak the convalescents and stores belonging to the regiments here, not forgetting the *Betsey* and *Polly*. I will take every opportunity of writing to you and shall be glad to hear as frequently as possible.

I am with the greatest regard, dear Balfour,
Your most faithfull servant and friend

CORNWALLIS

[*Subscribed*:]

Simcoe wishes much to have Captain Saunders as soon as he can be spared.

Balfour to Cornwallis, 21st May 1781

6(93): ALS

Charles Town
21st May 1781

I had the pleasure of receiving your Lordship's letters of the 3rd of this month[6], and with much concern I am obliged to inform you that since that period we have lost great part of this province and Georgia.

The approach of General Greene's army to Camden was apprehended only by Lord Rawdon, but his appearance before the post was sudden and unexpected, all your Lordship's

---

[5] *My letter..*: see p 286.

[6] *letters of the 3rd..*: they were of 30th April and 3rd May. See vol IV, pp 175-6.

letters having been intercepted. Colonel Lee, having come forward before the rebell army, joined Marrion near Black River and they proceeded immediately to attack a post at Wright's Bluff, which Watson had established there and which they carried after a very considerable resistance and great gallantry on the part of the officers, but the men's behaviour was by no means of the same kind.

This attack upon a post in the rear of Camden plainly evinced the intentions of the enemy, and Lord Rawdon, taking advantage of their having detached for provisions and being reinforced by the arrival of the South Carolinians from Ninety Six, marched out on the 25th of April in the morning and, having concealed his approach, attacked the rebell army on Hobkirk's Hill about two miles from Camden. Their left flank was gained and they were totaly beaten after a contested action of near an hour in which we lost about two hundred and twenty men and the enemy at least double that number. The great superiority of the enemy's cavalry prevented the victory being decisive and saved their army, which fell back to Rugely's Mills, being pursued for several miles towards that place. Their cannon narrowly escaped, being drawn into a swamp and concealed untill the return of our troops, who had passed them in the pursuit.

Lt Colonel Watson had moved from George Town for many weeks up the Pedee and we were at a loss to know where he was. However, having at length got at him, he was ordred instantly to Camden. At this period I had moved the 84th with a detachment of Hessians and convalescents, amounting to three hundred infantry and one hundred cavalry, to Eutaws in order to facilitate Lord Rawdon's retreat over the Santee, a measure I had earnestly and warmly pressed his Lordship to take but which, when Green had come before Camden, he could not adopt.

In my dispatch by a schooner which I had purchased for the purpose of communicating with your Lordship I had mentioned your coming into this province by the way of George Town and that I had placed a vessel with provisions there for the use of the army, as also had provided boats and flatts and stopped Watson's corps for a short time in order to support your passing the ferrys. McArthur with his corps at the Eutaws was also ordred to join you when he heared of your approach.

This vessel being unfortunately taken, and not being able to procure any mode of safe conveyance to you at that critical period, was most distressing, as your return would then, I presume, have been determined upon when you knew that it might have been so easily effected from these asistances.[7]

In a day or two after these arrangements were made, and while I waited with anxious and eager expectations of hearing from you, Broderick arrived with your dispatches[8] on the 27th. Lt Colonel Watson was immediately ordred to proceed to Camden and I again pressed Lord Rawdon's retreat the moment it was practicable. On the 29th of April we heared of Lord

---

[7] Balfour summarised in another letter (of 20th April, vol IV, p 170) his preparations for Cornwallis to return to South Carolina by land. Cornwallis received it nine days later.

[8] *your dispatches*: see vol IV, ch 45 and 46.

Rawdon's success, and I wrote by Broderick of it to Lord George Germain, but in a guarded and cautious manner. The *Delight* with Broderick sailed on the 3rd of May, taking an acount of all our situation, which then threatned fully enough to justify a strong picture and which I charged Broderick verbaly to represent.

Watson, having crossed on this side the Santee, crossed below Thomson's House on the same day that Lee and Marion came on this side the river on the 7th. He proceeded to Camden while they invested Motte's House, where unluckily a reinforcement from McArthur with provisions for Camden had arrived but a few hours before. The garrison ammounted to upwards of one hundred and twenty men commanded by McPherson[9]. They defended it until the enemy got near to the house by sapp and with combustibles set fire to it, which oblidged them to surrender at discretion on the 12th.

Watson having arrived at Camden, Lord Rawdon moved across the Watteree to attack the enemy, who had retired behind Sawney Creek and were posted so very strongly that his Lordship did not think proper to force them and therefore returned to Camden without Green's quitting his ground. The next day, the 10th, the army moved from Camden towards Nielson's Ferry, having set fire to the stores, and brought off all their wounded but thirty and those loyalists who wished to follow the army. On the 13th the whole crossed to this side the Santee without a shott being fired, and on the 14th I went up to communicate with Lord Rawdon upon the plan of future operations.

The general revolt of the province, the universal dissafection which shewed itself on every quarter, even in the heart of the town, stopped every idea of risking a march into the country, and nothing appeared to us so essential as the collecting the force and withdrawing the posts of Ninety Six and Augusta. Lord Rawdon wished to make a tryal to save Maxwell at the Congarees and marched on the 15th towards him, while I returned to town and messengers were dispatched to Cruger.

Foreseeing the obvious consequences of the enemy's superiority in this province, I had previously wrote to Cruger to be watchful and, when he heared that Camden was evacuated, that I wished him to retreat to Augusta and so to fall down upon Savannah. This letter he received on the 6th and I have the greatest hopes that it will be the means of saving him, for if he waits untill our last letters reach him, I fear it will be too late.

Brown at Augusta has been invested for some time past, but not closely, by Pickens and the Georgians who have also revolted.

On the 15th Lord Rawdon, having received intelligence that Green was on his march by Orangeburgh, returned to Nielson's Ferry and from thence to Monk's Corner, where he now is. I have detached a hundred and fifty men to a fortifyd church at Dorchester, and this has been our position since the 11th.

---

[9] MacPherson is said to have been Donald MacPherson, a lieutenant in the 2nd Battalion, 71st (Highland) Regiment, although the bulk of the battalion was serving with Cornwallis in Virginia. (*Army Lists*) For an eyewitness account of the taking of Fort Motte, see Lee, *Memoirs* 345-9.

Yesterday I received acounts of Maxwell's having surrendred, and this day I have sent vessells for the post at George Town, which has been kept as long as possible in case Tarlton's cavalry should still come that way, nor will that post be evacuated unless it is certain the enemy are in force against it. By my last intelligence Green was at the Congarees on the east side and had not crossed, that Sumpter had advanced betwixt Orangeburgh and Dorchester, Lee and Marion being betwixt Nielson's Ferry and the Corner on the banks of the Santee.

The consequences of Lord Rawdon's success at Camden being supposed greater than it was may, I fear, mislead Cruger and keep him in his post. If so, he must fall, but if he obeys my letter of the 29th, which I know he has received, and has tolerable intelligence, he will still get off.

The entreaties of Sir James Wright for asistance you may suppose, and I have told Lord Rawdon that, if the enemy make any movement southward, that we must send him some troops by sea.

The enemy having uniformly murdred in cold blood all our militia whom they have been able to get at, you will naturaly suppose the terror it has struck in the country, and it has not failed also to affect our town folks. I have therefore (having no other means left in my power to stop it) seized and put on board of ship all the remaining militia in Charles Town that were taken in it and have not come in or taken the oaths of allegiance, and have wrote them a letter, which is inclosed[10], and which I hope may have the effect. They have sent it out to Greene and I beg to know, if this horrid practice still continues, what we are to do and whether our threats should be put into execution.

I need not point out to your Lordship what the consequences must be if speedy asistance is not sent. The country may still be regained if we are in force sufficient to reposess it, but if the enemy are allowed to remain any time in it, they will anihilate every remaining vestige of loyalty and by the vigour of their measures prevent our being joined by a single man. At present the country, although in arms against us, yet are doubting and wavering much. They expect a change and that they are soon to see a British army again marching into their country, but this doubt must not long be cleared up. Their inclinations lead them to the rebels, and nothing but fear will check their exerting every means to keep the country. Rutlidge, who is a terror to them all, is expected every day and will no doubt adopt the most violent measures against our friends.

It appears to me clearly that there is little time to be lost in determining betwixt the posession of the provinces and that of the two capitals, and whether the first are objects in the war to employ an army to keep or if the last are only necessary.

Should it be determined to regain the country, a very great additional force must come here immediately, and if the capitals are only to be kept, the present will be nearly sufficient

---

[10] *a letter..*: the copy is not extant. Dated 17th May, the letter threatened retaliation on the detainees for the treatment of loyalist militia made prisoners. It is published in R W Gibbes, *Documentary History of the American Revolution...* (Columbia, SC, 1853), iii, 72-3.

for a time except against a foreign force, when they are certainly inadequate. I own to you that I feel infinitely for the miserable districts of loyalists in the Back Country, and, if it had been possible to avoid an evacuation, that we should not have been so totaly ruined as we now shall be in the attachment of those poorer people, who are indeed our only friends in the country. Should the regiments arrive from Europe or the West Indies, I beg to know what is to be done with them. I know you will send me instructions respecting every thing that will be necessary and I shall as usual continue to act for the best untill I hear from your Lordship, but the situation here now becomes indeed very distressing, and if the seat of war is to be transferred to the Chesapeak, some very general arrangements of the force to be left here will be necessary, as well as some officers of rank to command, provisions to be demanded, and the whole system to be changed. Yet I would still hope all this may be regained if you are near us and not gone to Virginia, but if that is the case, I must in the most earnest manner request to come to you myself and that some general officer may immediately be sent to take the command in the two provinces. The giving up the country, I own, I think should not if possible be determin'd upon. However, I do not presume to mention this opinion or to put it in competition with any plans made for carrying on the war to the southward. I only cannot help regretting the leaving a country where so many exertions have been made to keep it and establish our friends in it.

Lord Rawdon has been ill and I fear he will be obliged to come to town. If so, Watson must command – a horrid idea, and which cannot be admitted by any means. His Lordship will write you but I fear his letters will come too late to catch the *Richmond*.

I referr you to Lord Chewton and Colonel Yorke for particulars, and I can only add that you may depend upon every exertion in my power to keep as much as possible of the country with safety and that my most anxious wish is to prove myself worthy of the friendship and confidence you have placed in me, and am

Most gratefully yours

N BALFOUR

Balfour to Cornwallis, 7th June 1781   *6(200): LS*

Charles Town

June 7th 1781

Rt Hon Lt General Earl Cornwallis etc etc etc

My Lord

As Lord Rawdon has wrote you very fully upon our situation in this country[11], little remains for me to add but to congratulate your Lordship most sincerely upon your junction with the troops in Chesapeak.

---

[11] *As Lord Rawdon has wrote you..*: on 24th May and 5th and 7th June, pp 288-293.

Had my letters reach'd you that were wrote soon after your arrival at Wilmington and those of a later date, you would have been certainly informed of every material transaction since you left us, with the copies of all my letters to the Secretary of State. As they have miscarried, I have only to trust to my last by Lord Chewton[12], which was a kind of recapitulation of my former letters. Yours of the 20th May arrived two days ago, and I shall write a duplicate of this as well as my letter to Ross[13] by the return of the brig which brought your dispatches here. The want of every kind of naval assistance, even to the sending armed vessels with dispatches, is so distressing that infinite prejudice has arisen from it. However, in vain are all my complaints, and I beg if possible that either this vessel or *some other* may return with your dispatches here and be kept for that purpose only. If that cannot be done, you may be assur'd that, however critical and important the service may be, yet it will not be possible to communicate with your Lordship.

As the convalescents, clothing, stores etc will amount to a very considerable fleet, some strong convoy should be immediately sent from you for them, otherwise you may be assur'd they will not reach you.

Inclosed is a letter just receiv'd from Craig[14], by which you will see his activity and desire to distinguish himself. His plan appear'd to Lord Rawdon and me so very plausible and useful that in our answer we have desired he might try it if he thought it would be effected without keeping the men belonging to your army that were left with him, and at all events to send them here and wait the result of Lord Rawdon's movements, himself at Wilmington keeping Hamilton's corps, his own, and the Yagers. The cartel for an exchange of prisoners as settled by Captain Cornwallis[15] is now beginning to be put in execution, the rebel commissary having arriv'd here two days ago. I find we must give up all the Augustine gentry, as well as all the very violent and oppressive people, to go home upon their paroles as militia as we have not enough, I doubt[16], to exchange. However, I will try to keep them off that article as much as possible.

Our want of money increases to a very great degree. The expences of purchasing horses for the infantry, the sums paid to the distress'd refugees and militia, added to our other contingencies, swells the expenditure of public money to a very great amount. However, I trust that when the accounts are examin'd you will find them exactly agreeable to the instructions your Lordship in general has given me.

As Georgia has been threatened and much mischief already done there, I have wrote to Lt Colonel Clarke to come from St Augustine if he possibly can. The reinforcement of

---

[12] *my last..*: of 21st May, p 274.

[13] *my letter..*: no copy.

[14] *a letter..*: of 2nd June, p 307.

[15] *The cartel..*: see vol IV, p 88.

[16] *doubt*: used in the archaic sense of 'fear'.

Fanning's corps to that place Lord Rawdon will have mentioned.

In my letter to Ross I have mention'd every idea respecting matters here with that openess, warmth and confidence which your goodness and friendship to me must ever dictate. Your decision upon my requests will be received, as your commands have ever been, by

Your Lordship's most faithful and grateful

N BALFOUR

Balfour to Cornwallis, 9th June 1781　　　　　　　　　　　　　　6(222): ALS

Charles Town
9th June 1781

In my letter of the 7th June I forgot to mention to your Lordship Benson's application for leave to return to Europe.

He proposes to resign his majorship of brigade, and as he belongs to a regiment in Canada, he thinks there can be no objections to his quitting this part of America and returning to Europe. Indeed I do not see there can be any impediment or that the Commander in Chief could be offended with his going. However, he wishes to have your Lordship's permission before he takes either step.

Although I am certain that the service of this province will suffer exceedingly by Benson's leaving the situation, yet I cannot think of objecting to it, as his friends in Ireland under the administration of Lord Carlisle[17] have very considerable interest and influence and his presence there might be the means of his obtaining a very desirable situation. I own likewise that the prospect of my own movement soon from Charles Town makes me the more readily join in the request, as I assure you I could not go on as we have done without his asistance.

Could your Lordship give him any publick letters to mark his services, it would be only doing his merit justice, but as a favour done myself I would beg one in his favour from you to Lord Carlisle, to whom he looks in future. I am certain I need not say any more to induce you to grant both our requests, which will add to the numberless obligations bestowed on

Your sincere and faithful humble servant

N BALFOUR

---

[17] After leading a dissolute life, Frederick Howard (1748-1825), Earl of Carlisle, began to develop political ambitions as he approached his thirtieth birthday and in 1778 was named head of the peace mission dispatched to North America to try and negotiate a solution to the crisis. Accompanying him was William Eden, with whom he developed an effective relationship and who would remain a crucial adviser in the years ahead. After the failure of the mission both returned to England and on 29th November 1780 Carlisle was appointed Lord Lieutenant of Ireland (akin to governor general) with Eden, his trusted aide, as Chief Secretary. He would lose office on the fall of the North ministry in 1782, and apart from briefly serving as Lord Privy Seal in 1783, he would hold no other office of state during the rest of his life. (*ODNB*)

Balfour to Cornwallis, 10th June 1781 *6(208): ALS*

Charles Town
10th June 1781

Lord Cornwallis

By the express boat being detained I have an opportunity of sending your Lordship two letters just received from Lord Rawdon inclosed, also his Lordship's letter to me, by which you will see there is still a hope of our getting in time to save Cruger.

I have sent every person I could procure and offered large sums to get intelligence to 96 of the relief coming, and I have the greatest hopes that some of them will get in. God grant they may and all will still be well!

I ever am most faithfuly yours

N BALFOUR

Enclosure (1)
Rawdon to Balfour, 9th June 1781 *6(210): ALS*

Blake's Plantation
June 9th 1781

Lt Colonel Balfour etc

Sir

The enclosed is the copy of a letter which I have just received from Cruger. The messenger left the neighborhood of Ninety Six only on Wednesday last, tho' the letter is dated on Sunday. He says that the enemy had not at that time gained any advantage but were busy in building a cavalier to overlook the Star Redoubt. By the latest advices from Augusta, Browne still continued to defy the enemy. It was understood that they had attempted to undermine him but that he had countermined them and obliged them to give it up. We shall reach Four Hole Bridge this night. I have sent back the express to Cruger to tell him that we are coming.

I have the honor to be
Your very humble servant

RAWDON

Enclosure (2)
Cruger to Rawdon, 31st May 1781   6(212): C

31st May 1781

Lord Rawdon etc etc etc

By two different conveyances I informed your Lordship that Greene came here 22nd instant with about nine hundred men and three six pounders. He has been busy ever since building batteries and drawing lines round us. They appear to be advancing by regular approaches, working very industriously as if your Lordship was at hand, which important circumstance we are very anxious for as the only means of our safety. We begin tomorrow on our salt provisions, which will last a month with good management if the enemy does not take it from us, which we are all in full confidence your Lordship will very speedily put out of their power. Your Lordship's letter of the 5th instant is the last I have received. I have not since heard from Augusta. Greene since my last letter has been considerably reinforced by the militia of this country. He is now within one hundred and fifty yards of our Star Redoubt, the principal work, and approaching with great rapidity.

J H CRUGER

Enclosure (3)
Cruger to Rawdon, 3rd June 1781   6(213): C

Sunday evening
June 3rd 1781

Our neighbours continue industriously at work. They are within less than sixty yards of our Star Redoubt, at which distance they put up a log battery last night and fired from it this morning. Their great industry is a pleasing indication to us that your Lordship is not far off.

Our loss as yet is only one officer killed and eight soldiers wounded. We get no intelligence; no creature comes in to us. In a former letter I advised your Lordship that I had two hundred militia, pretty good and armed, and about an hundred old and helpless with their families. We were this day summoned to surrender and trust to the generosity of the American arms, which being rejected, a furious cannonading began from three one gun batteries.

I have the honor to be very respectfully, my Lord,
Your Lordship's most obedient humble servant

J H CRUGER
Lt Colonel commanding 96

Balfour to Cornwallis, 22nd June 1781　　　　　　　　　　　　6(249): LS

Charles Town
June 22nd 1781

Rt Hon Lt General Earl Cornwallis etc etc etc

My Lord

　　Agreeable to the cartel established between Lt Colonel Carrington and Captain Cornwallis, I have the honor to inform your Lordship that Lieutenant McKenzie of the 71st Regiment proceeds with four American officers and one hundred and ninety eight privates in order to receive an equal number of our troops in exchange. They are embarked on board the *Success Increase*, whereof Joseph Sanderson is master, and I am to request your Lordship will be pleased to give your directions for this vessel, when she has received the British prisoners in exchange for the Americans sent in her, proceeding to such near port as your Lordship shall judge agreeable to the cartel.

I have the honor to be, my Lord,
Your Lordship's most obedient and humble servant

N BALFOUR

Balfour to Cornwallis, 22nd June 1781　　　　　　　　　　　　6(251): LS

Charles Town
22nd June 1781

Rt Hon Lt General Earl Cornwallis etc etc etc

My Lord

　　Agreeable to the cartel established between Lt Colonel Carrington and Captain Cornwallis, I have the honor to inform your Lordship that Captain Duncanson is sent to receive the exchanged prisoners of the 71st Regiment, to which he belongs, and your Lordship's orders. One hundred and fifty five officers, Continentals and militia are embarked on board the *Two Brothers*, whereof Magnes Mariner is master, and I am to request your Lordship will be pleased to give your directions for this vessel, when she has received the British prisoners in exchange for the Americans sent in her, proceeding to such near port as your Lordship shall judge agreeable to the cartel.

I have the honor to be, my Lord,
Your Lordship's most obedient and humble servant

N BALFOUR

Balfour to Cornwallis, 22nd June 1781 6(257): LS

Charles Town
22nd June 1781

Rt Hon Lt General Earl Cornwallis etc etc etc

My Lord

Agreeable to the cartel established between Lt Colonel Carrington and Captain Cornwallis, I have the honor to inform your Lordship that the bearer, Mr Cooke, assistant commissary of prisoners, goes to receive the exchanged British prisoners and your Lordship's orders.

The whole number of prisoners sent in different ships, exclusive of officers paroled and liberated militia, amount to seven hundred and forty, as specified in the within return[18]. By the next conveyance your Lordship shall be furnished with the particulars of this transaction.

I have the honor to be, my Lord,
Your Lordship's most obedient and humble servant

N BALFOUR

Cornwallis to Balfour, 16th July 1781 88(20): C

Suffolk
16th July 1781

Lt Colonel Balfour

Dear Balfour

I wrote to you from Williamsburgh on the 28th of June[19], but I fancy the express vessel was taken[20]. Since that time reports from all quarters have relieved me from the most painfull anxiety for Ninety Six. Lord Rawdon's conduct will, I make no doubt, entitle him to praise and I conclude that Cruger's firmness and good sense have been highly meritorious.

Sir Henry Clinton in a dispatch to me of the 19th of June[21] acquiesces in the 3 regiments lately arrived remaining for the present in South Carolina, which I have by this opportunity

---

[18] *the within return*: not extant.

[19] *I wrote to you..*: no extant copy.

[20] *the express vessel was taken*: See Hudson to Leslie, 15th July, p 215.

[21] *a dispatch..*: see p 135.

notified to Colonel Gould, recommending at same time to him in the strongest manner to act in the most confidential manner with Lord Rawdon and you. I have likewise desired in the most pressing terms the same cordial and confidential assistance from Stewart.[22] You will find him good natured. He has seemed, and I believe is, perfectly well disposed towards me.

As the General's plan is only defensive in this quarter, where I can be of little use, I have offered to return to South Carolina, which I think very probable that he will approve of, but as good opportunities are sometimes rare, I wish you could prevail on Barklay to send back the *Carysfort* with yours and Lord Rawdon's dispatches, which might enable me to join you with little loss of time in case the General agrees to my proposition. It would likewise be a good opportunity to send the baggage and convalescents belonging to the regiments here, but you need not send the *Betsey* and *Polly* untill you hear again from me.

If Lord Rawdon's health should oblige him to leave you before my arrival (an event which I much fear) and operations should be necessary in the field, I recommend that Stewart and you should be with the army, Moncrieff acting as temporary Commandant and Colonel Gould remaining in Charlestown.

I tremble for *Craig's* plan and should have stopped it, only that my interference must have come too late if he availed himself of the conditional leave to carry it into execution.

Several of your cartel ships have arrived in James River. Recruiting of prisoners must of course cease when there are hopes of being able to exchange them. I had written to Captain Amherst by the dispatch vessell but have not time now. You will be so kind as notify this to him and to the other gentlemen from West Indies employed on that service and do every thing in your power to carry the terms of the cartel into speedy execution.

I have promised a passport for 400 hogsheads of tobacco to discharge the debts of the prisoners at Charlestown[23], and if you require it I will give further passeports for the same purpose, but I must beg that you will be very watchfull that the sales are applied to that purpose only and I should wish to put a stop to similar indulgences as soon as possible, for it is a commerce from which the rebels might derive very great advantages.

The Marquis and Wayne thought proper to attempt to disturb us in passing James River. After skirmishing all the afternoon of the 6th instant, they, I fancy supposing that we hid only a rearguard, produced about sunset in the front of our camp a body of Continentals with cannon, which we immediately attacked and beat, killing or taking about two hundred and two brass six pounders. The darkness of the evening prevented me from making use of the cavalry, or it is probable the Pennsylvania line would have been demolished. Our loss was not considerable and the 76th and 80th had an opportunity of distinguishing themselves particularly.

---

[22] For Cornwallis's letters of 16th July to Gould and Stewart, see pp 299-300.

[23] *I have promised..*: see Cornwallis to Lafayette, 28th June, p 237.

I address this letter to you as being nearest, concluding that as usual it is communicated to Lord Rawdon. I have only to add to him my most sincere congratulations on the success of his campaign and that he will always have my best and warmest wishes for his health and happiness, and believe me ever with greatest esteem and regard, my dear Balfour,

Your affectionate faithfull servant

[CORNWALLIS]

§ - §

2 - Between Cornwallis and Rawdon

Cornwallis to Rawdon, 20th May 1781[24] *86(41): C*

Petersburgh
20th May 1781

Rt Hon Lord Rawdon etc etc etc

My dearest Lord

I cannot describe my feelings on your most glorious victory, by far the most splendid of this war. My terrors for you had almost distracted me but served afterwards to heighten if possible my heartfelt satisfaction. I inclose an extract of my letter to the Commander in Chief[25] to prevent too sanguine expectations, which dearly bought experience has shewn me are not to be raised in consequence of victories in this country. My next apprehension is for your health; I hope you received my private letter written in the beginning of April on that subject[26]. I earnestly hope that you will not find it necessary to quit South Carolina, but if it should be otherways, Balfour must take the command of the troops in the country, altho I am convinced that his quitting the command of the town would be very hurtfull to the service, and Moncrief must be Commandant of Charlestown.

As to the extensive frontier which we have hitherto endeavoured to occupy, I am not certain whether we had not better relinquish it, even if Greene should move this way, but this I leave to your discretion or eventually to that of Balfour, promising my most hearty support

---

[24] An extended extract omitting the subscription and part of the first and last paragraphs is published in Ross ed, *Cornwallis Correspondence*, i, 97-8.

[25] *my letter..*: of 20th May, p 87.

[26] *my private letter..*: no copy.

against any criticism or interested representation. The perpetual instances of the weakness and treachery of our friends in South Carolina, and the impossibility of getting any military assistance from them, makes the possession of any part of the country of very little use except in supplying provisions for Charlestown. The situation of the province renders it impossible for us to avail ourselves of its rich produce, and a strong garrison in Charlestown with a small corps in the country will prevent the enemy from reaping any advantage from it unless they keep a considerable body of Continentals in the country for that purpose.

I this day formed a junction with the corps under Arnold at this place. You will conceive my distress at the loss of my poor friend Phillips. I cannot immediately say what measures I shall pursue. I am superior to La Fayette even after Wayne joins him, but the Commander in Chief has notified the sailing of the French fleet and 2,500 troops from Rhode Island. I understand that our post at Portsmouth is a bad one, and must consequently take care of my communication with it untill I hear something of the fleets.

Balfour sends me the most horrid accounts of the cruelty of the enemy and the numberless murders committed by them. If it should be in your power, I should hope that you would endeavour to put a stop to them by retaliation or such means as may appear most efficacious. That every happiness and success may attend you and that you may long enjoy the glory which you have so justly obtained is the sincere wish of

Your most faithfull and affectionate servant

CORNWALLIS

[*Subscribed*:]

I wish you had sent Doyle home on this occasion and desire you will do it in case of any future event of importance, informing the Minister and Commander in Chief that you had my directions to do so. If the reinforcement appears at Charlestown, you will detain what part of it you may think necessary.

Rawdon to Cornwallis, 2nd May 1781   6(25): ALS

Camden
May 2nd 1781

Earl Cornwallis etc etc etc

My dear Lord

Greene is still at Rugely's, I suppose waiting for succour. Lee and Marion I believe have joined him. Sumter is collecting provisions for him in the fork. McArthur, I find, is not to cross Santee but I have now some hope of Watson. Be assured every exertion shall be made but nothing done rashly. I have provisions for a fortnight and horses plenty. Our action cost us two hundred and twenty men. Greene lost at the very least five hundred. Continental deserters come in fast.

I have the honor to be with great respect
Your Lordship's most affectionate servant

RAWDON

Rawdon to Cornwallis, 24th May 1781

6(106): LS

Camp at Monk's Corner
May 24th 1781

Lt General Earl Cornwallis etc etc etc

My Lord

The situation of affairs in this province has made me judge it necessary for a time to withdraw my force from the Back Country and to assemble what troops I can collect at this point. I hope a recital of the circumstances which have led to this determination will satisfy your Lordship as to the expediency of the measure.

After the action on the 25th of April (an account of which I had the honor of transmitting to your Lordship) Major General Greene remained for some days behind the farthest branch of Granny's Quarter Creek. A second attempt upon his army could not in that situation be undertaken upon the principles which advised the former. In the first instance I made so short an excursion from my works that I could venture without hazard to leave them very slightly guarded, and I had the confidence that had fortune proved unfavorable we should easily have made good our retreat, and our loss in all probability would not have disabled us from the further defence of the place. To get at General Greene in his retired situation I must have made a very extensive circuit in order to head the creek, which would have presented to him the fairest opportunity of slipping by me to Camden, and he was still so superior to me in numbers that had I left such a garrison at my post as might enable it to stand an assault, my force for the field would have been totally unequal to cope with the enemy's army. I had much to hope from the arrival of reinforcement to me and little to fear from any probable addition to my antagonist's force. Whilst upon that principle I waited for my expected succors, General Greene retired from our front and, crossing the Wateree, took a position behind Twenty Five Mile Creek. On the 7th of May Lt Colonel Watson joined me with his detachment, much reduced in number thro' casualties, sickness and a reinforcement which he had left to strengthen the garrison at Georgetown. He had crossed the Santee near its mouth and had recrossed it a little below the entrance of the Congaree. By him I received the unwelcome intelligence that the whole interior country had revolted and that Marion and Lee (after reducing a small post where Lt Colonel Watson kept his baggage at Wright's Bluff) had crossed the Santee to support the insurgents upon the same night which he passed it to join me. Information reached me the same day that the post at Motte's House near the mouth of the Congaree was invested and batteries opened against it. I had been long sensible of the necessity for my retiring within the Santee, but whilst Lee and Marion were in a situation to retard my march in front at the same time that my rear was exposed to Greene, I conceived it impracticable without the disgrace of abandoning my stores and particularly my wounded at Camden. The measure even now could only be effected at Neilson's Ferry, which was sixty miles from me. I determined to undertake it immediately, but I thought it first requisite to attempt reaping some advantage from the additional strength which I had received. On the night of the 7th I crossed the Wateree at Camden Ferry, proposing to turn the flank and attack the rear of Greene's army, where the ground was not strong, tho' it was very much so in front. The troops had scarcely crossed the river when I received notice that Greene had moved early in the evening upon getting intimation of my being reinforced. I followed him by the direct road and found him posted behind Sawney's Creek. Having driven in his picquets, I examined every point of his situation. I found it everywhere so strong that I could not hope to force it without suffering such loss as must have crippled my force for any future enterprise, and the retreat lay so open for him that I could not hope victory would give us any advantage sufficiently decisive to counterbalance the loss. The creek (tho' slightly marked in the maps) runs very high into the country. Had I attempted to get round him he would have evaded me with ease, for as his numbers still exceeded mine, I could not separate my force to fix him in any point, and time (at this juncture most important to me) would have been thus unprofitably wasted. I therefore returned to Camden the same afternoon after having in vain attempted to decoy the enemy into action by affecting to conceal our retreat. On the 9th I published to the troops and to the militia my design of evacuating Camden, offering to such of the latter as chose to accompany me every assistance that we could afford them. During the ensuing night I sent off all our baggage etc under a strong escort, and destroyed the works, remaining at Camden with the rest of the troops till ten o'clock the next day in order to cover the march. On the night of the 13th I began to pass the river at Neilson's Ferry, and by the evening of the 14th every thing was safely across. Some mounted militia had attempted to harrass our rear guard on the march, but, a party of them having fallen into an ambuscade, the rest of them gave us no further trouble. We brought off all the sick and wounded excepting about thirty who were too ill to be moved, and for them I left an equal number of Continental prisoners in exchange. We brought off all the stores of any kind of value, destroying the rest, and we brought off not only the militia who had been with us in Camden but also all the well affected neighbors on our route, together with the wives, children, Negroes and baggage of almost all of them.

My first news upon my landing at Neilson's was that the post at Motte's House had fallen. It was a simple redoubt and had been attacked formally by sap. Lieutenant McPherson had maintained it gallantly till the house in the center of it was set in flames by fire arrows, which obliged his men to throw themselves into the ditch and surrender at discretion. The stroke was heavy upon me as all the provisions had been forwarded from Neilson's to that post for the supply of Camden. Lt Colonel Balfour was so good as to meet me at Neilson's. He took this measure that he might represent his circumstances to me. He stated that the revolt was universal; that from the little reason to apprehend this serious invasion the old works of Charlestown had been in part levelled to make way for new ones, which were not yet constructed; that his garrison was inadequate to oppose any force of consequence; and that the disaffection of the townspeople showed itself in a thousand instances. I agreed with him in the conclusion to be drawn from hence, that any misfortune happening to my corps might entail the loss of the province, but as Major McArthur had joined me with near three hundred foot and eighty dragoons, I conceived I might, without hazarding too far, endeavor to check the enemy's operations on the Congaree. On the 14th at night I marched from Neilson's, and on the evening of the 15th I reached the point where the road from Congarees and McCord's Ferry unite. Various information was brought to me thither by spies whom I had detached that Greene had passed the Congaree at McCord's Ferry and had pressed down the Orangebourgh Road. The accounts, tho' none of them positive or singly satisfactory, corresponded so much that I was led to believe them, and the matter was of such moment that it would not admit of my pausing for more certain information. Therefore, after having given the troops a little rest, I moved back to Eutaws the same night, but hearing nothing there, I pursued my march hither. I had been five days within the Santee before a single man of the country came near me. My first intelligence on this ground was that it had been only Sumter with his corps who had marched to Orangebourgh and that Greene had marched to Congarees, where the post (unable to oppose such force) had been surrendered to him on the 14th. I dispatched emissaries immediately to Ninety Six, desiring Lt Colonel Cruger to retire to Augusta, and I desired Lt Colonel Balfour to forward the same order by different routes. Should Lt Colonel Cruger not have received this order, I fear his situation will be dangerous. I did not think it practicable to assist him without running hazards which I judged the general state of the province would not allow. Besides, I had no deposit of provisions left on the frontier, and as to the expectation of gleaning them as I advanced in a wasted country and surrounded as I should have been by a swarm of light troops and mounted militia, I conceived that my whole force must have been so employed in procuring its daily subsistence that little else could have been effected with it.

By my present position I cover those districts from which Charlestown draws its principal supplies; I am in readiness to improve any favorable occurrence; and I guard against any untoward event. It is a secondary but not a triffling advantage that I have been able to supply the troops with necessaries, for the want of which (occasioned by the long interruption of our communication) they suffered serious distress. I am using every effort to augment our cavalry in hopes that the arrival of some force which may put Charlestown out of danger will speedily enable us to adopt a more active conduct, but the plundering parties of the enemy have so stripped the country of horses and there is such difficulty in getting swords and other appointments made at Charlestown that I get on but slowly in this undertaking.

I have the honor to be, my Lord, with great respect
Your Lordship's most obedient and very affectionate servant

RAWDON

Rawdon to Cornwallis, 5th June 1781[27]   6(174): ALS

Charlestown
June 5th 1781

Lt General Earl Cornwallis etc etc etc

My Lord

I had yesterday the honor of receiving your Lordship's letter dated from Petersburgh on the 20th of May.

---

[27] Extracts from this letter, taken from Almon's *Remembrancer 1781*, appear in Tarleton, *Campaigns*, 479.

General Greene invested Ninety Six on the 22nd of May. All my letters to Lt Colonel Cruger failed, so that he thought himself bound to maintain the post. To my great satisfaction, however, I learn (by messages which I have found means to interchange with Lt Colonel Cruger) that Ninety Six is in a very different state from what I supposed. The new works were completed before the enemy's approach, the garrison is ample for the extent, and the fire of the enemy had no effect. Lt Colonel Cruger therefore only apprehends that relief may not arrive before his provisions are expended. Fortunately we are now in a condition to undertake succouring him without exposing a more valuable stake, and from the report of his provisions which he sent to me I trust we shall be fully in time. Augusta is likewise besieged, but I hope in little danger. Sir James Wright represented so strongly the want of troops at Savannah that I thought it necessary to send the King's American Regiment thither with all dispatch, tho' at that time we could ill spare them. No convoy could be procured for them. Therefore I was obliged to hazard them in small vessels, but I thought the case required that risque, and since their departure I have heard nothing to make me apprehend any accident.

On the 3rd instant the fleet from Ireland arrived, having aboard the 3rd, 19th and 30th Regiments, a detachment from the Guards, and a considerable body of recruits, the whole under the command of Colonel Gould of the 30th. Lt Colonel Balfour and I immediately made known to Colonel Gould the powers which your Lordship had given to us for detaining such part of the expected reinforcement as we might conceive the service required. We represented as our joint opinion that two complete regiments were indispensibly necessary for the safety of the province at this particular juncture, but difficulties having arisen respecting the separation of those three regiments, it has been settled that they shall all remain here until your Lordship signifies your pleasure respecting them. The recruits (excepting those for the Southern District) proceed to New York, and the detachment of the Guards, taking advantage of the convoy as far as the Capes of Virginia, will endeavor to join your Lordship immediately by way of Portsmouth.

Intelligence was given to me very early, from a quarter which stamped authority in the information, that General Greene expected the cooperation of a foreign force upon the coast. It was this consideration which principally induced me to decline at that time the attempt of further opposition to General Greene in the Back Country. The hint which your Lordship has given me respecting the sailing of a French fleet with troops from Rhode Island corresponds with the above intelligence, yet had they been destined against this province, I think that by this time they would have made their appearance. I shall march on the 7th towards Ninety Six, having been reinforced by the flank companies of the three new regiments. If I am in time to save that post, it will be a very fortunate circumstance, but I much doubt whether it would be adviseable to maintain it. By making the Congaree our frontier and transplanting our friends from the Back Country to the rich plantations within that boundary whose owners are in arms against us, I think we may with few troops secure and command a tract which must in the end give law to the rest of the province.

I am happy in mentioning to your Lordship a handsome testimony of zeal for His Majesty's interests which has just occurred here. Considerable difficulty having arisen in the formation of cavalry, some of the principal inhabitants of this town made a subscription amounting to near three thousand guineas, which sum they requested I would apply to the purpose of equipping a corps of dragoons in the manner I might judge most expedient. As I had no means of forming such a corps but by drafts from the infantry, I thought your

Lordship would be pleased that a compliment should be paid to the loyalty of the gentlemen abovementioned by fixing upon men connected with the province. I have therefore ordered the Royal South Carolina Regiment to be converted into cavalry and I have the prospect of their being mounted and completely appointed in a very few days.

I have the honor to be, my Lord, with great respect
Your Lordship's very faithful and affectionate servant

RAWDON

June 6th

I have just had the satisfaction to learn that the King's American Regiment arrived safe at Savannah.

Rawdon to Cornwallis, 7th June 1781   6(194): ALS

Charlestown
June 7th 1781

Earl Cornwallis etc etc etc

I send to you, my dear Lord, a formal account of my transactions, so very voluminous that I am almost ashamed of it. I could not, however, reduce it into less compass without suppressing many circumstances which it is very interesting to me that you should know and which would probably be satisfactory to you. I must apologize that two of the letters are not written with my own hand, but I was thro' illness obliged to dictate them to another person. I have sent copies of them to the Commander in Chief and have left others with Lt Colonel Balfour to be transmitted to Lord George Germain when he has an opportunity of writing to England.

Let me now, my dear Lord, express to you what happiness your most kind letter from Petersburgh has given to me. You have overrated our success, which you will find has had little other effect than to give me the passage of the Santee, and the warm interest which you have so obligingly expressed in my personal advantage far overpays any share that I had in the business. Balfour and I have done all manner of *strong* things. If we have acted consonantly to your wishes, we shall feel the highest satisfaction. If we have erred, you will at least believe that we studied to do what might be agreable to your sentiments. We have had miserable trouble with Gould. He himself is well disposed to make matters easy, I am well convinced, but he does not act from his own opinions. Lt Colonel Stewart of the 3rd Regiment bears the character of a good officer, and upon the strength of it, I can plainly perceive, has influenced Gould to run rusty[28]. The case is Stewart has too high an opinion of himself to conceive that he ought even indirectly to give way to me, a Provincial colonel, and from that idea he has made Gould fight hard that none of the new troops should be

---

[28] *run rusty*: become intractable or obstinate.

employed in this province. Balfour and I wanted to detain two regiments and to send the other to Portsmouth with the Guards, but in spite of all reasoning or representation Gould persisted that he would keep his brigade together, and we must keep all or none. As the not making an effort when we had it in our power would be nearly equivalent to an absolute cession of the province, Balfour and I have decided to keep the whole till further orders arrive. By the time that your Lordship's instructions come I hope that we shall not want more than one *battalion* of them. I wished now to have sent you some convalescents and the detachment of the 17th Regiment, but I could not well spare them, for Gould would let me have nothing but the flank companies, and to march into the Back Country with a force which I did not feel equal to the task would be doing serious mischief to the service. I shall have near 1,800 infantry, and I hope near 200 cavalry, *tels qu'ils sont*. If Greene retires, I shall instantly send back the flank companies. I march this night and have great hopes of saving Cruger. In the mean time the town and lower districts are safe against any French force. To get any assistance from Gould, Balfour and I were obliged to write a formal letter declaring ourselves charged with the care of the province and in that capacity requiring assistance according to the powers which we produced. Still, a thousand demurs arise, and we are glad to make any compromise by which the service can be carried on. Craig has written so anxiously from Wilmington respecting the distress of the inhabitants for fear of being abandoned, and has held forth so fair a prospect of doing service there, that we have ventured to suspend your Lordship's order for recalling him, provided always that he can effect his purpose with the 82nd, Royal North Carolina Regiment and Yagers, for we have ordered the convalescents hither immediately. It will be necessary that a convoy should be sent for them and such of the troops as your Lordship orders to join you.

I am now, my dear Lord, with great pain to tell you that Hayes declares to me I could not outlive the summer in this climate. I am by no means now in a state of health fit to undertake the business upon which I am going, but as my knowledge of the country and my acquaintance with the inhabitants make me think that I can effect it better than any person here, I am determined to attempt it. Let me say, my dear Lord, very sincerely that zeal for the public service or any view towards my own credit do not urge me to this resolution more strongly than anxiety lest the distresses of this province should personally embarrass you. It is no unpleasing reflection for you that your kindness to the officers who have been serving under you has produced more exertion on their part than could have arisen from any other motive. I think I shall hold out as long as my service is particularly requisite here, and then I shall think of getting a thorough repair. I mentioned to Gould that as my health was so precarious, I wished to have a lt colonel with me who should take the command of the army in case of accidents, as it would now devolve on Doyle, Watson being recalled by the Commander in Chief. I could not, however, prevail, and I must only resolve neither to be ill nor to be killed. Doyle is possibly as equal to command as a lt colonel just come from Europe, but I do not think it becoming. You must excuse, my dear Lord, the haste in which this is written, as Elphinstone is aboard and just going to sail. I should be ashamed of sending such a scrawl were I not so confident in your indulgence on every point to

Your most faithful and affectionate servant

RAWDON

§ - §

3 - Between Cornwallis and Gould or Stewart

Gould to Cornwallis etc, 2nd June 1781 *6(153): ALS*

Sampson transport
At sea of Charles Town Bar
2nd June 1781

The Rt Hon Earl Cornwallis or officer commanding
His Majesty's troops in the Southern District

My Lord

Captain Elphinston commanding the convoy having been so obliging as to send to me to let me know he was going to send a boat to Charles Town, I was happy to embrace the earliest opportunity of informing your Lordship of my arrival off the coast with the 3rd, 19th and 30th Regiments of Foot, a detachment of the Foot Guards, and corps of recruits for the army. Having received His Majesty's commands, signified to me by Lord George Germaine, to put myself under the command of your Lordship or the Commander in Chief in the Southern Provinces untill I shall receive orders from Sir Henry Clinton or the Commander in Chief of His Majesty's forces in North America for my further proceedings, I hope soon to have the honor of receiving your Lordship's orders and instructions.

As soon as the fleet comes to an anchor and I can get the returns of the state of the troops, I shall do myself the honor of sending them to your Lordship.

I have the honor to be with the greatest respect, my Lord,
Your Lordship's most obedient and most humble servant

PASTON GOULD[29]
Lt Colonel 30th Regiment
Colonel in the Army

---

[29] Paston Gould (?-1783) had been serving as Lt Colonel of the 30th Regiment since 28th March 1764 and had been promoted to colonel in the army on 29th August 1777. Now in overall command of the reinforcement just arrived from Ireland, he would, for the most part, fail to cooperate in the attempt to relieve Ninety Six. 'We have had miserable trouble with Gould,' remarked Rawdon. 'He himself is well disposed to make matters easy, I am well convinced, but he does not act from his own opinions.' Influenced by the forceful personality of Alexander Stewart (see below), he chose 'to run rusty'. He would be promoted almost immediately by Clinton to the local rank of brigadier general, but a weak man, he would not be considered by Cornwallis as suitable to command to the southward. For this reason, as Cornwallis explained, when bidding farewell to Rawdon, 'it became absolutely necessary to send Leslie [*to Charlestown*] lest the command should have devolved on Gould.' By early September Gould would have been elevated to the local rank of major general, but apart from going to the relief of John Coates at Shubrick's plantation in mid July, he left the command in the field largely to Stewart. On 8th November Leslie would arrive. In 1782 Gould was invalided out of the army and died one year later. (*Army Lists*; *The Cornwallis Papers*; Boatner, *Encyclopedia*, 441)

Stewart to Cornwallis, 6th June 1781 6(188): *ALS*

Charles Town
6th June 1781

Lord Cornwallis

My Lord

I did myself the honor of writing you some time ago from Ireland, informing you how happy I was from the prospect of being soon under your command and the pleasure it would give me to be of any use to you with any little ability or military knowledge I may be possesed of. I was not a little disapointed on our arrival here to find your Lordship had left this province, but as I think it is probable some part of the reinforcement lately arrived may join your Lordship in Virginia, I hope the Buffs will be part of it. In my former letter I took the liberty to mention my wish to have the flank companys of the three regiments from Ireland formed into a kind of brigade along with the Buffs and that I might have that command. If that could be accomplished, it would make me very happy, and I hope my rank in the army will entitle me to some small command as I find Lt Colonels Clark, Balfour and Lord Rawdon have seperate commands; but that I entierly submit to your Lordship's judgement and rely on the goodness and friendship you have always showen me, for which I ever shall be gratefull. I sincerely congratulate you on the glorious victorys you have lately obtain'd and hope you'll continue in good health.

With respect and regard I have the honor to be
Your Lordship's most obedient and much obliged humble servant

ALEX[R] STEWART[30]

---

[30] A native of Ayrshire, Alexander Stewart (*c*. 1739-1794) had been commissioned an ensign in the 37th Regiment on 8th April 1755 and served in Germany during the Seven Years' War. By now Lt Colonel of the 3rd Regiment (the Buffs), he had arrived with it at Charlestown in early June as part of a reinforcement from Ireland under the overall command of Colonel Paston Gould (see above). In early July he would lead his regiment to a junction with Rawdon at Orangeburg, where Rawdon, who was returning on sick leave to England, handed over to him command of the troops on the frontier. On 8th September he would lead them bravely in the Battle of Eutaw Springs. He nevertheless does not emerge from these Papers in an entirely creditable light. Admittedly beset with personal problems of a financial nature, he comes across as a forceful personality overly preoccupied with rank, advancement and reward — as one who, in his letters to Cornwallis, is not averse to leaning on their past acquaintance to try and obtain preferment. Had these preoccupations not affected the conduct of the King's service, then all would have been well, but on at least one occasion they did. In a damning letter of 7th June (p 292) Rawdon explains to Cornwallis how and why Stewart influenced Gould 'to run rusty' by refusing to cooperate in the attempt to relieve Ninety Six. It was left almost entirely to the exertions of Rawdon and Balfour that the successful attempt was made. Cornwallis, for his part, plainly understood the nature of the creature with which he was dealing, as may be read between the lines of his letter to Stewart of 16th July (p 299). In December 1781 Stewart would achieve his cherished promotion to brigadier general and in 1782-3 serve in Jamaica. In 1786 he entered the Commons as the Member for Kircudbright Stewartry, a seat which he would hold till his death, but lost his chance of preferment by opposing Pitt's Regency Bill in 1788. Two years later he became a major general. (Valentine, *The British Establishment*, ii, 825; *The Cornwallis Papers*; *The Greene Papers*, ix, 310n; *Army Lists*)

Gould to Cornwallis, 7th June 1781 — 6(206): ALS

Charles Town
7th June 1781

The Rt Hon Earl Cornwallis
Commander in Chief of the Southern Army in North America

My Lord

I have the honor to acquaint your Lordship that on the 5th in the evening I arrived here with the 3rd, 19th and 30th Regiments under my command, a detachment of the Foot Guards, and a corps of recruits for the army.

I transmit enclosed a return of the state of the said regiments. My orders are to put myself under the command of Earl Cornwallis or the Commander in Chief of His Majesty's troops in the Southern Provinces untill I shall receive orders from Sir Henry Clinton or the Commander in Chief of His Majesty's forces in North America for my farther proceedings.

Immediately on my arrival, on a requisition from Lord Rawdon, I put under his Lordship's command the flank companies of the three regiments to march for the relief of Ninety Six. The 3rd Regiment is marched to take post at Monk's Corner, the 19th Regiment disembarks tomorrow and marches to take post at Dorchester, and the 30th Regiment will disembark the day after tomorrow and be quartered in Charles Town. I hope soon to receive your Lordship's commands.

The detachment of Foot Guards I sent to join your Lordship at Portsmouth in the Chesapeak under convoy of the *Warwick*, and the recruits for the northern army I sent to New York. All this I did by the advice of Lt Colonel Balfour, Commandant of Charles Town, which I hope you will approve of.

I hope to have the honor of soon receiving your Lordship's commands, and am with the greatest respect, my Lord,

Your Lordship's most obedient and most humble servant

PASTON GOULD
Lt Colonel 30th Regiment
Colonel in the Army

Enclosure
State of the troops embarked under Gould 6(155): DS

STATE of the Troops embarked under the command of Colonel Gould, Cove of Cork, 18th March 1781						
Ranks	Regiments and Corps					Total
	Foot Guards	3rd Regiment or Buffs	19th Regiment	30th Regiment	Detachment of Recruits	
Officers present						
Commissioned						
Colonels						
Lt colonels		1	1	1		3
Majors		1	1	1	1	4
Captains	4	8	8	8		28
Lieutenants	4	11	11	11	2	39
Ensigns	3	7	6	8	11	35
Staff						
Chaplins						
Adjutants		1	1	1		3
Quarter Masters		1	1	1		3
Surgeons		1	1	1		3
Mates	1	1	1	1	2	6
Serjeants	3	30	30	30		93
Drummers and Fifers	1	22	22	22		67
Effective rank and file						
Present and fit for duty	150	710	710	710	777	3,057
Sick	4					4
TOTAL	154	710	710	710	777	3,061
Casualties since the regiments and corps embarked						
Deserted					30	30
Dead					11	11

Drowned					3	3
Discharged					1	1
Sick at Portsmouth					17	17
TOTAL rank and file - embarked	154	710	710	710	839	3,123

PASTON GOULD
Lt Colonel 30th Regiment
Colonel in the Army

Cornwallis to Gould, 28th June 1781[31]

87(23):C

Williamsburgh
June 28th 1781

Colonel Gould
South Carolina

Sir

I must desire that you will please to embark, as soon as Captain Barklay can provide a sufficient convoy, with the battalion companies of the 19th and 30th Regiments and proceed immediately to join Sir Henry Clinton at New York, leaving the 3rd Regiment and the six flank companies to serve in South Carolina. If, however, it should appear to Lord Rawdon and Lt Colonel Balfour, or, in the case of Lord Rawdon's absence, to Lt Colonel Balfour, that the situation of South Carolina is so critical and dangerous that the removal of the 19th and 30th Regiments would be prejudicial to the King's Service, you will then proceed to New York with the 8 companies of the 30th Regiment only and leave those of the 19th untill further directions can be sent from Sir Henry Clinton or myself.

I flatter myself that you will not conceive that I can possibly mean by this order to do any thing disagreeable to you. I am confident that on your arrival at New York Sir Henry Clinton will appoint you to the command of a suitable brigade, but as the direction of affairs in South Carolina is very intricate as it depends much on the knowledge of the climate, country and temper of the inhabitants, which nothing but a long local experience can give, and as much civil management is connected with it, you will not be surprized that at this alarming crisis I should wish to employ those who have acted confidentially with me for this last twelvemonth and who are fully in possession of my sentiments on any material event that may occur.

---

[31] This letter miscarried. See following letter, together with Hudson to Leslie, 15th July, p 215.

As soon as a frigate can be procured, I propose sending Major General Leslie to Charlestown, but as Sir Henry Clinton is very pressing to have troops sent to New York and as I cannot supply from hence so many as he desires, I must beg that you will lose no time in proceeding thither as soon as such a convoy is prepared as may appear to the commanding officer of the navy to be sufficient.

I am, sir, with great regard
Your most obedient and most humble servant

[CORNWALLIS]

Cornwallis to Gould, 16th July 1781　　　　　　　　　　　　　　88(22): C

Suffolk
16th July 1781

Colonel Gould

Sir

I embrace the opportunity of the *Carysfort* to write a few lines, for I believe the express vessell with my dispatches of the 28th June has been taken.

By a dispatch to me from Sir Henry Clinton of the 19th June it appears to be his wish, which entirely coincides with mine, that the three regiments under your command should for the present remain in South Carolina. It is probable that I shall soon join you, and in the mean time I strongly recommend it and shall think myself much obliged to you if you will act in perfect concert and in the most confidential manner with Lord Rawdon and Lt Colonel Balfour in carrying on the service. You will find them men of integrity and abilities, thoroughly acquainted with the disposition of the people and the nature of the country, and they are well informed of my sentiments relative to the conduct of the publick business in that district.

[CORNWALLIS]

Cornwallis to Stewart, 16th July 1781　　　　　　　　　　　　　　88(26): C

Suffolk
16th July 1781

Lt Colonel Stewart
3rd Regiment

Dear Stewart

I had written to you on the 28th of June[32], but I fancy the express vessell has been taken.

---

[32] *I had written..*: no extant copy.

It is not improbable that I shall soon be with you in South Carolina, where I am well convinced from our old acquaintance and friendship I shall receive the most cordial assistance from you. In the mean time I must beg that you will act in the most confidential manner with Lord Rawdon and Lt Colonel Balfour, who are most perfectly acquainted with my sentiments and to whose ability and zealous attachment I owe much of the success that has attended my command. In case Lord Rawdon's health should not permit him to serve 'till I arrive (which I much doubt[33]), you cannot oblige me more than by acting most cordially and heartily with Balfour, and you may be assured that it will give me pleasure when in my power during the course of the service to place you in eligible and creditable situations.

[CORNWALLIS]

§ - §

4 - From Cornwallis to Craig

Cornwallis to Craig, 20th May 1781[34]   *86(39): C*

Petersburgh
May 20th 1781

Major Craig

Dear Sir

I sent off as many letters to you from Halifax as it was possible to get messengers to carry[35], and hope one may have arrived safely at Wilmington. For fear of the worst I have desired the commanding officer of the navy to send a ship of war. You will of course immediately fall down to Bald Head and proceed as soon as possible to Charlestown. Things looked very black when I wrote to you on the 3rd and 4th of this month[36], but the prospect soon brightened and Lord Rawdon has dispelled all the clouds. The death of my friend General Phillips has given me the most sensible affliction.

I am with great regard
Your most obedient and faithfull servant

CORNWALLIS

---

[33] *doubt*: used in the now archaic sense of 'fear'.

[34] Received by Craig on 2nd June. See Craig to Balfour of that date, p 307.

[35] *I sent off as many letters..*: see vol IV, p 168.

[36] *when I wrote to you..*: see vol IV, p 166.

Cornwallis to Craig, 25th May 1781[37]

86(49): C

Byrd's Plantation
25th May

Major Craig

The junction was effected the 20th at Petersburgh. You will return to Charlestown as soon as possible.

CORNWALLIS

[*Subscribed*:]

Ten guineas to the bearer.

Cornwallis to Craig, 17th July 1781

88(28): C

Suffolk
17th July 1781

Major Craig

Dear Sir

I feel most exceedingly for the situation of our friends in and near Wilmington, but I own I wish of all things that you and your detachment were safe at Charlestown and therefore beg that you will evacuate Wilmington and Cape Fear River and repair to Charlestown as soon as possible unless you have begun any operations in consequence of orders or permission from Lord Rawdon or Lt Colonel Balfour. In that case you will follow their future directions.

I am with great regard etc

[CORNWALLIS]

§ - §

---

[37] Annotated: 'This letter was not delivered. The bearer returned.'

5 - From Craig to Balfour

Craig to Balfour, 18th May 1781   6(82): ALS

Willmington
18th May 1781

Dear Sir

I have receiv'd your letters of the 12th as also one wrote by Colonel Moncrief's directions on the 13th. The intelligence contain'd in the latter I looked on as being of the utmost consequence and have consequently dispatch'd as many messengers as affection or money could procure in order to ensure its arrival to Lord Cornwallis[38]. From the tenor of the last letters I had then receiv'd from him I did not imagine he would have been so far advanc'd as I now find by one I got yesterday. It was dated from Halifax the 12th instant[39]. I inclose you a copy of it. I am afraid that General Phillips's progress was suppos'd rather more rapid than it really was, as I think Lord Cornwallis must have heard of him if he was within sixty miles, or else that the reports now about the country of the arrival of a second French fleet in the Chesapeak may be better founded than the many similar ones have hitherto been. All thoughts of embarkation here[40] now seem to be at an end, but you will observe that observation in Lord Cornwallis's letter is founded on the idea of Lord Rawdon's victory having had more favourable consequences than your letters give us reason to hope for. I have sent him the substance of all your letters relative to the state of your province[41] that he may have the best information to ground his resolutions on. I cannot bring myself to think that he will not afford you some assistance if his junction with General Phillips takes place at Halifax. The most effectual way would certainly be by returning on Greene's back and crushing him effectually or, if he is fortunate enough to escape, by driving him into Virginia, but at least I think he will send a reinforcement to you, which can only be done by embarkation from this place. I have wrote to him on this idea[42], and that I should not think of stirring till I got an answer to that letter. At all events the *circumstances already settled between us*, mentioned in his letter, is his passing the Roanoke to form his junction with Phillips in Virginia, but his junction now taking place probably at Halifax and the situation of South Carolina may make such a material alteration in his intentions as may render my stay here necessary for a longer time, and I cannot bring myself to think but one or other of the methods for your relief above stated will take place. I shall be able, I think, to get an answer in 10 or 11 days, which will immediately determine me, or if in the mean time I receive

---

[38] If in written form, the intelligence miscarried.

[39] See vol IV, p 168.

[40] *embarkation here*: of Cornwallis and his corps from Wilmington to Charlestown.

[41] *I have sent him..*: see Craig to Cornwallis, vol IV, pp 165 to 170.

[42] *I have wrote to him..*: the letter miscarried.

accounts from him that he passes the Roanoke to form his junction in Virginia, I shall then begin my embarkation, which will be a work of some time from the impossibility of the vessels coming within some miles of us and the opportunity I am determin'd to give, to every body who chuses, to come with us to atone as much as possible for the disappointment we so frequently subject them to. At present I see no probability of our being molested as there are not fifty men in arms within twice as many miles, but should the idea of our evacuating the post, which from the circumstances of the empty transports coming has already gone about the country, be confirm'd, there is no knowing whether they may not have it in their power to assemble a sufficient number to be troublesome. I am therefore carefull to conceal my intentions, tho' it goes to my heart as I am confident many will suffer, particularly some who in spite of my endeavours have taken arms and yesterday brought me in some prisoners of consequence.

Believe me, your last letter of the 12th as well as my earnest wish to profit of your friendly intentions to myself would induce me to stretch every point to join you immediately, but when I do by the by I shall not carry you much active assistance. Neither my own people nor those with me are capable of it, Lord Cornwallis having stript me of my light company as well as of that of Hamilton's corps. However such as we are, I regret our situation depriving us of the opportunity of being of the little service we might be of. I shall endeavour to have every thing in that state as to take as little time as possible after I receive my directions, and shall contrive, I hope, to detain the *Carysfort* for convoy. I beg you to dispatch the pilot boat back with further accounts of your situation as soon as possible, as I will still continue to send after Lord Cornwallis to the last moment, being confident of his anxiety.

Have you such a thing as a few cavalry appointments to spare me? If you have, and have any opportunity of sending me 30 or 40, I should be much oblig'd to you. I believe I shall be able to carry near 50 very well mounted men with me, which might be of use. If circumstances oblige me to make any longer stay here, I cannot do without them, and if not, and any difficulty should occur in transporting them by sea, I mean to push with them for George Town, but this can only be, provided they have each *a sword at least*, which I cannot give them at present. Should this ever take place, I shall go with them myself. If the *Otter* should be sail'd, I am so distress'd for them that I should even beg you to risk them in the pilot boat, only let the swords be kept at hand to throw over with the letter in case of misfortune, as there is nothing the rebels want so much. I have no accounts yet of the *Columbine*.

I congratulate you on Lord Rawdon's quitting Camden, which from the first I look'd on as a necessary and deciding step. After a victory which does him such infinite honour, every body would doubly regret any misfortune happening him. I wish I could also hear of the garrison of Ninety Six being added to your force. In a general revolt like the present, it is not a single post [that] can contain a country or be of any service. Your united force may do great things and I shall never despair while I hear of its being collected.

I am with the sincerest regard, dear sir,
Your most faithfull humble servant

J H CRAIG

[*Subscribed*:]

9 o'clock at night

The *Columbine* is just come up but does not bring any thing near the quantity of provisions you mention.

Craig to Balfour, 28th May 1781 *6(129): ALS*

Willmington
28th May 1781

Dear Sir

I wrote to you on the 18th by Lieutenant Cunningham of the 82nd, duplicate of which inclos'd. Since that, Cane return'd from the Chesapeak and I detain'd him in expectation of having something to send you of consequence. However, as I now expect you will send the other boat back soon, I shall not keep him any longer.

Lord Cornwallis pass'd the Roanoke at Halifax on the 15th, and by a man who carried one of my letters and is this instant return'd, tho' without any letter from his Lordship, he was left on the Nottaway within five and twenty miles of Petersburgh on the 19th in the morning early and probably reach'd that place the 21st. General Arnold was with him, and it is with real concern I add the man's report that General Phillips died in Petersburgh the Sunday before, which I am afraid is but too true, as he was oblig'd on account of indisposition to employ another hand to write a private letter I have from him dated the 6th. I have already mention'd the man brings no letter, but the general report was that La Fayette was at Williamsburgh and an action was expected to take place immediately. If the former part of the report is true, the latter is most probably so also, as by an inspection of the map his avoiding it seems impossible. This is all I know at present concerning Lord Cornwallis's movements, and before I proceed on my own situation, I must give you a piece of intelligence brought me yesterday, in which I shall be particular, as it nearly concerns your situation, is the principal cause of my dispatching Cane, and, being only circumstantial confirmation of a report in the country, I wish to enable you to judge of the probability of it. A very sensible young man who has been much employ'd by Lord Cornwallis and lately by myself came in yesterday from within 25 miles of the Little Pedee, which he left on the 24th. He says it was currently reported and believ'd in the country that Grene meant to retire immediately to Virginia. The young man is so well accustom'd to collecting intelligence that I place great dependance on him. He believes it himself and thinks the report confirm'd by finding the people busily employ'd in collecting and driving the cattle to different parts of that road, and in Cross Creek he found the people collecting corn for the same purpose. His own and brothers' cattle have been drove off from their farms. The country people said they had directions from Grene himself to retire into Virginia and seize and carry with them all the Torys' cattle, and that they should have the milch cows and other cattle which he did not use for their trouble. The young man is so fairly worn out with fatigue, having rode above 800 miles in our service since the army march'd, that I could not send him back, but I have taken every other method I could think of to get at the certainty, of which you shall have the earliest intelligence, even tho' I should think it probable that you have known it before. My informer adds that he could not get any certain accounts of where Grene was then, as reports were so various, one even making him to be at Colson's Ferry, but he is certain *that* is one of the places to which they were driving the cattle.

Lord Cornwallis's passing the Roanoke, of which I also receiv'd the accounts yesterday, was the circumstance agreed on between us on the information of which I was to begin to embark, but the situation of affairs has varied so much since that was determin'd on that I have wrote to him that I should take on me to remain till I receiv'd an answer to that letter, which I am now in hourly expectation of. You can have no idea of the consternation which seized the country on the arrival of the empty transports from the notion, which immediately spread, that we were going away. Had I remain'd, as was at first suppos'd, only a few weeks for the supply of Lord Cornwallis's army, my going would not have been attended with such circumstances as it will now after being here four months. Now it will add one to the many instances of the same kind which have rais'd such a clamour against us, and should Grene abandon his attempt on South Carolina, which I think probable, the possession of this place will (I think) be absolutely necessary, as I can almost answer for the submission of the lower part of the country at least. All my endeavours, which have been strenuously exerted for the purpose, have not been sufficient to keep the people from rising. Some hundreds are in arms and many more wait only for the word from me to rise. Whether I should ever assemble them so as to employ them to any effect should armies from the other provinces enter this I cannot say, but I am pretty confident, even with what force I have, I could encourage and support them so as to become masters of the country and disarm the rebels; probably, at least I am led by circumstances to think so. Many would inlist so as to form corps, one gentleman here to whom Lord Cornwallis gave permission to try having already underhand nearly compleated an independant company. In short, tho' the advantages which may be deriv'd from them cannot be foreseen yet, I dread, and most sincerely feel the being reproach'd as the cause of, the miseries these poor people will be expos'd to the moment I quit them, tho' in the present instance it will be unjustly, because so far from encouraging them in rising I have done every thing I could (except telling them I was to leave them) to dissuade them from it. Still, it was our coming here that caus'd it and it will be cruel to abandon without one effort to save them.

A few days ago a party who had particular directions from me to remain quiet brought me in seven prisoners whom they seiz'd because they came into their settlement to force them to take arms with the usual denunciations of plunder and devastation. They, however, brought them to me without injuring them or even taking their arms from them. As I wish'd to stop this kind of business of *forcing* people, I put the prisoners (tho' 3 or 4 of the gentlemen of the neighbourhood were among them) into the prison ship. Since then I have receiv'd pretty good information that five of these unfortunate people have been taken and carried to a General Caswell's camp, who has not 50 men with him, who deliberately order'd them to be shot. I have put my prisoners in irons and have given them to understand that their fate depends on a confirmation of my account of Mr Caswell's treatment of these people, a threat I should not hesitate one moment to execute did I not think it a step of too much consequence to be taken without a sanction of my superior. Indeed, were I fix'd to remain here, I believe, serious as it is, I should take it on me. However, it seems likely to produce some consequences among themselves, for a very considerable body of the inhabitants between

Kingstone and Halifax who had been parol'd by Lord Cornwallis in his passage assembled the next day to the number as said of near 500 and march'd to Mr Caswell's to know the reason of the execution. I have not had time to hear the result. I must add one to the many reasons I have urg'd why I now think the possession of this place of consequence, viz, that it is the port to which they look up for French succour and indeed the only one by which they can communicate with the sea in a vessel of any size to the southward of the Delaware. I could soon repair or rather rebuild Fort Johnson at a very small expence, and if I get any assistance from the country, which I think I should, I could garrison it and defend this post, bad as it is. The trade would also be very considerable. Lord Cornwallis parol'd near 3,000 men on this side of Halifax.

I have endeavour'd as well as could be done in cypher to explain all this to Lord Cornwallis and only wait for a confirmation of Grene's movement to send him an account of that also, which may be of consequence to him to know. I hope you will send back one of the pilot boats, as I should wish to let you know the moment my moving is determin'd on as also if I get any account of an action with La Fayette.

I am with great regard, dear sir,
Your most obedient and faithfull servant

J H CRAIG

[*Subscribed*:]

The *Columbine* from George Town with provisions is arriv'd.

Craig to Balfour, 28th May 1781   6(127): ALS

Willmington
28th May 1781

Dear Balfour

A very long letter which is just finish'd is not wrote with my usual freedom from the probability of your being out of town and its being open'd by others. From every circumstance I put confidence in the intelligence I have sent you concerning Grene, tho' I by no means give it you as certain. I wish I could, as I should add my most hearty congratulations. It would, I think, ensure the future tranquillity both of your and this province. I was in haste to send it you that you might take measures to find out whether it is so or no, as I think he might leave his militia with his cavalry before Lord Rawdon and by that means keep him ignorant of his march some days. The latter might follow and the former he does not care about.

Lord Chewton, who was off the barr and has proceeded to the Chesapeak, wrote me that the reinforcement from Europe was expected at Charles Town daily as well as some regiments from the West Indies. Is this true?

This country is in a glorious situation for cutting one another's throats. I am very sincere in my endeavours to prevent it, which, however, have not in every instance been effectual. The Tories are the most numerous, and was I to give the word, a fine scene would begin. However, I think it cruelty without a certainty of being ready to support them. If I had that, I should soon begin. I am confident, if suffer'd to remain here, I could do much, and want only a few cavalry appointments. The men who were left behind recover fast and, tho' not fit for active service yet, are more than equal to our defence, was the whole country assembled together to come against us.

There is a rascally little place call'd Beauford near Cape Look Out where they fit out a number of little piccarroon privateers and do much mischief on your coast. There are no less than five row boats fitting out now. I wish to destroy it but dare not undertake it in my present situation. If I should remain here, it will be one of the first things I do.

Lord Cornwallis's idea when here seem'd to be to raise independant companies and not corps. It is a much better scheme. Governor Martin's corps has got but 50 men. Indeed they have not had much time, but I don't think they will ever compleat. Country people don't like to have their neighbours and former companions for their officers. However, they should have a fair trial, which they have not had yet.

God bless and deliver you from your present troubles. I think the prospect now so fair I have no doubt of success. What think you of Lord Cornwallis beating La Fayette? If you see Lord Rawdon, make my most respectfull compliments to him.

Yours very sincerely

J H CRAIG

Craig to Balfour, 2nd June 1781   6(151): ALS

Willmington
2nd June 1781

Dear Balfour

The general willingness I find in (or rather which is declar'd to me by) all ranks of people here to take arms in the King's favour encourages me to offer a project to you which has appear'd every moment more plausible since I sent the pilot boat off. My present situation and the probability of my quitting them soon has made me extremely cautious how I encourag'd this spirit, tho' I am almost convinc'd it exists and in your exigency I think should be tried. The service a body of *Tories* will do is, you know, so very precarious that the man who proposes to use them risks his person and reputation with considerable odds against him. However, if Lord Rawdon will give the word, I am ready to stake them.

I find our men recover so fast that I can march out about 300 men and still leave almost as many to defend the post as I had before the arrival of Lord Cornwallis. With these I propose going first towards the Nuse near New Berne, where some hundreds of Tories are I believe ready to join me. From thence I would march towards Duplin Court House, where I am taught to believe I shall meet many more. Higher up I should still become stronger, but that would carry me too far from my principal object, which is to engage as many as I could to follow me and with them cross the NW Branch of the Cape Fear River, between which and the Pedee the country swarms with our friends, from many of whom I have had messages. I am apt, I know, to be sanguine in my projects, but in matters of this consequence I am on my guard against my own disposition. Could I appear on the Pedee at the head of 1,200 men, three [hundred] of which would be regular troops, it might perhaps startle Mr Grene and be of essential service. Unless I engag'd *near* that number, I should not think of advancing far, and George Town or this place would always furnish me a retreat.

I have here in all about 700 stand of arms and plenty of ammunition but not a bayonet. I have my two three pounders, which are sufficient (tho' I should like one six or a howitzer added to them), and I have about thirty mounted men, not bad but wanting swords etc which I wrote to you for by Lieutenant Cunningham. Our fall will not be very considerable and I should hope will cost dear. I should mean, however, to act with a little caution at first, tho' apparently otherwise, so as to *bully* if possible where I found real strength deficient.

You have now my project, the execution of which depends on Lord Rawdon and your idea of its utility and propriety. If you think fit to risk it, only give me the word and a power to be liberal to my friends in the article of blankets and other stores which are absolutely necessary and I will proceed immediately.

I have just been call'd off to receive a letter from Lord Cornwallis dated at Petersburgh the 20th ultimo[43], which was only wrote in case those he sent me from Halifax should have miscarried. Therefore alters nothing in my intentions as he could not have receiv'd any of mine. However, it makes the receiving them at all more improbable and furnishes me with a proper vessell to send this by. I shall now wait till next Sunday (tomorrow) se'ennight, before which if ever I shall receive an answer. In the mean time I shall be more determin'd by yours with respect to this proposal. If you and Lord Rawdon think it can be of material service or rather that it is worth risking, I am most ready to undertake it. You must be the judges whether it promises better than the assistance of about 300 men, which are all I shall carry you. Eighty men are this moment come in to me. Seventy came in a few days ago. All these must be abandon'd to the mercy of *most merciless rascals*.

I need not mention how necessary it is that I should get the answer as soon as possible. I would wish even duplicates were sent. Remember, no letter I receive in the mean time wrote before I can suppose you to have got this will induce me to alter my resolutions.

I am with the sincerest regard
Your ever faithfull and oblig'd servant

J H CRAIG

---

[43] *a letter..*: see p 300.

Craig to Balfour, 12th June 1781　　　　　　　　　　　　　　　　6(238): CS

Willmington
12th June 1781

Dear Sir

This morning I was favor'd with your answer to mine of the 2nd instant and am very happy in having my idea of the movement I propos'd approved of by Lord Rawdon and yourself. I therefore cannot help feeling myself doubly mortified at being at the same moment depriv'd of the means of executing it. I inclose you a return of the men I shall have after sending to Charlestown the convalescents of Lord Cornwallis's army[44]. This I do not hesitate one moment to pronounce totally inadequate to the object I had in view, and will be barely sufficient for the maintenance of this post, the ordinary duty of which will be done with extreme difficulty. I proposed that scheme in the confidence that I should not have been deprived of the men of Lord Cornwallis's army so soon. Long I knew I could not keep them, but as a very considerable number are still totally unfit for duty and as the General Hospital here is in a very fine and healthy situation, I thought they would not have been mov'd till they recover'd, and in the mean time I could have made use of those who are well, which would I think have been sufficient at least to have justified the attempt.

The probability of collecting the number of friends I mentioned in my former letters appears the greater every day. I have had near 250 with me already whom the uncertainty of my movements oblig'd me to send home again. Having constantly made a point of not deceiving them, I have acquired their confidence, I believe, and have their promise of joining me the moment I go out and of such of them as I chuse continuing with me to any part of the province. They give me the highest reasons to expect many more from the parts contiguous to their settlements, which are all near me, while I have equal offers and promises from other parts more remote. On the whole I think I may with confidence say that could I have gone even with the 300 men I propos'd, I should very soon have exceeded the numbers I gave you reason to hope for in my former letter, but I can with almost certainty say now that 500 troops exclusive of the number necessary to be left here would ensure me the whole lower part of the province and perhaps have enabled me to appear in Green's rear. The people seem hearty and well dispos'd. Experience can alone determine the degree of efficacy with which they would act, but I believe proper treatment might make something of them. I would in a particular manner propose paying the militia while embodied, which I know would have a very good effect.

The impossibility of making the propos'd movement has put me into a terrible dilemma with respect to the friends of Government, nor can I at present determine on what to do or how to put them off till I receive your answer. At this moment the thing would be of double consequence because the rebels are making every possible effort to raise 2,700 for twelve months' men. In this they would certainly fail could I go out and offer a protection to those who did not chuse to engage with them, but by delaying it they may collect some, which may prove the means of getting others who would not join them could they avoid it. Caswell has

---

[44] *a return..*: no copy.

about 300 men at Kingston and a few more are collected in Duplin County. The moment they hear of so considerable a part of our force going away, they will collect as strong as they can and come down to a strong position about 25 miles off, possibly nearer. My communication with the country will then be cut off as it was before Lord Cornwallis's arrival and any future attempt be very difficult. Besides that, they will inevitably ruin all the friends who have been here.

I cannot help offering my own opinion and I hope it will be look'd on as proceeding only from a sincere desire of being of as much service as my situation will allow. At least I rest in assur'd confidence that both Lord Rawdon and yourself will do me the justice to believe I do it with the most respectful deference to your judgements and acquit one of any other presumption than what arises from a strict attention to the state of the country and an opinion in which I may be mistaken but which has been founded only on that. I cannot then help thinking that the arming the friends of Government here and supporting them with a small body may at this time be attended with every beneficial consequence exclusive of the reduction of this province and assisting in crushing Green. The affairs of the rebels are certainly at a critical period, and a beginning is perhaps only wanted. A majority of the people declaring themselves in one province may induce others to follow the example and might perhaps have the greater effect when supported by no more than the necessary number of troops from the greater appearance it would have of being voluntary.

I have now hazarded my opinion, and having already informed you that I do not look on myself as at all adequate to the execution, I submit it to you to determine on the propriety of enabling me to attempt it, which can only be done by sending something here in the room of the force I am deprived of, something more considerable, as 4 or 500 would insure, I think, success. I should not, however, hesitate to undertake it with 250. However flattering command may be to a young man whose whole views are military, I request my pretensions to it may not interfere in the smallest manner on this occasion, as you may be assur'd I shall serve with equal readiness should it be thought necessary to send a senior officer here.

The Assembly of the province is called to meet by the rebel Governor on the 15th instant and is one additional motive for my pressing that whatever the determination may be may take place immediately. Could the reinforcement be spared, it would be of infinite consequence that it should come before Lord Cornwallis's men sail. As I have not yet seen Captain Peacock, I can say nothing on that subject but that they shall embark the moment he pleases.

A convoy of twenty eight waggons loaded chiefly with ammunition and salt has lately pass'd thro' the upper country escorted by about 250 or 300 Maryland eighteen months' men for Green's army. I had their route, tho' too late, even had I been strong enough to have attempt'd it. I suppose you are well acquainted with Greene's strength. However, it may not be improper to mention that from every information he cannot have 800 Continental troops with him.

J H CRAIG

Craig to Balfour, 13th June 1781

6(240): CS

Wilmington
13th June 1781

Lt Colonel Balfour etc etc etc

Dear Sir

The small boat which carried the original of the enclosed duplicate sailed last night, and this morning Mr Magridge in the pilot boat arrived and delivered me the duplicate of yours of the 7th instant. I dispatch him back instantly, both as a second opportunity for conveying mine and as it furnishes me one for adding what has occurred to me since on the subject. The more I think of it, the more I am confident of the success of my plan if enabled to execute it, but I cannot without further assistance. I observe your postscript and shall do my utmost to induce our friends above to intercept Green's supplies, but you may be assured they will never be brought to act of themselves to any effect. They will only get cut to pieces if they do attempt any thing. It is almost cruelty to persuade them. If reinforced to the utmost of my request, viz, 400 men, I would almost engage to be between Hilsborough and Salisbury in a month's time at the head of 2,000. I would attempt it with less, but with proportionally less probability of success, as I know the numbers would increase in proportion to the support, which these people look up to.

On seriously considering the consequences of embarking the convalescents of Lord Cornwallis's army, I have ventured to take on me to delay it till I hear from you again. Probably, indeed, they might not be able to sail before then, and every other circumstance will be ready except the actual embarkation, which I keep secret. That can take place, if required, in four hours after. If you should think proper for me to attempt the movement I propose, I can assure you that the delay of the embarkation may be of the greatest consequence, as the loosing so very considerable a part of my force will discourage these people in a manner you can have no idea of and throw instantly the wavering into the rebel levies, in which they are exerting themselves as much as possible, not sparing the most infamous and cruel methods to force the people into them. If I am to remain a mere guard on Wilmington, I must still hope the delay I shall have occasioned will not be attended with any bad consequences. Captain Peacock, who shews the utmost readiness to concur in every thing I propose and to whom I have opened myself on the subject, approved of my reasons and instantly complied with my request of waiting; and should no other vessel be at hand to convoy the reinforcement, if thought proper to send it, I am sure he would be off of Charles Town Bar for the purpose in four and twenty hours after I informed him of it. He lays without this bar and would almost work it in the time. He would then convoy from this the men of Lord Cornwallis's army and empty vessels. I cannot help repeating that expedition is on this occasion of the utmost consequence. Every day brings fresh accounts of the *Tories* being in arms in almost every part of the province, but they want both arms and ammunition and leaders. They cannot get to me to be supplied and must fall very soon if left to themselves. The only thing I should be in want of is bayonets to give them a confident superiority over the rebels. Of them I have not one.

J H CRAIG

Craig to Balfour, 21st June 1781   6(253): ALS

Willmington
21st June 1781

Lt Colonel Balfour

Dear Sir

I have received accounts of the capture of Maggridge's pilot boat, which carried the letters of which the inclos'd are duplicates. This is a very severe stroke on me from the expectation I was in of almost receiving the answer which was to determine my conduct by this time, and has given rise to the most serious deliberation on the part I should now act. I have at length come to a determination founded only on the most perfect conviction of its utility and the material assistance it will afford Lord Rawdon. Grene has certainly sent orders to Caswell to collect every man he can in this province and to march immediately to join him. Marion, who was near George Town, has the same directions. They are to march to Hugeley's Ferry on the Pedee, and I have been even told from one quarter that Grene was already arriv'd at the Cheraws, where I suppose they are to join. This latter part is, however, not to be depended on. The former I believe is, and the utmost efforts are making for the purpose, which will be back'd by every possible degree of authority which can be afforded by the Governor and House of Assembly, who are now at Wake Court House. I have already wrote them to you so fully that it is unnecessary to repeat to you the advantages I expect from a move into the country, but I must add I think and am convinc'd this is a *critical* moment, as it will most certainly prevent Grene's getting a man to join him from this and, should my expectations with respect to the junction of the country people be answer'd, may enable me to stop his supplies from the upper country and to cooperate with Lord Rawdon. In short, such advantages appear to me probable to arise from it, whether Lord Rawdon confines his views to the preservation of South Carolina only or pursues Grene in order to drive him out of and reduce this province, that I cannot but persuade myself my determination will be approv'd of, tho' in order to enable me to execute it I am oblig'd to detain Lord Cornwallis's men. His Lordship's wish to have them sent to him is founded on his expectation of my being at Charlestown with them and of Lord Rawdon's victory at Camden having rendered them unnecessary. Certainly the detaining them a few days can create no great inconveniency to him and enables me to execute a plan of confessed utility. If you should think proper to send me any reinforcement in their room, they can return and embark immediately on its arrival, or if you should not adopt that measure but should think it right that they should be sent to Lord Cornwallis, we can all return and I can send them to you. I shall not by the time I receive your letter be above 4 or 5 days' march off, so that the utmost harm I can do will be delaying the embarkation a few days.

I shall march tomorrow with near 400 men and shall first direct my route towards Kingston and mean from thence to come to some part towards Duplin Court House. My object at present is to collect friends, disarm rebels and prevent their assembling. My success in these and your answer must determine my further operations. However, it is impossible to determine exactly on my movements, yet one thing you may rely on, that I will not go beyond 5 or 6 days' march from this till I hear from you so as to be always at hand to exchange Lord Cornwallis's men or to bring them back immediately on the receipt of your letter, as you shall think necessary. If they are to go without any body coming in their room, we must all return and shut ourselves up in our redouts again, for with what will remain I must be satisfied if I defend myself.

I have every reason still to expect I shall be join'd by a very considerable number of men, tho' if Grene comes near the Pedee he will cut me off from one great resource. A gentleman here to whom Lord Cornwallis gave permission to raise an independant company has 25 of his men without stirring out of town and the remainder are engag'd very near us. I wish'd to convert them into light dragoons, in which capacity they would be of infinite use, but am at a loss for accoutrements, particularly swords. If no other method can be fallen on to supply me, I wish you would be good enough to order to be sent me by the first oppertunity about four hundred weight of the best steel that can be procur'd with a quantity of sheet iron sufficient for chapes etc for 100 swords. I can get very good ones made here at a very trifling expence. One man has made me a very good one for a pattern.

Captain Peacock has this moment left me. It is impossible for me to say enough of his readiness to assist me in every instance. On my explaining my present difficulty and regretting the uncertainty of small vessels, he instantly offer'd to carry this himself and assures me, should there be a necessity, he will be back in three or four days with your answer. This will only alter my plan in this respect, that I shall not advance above 30 miles till I hear from you, and puts me more at my ease with respect to the delay. If you think as I do with regard to the movement, the best method will be to send a reinforcement under convoy of the *Carysfort* and let her return from this with Lord Cornwallis's men, but as Grene now retreats before Lord Rawdon and of course comes nearer us, I must hope (whether I retain the command of it or not) that it will not be short of 400 men. The effect now will not be greater than that of 250 three weeks ago. If it is not possible to send any reinforcement, the sooner the *Carysfort* returns the better and not a moment shall be lost in the embarkation of Lord Cornwallis's men.

We have no sick of any consequence here. The wounded men who have not yet recover'd form by far the most considerable part. Our hospital is the finest and in the best situation I ever saw.

I am with the greatest regard, dear sir,
Your most obedient and very humble servant

J H CRAIG

[*Subscribed*:]

There has not been a moment's wind with which the convoy could have sailed since I received your letter.

§ - §

6 - Proposed enlistment of prisoners at Charlestown for the West Indies

Amherst to Cornwallis, 19th May 1781 6(88): ALS

Charles Town
19th May 1781

Rt Hon Earl Cornwallis

My Lord

The enclosed letters from their Excellencies General Dalling and General Robertson[45], together with General Dalling's instructions to me, will explain to your Lordship the views with which I came to this country and the motives for my presuming to trouble your Lordship with this.

The field for exertions in the service I was sent upon was so small in New York as to afford me but little prospect of success by remaining there, although latterly the Commander in Chief had granted me the permission to raise from what prisoners were there.

In consequence of some advices I understood the Commander in Chief had received from the Secretary of State expressive of the King's wish that encouragement should be given to the rebel prisoners to enlist for the southern service, I made application to his Excellency that he would be pleased to furnish me with the necessary credentials to your Lordship so that General Dalling's views should be accomplished in the raising of the prisoners at Charles Town. The answer I received from the Commander in Chief was that he had referred this service altogether to your Lordship for many motives, which he did me the honor to explain to me. He was pleased to give me a letter on this subject and to entrust me with his dispatches to your Lordship. I had flattered myself in the honor of delivering them myself, but unfortunately for me the ship I was in could not get over this bar.

To fulfill the views of my General and to be relieved from an anxious state of suspense I hope will be sufficient pleas with your Lordship to excuse me for the liberty I take in entreating your Lordship, either for the permission to enlist the prisoners who all express an inclination for the service and for instructions to the Commandant so that General Dalling's requisition may be fully complied with, or otherwise that I may have a decisive answer to the contrary.

---

[45] *The enclosed letters..*: Robertson's is a copy of his to Cornwallis of 4th March, p 152.

The permission that has been granted to Major Odell and myself at New York and that which has been obtained by Lord Charles Montagu[46] here for the same service will I hope be the means of having my present request complied with.

I have the honor to be, my Lord, with the greatest respect and esteem
Your Lordship's most obedient humble servant

JEFF AMHERST[47]

Enclosure (1)
Dalling to Cornwallis, 4th November 1780   *66(1): LS*

Jamaica
November the 4th 1780

The Rt Hon Earl Cornwallis

My Lord

I felicitate my country on the late signal victory gained over the rebel forces on the 16th of August ultimo by your Lordship, and truly happy I am to hear of your Lordship's health.

The service in consequence of climate requiring men for farther exertions on the Main, I most earnestly urge your Lordship to forward to me as readily as possible as many of those who have fallen into your hands as may be willing to serve under my command. Even a few hundreds will be of the greatest consequence to the King's Service and, tho' not of equal discipline with regular troops, yet will be of infinite utility in the quarter they are intended for.

---

[46] The second son of the third Duke of Manchester, Lord Charles Montagu (1741-1784) had served as Governor of South Carolina between 1766 and 1773, a period in which tensions between the American colonies and Britain had markedly increased. Towards the end of his administration he had had to dissolve the South Carolina legislative assembly time and again, the Commons House of which had become increasingly hostile to interference by the Governor and HM Council in the House's disposition of public money. By February 1781 he had arrived back at Charlestown with instructions from Governor Dalling to seek to enlist revolutionary prisoners for service at Jamaica and on the Spanish Main. Unable to get a decision out of Clinton or Cornwallis, Balfour took it upon himself to give consent and by early May Montagu had completed a corps of 500 men and engaged transports for carrying them to Jamaica. With Montagu as lt colonel, the corps became the 1st Battalion, Duke of Cumberland's Regiment on the Provincial establishment. When it was disbanded at the close of the war, he and a number of his men settled in Nova Scotia, where he soon died at Halifax and was buried there in St Paul's Churchyard. (*ODNB*; *The Cornwallis Papers*; Treasury 64/23(23) (National Archives, Kew))

[47] Jeffery Amherst (c. 1753-1815) was the illegitimate son of Jeffery Lord Amherst (see vol II, p 21, note 16) by a mother whose identity is uncertain. On 2nd June 1771 he was commissioned an ensign in the 60th (Royal American) Regiment, of which his father was Colonel in Chief. Some two years later he was promoted to lieutenant in the 1st Battalion and on 2nd August 1777 he became a captain there. He was now serving as aide-de-camp to Major General John Dalling, the Governor of Jamaica, and was charged with the mission which this and the following letters describe. He died a major general. (*DCB*; *Army Lists*)

Give me leave, my Lord, to introduce to your Lordship the bearer hereof, my aid de camp Captain Amherst of the Royal Americans, an approved and good officer, being firmly confident that you will give him every possible assistance in promoting the service he is sent on.

For the intended service a number of able men will be wanting to work the bateaux under proper officers, the appointment of whom as likewise the appointment of the officers to the intended new rais'd corps from the district under your command I entirely leave to your Lordship.

I have the honor to be with great respect, my Lord,
Your Lordship's most obedient and most humble servant

JOHN DALLING

Enclosure (2)
Dalling to Amherst, 11th November 1780

6(90): C

Jamaica
11th November 1780

Captain Amherst

You are immediately to proceed to New York, where you will wait upon the Commander in Chief of His Majesty's forces or the commanding officer of the troops in that district with my dispatches.

You will inform yourself of what progress has been made by Major Odell in raising recruits for the service in this island, the number raised, their condition, readiness to embark, and all the information you can receive, [which] together with an account of your arrival you are to transmit to me by the earliest opportunity.

After aiding all in your power, and urging in the most pressing manner, the raising of troops there, you are to proceed to the southward and deliver my dispatches to Lt General Earl Cornwallis or the officer commanding His Majesty's troops in the Southern District, to whom you are to make application for every kind of assistance in raising, paying and embarking such people as through his assistance you shall be able to raise. You are to endeavour as much as in your power to get these people armed and clothed in America and give me from time to time by every opportunity an account of your progress.

You are to make particular enquiries into the footing the American corps in our service are upon that you may embrace every opportunity of offering a relative situation to induce the people to enter.

If, however, you find you can effect the intended service by raising men at New York, you need not proceed to the southward but forward my dispatches by the first opportunity.

In endeavouring to raise a corps, of which I intend you shall have the command, you are to follow the plan of the Provincial corps already raised for His Majesty's Service in America, offering rank to the respective officers on their raising the proportionate number of men, which rank I request the Commander in Chief to grant immediately on the passing such corps as you may be able to raise, requesting that he will afford you every assistance in raising, paying and embarking them for the service intended.

Should you, however, find that you cannot effect the intended service, you are, after giving all the assistance in your power to the different parties, to return to me without further loss of time.

JOHN DALLING
Major General

Odell to Cornwallis, 19th May 1781   6(91): LS

Charlestown
19th May 1781

My Lord

On my arrival here I did myself the honor of informing your Lordship that I had received the Commander in Chief's permission to attend your Lordship's pleasure for inlisting of prisoners for the service of the West Indies, this measure having been recommended by administration, as his Excellency's dispatches will explain. Your Lordship's removal from Wilmingtown before these could have reached you will excuse my presumption in representing to your Lordship that the few men wanted to compleat this battalion (having already sent upwards of three hundred to Jamaica) will, I flatter myself, not interfere with any prospect of exchange as in all probability a short confinement in the approaching summer might lose the number required.

If your Lordship's views for the general wellfare of the service will not admit of the obligation to General Dalling in the full extent wished by him, I most respectfully hope the above indulgence may be signified to Colonel Balfour, who does me the honor to mention the subject.

I am with the truest respect
Your Lordship's most devoted and obedient servant

WILLIAM ODELL
Lt Colonel commanding Loyal American Rangers[48]

---

[48] Odell had been dispatched to New York by Governor Dalling in June 1780. He had enlisted some 300 men from the navy prison ships by promising service against the Spanish instead of the American revolutionaries and by holding out the prospect of acquiring Spanish doubloons. This meagre source of recruits had now dried up. Like Jeffery Amherst, he would not be allowed to recruit from prisoners at Charlestown in view of the cartel with Greene. He died in 1783, perhaps at Jamaica, sometime before the christening of his son there in mid September.

Amherst to Cornwallis, 6th June 1781[49]   *6(178): ALS*

Charles Town
6th June 1781

Rt Hon Earl Cornwallis

My Lord

Some late letters from General Dalling commanding in the strongest manner my exertions in the recruiting service, as the future operations on the Spanish Main depend in a great measure on the numbers of men to be procured here, I find myself again under the necessity of troubling your Lordship and, for fear of any accident arriving to my first letters, to take the liberty of sending duplicates of them. As General Robertson's letter to your Lordship was delivered to me under a flying seal, I was enabled to take a copy of it. General Dalling's not being so, I could not know perfectly the contents.

I need not again entreat your Lordship for an answer on this subject. Your Lordship's goodness, I am convinced, renders it unnecessary.

I have the honor to be, my Lord, with the highest respect and esteem
Your Lordship's most obedient and most humble servant

JEFFERY AMHERST

Cornwallis to Amherst, 28th June 1781[50]   *87(19): C*

Williamsburgh
28th June 1781

Captain Amherst
60th Regiment

Sir

While the enemy persisted in delaying the exchange of prisoners I judged it expedient to encourage the enlisting them for the service in the West Indies to relieve the publick from the enormous expence and trouble of keeping them, but since a cartel is settled between General

---

(*The Cornwallis Papers*; Philip Ranlet, 'In the Hands of the British: The Treatment of American POWs during the War of Independence', *The Historian*, 22nd June 2000)

[49] Annotated: 'Received 26th June 1781.'

[50] This letter miscarried. See Hudson to Leslie, 15th July, p 215. Cornwallis gave a further reply to both Amherst and Odell in his letter of 16th July to Balfour, p 284.

Greene and me, there is a probability of redeeming our soldiers from captivity, which obliges me to decline giving my consent to any more of those people being enlisted.

I am etc

CORNWALLIS

Amherst to Cornwallis, 2nd July 1781   6(292): ALS

Charles Town
2nd July 1781

Rt Hon Earl Cornwallis

My Lord

An opportunity offering of some vessels bound to James's River, I again presume to take the liberty to address your Lordship on the subject of the service I am sent upon by General Dalling.

The exchange of prisoners being finally settled here, and consequently no further opening at present left for exertions in the recruiting service in this place, I have desired the bearer, Captain Cook, to solicit your Lordship's permission to enlist any prisoners or others that may be with your Lordship or elsewhere who do not come under the terms of the cartel by a subsequent capture to it.

As General Dalling has great hopes from this quarter and expects considerable reinforcements from the exertions of his officers, I flatter myself your Lordship will excuse the trouble I give in steps that seem the most promising to his views.

I have the honor to be, my Lord,
Your Lordship's most obedient and most humble servant

JEFF AMHERST

§ - §

7 - With the public departments

Townsend to Cornwallis, 14th April 1781   5(217): ALS

Charles Town
14th April 1781

The Rt Hon Earl Cornwallis

My Lord

I had the great satisfaction last evening to hear from Mr Knecht of your Lordship's safe arrival in good health near Wilmington. It appears by the returns from thence, 26th March, there are for 6,000 men *bread and flour sixty nine days, pork and beef thirty three days, rum 69 days*, and a good supply of salt, which I hope with the help of cattle from the country will make up the deficiency of salt provisions. There is in store here *bread and flour for 10,000 men 150 days, beef and pork 140 days, rum 200 days*. St Augustine is victualed for 800 men to the last of August, Savannah for 1,800 men to the last of June. The demands for bread, pork and rum for Monk's Corner to supply that post and send forward are very considerable of late. If all the posts depend on the stores here, the daily consumption will exceed ten thousand rations.

I think it my duty to inform your Lordship that Major Morrison arrived here from New York the 5th instant and brought me orders from Mr Wier to deliver over the stores and provisions in my possession to the major and return to New York the first good conveyance. I have fix'd on the 24th instant to give up my charge here and shall hold myself in readiness to embrace the first opportunity for New York. Permit me, my Lord, to express my warmest gratitude for your Lordship's kindness and attention to me. Nothing can add more to my happiness than the assurance that my conduct on this station is honor'd with your Lordship's approbation.

I have the honor to be with the utmost respect, my Lord,
Your Lordship's very obedient and most humble servant

G TOWNSEND
Captain

[*Subscribed*:]

There are seven boxes of essence of spruce which will be left with Major Morrison.

Enclosure
Returns from HM Stores in Charlestown, 18th to 31st March 1781 103: DS

	Remaining in store as per last Return	*Purchased of Messrs James & Edward Penman*	*Received from the Montague transport*	*Purchased between 17th & 31st March 1781*	*Totals*
* STATE of Provisions and Rum in His Majesty's Magazine in Charles Town, South Carolina, between 18th and 31st March 1781 *					
Pounds of:					
Flour	1,686,960				1,686,960
Biscuit	52,528		592		53,120
Rice	464,390	47,133	471		511,994
Beef	138,180				138,180
Pork	859,872		460		860,332
Butter	76,776				76,776
Oatmeal	178,976				178,976
Bushels:					
Salt	2,250		2½		2,252½
Pease	16,175				16,175
Gallons of:					
Vinegar	4,950		47		4,997
Oil	425				425
Rum	92,190		49		92,239
Live stock:					
Cattle	26			51	77
Sheep	100				100

ABSTRACT of Provisions and Rum issued from His Majesty's Magazine in Charles Town, South Carolina, between 18th and 31st March 1781

	Charles Town, Issuing Store, Jnº Morison	Monk's Corner, QMG's boats	George Town per sloop Polly and Charles Town packet	New York per ship Robert	Ninety Six per waggons	St Augustine per sloop Recovery	Savannah per brigantine Friendship	Totals	Remaining
Pounds of:									
Flour	88,726	24,660				27,400		140,786	1,546,174

321

Biscuit	5,055							5,055	48,065
Rice	35,053			152,015				187,068	324,926
Beef	10,710							10,710	127,470
Pork	36,028	14,560	4,160		3,536	15,600	67,600	141,484	718,848
Butter	12,005					1,506		13,511	63,255
Oatmeal	280							280	178,696
Bushels:									
Salt	15	50						65	2,187½
Pease	305		50					355	15,820
Gallons of:									
Vinegar	551		60					611	4,386
Oil									425
Rum	4,103	1,801				1,341	3,386	10,631	81,608
Live stock:									
Cattle	54							54	23
Sheep	3							3	97

To His Excellency Lt General Earl Cornwallis etc etc etc

G TOWNSEND
Captain
Commissary General

Haldane to Deputy Paymaster General, Charlestown, 28th June 1781[51]

87(29): *ADfS*

Head Quarters
Williamsburgh
28th June 1781

Deputy Paymaster General at Charlestown

Sir

I am directed by Lord Cornwallis to desire you will be pleased to order Mr Gale or some person from the Office of the Paymaster General to come to the Chesapeake by the first opportunity to transact business with this army.

---

[51] This letter miscarried. See Hudson to Leslie, 15th July, p 215.

His Lordship desires you will transmit to him by the same opportunity an abstract of the sums issued by you on the several warrants granted by him, Major General Leslie and Lt Colonel Balfour during his command in the southern provinces.

I am, sir,
Your most obedient and most humble servant

HENRY HALDANE
Aide-de-camp

§ - §

CHAPTER 56

Letters from Georgia or East Florida

1 - From Sir James Wright

Wright to Cornwallis, 2nd April 1781   5(153): ALS

Savanah in Georgia
the 2nd of April 1781

The Rt Hon Earl Cornwallis
Commander in Chief of His Majesty's forces etc etc etc

My Lord

Give me leave with the utmost pleasure to congratulate your Lordship on the signal victory you obtained over the rebel General Green and his army on the 15th of last month near Guildford in North Carolina. Such zeal and indefatigable efforts I am very hopefull will soon compel the colonies to return to their allegiance and obedience to His Majesty's Government, and give us peace and quietness.

Permit me now, my Lord, to acquaint you how much I lament Colonel Clarke's being under the necessity of leaving us and going to St Augustine. I have been perfectly happy with this gentleman for the ten months he has had the command here, and what makes his leaving us at this time the more to be regretted is that the command will devolve on a gentleman who is a foreigner and totally unacquainted with the Laws of England and the nature of the British Government. How far this may be proper in a province where the King has thought fit to re-establish His civil Government and to order out His Governor and other Crown officers for that purpose I need not comment upon but submit to your Lordship's wisdom to determine.

I have the honor to be with perfect esteem, my Lord,
Your Lordship's most obedient humble servant

JA WRIGHT

Wright to Cornwallis, 6th April 1781   5(167): ALS

Savanah in Georgia
the 6th of April 81

Earl Cornwallis etc etc etc

My Lord

I have the honor to inclose your Lordship an address from both Houses of Legislature in this province, in which I most heartily join, and have the honor to be with perfect esteem, my Lord,

Your Lordship's most obedient servant

JA WRIGHT

Enclosure
Address of the Houses of Assembly, Georgia, 4th April 1781   5(169): DS

To the Rt Hon Charles Earl Cornwallis, Lt General of His Majesty's forces etc etc etc

The address of the Upper and Commons Houses of Assembly of the Province of Georgia

May it please your Lordship

We, His Majesty's most dutiful and loyal subjects, the Upper and Commons Houses of Assembly of the Province of Georgia now in General Assembly met, beg leave to offer to your Lordship our most grateful congratulations on the late important victory gained by His Majesty's forces under your command over the rebel army on the 15th of last month.

The reduction of this province and that of South Carolina we consider not only as matters of the greatest importance to the British Empire but as a happy presage of still more important successes.

The same zeal, gallantry and good conduct which so eminently distinguished your Lordship in the glorious victories of Cambden and Guilford cannot fail, under the influence of divine providence, of extending His Majesty's benign authority over those unhappy provinces that are still in arms against His Majesty and of putting an honorable end to this unnatural rebellion.

That your Lordship's future exertions for the service of your King and country may be crowned with success equal to the distinguished abilities and activity so conspicuous in all your operations, and that you may receive from our most gracious Sovereign such marks of His royal approbation as your Lordship's eminent services so truly merit, are our ardent wishes and prayers.

By order of the Upper House of Assembly   Savannah, Georgia
                                                           4th April 1781

JOHN GRAHAME[1], President

By order of the Commons-house of Assembly

SAM FARLEY[2], Speaker

Wright to Cornwallis, 23rd April 1781[3]   5(247): LS

Savannah in Georgia
the 23rd April 1781

Earl Cornwallis
Commander in Chief of His Majesty's forces etc etc etc

My Lord

On the 2nd instant I had the honor to write to your Lordship on the subject of your Lordship's signal victory over the rebel General Green and of Colonel Clarke's leaving this province and going to St Augustine. The number of men who were ordered from hence to that place I presume your Lordship has been informed of, I think upwards of 140, since which, my Lord, affairs in South Carolina and this province (according to the intelligence I have received) have taken a very unfavourable turn and of which, as far as it concerns Georgia, it is my duty to acquaint your Lordship.

---

[1] As Lt Governor of Georgia, John Graham served as President of HM Council there when it acted as the upper house of the royal assembly.

[2] Samuel Farley was an Englishman who before the revolution had acted as an attorney at a Savannah law firm which he owned. In 1775 his state of health and a desire to avoid the troubles led him to return to England, from where he moved to East Florida three years later. When civil government under the Crown was reinstated in Georgia in July 1779, he returned to act as Speaker of the lower house of the royal assembly, captain in the royal militia at Savannah, and 'Chief Magistrate of Police'. On the evacuation of Savannah in the summer of 1782 he repaired again to East Florida, having been banished and subjected to confiscation by act of the Georgia revolutionary assembly. He proceeded to serve there as a chief magistrate and judge until the province was ceded to Spain. He then settled with his family at New Providence, visited England to press his claim for compensation, and, on returning to the Bahamas, died at Nassau in December 1785. (Coldham, *Loyalist Claims*, i, 149; Cashin, *The King's Ranger*, 153; The Georgia Banishment and Confiscation Act 1782)

[3] Published with inconsequential differences in Davies ed, *Docs of the Am Rev*, xx, 117-9.

About the middle of February a party of from 60 to 70 rebels came over Savannah River from the Long Canes settlement and assassinated eleven persons in their houses, and some in their beds, and those all pickt out from amongst the most zealous loyal subjects, and no others were meddled with. And yesterday, my Lord, I received a letter from Colonel Greirson (who commands the militia at Augusta) in which he acquaints me that a party of rebels from 200 to 250 under the command of Shelvey from over the mountains and others had come into the Ceded Lands and down towards Augusta and Wrightsborough and assassinated upwards of 40 people whose names are mentioned, these also pickt men and such as they thought were most firm in their loyalty and allegiance, and they came so suddenly on the inhabitants that they had not the least notice or time to collect or be on their guard, and the unheard of cruelty of the rebels was so shocking that the generality of the people took to the swamps for shelter against these worse than savages, who say they will murder every loyal subject in the province. Greirson writes that Colonel Brown's corps and his militia were so much weakened by the partys sent to protect the boats which were going from hence to Augusta with provisions, stores, ammunition etc etc that they could not send out any men to oppose this vile rebel party, and that the boats were then from 40 to 50 miles below Augusta, say, on the 18th.

It's a cruel, hard case, my Lord, that loyal subjects struggling to support His Majesty's Government against rebellion should be suffered to be thus murdered for want of a few troops to support and protect them. I am persuaded for the numbers in this province there are far more loyal subjects than in the next, but being doomed to death and destruction for that very reason is poor encouragement for them to persevere in their loyalty.

Colonel Porbeck received a rolled up note from Colonel Brown to the same purpose and adding that he had received a letter from Colonel Cruger in which he writes (as I recollect) that he can give him no assistance and he must expect none; that Pickens and Clarke were between Tyger River and the Enoree with 300 men, but the latter down with the small pox; that Sumpter was some where about Fish Dam Ford on Broad River, but don't mention any number of men he has with him; that Baker[4], Marion etc were collecting men in Carolina and, it was said, had then near 600 and intended to join the others and then *look* at 96; but with respect to the situation of affairs in South Carolina I presume your Lordship will be particularly informed by others. We are also threatened by another party from Zubly's Ferry and Purysburgh, where by my information there was near 300 at the former place and 100 at the latter place, although it's very like the numbers may be exaggerated; and they told some whom they took prisoners and let go again that they intended to come over into this province and lay waste the whole lower part of the country, that they knew our force and strength as well as we do ourselves, and that it's not in our power to prevent them; and a party of 16 under the command of one Johnston did actually come over, well mounted, and plundered some houses within 8 miles of the town and made off again, which shows the necessity of our having a troop of horse; and your Lordship knows the garrison is reduced to a small number, and we can do but little with the militia, who are now quite fatigued and worn out with

---

[4] John Baker (?-1792) was a colonel in the Georgia revolutionary militia. In May 1777 he had been routed when ambushed by Thomas Brown in the country above the St Johns River, East Florida. Now active in South Carolina, he would, according to Marion, 'do no other service than plunder the inhabitants, which will make more enemys'. An affluent farmer and Indian fighter, who represented Liberty County in the Georgia House of Representatives, he is not to be confused with his namesake who was a colonel in the North Carolina revolutionary militia. Baker County, Georgia, is named after him. (Cashin, *The King's Ranger*, 64-5; *The Greene Papers*, vii, 230n)

almost constant alarms and duty and without *either pay or subsistance*. Upon the whole, my Lord, on a general view of all circumstances and appearances things are very alarming and I must consider this province as reduced to a precarious and dangerous situation.

I most heartily wish your Lordship health and a continuance of success, and have the honor to be with the utmost regard

Your Lordship's most obedient servant

JA WRIGHT

§ - §

2 - From Clarke

Clarke to Balfour, 13th January 1781 *62(22): ALS*

Savannah
January 13th 1781

Lt Colonel Balfour etc

My dear Balfour

I long much to hear from you. Enclosed I send a letter from a prisoner at St Augustine[5] which came here by the post sealed. I took the liberty of opening of it and thought the contents so indecent and so little consonant to the tenor of his parole that instead of forwarding it as directed I send it for your perusal and condemnation or otherwise. I have in consequence of it written to Major Glasier and ordered that no letters should be sent from any prisoner without having been read by the commissary and approved of by himself.

I am, my dear Balfour, *in great anxiety*
Ever yours

ALURED CLARKE

[*Annotated on receipt, but not in Balfour's hand*:]

Jacob Reed not to carry on any kind of correspondence with this place, Pinckney under cover to Mr Winstenly, which points out the necessity of all prisoners' letters being most

---

[5] *a letter..*: not extant.

strictly examined, and to confine him to his house for breach of parole by letter to Augustine.[6]

Clarke to Balfour, 24th January 1781   62(24): ALS

Savannah
January 24th 1781

My dear Balfour

Some time ago Governor Tonyn intimated to me his intention of sending a flag of truce to the Havannah when a *convenient opportunity should offer.* This he has done by an intelligent young man (a Mr Forbes[7]), who left that place on the 7th and arrived at St Augustine on the 14th of this month with the intelligence contained in the Governor's letter to me[8] and the paper of questions and answers sent by Lt Colonel Glasier, copies of which I enclose for your information in order that you may give me every assistance towards the defence of East Florida, which I am confident will be attacked after the reduction of Pensacola, and also that you may forward such parts of their contents to the Admiral or officer commanding the navy as you may think useful to him. I am in constant expectation of accounts from General Campbell and shall set off for Augustine the moment he announces the appearance of the Spaniards before him. Whilst you was very weak in South Carolina I never made a difficulty about the numbers being too small for the defence of the place because I foresaw the distress it would be to Lord Cornwallis to part with any more troops, but as the case is altered in some degree by the arrival of General Leslie and will be considerably so, in all probability very soon, by the arrival of the three regiments from Europe, I must request that you will contrive to spare me *at least* one hundred men, and as my motive is merely the service *immediately* in question, if you was to let it be a *detachment* composed for the purpose, there would be no probability of their being detained longer than

---

[6] Considered a firebrand by the British, Jacob Read was one of the prominent Charlestonians who had been transported to St Augustine for behaviour incompatible with their paroles. The letter which now caused offence had been ostensibly written by Read to his friend Thomas Winstanley (see vol II, p 317, note 4) but was actually intended for one of Read's other friends, Colonel Charles Cotesworth Pinckney (see vol II, p 111, note 103), a Continental prisoner. A member of the revolutionary party was later to describe the episode in typically partisan language, putting the worst complexion on it: 'Naught but the determination to give to malignity a sharper sting caused the Commandant of St Augustine to sentence Captain Jacob Read to rigourous and solitary confinement for no other offence alleged against him than having transmitted to a friend in Charleston an extract from a Jamaica paper giving intelligence of an advantage gained by a Spanish squadron over a fleet of British transports in the West Indies.' Read was exchanged in the summer of 1781 under the cartel with Greene. (McCowen Jr, *Charleston, 1780-82*, 75; Garden, *Anecdotes* (1st series), 266)

[7] An enterprising, sensible young Scot, Thomas Forbes was a resident of East Florida who was involved in the mercantile line. By July 1783 he had taken passage to London, where he described himself as a merchant, but by March 1789 had moved on to Nassau in the Bahamas. He was eventually granted land on Great Exuma Island, where the small farming town of Forbes Hill is named after him. (Coldham, *Loyalist Claims*, 92, 298, 364; Ruby Dusek, 'The Papers of Panton Leslie and Company', *The CLF Newsletter* (Clayton Library Friends, Houston TX), x (February 1996), 3-4)

[8] *Governor's letter to me*: of 22nd January, p 342.

the business now before us requires. It surely is requisite that another artillery officer should be sent and I do suppose one might be spared from Charles Town without any great inconvenience. Therefore pray speak to Traile about it, and also that some articles may be supplied that are absolutely necessary, and of which I will send an account. The garrison of St Augustine at present consists of about 450 men. 100 I propose taking from hence, which, with what I have requested of you, will only make 650, a number by no means equal to what it ought to have but with which, and such of the inhabitants as may be *scraped* together, I would endeavour to make the best defence possible. Pray speak to Moncrief on this subject and I am convinced you will find his opinion coincide with mine. The article of provisions is also so necessary to be attended to that I must beg of you to speak *strongly* to Mr Townshend on the subject and beg of him not to neglect keeping up the stock as complete as possible, adverting always to the number of prisoners when he sends supplies. I shall write a few lines to Lord Cornwallis, which I request you will forward to him with copies of the papers of intelligence that I send you. I will mention to him my application to you for the men above requested and make no doubt of its meeting with his Lordship's approbation. The two 36 pounders at Augustine are guns of infinite importance and there are very few shot for them. Therefore beg some may be sent, as I am informed you have them at Charles Town. I cannot conclude without again begging you will press Major Traile and Mr Townshend to do every thing requisite.

I am, my dear Balfour,
Yours most truly

ALURED CLARKE

[*Subscribed*:]

Although I write to Traile, I enclose the ordnance returns[9] for you to give him, thinking that may assist matters. One of them is sent from Augustine, and the demand such as to complete the garrison to its full allowance. The other I have made out here and hope that may be complied with if the other is beyond your abilities.

I have mentioned to Lord Cornwallis that you would send a copy of Governor Tonyn's letter and the other paper to him, so beg you will do it.

Enclosure
Intelligence from Havana, January 1781[10]   *67(73): C*

Colonel Glazier's compliments to Mr Forbes, and begs the favour of him to inform Lieutenant Floyer what he knows of Don Galvez's expedition or any other interesting news.

---

[9] *ordnance returns*: no copies.

[10] For further details of Forbes' expedition, see Tonyn to Cornwallis, 29th January, and enclosures, pp 337-350.

Questions to ask Mr Forbes

Q: What time did Don Galvez sail from the Havannah?

A: General Galvez was to sail for Mobile the 11th or 12th instant in a single frigate. Troops had sail'd by detachments before and others were order'd to join him there from Campeachey, Orleans etc, in all imagin'd 4 or 5,000.

Q: How many King's ships and of what rates?

A: The squadron station'd at Havannah consists of 13 sail of the line, 2 of which are 80 guns, 5 of 74, and 6 of 64 guns. A French squadron had come there 8 days before our departure, consisting of 3 ships of the line and 2 frigates.

Q: How many transports and victuallers and what number of troops?

A: There are many transports at Havannah always kept in readiness. The troops there now, after the armament fitted out against Pensacola, may be 5 or 6,000 men.

Q: Where did the gale of wind take them and how long after they sail'd?

A: In the bay, 2 days after their departure on the former expedition, which proved abortive. 3 of the line and one frigate return'd dismasted. The transports were totally dispersed.

Q: When did they return, how many, and in what condition?

A: At many different times. Not half of the transports got back to Havannah but [some], according to their information, had reach'd Campeachey, Orleans, Mobile etc.

Q: How did they account for the rest of their fleet?

A: They acknowledge 3 wrecked, 3 carried into Pensacola, and the rest arrived as mention'd above.

Q: When did the third expedition sail, and how many ships of war and transports, and how many troops on board?

A: The troops were collected as before mention'd – may amount to 4 or 5,000 men. The last detachment sail'd a fortnight before us under one ship and one frigate.

Q: Where was it said they were bound?

A: To Mobile, there to wait the General's arrival, and to march against Pensacola as occasion may offer or to defend their own possessions if in danger from us.

Q: Wheather Don Galvez talk'd of a second expedition to Pensacola?

A: Answer'd above.

Q: Weather he talk'd of coming here, and Mr Forbes' remarks upon the whole?

A: No one imagin'd General Galvez had intentions of coming here, though him or others will do so if Pensacola falls.

Clarke to Cornwallis, 26th January 1781   5(64): ALS

Savannah
January 26th 1781

Earl Cornwallis etc etc etc

My Lord

Some time ago Governor Tonyn intimated to me his intention of sending a flag of truce to the Havannah when a *favorable opportunity should offer*. This he has done, and it returned to St Augustine on the 14th of this month with the intelligence contained in the Governor's letter to me[11] and that which you will find in a paper of questions put by Major Glasier with Mr Forbes' answers to them[12]. Mr Forbes is a sensible young man and I have no doubt of the authenticity of his information, which keeps me in hourly expectation of accounts from General Campbell, on the arrival of which I shall go immediately to St Augustine.

Whilst your Lordship's numbers were so inadequate to the great task you had on hand in South Carolina, I never made difficulties about the numbers in East Florida being too small for the defence of that place, sensible that your force would not admit of the smallest dimunition, but as the arrival of General Leslie has altered that circumstance in some degree, and as in all probability it will be considerably more so soon by the arrival of the expected regiments from Europe, I have requested of Balfour to spare me at least one hundred men for the garrison of St Augustine (to stay there no longer than the appearance of the present intended attack continues), which, with those already there and one hundred men that I propose taking from hence, will amount to six hundred and fifty, a number which I am persuaded your Lordship would think too small for the extent of the place if more could be afforded, but with which and such of the inhabitants as may be collected I will make the best defence in my power.

I am perplext extremely by the frequent demands made by the proprietors of houses which have been occupied by the officers and soldiers in this town since the reduction of the province. Many of them even threaten us with *lawsuits* for the recovery of their rent. Those who are friendly and more proper in their behaviour present memorials to me and request that I will set forth their pretentions to your Lordship, which I propose doing when a proper

---

[11] *letter to me*: of 22nd January, p 342.

[12] See the preceding enclosure.

opportunity offers. And as attachments against the houses at present occupied by the troops will dispossess us of them all in a month or two, I wish to have your directions how I had best act. I think the least expensive mode to Government (though not the most eligible for the troops) will be to apply to the Governor for billets on the inhabitants, which I shall do when forced by necessity unless any other plan from your Lordship arrives before that happens.

It having been necessary for Sir James Wright to employ the militia in consequence of the armed boats that at times infested this coast lately, he has applied to me in order that provisions might be issued to them from the King's Stores, which not feeling myself authorised to comply with, I wrote to Balfour to know your Lordship's pleasure on that head, who not being able to give me a satisfactory answer relative to *this province*, I am induced to trouble you on the subject that I may be guided by your will in future.

With the warmest wishes for your Lordship's health and happiness, and that brilliant success may attend all your operations, I have the honor to remain, my Lord,
Your Lordship's most obedient and most faithful humble servant

ALURED CLARKE

Clarke to Cornwallis, 31st March 1781   69(25): ALS

Savannah
March 31st 1781

Earl Cornwallis

My Lord

In a letter of the 26th of January I did myself the honor of mentioning to your Lordship some circumstances relative to the quarters of the troops in this garrison and at the same time informed you that several memorials had been presented to me by persons who requested I would lay them before your Lordship and say as much in their behalf as on enquiry I thought they merited. I have therefore endeavoured to make myself acquainted with their respective situations and deserts that I might be able to represent their pretentions to your Lordship, which is done on the different memorials.[13]

I have the honor to be with great respect, my Lord,
Your Lordship's most obedient and most faithful humble servant

ALURED CLARKE
Lt Colonel

---

[13] Clarke encloses nine memorials (69(27) to (52)). Most seek rent for property used by British forces in Savannah. A few also seek payment for damages to it. One is from a British officer seeking reimbursement for losses incurred on an overland journey from Pensacola to St Augustine. Clarke recommends all to Cornwallis's favourable consideration.

Clarke to Cornwallis, 6th April 1781   5(171): ALS

Savannah
April 6th 1781

My Lord

It is with the utmost satisfaction I congratulate you on the glorious success which has attended His Majesty's arms under your auspices and on the signal advantages which must accrue to your Lordship as well as to your country from the late brilliant action at Guilford. In addition to the intelligence sent by Captain McNamara[14] of the *Hound* sloop of war, I have received other accounts which convince me of the Spaniards having arrived before Pensacola about the 10th of last month. This has determined me to go to St Augustine directly with a detachment of 120 men, which is all that can possibly be spared from the immediate duty of this garrison. And Lt Colonel Balfour having assured me that he will send some troops to this province in the event of its being seriously threatened, I have informed the Governor of it in order to reconcile him to the departure of those going from hence. And I flatter myself your Lordship will approve of what I have done, as the numbers at St Augustine (even with the addition I am now making) will fall very short of what ought to be there if it should be attacked, but being convinced that the numbers in South Carolina will not admit of more being sent from the service of that province at present, I cannot expect it but shall by every exertion in my power endeavour to prove that my idea of the numbers in East Florida being insufficient was ill founded. During my absence Colonel de Porbeck will command, at which the Governor seemed a little uneasy. However, I believe he is better reconciled to it since we had a meeting at which Colonel de Porbeck expressed (in the best manner indifferent English would admit of) his intention to promote the service as far as he was able and not to interfere with the civil power. The Governor, who acts with great caution in most matters, has shewn me a letter he has written to your Lordship on this subject[15], and his motive for so doing, he says, was, in case of any thing unpleasant happening, it might appear that he had represented the matter. Lt Colonel De Lancey[16] having been represented to me in so bad a state of health as to make his going to a more northern climate indispensibly necessary, I have given him leave to go to New York for six months, which I hope will meet with your Lordship's concurrence. I cannot conclude this letter without

---

[14] Commissioned a lieutenant in the Royal Navy on 25th June 1761, James McNamara (?-1802) had been promoted to commander on 2nd May 1779 and to post-captain on 5th February 1781. Commanding the *Hound*, a 14-gun sloop of war launched at Deptford in 1776, he was presently serving on the Pensacola station. He would die a superannuated rear admiral. (Syrett and DiNardo eds, *The Commissioned Sea Officers*, 293; Michael Phillips, 'Ships of the Old Navy 2' (Internet, 13th September 2006); *The Cornwallis Papers*)

[15] *a letter..*: of 2nd April, p 324.

[16] A brother of Oliver De Lancey Jr, Stephen De Lancey (1749-1798) had been serving as Lt Colonel of the 2nd Battalion, De Lancey's Brigade, since 5th September 1776. He would later become Lt Colonel of the 1st Battalion, New Jersey Volunteers. Placed on the Provincial half-pay list at the end of the war, he was appointed Chief Justice of the Bahamas and went on to become Governor of Tobago. Having begun to suffer from impaired health while holding the latter office, he took passage for England but grew rapidly worse during the voyage. Transferring at his own request to an American vessel bound for Portsmouth, New Hampshire, he died there and was buried a few days after his arrival. (Raymond, 'British American Corps'; Treasury 64/23(6), WO 65/164(35), and WO 65/165(6) (National Archives, Kew); *Appletons'*)

mentioning a very disagreeable subject, in lamenting the misfortunes of the poor Fusiliers[17] and expressing my earnest hopes that in their present distressful situation they may find a friend and advocate in your Lordship. Words cannot describe what I have felt on their account, and from your Lordship's kind patronage alone I am to expect consolation and the regiment, I hope, receive such assistance as may be most likely to reconcile it to the mortifying loss it has sustained, I need not say I mean its colours.

I must take the liberty of requesting that your Lordship will give my best wishes to my friend Ross, and have the honor to remain with the utmost respect and regard, my Lord,

Your Lordship's most obedient and most faithful humble servant

ALURED CLARKE

PS

I should be very ungrateful if I did not inform your Lordship how much attention my friend Balfour pays to all my wishes and wants respecting this command.

Clarke to Cornwallis, 3rd May 1781   6(31): ALS

St Augustine
May 3rd 1781

Earl Cornwallis

My Lord

I arrived here on the eleventh of last month, and having sent Lieutenant Dunford of the Engineers some time before me, I was happy to find that he had (by the assistance of some Negroes furnish'd from the province) done a good deal towards completing the works according to the plan fixt on by Lt Colonel Moncrief, but as the lines were much out of repair, the labour has been considerably greater than was at first apprehended. There is now a bill before the legislature empowering the Governor to employ Negroes etc in the defence of the province, and when it has passed, he intends to furnish us with such a number on the publick works as shall be thought sufficient to complete them in a short time. Which done, I think the place will be very strong and want only an additional number of troops to make it *perfectly* secure.

Since my leaving Georgia I have received two letters from Sir James Wright, and also from Mr Graham, strongly expressing their apprehensions for the safety of the plantations and inhabitants in the lower part of the province, some parties of rebels having been within ten miles of Savannah. This gives me great uneasiness from the impossibility of my affording them the smallest assistance. However, I am not without hopes that Colonel Balfour may (by

---

[17] Clarke was Lt Colonel of the 7th Regiment (Royal Fusiliers), which had been captured with its colours at the Battle of Cowpens.

an exertion in South Carolina) give them a little relief, as I understand he has sent Major McArthur with a detachment to Pocotaligo, which is not very distant from the part of the river where they cross.

By a letter from Lord George Germain to the Superintendant of Indian Affairs I have been given to understand that the *Seminolies* were to be provided by, and wholly dependant on, the Governor of East Florida, 'he having a fund for that purpose', and Colonel Brown being forbid to interfere with or incur any expense on their account. But a body of those people amounting to near one hundred having come down since my arrival here, Governor Tonyn has applied to me to furnish them with provisions etc, which I foresee must be attended with a very heavy expense, as the *quantity* of provisions in the King's Stores will not admit of any *extra* diminution of them without great risk to the security of the place if it should be invested and the articles they are accustomed to receive cannot be purchased but at a high price. However, the Governor having convinced me by the strongest assurances that he has no allowance whatever on this account, and coinciding with him in opinion that it would be very impolitic to disgust these people at this particular crisis, I have on his urgent application consented to defray the present expense, at the same time declaring my inability to continue so doing untill I have some instructions from your Lordship on this head[18], which I hope you will be so kind as to honor me with as soon as possible. The situation of this place is such that Indians may be very useful indeed if the Spaniards should attack it. I have therefore desired that Colonel Brown will afford us all the assistance in his power the moment he hears such an event has taken place, which measure I hope will meet with your Lordship's approbation when I assure you that the expense shall be made as moderate as the nature of the service will admit of.

I am extremely anxious to hear that your Lordship has reaped all the benefits that were to be expected from the glorious victory of Guilford Court House, and have the honor to remain with the utmost respect and regard, my Lord,

Your Lordship's most obedient and most faithful humble servant

ALURED CLARKE

PS

Since writing my letter, Governor Tonyn has come to a resolution to provide for the expense (occasioned by the Seminolies) himself untill he hears further concerning them, but I am nevertheless anxious to have full instructions from your Lordship (as soon as possible) on this head that I may know how to act if the Governor should make a future application to me on the subject, which I don't think improbable.

I must take the liberty of requesting that your Lordship will remember me to my *old friend Ross*.

§ - §

---

[18] For Clarke's correspondence with Tonyn, see pp 354-7.

3 - From Tonyn

Tonyn to Cornwallis, 29th January 1781 *67(35): ALS*

St Augustine
29th January 1781

Rt Hon Earl of Cornwallis

My Lord

Actuated by powerful motives, I had the best reasons for sending a gentleman in whom I could confide to the Havanna in a flag of truce for exchanging some prisoners of war, and I have the honour of inclosing a translated copy of Don Jego Joseph Navarro the Governor's letter to me and the terms of exchange, and your Lordship will observe the twenty five soldiers of the 60th Regiment are sent upon good faith. I shall not dismiss the Spanish vessel untill I have your Lordship's commands.

As this gentleman from connections and other circumstances had the means of geting the best information, I have the honour of communicating to your Lordship most interesting intelligence which may be relied upon.

A plan for the conquest of the Floridas and Bahama Islands has been sent out by the Court of Madrid to the Havanna.

The second formidable armament against Pensacola has been defeated by a storm, and altho' disapointed, they persevere in forming a third attempt.

Don Galvez was to sail about the 12th instant from the Havanna with two ships of the line, some frigates and transports and assemble an army at Mobile of five thousand strong with design of besieging Pensacola.

Confident of success, it is determined to attack this province, for which purpose preparations are making, and four ships of the line, three frigates and twelve new gallies, each carrying one twenty four pounder and calculated for the East Florida navigation, it was thought might be ready to sail in March with six regiments and irregulars together amounting to five thousand men, and Don Victor Navia[19] is to command the expedition.

---

[19] Don Victorio de Navia was a lt general commanding the so-called *Ejército de operaciones de América*, an expeditionary corps of 10,000 men which had left Cadiz on 28th April 1780 in a convoy of eighty-two transports, twelve ships of the line, three frigates, and four sloops of war. After a passage of three months he dropped off part of the corps at several Caribbean ports before disembarking the rest at Havana. Much reduced by scurvy and other diseases, some effectives were quartered on the Campo de Marte in humid and unsuitable barracks hastily erected on the site while others were billeted in the welcoming homes of the people of Havana. The many sick – both soldiers and sailors – were brought to the hospital of San Juan de Dios, the hospital of San Ambrosio, and the convent of Belén. (Sergio Guerra Vilaboy, 'Miranda en Cuba: Un capítulo decisivo en la vida del precursor de la Independencia de América Latina', *Cuadernos Americanos: Nueva Epoca*, iii, Nº 111 (2005), 85-102)

A fleet of 36 sail with eighteen millions of dollars for the King and twelve millions and merchandize for the merchants, convoyed by three ships of the line besides others of observation, were expected to sail from La Vera Cruz about the end of this month and probably would leave the Havanna for Spain early in the summer.

Monsieur Montell[20] with three French ships of the line and two frigates arrived from Cape François as an additional security for the flota.

At the Havanna there were two ships of eighty guns, five of seventy four, six of sixty four, seven frigates, thirty large transports, and ten thousand troops.

The Morro[21] is altered and strengthened. The Cavagne[22], a new work, answers equally as a citadell more extensive than the Morro. The lines of the town have had no alteration, but to defend them two new forts have been erected: Arostigne[23] upon an eminence towards the sea; the other, Dalteres[24], on a hill protects the ship-yard, magazines and town.

As your Lordship is acquainted with the state of this garrison and fortifications, I have only to suggest that by His Majesty's instructions I am to apply to the Commanders in Chief for military protection and expenditures and for the necessary repairs of fortifications.

I am confident your Lordship's zeal for the service will lead you to give the necessary directions. For some time the repairs have been at a stand, and some works must be established. I find, my Lord, innumerable embarrassments from the imperfect state of my situation.

---

[20] Entering the French navy as a *garde de la marine* in 1741, François-Aymar, Baron de Monteil (1725-1787) had been promoted to *lieutenant de vaisseau* in 1756, *capitaine de vaisseau* in 1762, and *chef d'escadre* in 1779. When de Guichen and de Grasse left the West Indies in August 1780, de Monteil assumed command of the French navy there, raising his flag aboard the 74-gun man of war *Le Palmier*. With it and three other men of war (*l'Intrépide* (74), *le Destin* (74), and *le Triton* (64)) he took part in de Gálvez's expedition which led to the reduction of Pensacola in May 1781. Later in the year, while commanding the 80-gun *le Languedoc*, he accompanied de Grasse to the Chesapeake and commanded the rear guard in the Battle of the Virginia Capes on 5th September. Back in the West Indies after Yorktown, he distinguished himself in the capture of Saint-Christophe in January 1782. Soon afterwards he returned ill to France and in 1783 was promoted to *lieutenant-général*. (*Expédition Particulière* Commemorative Cantonment Society, 'French Naval Leaders and the French Navy in the American War for Independence' (Internet, 3rd August 2006))

[21] *The Morro*: designed by Bautista Antonelli, the Castillo de los Tres Reyes del Morro was constructed in 1589 and overlooks the entrance to the Bay of Havana on the eastern side. It was carried by the British in 1762 when they occupied the town. It is complemented by the Castillo de San Salvador de la Punta, constructed at the same time on the western side.

[22] *The Cavagne*: the Fortaleza de San Carlo de la Cabaña adjoins the Morro. It was constructed after the close of the Seven Years' War.

[23] As Forbes later makes clear, 'Arostigne' is not the name of the fort but of the eminence on which it was being constructed. The fort has not been identified.

[24] *Dalteres*: the Castillo de Atarés is located to the south of the old town, overlooking the Bay of Havana from the west.

With my warmest wishes for a continuation of your Lordship's successes in reducing the rebellious colonies and restoring peace, I have the honour to be with the greatest respect and esteem, my Lord,
Your Lordship's most obedient and most humble servant

PAT TONYN

PS

Upon the first intimation of this intelligence I apprised Lt Colonel Clerk of it and I have the honour to inclose copies of two letters I have written to the Colonel upon the subject.

Permit me to beg of your Lordship to forward the inclosed letter for Lord George Germain with all possible dispatch.

Enclosure (1)
Navarro to Tonyn, 30th December 1780   *67(37): C*

Havannah
30th December 1780

Sir

Mr Thomas Forbes, commissary appointed by your Excellency for the exchange of Spanish prisoners brought to this port in the flag of truce under his command, has delivered me your Excellency's letter of the 10th of October last, by which I acknowledge your Excellency, having been moved by the unhappy situation of the unfortunate prisoners, did dispatch the said flag with them. I am sorry to find myself without orders from my Court to establish flags of truce for the relief of unfortunate subjects of both Crowns, and in the interim I have taken what steps I can with other Governors of His Britainick Majesty's dominions untill such orders come to me.

By the inclosed list your Excellency will be informed that the number of prisoners brought by Mr Thomas Forbes are regularly exchanged, and that separately goes also exchanged Lieutenant William McDonald of the 60th Regiment, and that in consequence of your Excellency's request and that of the commander in chief of the said regiment [I] have condescended that the number of soldiers specified in the said list may be embarked on board of the said flag, who are not to take up arms untill others are properly exchanged for them.

Mr Forbes having represented to me that the flag of truce was obliged to be repaired and that he was unprovided with money for to pay the expences and also for fresh provisions had daily from markett for the said flag of truce, I have on the King's account, and to be accounted for on account of prisoners of His Britainick Majesty, supplied him with the sum of three hundred and ninety four dollars four reals.[25]

---

[25] A real was worth one eighth of a Spanish milled dollar (*peso duro*).

Lastly, the said Mr Forbes, finding that the said flag of truce was not sufficient to proceed on her voyage in the present season with the number of prisoners that are to be given to him, beged I would furnish him with a proper Spanish vessell to perform the voyage. Anxious of contributing to the good of both nations, [I] have therefore furnished him with the Spanish sloop named the *Industrious*, commanded by Don Joaq[n] Escalona, giving him a proper passport for his safe navigation as flag of truce, and for his return I beg your Excellency will give him such as may be necessary.

I thank your Excellency for the kind expressions of your letter in wishing peace once more established. We may have reason to correspond mutually.

God preserve your Excellency in good health many years.

I am your Excellency's most sincere humble servant

JAMES JOSEPH NAVARRO[26]

Enclosure (2)
Prisoners delivered to Forbes   *67(39): C*

Havannah
30th December 1780

List of 16 English prisoners delivered to Mr Thomas Forbes, commissary of prisoners from East Florida, in exchange for the like number of Spanish prisoners he brought into this port, viz:

Captains:	N° 1	William Barnes
	2	Edward Ross
	3	Hamilton Wood
Pilots:	4	George Elliott
	5	Matthew Buckhanan
	6	Henry Huton
	7	Christopher Fisher
	8	Richard England
Passengers and sailors:	9	John Jarle
	10	David Drew
	11	Thomas Moore
	12	William Miller
	13	Henry Lane
	14	John Turpin

---

[26] A lt general, Don Diego José Navarro had become Capitán General (Governor) of Cuba in June 1777, succeeding the popular Felipe Fondesviela, Marqués de la Torre. Navarro would in turn be succeeded by Don Juan Manuel de Cagigal on 4th June 1781.

15   Samuel Ingram
16   Daniel Ashman

NB: Besides the above number which have been exchanged, William McDonald, lieutenant of the 60th Regiment, who was a prisoner at Mobile, and James Buchanan, passenger on board of the merchant ship named the *Nancy*, who was taken by the ship of war named the *Nuestra Seňora de O*, the first exchanged instead of Don Joseph Eugenio Rey, lieutenant of the Royal Artillery, and the other instead of Don Francisco Casas, who was a passenger on board of the merchant ship called the *Hope* and was taken by the ship of war named the *Cyclops*, for which said two gentlemen the aforesaid commissary has given certificates.

Also there has been delivered to the said commissary, Mr Thomas Forbes, the 25 soldiers following, to be exchanged in their equal ranks under the conditions that they are not to take up arms 'til their exchange is verified, viz:

Serjeants: Nº 1   John Gun
              2   Henry Coomber
              3   Jacob Rock

Corporals: 4   John Hundy
              5   William Brocon

Drums: 6   Joseph Gibbon
              7   John Wagg
              8   William Arnfield

Soldiers: 9   Philip Zimer
              10   William Hugues
              11   George Spencer
              12   John Wynn
              13   James Beaman
              14   William Baker
              15   John Owen
              16   Edward Russell
              17   Thomas Jobbins
              18   Charles Woodhead
              19   James Man
              20   William Gardner
              21   Samuel Robing
              22   John Small
              23   John Sams
              24   Edward Gardner

Artillery: 25   George Atkinson

In the same manner and form has been delivered the said commissary Mr Richard Loyd, in whose stead a Spanish gentleman of the same rank is to be received.

Enclosure (3)
Tonyn to Clarke, 22nd January 1781   67(42): CS

St Augustine
22nd January 1781

Dear Sir

I have been honoured with some of your letters and I am much obliged for the particulars.

The reinforcement under General Leslie having effectuated a junction with the Earl of Cornwallis is a very material point gained. This additional strength directed by his Lordship's zeal and military capacity will, I hope, surmount every opposition which can be attempted by the rebels in the prosecution of his plans.

At the very moment I had the honor of receiving your last favour dated the 4th instant I had circumstantial and authentic intelligence of the undoubted intentions of the Spaniards to invade West Florida notwithstanding the late disasters and losses of their second attempt occasioned by a violent storm.

A few transports excepted, the heavy ships have arrived at the Havannah, and the lighter armed vessels and transports at Campeachy, and have sailed again from every quarter to assemble at Mobille to carry on from thence their further operations, and Don Galvez it was expected would sail from the Havannah about the 12th instant for Mobille to take upon himself the command of the expedition.

This plan has been received from the Spanish Court with orders to be put into immediate execution for the reduction of and reuniting the two Floridas to the Crown of Spain.

As you will be more particularly informed by Lt Colonel Glazier, who has stated some questions and answers respecting the strength of the forces and Spanish Marine[27], I shall not trouble you with any further relation untill another opportunity, as I would not detain the vessel sailing and prevent your having the earliest notice of the certain preparations at the Havannah to attack St Augustine immediately after the reduction of Pensacola. In the success of this last they have the greatest confidence.

This garrison being exactly in the same weak state of which you was a witness in August last, and no engineer having been here to repair or strengthen the fortifications, it is needless to trouble you with any observations upon the subject, who know the wants and necessities and that an engineer ought to have been sent to put the garrison in a more respectable situation.

Besides the insufficiency of numbers to maintain a post where at least twelve hundred men should be stationed, I therefore hope that proper steps will be taken upon these threatening appearances to put the province on a more defensible footing.

---

[27] *some questions and answers...*: see pp 330-2.

Wishing you every happiness in this and many returning years, I have the honour to be, sir, Most sincerely yours

PAT TONYN

Enclosure (4)
Tonyn to Clarke, 29th January 1781　　　　　　　　　　　　　　　　*67(44): CS*

St Augustine
29th January 1781

Lt Colonel Alured Clark

Dear Sir

I have the honor, in addition to my last of the 22nd instant, to confirm that it is the determined intentions of the Spaniards to attack this province, for which purpose preparations are making at the Havanna, and four ships of the line, three frigates, and twelve new gallies each carrying one twenty four pounder and calculated for the East Florida navigation it was thought might be ready to sail in March, with six regiments and irregulars together amounting to five thousand, and Don Victor Navia is to command the expedition.

As this information may be depended upon, I am confident you will send Lt Colonel Glazier the necessary orders and an engineer, as you are acquainted with the state of the garrison and our situation, and with as much dispatch as circumstances will permit.

At present there is not a single armed vessel in our harbours to be sent to the southward for observation or to go express. In short, the province is entirely without any naval support. It would be very convenient if an inland communication could be kept up by establishing a post to go between this place and Savanna with dispatches, as our correspondence is precarious and the opportunities uncertain.

I have ever been assured that a store of provisions of six months in advance for fifteen hundred men should be constantly kept up by the commissaries in this garrison, and that our friendly Indians were to be supplied out of the King's Stores. Major General Prevost directed the commissary's agent to issue provisions for the Indians, and when there was none in the King's Store, I was compelled to purchase at a most enormous price. Although Colonel Glazier is very obliging in supplying the main body of Indians of the Nation, yet at this crisis it would be satisfactory to me if you would be pleased to direct him to supply me likewise with provisions for the Seminoly Indians as my fund is altogether inadequate for that purpose and I have received instructions to apply to the military department for such supplies, protection and expenditure.

I have the honor to be with every sentiment of regard and esteem, dear sir,
Your most obedient etc

PAT TONYN

Enclosure (5)
Tonyn to Germain, 27th January 1781[28]

67(48): CS

Nº 108

St Augustine
27th January 81

Rt Hon Lord George Germain

My Lord

I have the honor of informing your Lordship that for very good reasons I thought it proper to send Mr Thomas Forbes in November last with a flag of truce to the Havanna. He is just returned and brings me the inclosed interesting intelligence, which I send express to Admiral Arbuthnot to be transmitted to your Lordship.

By means of his late uncle, Mr Gordon of Charlestown, Mr Forbes is connected with some families of distinction there and I am confident his information can be relied upon. It is in substance this.

The Court of Madrid have established a plan for the conquest of the Floridas and Bahama Islands.

Last October a fleet of six sail of the line, four frigates and transports with four thousand troops sailed from the Havanna under the command of Don Galvez with a design to besiege Pensacola. This fleet was dispersed by a storm and considerably damaged. Some transports were lost, three decoyed into the port of Pensacola and captured, two vessels with ordnance stores were taken by His Majesty's Ship the *Mentor*, and five arrived safe at Mobille.

The 7th of December five hundred men sailed from the Havanna for Mobille, and on the 13th a thousand more. Don Galvez with two ships of the line and transports were to sail about the 12th of January against Pensacola.

Confident of success, it is intended immediately to attack this province, for which purpose four ships of the line, three frigates, and twelve new gallies each carrying one twenty four pounder and calculated for the East Florida navigation are prepared and it was thought might be ready to sail in March, with six regiments and irregulars together amounting to five thousand men under the command of Don Victor Navia, and that they mean to send Indians upon our back settlements.

A fleet of thirty six sail with eighteen millions of dollars for the King and twelve millions of dollars and merchandize for the merchants under convoy of three ships of the line, besides others of observation, were expected to sail from La Vera Cruz about the end of this month and would probably leave the Havanna for Spain early in the summer.

---

[28] Published without enclosure (6) in Davies ed, op cit, xx, 46-7. There are no other material differences.

Monsieur Montell with three French ships of the line and two frigates arrived in December from Cape François as an additional security to the flota. These ships were crouded with troops but very deficient in seamen.

Of twelve thousand troops from Spain, four thousand were lost by sickness.

At the Havanna there were two ships of eighty guns, five of seventy four, six of sixty four, seven frigates, thirty transports and ten thousand troops.

The Morro is altered and strengthened. The Cavagne, a new work, answers equally as a citadel more extensive than the Morro. The lines of the town have had no alteration, but to defend them two new forts have been erected: Arostigne upon an eminence towards the sea; the other, Dalteres, on a hill protects the ship-yard, magazines and town.

The people of Cuba wish much for peace and feel the hardships of war in a stop to commerce.

In my letter N° 103 of 9th December[29], of which a duplicate goes by this opportunity, I had the honor to lay before your Lordship a state of the province and garrison. I now in cooperation with the commanding officer take every step in my power to strengthen our situation. I am only apprehensive my zeal for His Majesty's Service may lead me to exceed the limits of His Majesty's instructions concerning expenditure.

The ordnance vessel mentioned in your Lordship's letter of the 3rd of August, N° 15[30], is not arrived.

I have thought proper to communicate to the Commanders in Chief of His Majesty's forces the necessary information upon these threatenings of the Spaniards.

I have the honor to be with the greatest respect, my Lord,
Your Lordship's most obedient and most humble servant

PAT TONYN

---

[29] *my letter..*: published in Davies ed, op cit, xviii, 252-5.

[30] *your Lordship's letter..*: published in Davies ed, op cit, xvi, N° 2371.

Enclosure (6)
Forbes' report, January 1781   *67(50): C*

*REPORT of sundry occurrences at Havanna from 6th November 1780
to my departure on the 7th January 1781*

On my arrival I found them much disappointed by the failure of an expedition which sail'd from thence against Pensacola on the 2nd of last October. It consisted of six sail of the line and four frigates commanded by Señor Solano[31] and transports carrying four thousand troops with artillery and stores of every kind under General Galvez. My advantageous situation soon gave me an opportunity of knowing that this expedition was undertaken in consequence of orders from Spain to improve the success lately gain'd by Galvez upon the Micissippi and at Mobile, and that it was a prelude to their hostile intentions against this province and New Providence. In the hurricane which reached this fleet on the 5th of October they had three ships of the line and one frigate totally dismasted and their transports dispersed beyond a possibility of collecting them again. In this condition the four dismasted ships were brought back to Havanna, on the 12th day after their departure, by two of the unhurt men o' war, a frigate and an hospital ship.

On the 10th November I had certain information of their design against East Florida, which they determine to put in execution when the fate of Pensacola is decided. Besides a convoy of men o' war and frigates I had an opportunity at this time to see three of twelve galleys intended for this business, each to carry a 24 pounder, and in my judgement these vessels are well constructed for the purpose. The Commander in Chief, Don Victor Navia, Generals Waughan[32] and Cagigal[33] are to be employ'd in this service. The regiments named for it are those of Ell Rei, Soria, Guadalaxara, Hibernia, Aragon and Segunda Cataluña, besides detachments from the artillery, muleatto and Negro regiments, the whole to make up five thousand effective men.

---

[31] Don José Solano y Bote (1725-1806) was a *jefe de escuadra* (commodore) in the Spanish *armada real*. On 19th April he and de Monteil (see note 20 above) would arrive off the island of Santa Rosa to reinforce de Gálvez in his attempt to reduce Pensacola. With them they brought fifteen ships of the line, three frigates, and other vessels, together with a landing party of 1,600 men under the command of Don Juan Manuel de Cagigal (see note 33 below). In later life Solano would be created Marqués del Socorro and die a *capitán general*. (José Luis Santaló Rodríguez de Viguri, *Don José Solano y Bote, Primer Marqués del Socorro, Capitán General de la Armada (1725-1806)* (Instituto Histórico de la Marina, Madrid, 1973); Bernado de Gálvez, 'Diary of the Operations against Pensacola', *Louisiana Historical Quarterly*, i (January 1917), 44-84)

[32] Waughan has not been identified. The spelling may be an inadvertent anglicization of 'Juan'.

[33] Born in Santiago de Cuba, Don Juan Manuel de Cagigal (1739-1811) was by now a major general in the Spanish army. In April he would reinforce de Gálvez at Pensacola, where his conduct led to his promotion to lt general. Amost immediately after the reduction of the town, he succeeded Navarro on 4th June as *Capitán General* (Governor) of Cuba and was in due course promoted to *mariscal de campo* (field marshal). In 1782 he proceeded to occupy the defenceless Bahama Islands, which capitulated on 8th May. Soon afterwards he was recalled to Spain for political ineptitude and confined in a castle near Cadiz for four years. (*Appletons'*; Francisco Calcagno, *Diccionario biográfico cubano* (New York, 1878-1886))

On the 17th November General Galvez return'd in the *La O'* frigate accompanied by the *Santa Rosalia* (on board of which Solano had hoisted his flag after the storm), an 18 gun snow and two English prizes which they accidentally mett with in cruising for their transports.

On the 30th November the *Dragon* man o' war of 64 guns (being the last of the six convoy ships) came in from Mobile, where she had safely conducted five sail of the transports. At this date they had certain information of twenty three sail more being safe at Campeachy. They admitt that one with every soul on board perished on that coast; two more were stranded. One ship with troops and two small vessels with stores were carried into Pensacola. (NB: By my list thirteen transports are still missing.)

On the 7th December five hundred troops were embarked and sail'd immediately for Mobile to prevent in the mean time any attempt against it from Pensacola.

On the 11th I was informed that much altercation has prevail'd in the daily councils held at the Governor's by the general officers since the return of General Galvez. Mutual accusations are thrown out on the one hand by Señor Navia against the expensive and ill conducted plans of Galvez, who on the other retorts upon the Governor and General for their feeble and dilatory proceedings in complying with the King's orders.

On the 13th December one thousand troops more sail'd for Mobile in consequence of General Galvez having gain'd his point in council and becoming answerable for the event of another attempt against Pensacola. The General himself will not embark till after the holidays, having to wait the arrival of the transports from Campeachy at Mobile before any movement is made from thence.

On the 27th December arrived from Cape Françoise a French fleet consisting of three ships of the line, two frigates and one copper bottom'd cutter, commanded by Monsieur Montell. This fleet was sent for by the Spanish Admiral (Bonney[34]) to strengthen the convoy expected to sail from La Vera Cruz about this time. They had a heavy gale on their passage, in which one sixty four parted company and is still missing. These ships have not half their complement of seamen but are crouded with troops. The *Comodore* is so leaky that 150 slaves are hired to assist in keeping her clear till the guns are taken out and the ship prepared

---

[34] A *comandante general* (rear admiral) in the Spanish *armada real*, Don Juan Bautista Bonet (c. 1709-1785) was presently in charge of the Havana station. Born in Cartagena, he was commissioned an *alférez de fregata* (lieutenant) in November 1728 and went on to sail the seven seas, gaining very wide experience in nautical matters. In view of his interest in engineering he was then assigned to the arsenal of Cartagena, where he took charge of nautical engineering. Promoted to *capitán de fregata* in November 1746, he was given the command of Admiral Spinola's flagship, the 70-gun *Invencible*, which formed part of Admiral Regio's squadron. While sailing not far from Havana on 12th October 1748, the squadron fell in with that of Rear Admiral Charles Knowles and in the ensuing engagement Bonet was wounded. Upon his recovery he served for the next twenty years in the Pacific, commanding the naval forces at Chile and Peru. Besides protecting maritime traffic, he charted the coastal waters, bringing about much safer navigation. By now a *jefe de escuadra* (commodore), he moved on promotion to his present command at Havana, which he invigorated. An arsenal was renovated and a shipyard converted, from which were launched numerous vessels, including various large ships of the line. In recognition of his services he was promoted to *teniente general* (vice admiral). He ended his naval career in 1782 as second in command of Córdova's squadron, taking part in the Channel campaign and the blockade of Gibraltar. He died at Cartagena. (*Enciclopedia General del Mar* (Ediciones Garriga, Barcelona))

for heaving down. A gentleman of rank told me the Monsieurs had not been so ready in their compliance if their ships had not wanted many repairs and materials which are not to be procured at the Cape.

On the 31st December arrived a frigate which convoyed the embarkation of the 7th to Mobile.

On the 4th of January arrived a packet from Cadiz, which she left the 6th November. They call the combined fleet seventy sail of the line, commanded by d'Estaigne, Cordova[35] and Guichen. The British they admit to be fifty sail and upwards under command of my Lord Howe — that the English fleet were coming to succour Gibraltar.[36] The Count, determined to prevent this, was to blockade that fortress and risk a decisive action. They admit that overtures of peace from England had been seriously attended to at Madrid, and that Monsieur Necker[37] had with much difficulty prevail'd with their Court to continue the war one year longer, in which time he persuaded them that the British finances must be ruin'd and exhausted and that she must submit to any accomodation they should dictate. Politicians here are still of opinion, notwithstanding, that a seperate peace will soon take place between the Courts of Madrid and London, an event which all ranks of people at Havanna wish and pray for.

On the 6th of January three Spanish and two French ships of the line with three frigates and a small tender sail'd under command of Señor Solano to meet and convoy the flota from La Vera Cruz. This fleet has on board eighteen millions of dollars for the King and twelve millions of private property besides merchandize to a large amount. The King to encourage the importation of money on the present occasion has relinquished the usual dutys. There are three men o' war to sail with this fleet from La Vera Cruz, three more have sail'd at different times since my arrival to cruise for them in the sound, besides the fleet which sail'd this morning. The time they may sail from Havanna for Europe is very uncertain, but when they

---

[35] Born in Segovia, Don Luis de Córdova (1706-1796) had entered the Spanish navy in 1721. By now a *teniente general* (vice admiral), he had commanded the Spanish squadron which in 1779 had formed part of the combined Franco-Spanish fleet in the Channel campaign. The following year he had captured a British convoy of more than fifty-five sail off Cape Santa Maria. He would soon go on to take part in a Franco-Spanish fleet in the second Channel campaign and in 1782 command the naval forces blockading Gibraltar. Having been appointed Director General of the Navy in 1780, he became its *Capitán General* three years later. He died at San Fernando, a small town near Cadiz.

[36] It was Rodney who relieved Gibraltar. On 29th December 1780 he left Plymouth with twenty-one sail of the line, the normal complement of frigates, some three hundred store ships, and a fleet of transports. On 16th January he defeated a smaller Spanish squadron off Cape St Vincent and went on to complete his mission successfully. (Boatner, *Encyclopedia*, 943)

[37] Born in Geneva, Jacques Necker (1732-1804) moved to Paris in 1747 and became a banker and very wealthy man. Despite being a Protestant, he was appointed France's Finance Minister in October 1776 and became popular, particularly after France's entry into war with Britain, when he adopted a policy of borrowing rather than raising taxes to finance the increased burden of expenditure. In May 1781 he would be dismissed from office, partly due to the influence of Marie Antoinette, whose schemes for benefitting the Duc de Guines he had thwarted. In 1788, as France's finances unravelled, he again became Finance Minister, adopting policies which in some quarters are thought to have precipitated the French Revolution. In September 1790 he resigned and retired to Coppet, his estate near Geneva, where he died. (Jean de Viguerie, *Histoire et dictionnaire du temps des Lumières, 1715-1789* (Collections Bouquins, Paris, 2003); *Encyclopædia Britannica* (11th edition))

do, it will be a very numerous and rich fleet, no property having gone from this port since the commencement of hostilities.

On the 7th January I saw some transports fall down the harbour and am told that General Galvez will certainly sail in four days.

MEMORANDUM

Their fleet which so narrowly escaped from Admiral Rhodney to windward, after landing fifteen hundred sick at Martinique, arrived here in August last with nine thousand troops, which were landed in a most wretched condition. These regiments, which all consist of two batallions and, when embark'd, had each fifteen hundred men, can hardly muster five hundred healthy men now. I saw that of Hibernia twice paraded and am certain they did not come up to that number — others much less. Of twelve thousand troops embark'd in this fleet from Spain, they have at this time lost by sickness upwards of four thousand, and many of the hospitals are still full.

On my arrival they had in this port (including the dismasted ships) two of 80, five of 74, and six ships of sixty four guns, seven or eight frigates of all sizes, and about thirty sail of transports or large merchantmen, mostly armed. I was on board both the 80 gun ships (call'd the *St Louis* and *St Nicholas*). They are fine ships, carry only 24 pounders on the lower deck, and are very deficient of seamen. Many of their cannon are old and upon the long construction.

They have at present two batallions of black and two of mullatto soldiers raised in the island. They are well appointed and commanded by experienc'd officers. I saw the blacks reviewed. Besides these they have two regiments of horse well accoutred and mounted on small sprightly and tractable horses. These I also saw reviewed to the number of seven hundred. They are call'd militia but are train'd by officers from the regular service. From the number of churches and other buildings still occupied by the troops I conjecture their whole force at Havanna (including these regiments) may amount to ten thousand men.

This place in the improved state of its fortifications is exceeding strong — in the hands of ten thousand *British*, perhaps impregnable to any attack. The Morro is altered and strengthen'd. The Cavagna is much more extensive than the Morro and will be equally strong when the rising ground behind it is removed. Five or six hundred slaves and malefactors are daily employ'd upon this work, which, when accomplish'd, will give full range to the guns of the Cavagna upon the only accessible side.

The Punta[38] on the other side of the harbour is repair'd and now has casemates and magazines which are bomb proof.

---

[38] *The Punta*: see p 338, note 21.

The lines of the town have undergone no manner of alteration, but to defend the approach of an enemy this way they have built two entire new forts since the last seige. One stands towards the sea upon an eminence call'd Arostigny and is not quite finish'd. This is a large and respectable work. The other, call'd Dalteres, commands the ship yard, magazines and town upon that side, crosses its fire with that of Arostigny, and is completely finish'd. This last is said to be exceeding strong from its situation on a hill which is or may be very easily surrounded with water. This fort is smaller than the other, but both are furnish'd with casemates, reservoirs and magazines all bomb proof.

Tonyn to Balfour, 30th January 1781   67(55): ACS

St Augustine
30th January 81

Lt Colonel Nesbit Balfour

Sir

Duplicates of my letters sent by the *Sandwich* go by this opportunity.

As my letters to Earl Cornwallis are of the greatest importance, give me leave to request that you will forward them to his Lordship with all haste.

Being much hurried, I hope you will pardon my transmitting copies of two letters written to Lt Colonel Clerk[39] which will acquaint you of the important subject of my letters to the Commanders in Chief.

In other matters here we are perfectly quiet.

I have the honour to be with great respect and regard, sir,
Your most obedient and most humble servant

PAT TONYN

Forbes to Tonyn, 5th February 1781   67(46): C

St Augustine
5th February 1781

Sir

I take the liberty to send your Excellency the names of three Spanish prisoners who were said at the Havannah to be in Carolina. It was requested of me that they might be relieved

---

[39] *two letters..*: of 22nd and 29th January, pp 342-3.

and sent home by return of the present cartel. Their names are Vizente Perez, Pedro Perez and Thomas de Noa. From the difficulty I had in procuring so advantageous an exchange your Excellency will no doubt be induced to observe as much punctuality as possible in the discharge of those engagements I entered into upon account of the soldiers belonging to His Majesty's 60th Regiment.

Should it be found expedient for His Majesty's Service to send another flag to Havannah for the relief of the British prisoners still remaining there, I think it may be in my power to obtain an exchange for those Spanish prisoners sent from Charlestown soon after the reduction of that place.

The want of instructions from Spain concerning prisoners made them at that time particularly cautious of admitting British cartels and is still their greatest objection to a general exchange.

I think this difficulty may be got over by proper management, at least so far as extends to the relief of such prisoners as can be sent them from America or Jamaica.

I have furnished your Excellency with my reasons for thinking that no person from this country can so readily execute this business as myself in the present state of affairs, but to facilitate the matter I must have permission to send by return of this sloop one thousand bushels of salt at least, some cordage, nails and coarse linens with some trifling commissions for private gentlemen of my acquaintance, who are persons of some consequence there.

This is the only method which can procure me a good reception and sufficient interest, and, if approved by your Excellency, would make it worth my attention to undertake the business. I should not in this case propose to go by this sloop, but to follow soon after in a vessel adapted for the purpose of bringing off as many prisoners as I could procure.

On the score of intelligence your Excellency can judge from what I have already obtained if I can render His Majesty's Service any further good.

I have the honor to be, sir, with great respect
Your Excellency's most obedient and most humble servant

THO[S] FORBES

[*Superscribed in Tonyn's hand*:]

Private and confidential

Governor Tonyn presents his best compliments to Earl Cornwallis and has the honour in confidence of transmitting to his Lordship a copy of a letter to him which discloses the channel of intelligence he has established, and begs it may be for your Lordship's perusal only, as it might be attended with some hazard to Mr Forbes.

Enclosure
Return of British prisoners at Havana, 1st January 1781   *67(63): C*

ACCOUNT *of British troops and seamen, prisoners at Havannah, the 1st of January 1781*

16th Regiment		60th Regiment		Waldecks		Loyalists		Independants		Artillery		Total	
Captains:		*Captains:*		*Captains:*		*Serjeants*	1	*Lieutenants:*		*Corporals*	1	*Captains*	5
Fitsmorris Conner		John Christie		Hawke		*Corporals*	2	McGibbin		*Bombardiers*	1	*Lieutenants*	5
William Barker		*Serjeants*	2	Alberty		*Privates*	12	*Serjeants*	1	*Gunners*	10	*Ensigns*	1
Lieutenants:		*Drums*	2	*Lieutenants:*		*TOTAL*	15	*Corporals*	1	*TOTAL*	12	*Surgeons*	1
Nath.l Lindergreen		*Privates*	15	Stroughbury				*Drummers*	1			*Serjeants*	17
William Barwell		*Women*	5	Bromhart				*Privates*	1			*Corporals*	19
Ensigns:		*TOTAL*	25	*Surgeon:*				*TOTAL*	5			*Drums*	7
Hambleton				Daniel Beck								*Bombardiers*	1
Serjeants	7			*Serjeants*	6							*Gunners*	10
Corporals	6			*Corporals*	9							*Privates*	197
Drums	4			*Privates*	102							*Women & children*	27
Privates	67			*Women*	5							*TOTAL*	290
Women & children	17			*TOTAL*	127								
TOTAL	106												

NB: I compute the seamen prisoners at least 250 men.

THO.s FORBES

352

Tonyn to Cornwallis, 5th May 1781 6(50): ALS

St Augustine
5th May 1781

Rt Hon Earl Cornwallis

My Lord

In my letter of the 29th January last I had the honour of mentioning to your Lordship that by the King's instructions I am to apply to the Commanders in Chief of His forces for protection and expenditures; and as the annual grant of Parliament for the contingent expences of the Seminolie Indians of this province hath been stoped since the 24th of June 1779, there is no fund for discharging their expences which are unavoidable; and the Superintendent has directions to send to me necessary supplies of presents and to leave these Indians to the management of the Governor. Lt Colonel Brown informs me that he has forwarded these presents, but they are, my Lord, taken possession of by the military department and I could not be supplied with any for a party that at the desire of the commanding officer was by invitation brought here, and they are reserved for presents in case of the arrival of the Creek Indians from the Nation. The case is similar with respect to provisions for the Seminolies out of the King's Stores. Upon my representations of the state of provisions the Secretary of State acquainted me that there would be in advance constantly for fifteen hundred men six months in the King's Stores and that the Indians would be supplied out of it.

I have the honour of inclosing for your Lordship's satisfaction my correspondence with Colonel Clark upon these subjects, and I should have been at a very great loss or must have sent the Indians away out of humour, when the object of their visit was their assistance in case of invasion by the Spaniards, if I had not husbanded presents which were to be expended in 1779. And as their reception would not have been what they were accustomed too, I thought it prudent not to risk their friendship for us and attachment to His Majesty and therefore made provision for them, which expences I shall have the honor of transmitting to your Lordship. And they have engaged to watch the coast from this place to the southward and give the earliest information, with the strongest assurances of friendship and assistance against all our enemies.

By a letter received the 20th of April from a Mr Barnes dated 21st March near Pensacola, the Spaniards had made a descent upon Rose Island, their army was three thousand men, and their fleet were got into the harbour. The Choctaws and Chickasaws Indians have skirmished with some attempting to land on the main, which was not effected, and that the Creeks were not arrived to their assistance but were expected. Later accounts mention that they have besieged the fort near to the cliffs and have gained no advantage. I trust the Admiral at Jamaica will get in time to relieve it.

I most sincerely congratulate your Lordship upon your glorious victories and extraordinary repeated successes over the rebellious provinces. Such renowned actions will transmit your fame with admiration to posterity and you will thereby be rendered dear in the hearts of the nation.

I have the honour to be with the greatest respect and esteem, my Lord,
Your Lordship's most obedient and most humble servant

PAT TONYN

Enclosure (1)
Tonyn to Clarke, 30th April 1781   5(274): C

St Augustine
30th April 1781

Lt Colonel Alured Clarke

Dear Sir

In consequence of the expedience of the invitation to the Cowkeeper and some of the Chiefs of the Seminoly Indians they have arrived last night, and I am under the necessity of applying to you for supplying them with provisions out of the King's Stores.

I had the honor in a former letter dated 29th January of mentioning the assurances given me that a sufficient quantity of provisions for such purposes were expected to be stored in the magazines, and that I had received instructions to apply to the military department for such supplies and protection and expenditure.

As I have no fund whatever for Indian contingencies, the Provincial annual allowance for that service voted by Parliament having been struck off last year and most probably will not again be restored, and as it is absolutely necessary that the Indians must be supported and their alliance to His Majesty courted, more particularly at this crisis, I have to request that you will be so good to order the commissary's agent to issue rations for the Indians, and the Indian commissary shall wait upon you with a list of the number of Indians present, and to receive your commands.

It has been customary to issue baked bread to the Indians in the same manner as delivered to the soldiers, sometimes fresh meat, and they have also rum given to them occasionally, and to the Cowkeeper (who is in advanced years) some wine and coffee and sugar, and to some of the Chiefs the two latter articles; and I beg, sir, they may have the usual hospitable and friendly reception.

The Cowkeeper is considered as the principal of the Seminolies and his influence guides in general. It will therefore be proper to fix a plan for their conduct in cases of future exigencies and to endeavour to impress them with the urgency of adopting such measures. It will therefore give me great pleasure to know your sentiments upon this subject and to do all in my power to forward your views.

I have the honor to be, sir, etc

PAT TONYN

Enclosure (2)
Clarke to Tonyn, 1st May 1781 6(17): C

St Augustine
May 1st 1781

His Excellency Governor Tonyn

Dear Sir

I have been honored by the receipt of your Excellency's letter and in answer to the first part of it am sorry to observe that the small quantity of provisions in His Majesty's Stores will not admit of the least *extra* diminition of them without manifest risk to the security of the garrison, but as the expediency of keeping the Indians firm in His Majesty's interest at this crisis is obvious and your Excellency assures me you have no fund whatever for Indian contingencies (that formerly allow'd by Parliament having been struck off), I shall think it my duty to order Mr Moore, the Superintendent's deputy in this province, to furnish the Cowkeeper and his attendants now here with such articles as seem necessary, at the same time observing it must be done with as sparing a hand as possible, not feeling myself justifiable in incurring a heavy expence on this account unless the security of the province should be immediately in question. I will do myself the honour to call upon your Excellency in order to determine on such a line of conduct for the Seminolies as may appear most likely to render them serviceable and as little burthensome as possible if St Augustine should be attacked, and I shall on all occasions be happy to concur with you, sir, in such measures as seem calculated to promote His Majesty's Service, having the honor to remain with great respect and regard, dear sir,

Your Excellencies most obedient and most faithful humble servant

ALURED CLARKE

Enclosure (3)
Tonyn to Clarke, 4th May 1781 6(43): C

St Augustine
4th May 1781

Lt Colonel Alured Clarke

Dear Sir

The insufficiency in the King's Stores for supplying the Indians with provisions mentioned in your letter, which I have the honour of receiving, is very embarrassing, and as the attachment of the Indians is highly necessary, the best means must be used of preserving their fidelity to His Majesty, and although they have ever been treated here with some indulgencies, it hath constantly been done with frugality, and a deviation of their accustomed receptions may be dangerous. My instructions refer me to the army department for defraying such expenditure. I must therefore necessarily apply to the Commander in Chief of His Majesty's troops for that purpose, and as our intelligence of the Spanish designs is actually in part fulfilled by the invasion of West Florida, we ought to be prepared to repel the intended attack of this province. The intire want of cruizing vessels deprives us of any previous information of an enemy's approach until they are seen from the coast, a period too late to have the assistance of the Indians without they are properly prepared for such an event. If you approve of it, I shall this day apprize them of the prospect there is of such necessary service for them and the advantage of their being stationed at Anastasia, Matanza and the Mosketoes. This will incur a constant expence for provisions and fit leaders to conduct them.

I should not hold myself blameless was I not to propose the adopting measures for meeting the enemy at every point where attacks are most likely to happen, and the ostensive threatnings of the enemy sufficiently warn us to be prepared.

It would be very convenient, and I should be much obliged, if you will order Mr Moore to make out a proper assortment of presents to deliver to the Indians this afternoon that they may be sent away to their towns tomorrow.

The Cowkeeper has desired that his son may be dignified with the highest marks of distinction. I have ordered a commission to be made out for him of the first rank amongst them, and as it has been customary to anounce such honour conferred at the head of a captain's command and [with] a discharge of artillery, I beg leave to request that a similar command may be ordered with two field pieces on the parade at twelve o'clock, and, after the commission is proclaimed, that the guns may fire a salute and the command three volies.

I beg leave to request a return of provisions in the King's Stores and for what time they will supply the troops in garrison.

Upon all occasions I shall be happy to give you the strongest testimonies that

I have the honor to be with every sentiment of regard and esteem, sir, etc

PAT TONYN

Enclosure (4)
Clarke to Tonyn, 4th May 1781 6(52): C

St Augustine
May 4th 1781

His Excellency Governor Tonyn

Dear Sir

I am this moment honor'd by the receipt of your letter and must beg leave to join in opinion with your Excellency that every obstruction should be thrown in the way of the enemy, consequently that a body of Indians being in readiness to oppose any attempt the Spaniards may make to land would be very beneficial, and I am sorry that not feeling myself authorized to enter upon a considerable expence on account of the Seminolies without further instructions from Lord Cornwallis should occasion you having the trouble of writing a second letter on the subject. At your Excellency's request I have given the necessary orders for a captain's party and two field pieces to attend at the proclamation of the Cowkeeper's son's commission.

Fully aware of the propriety of being prepared to oppose the enemy in every possible situation, I shall at all times attend to your Excellencies sentiments and wishes on this head, and I trust that no zeal will be wanting on my part in the execution of such measures as may appear most condusive to His Majesty's Service.

I will do myself the honor of calling on you this morning to talk about the presents, of which I understand there are but a small quantity in publick store, and in the mean time

I have the honor to remain with great respect and regard, dear sir,
Your Excellency's most obedient and most faithful humble servant

ALURED CLARKE

§ - §

4 - Between Brown and Balfour

Brown to Balfour, 23rd January 1781 *62(2): ALS*

Augusta
January 23rd 1780[40]

Sir

I have the honor to acquaint you that, on receiving information the public boats had been robbed by McKay's party and the inhabitants of Beaufort District and that Lieutenant Camp, whom I had ordered with ten rangers to see that the militia furnished proper excortes, had been deserted by the militia on the appearance of the rebels and, after being taken prisoner, had been murdered in cool blood with five of his men, I detached Captain Wylly[41] with 40

---

[40] *1780*: a slip. It should read '1781'. As so often happens, Brown was not yet used to writing the new year.

[41] Alexander Campbell Wylly (1760-?) was a Georgian who had been commissioned a captain in the King's Rangers on 1st December 1778. His father, Alexander, was the prewar partner of Dr Lewis Johnston (see vol I, p 281, note 68) and would soon serve as Speaker in the Commons House of the Georgia royal assembly. Alexander, the son,

rangers and 30 Indians with orders to procure what assistance he could from the loyal part of the militia and endeavour to drive those villainous banditti out off the country. On his marching as low as Matthews's Bluff, he received information that all the different companies of the district with their officers were in arms under a Colonel Harden, amounting to 500 men.

Apprehending a general insurrection in the country from a knowledge of the conduct and principles of the inhabitants, I immediately marched with 40 rangers and about the same number of Indians and militia, not judging it prudent to take more men from this post.

Captain Wylly, on finding the rebels in such force, very prudently retreated. After marching 30 miles each day, I effected a junction with him. One hundred militia having joined us, I immediately continued my march to one Wigan's plantation, where I encamped. About three hours before break of day the rebels attacked the militia I had posted on my left, who, without returning a shot, I am sorry to say, fled into camp in the greatest disorder and confusion imaginable. Being in consequence obliged to change our front, at some distance from our fires, we permitted them to advance and instantly repulsed them.

Confiding in their numbers, about 8 o'clock in the morning they made their appearance on our right and, having dismounted, advanced to attack us (our militia either through fear or dissaffection, ten only excepted, immediately fled) after annoying us a little at a distance of 200 yards. We charged, dispersed and (with the Indians) pursued them 2 or 3 miles.

The loss the rebels sustained I cannot ascertain but believe it considerable. The number left on the field after the second action did not exceed 10. They were principally indebted to the speed of their horses for their escape. A Captain Johnson is since dead of his wounds.

Our loss in the two actions is 1 serjeant and 4 rank and file killed, 1 lieutenant and eight wounded. Of the Indians, 1 Chickesaw, 2 Creeks (viz, the Dog King and Far Off King of the Cussetas), and 3 Cherokees — and five wounded.

About 150 of the rebels fled by the upper part of the lower Three Runs on their way to the rebel army. Colonel Harden it is said with a party fled by the Saltketcher Road towards Santee. McKoy and the plunderers from the Georgia side recrossed Savannah River. The rest took such routes as I suppose they imagined would be the safest.

In or near every house within an extent of 30 miles we have found some of the King's stores. I have made a severe example of some notorious murderers and plunderers, which I hope will deter other villains from a commission of similar outrages.

---

would shortly be dispatched on command to seek support from the Cherokees as the revolutionary forces closed in on Augusta. He may therefore have evaded capture when the post capitulated to Lee and Pickens. At the close of the war he was placed on the Provincial half-pay list and settled on Abaco, a narrow, irregular and crescent-shaped island at the northern end of the Bahamas. Although included in the Georgia Banishment and Confiscation Act passed by the revolutionary assembly in May 1782, he was eventually pardoned and returned to St Simons Island, where he lived out the rest of his life among the plantation gentry of the Georgia low country. (Treasury 64/23(16), WO 65/164(42), and WO 65/165(11) (National Archives, Kew); Cashin, *The King's Ranger*, 17, 130, 144, 175, 191; Clark, *Loyalists in the Southern Campaign*, i, 80-4, 445; The Georgia Banishment and Confiscation Act 1782)

From every information I have received, the rebels in Beaufort District had received orders from a General Green to assemble and were to have been supported by a Colonel Marion from some part of Santee whilst a General Morgan made a diversion in their favor towards Ninety Six. I presume the march of General Leslie disconcerted their plan of operation.

It will now I presume occur to you, sir, the necessity of the militia under the command of Colonel Lechmere doing occasional duty on Savannah River for the security of the navigation.

If the companies near Matthew's Bluff at the crossing place and at Summerlin's Ferry were to form a stockade near the river at each place, which might be done with poles in half a day, and keep twenty men with an officer to be relieved once a fortnight, the boats in time of danger might lay with safety at either of these places and the loyal militia repair there whenever their services are required.

In a letter I had the honor to receive from you the other day you mention the establishing a post on Savannah River. If a company of 40 men only is posted on the river near the mouth of Briar Creek, the inhabitants in that quarter who are great villains will be cautious how they harbour any of McKoy's gang. This place is centrical and well adapted for the Georgia militia of St George's Parish to assemble at when necessary.

If Captain McKinnen[42], who commands at Pocotaligo, is a little rigid with the militia in that quarter, I believe they may be brought to do their duty.

I beg leave to mention to you, sir, that the King's Rangers have within a short time twice lost their necessaries: at Augusta when Clarke paid us a visit, and in the boats which were plundered. I should imagine we are entitled to that return which I am informed is sometimes made on such occasions. I should be much obliged to you, sir, for your good offices in procuring us some compensation, as the men are now half naked. On the first occasion they only saved what they had on their backs; on the last we had a supply coming up the river of two shirts, two pair of overhalls and a pair of shoes for every man with all our camp equipage.

Our friends[43] are generally employed. The Virginians and inhabitants from the back parts of Pensylvania are assembled in force and talk of an expedition against them. I believe they meditate an attack against some of the upper towns. As it is a quarter that has been long dissaffected, it will be of service to our concerns rather than prejudice if they destroy them, as it will fix the inhabitants firmly in our interest and stimulate them to take an active part.

I hope the Dons will drop all thoughts of an expedition against Pensacola from the loss they have sustained in a gale of wind. Should they abandon their design against that place,

---

[42] Commissioned a captain in the 2nd Battalion, 84th Regiment on 14th June 1775, Ranold McKinnon had accompanied it south as part of Leslie's reinforcement and was now commanding its light company at Pocotaligo. Like his commanding officer, John Small, he would gain a reputation for benevolence and humanity. His first name is frequently misspelt as Ronald. (*Army Lists*; McCrady, *SC in the Rev 1780-1783*, 261)

[43] *Our friends*: native Americans.

I can employ my myrmidons[44] in a different quarter.

What greatly prevents my carrying into execution the plan you proposed with vigor and spirit is the want of means to defray the charge. My last year's expences are yet unsettled, which is really a heavy load on my shoulders and very prejudicial to my private fortune. Lord Cornwallis has not informed me to whom I must present my accounts for payment in his absence and I have hitherto pushed my credit, I believe to the great inconvenience of many. You will please to inform me, sir, to whom I must present my account of charges for extra officers, subsistence of Indians, rum, tobacco, repair of arms, expresses etc etc, which nearly amounts to £6,000. I wrote to Lord Cornwallis on this subject[45], but have not yet been favored with an answer as I presume his Lordship has signified his pleasure to you respecting this matter in the same manner as to other concerns.

I shall send off 50 or 60 packhorses in a few days to Savannah for ammunition for the Cherokees, as we have sustained such a loss in the boats. I beg you will be so kind as order the Acting Quarter Master General to give us what assistance he can in boats, as I fear he thinks such duty without the line of his office.

Five hundred of the inhabitants on Holstein profess themselves friends to Government. Do you think, sir, it will [be] prudent to receive them? I can prevail on the Cherokees to assist them on their road through the Nation. Above 30 have passed through the Cherokees. By them I have receiv'd this information and that the people above mentioned will serve under me during the war.

When a safe opportunity offers, I would recommend sending the vessel with Indian presents round to Savannah, as it will be difficult to procure waggons from Charlestown to this place with the necessary escortes.

I send this by Lieutenant Smith[46] of the King's Rangers on recruiting service. I have given him strict orders to avoid receiving any sailors or men who are prisoners.

Major Prevost, if I am not mistaken, mentioned you were in want of some bearskins. I expect some by the Indian packhorses, which I shall forward the first opportunity.

I am, sir, with every sentiment of esteem and respect
Your most obedient and most humble servant

THO\[S] BROWN, Lt Colonel commanding King's Rangers

---

[44] *myrmidons*: warlike native Americans.

[45] *I wrote..*: on 17th December 1780, vol III, p 295.

[46] Of James Smith (1759-?) little is known. Born in England, he was commissioned a lieutenant in the King's Rangers on 22nd November 1780 and by October 1782 was posted with part of his regiment to St John's Island outside Charlestown, awaiting passage to East Florida. At the close of the war he was placed on the Provincial half-pay list. (Treasury 64/23(16), WO 65/164(42), and WO 65/165(11) (National Archives, Kew); Clark, *Loyalists in the Southern Campaign*, i, 66-7, 466; Cashin, *The King's Ranger*, 156)

Balfour to Brown, 9th February 1781

109(13): C

Charles Town
February 9th 1781

Lt Colonel Brown commanding at Augusta

Sir

I am honoured with yours of the 23rd ultimo and am sincerely to thank you for your judgment and activity in surprizing and defeating Colonel Harden with his party, and am truly happy that in the present distracted state of this country the essential post of Augusta is in such hands that the enemy can form to themselves but little hopes from attempting it.

I shall write most fully to Colonel Clarke on the subject of establishing a post near the mouth of Briar Creek and likewise mention to Colonel Lechmere the necessity of his militia acting on Savannah River, as you point out, for the support of its communication, but I have scarce any hope they can be made to acquiesce in such a measure, tho' so much for their own security and advantage.

As the case of the King's Rangers having twice lost their necessaries on service is very hard on them, and their plea to be reimbursed strong, I shall not fail to represent it to Lord Cornwallis whenever a good opportunity offers.

I have no doubt that under your direction *our friends* will act with spirit and deserve well, and as on this account I have in orders from my Lord Cornwallis to give you a certain credit, I shall grant a warrant in your favour for two thousand pounds, which I hope will enable you in part to discharge present debts and carry on the service until I am more fully instructed on this head by his Lordship. It will therefore be necessary for you to send an assignment to some one here to receive this or any future sums granted you on the Paymaster General at this place.

I wou'd gladly give directions to the Quarter Master General, as you desire, to supply you with boats, but think it wou'd be better done for you by some branch of that department at Savannah.

The offers which have been made you by the inhabitants of Holstein are of too much consequence to be neglected, and on this and every other account I wish you success in it.

The vessel with Indian presents will be sent round to Savannah as soon as possible, but the necessity of the service has obliged me to take out of it some sadlery and spurs, the account of which will be transmitted you by the vessel.

I have the honor to be, sir,
Your most obedient humble servant

N BALFOUR

§ - §

5 - From Kirkland

Kirkland to Cornwallis, 22nd February 1781 67(83): LS

Augusta
Febuary 22nd 1781

The Rt Hon Earl Cornwallis etc etc etc

Sir

As I was on my way to Savannah, I received your Lordship's very genteel and perlite letter dated at Wynnes borough November 30th[47], which will ever do me honour. And I humbly beg that your Excellency will be pleased to except my sincere thanks, particular in the note inclosed to Major Frazer, but am sorry to inform your Lordship that after Major Frazer had detain'd me 12 days waiting on him in Savannah, he then refused to settle with me[48], made an excuse that he had not the money, and I raley suffer for the want of it, as I have not received any pay for three years past.

I make not the least doubt but your Lordship's appointment of Brigadier General Cunningham was purely intended for the good of His Majesty's Service, but I could never think of taking any command under a man who had so much neglected His Majesty's Service, and he stills continues to do and worse. Ten days ago I set out to come to your Lordship to offer my service if I could be any other way enploy'd than receiving orders from him. I got as far as Major Maxwell's at the Congerees, but, finding the road forward so invested with small parties of the rebels, thought it prudent to return and went up Saluda to 96, but, finding that way full as difficult as the other, am now on my way back to Savannah, where I shall remain to wait your Lordship's commands. I beg leave to conclude with my best wishes to your Lordship, and am, sir,

Your most obedient and very humble servent

MOSES KIRKLAND

§ - §

---

[47] For the letter and note referred to later, see vol III, p 387.

[48] Fraser gives his reasons in a letter to Cornwallis of 12th January, vol III, p 388.

Index[1]

Abercromby, Robert (III, 444), 15, 124-5
Actions —
    off the Capes of Virginia, 15n, 17, 23;
    at Charles City Court House, 78;
    at the Cross Roads two miles from Hood's Point, 78-9;
    at Green Spring, 4, 116-7, 179, 285;
    at Mackie's Mill, 79;
    at Spencer's Ordinary, 104-5;
    at Wiggan's plantation, 358
Alexander, ——: *see* 'Rankin, William'
Allen, Ethan (I, 195), 62, 75, 84
Alston, Andrew, 183n
Amherst, Jeffery, 87, 152-3, 285, 314-5n, 316-9
Amiel, Henry or Otho, 105, 166n, 176-7
Anderson, Robert (IV, 167), 67
Aplin, Peter, 117n, 191, 212, 217
Arbuthnot, Marriot (I, 7), 8-12, 15, 18, 21-4, 28, 36, 50, 53, 60, 62-3, 70, 75, 83-5, 95, 97, 122, 136, 144-5, 208, 329, 344 —
    assures Clinton that every measure will be taken to protect British operations in the Chesapeake, 123;
    in hourly expectation of being relieved, 144-5
Armistead, Moss, 253n
Arnold, Benedict (III, 55), 7-9, 11-16, 26, 28, 37, 41, 44-55, 60-1, 63, 65, 66-7, 84, 87-8, 90, 95, 119, 125, 127, 132, 136, 140, 150-1, 250, 266, 287, 304
    — his operations on first entering Virginia, 76-83;
    his return to New York, 89, 91, 124, 163
Atarés, Castillo de, 338n, 345, 350
Augusta —
    enemy marching against, 108, 110;
    siege of, 276, 281;
    captured by the enemy, 180
Austin, ——, 210n

Baker, John, 327n
Balfour, Nisbet (I, 35-7), 6, 10, 75, 90, 98-9, 101-3, 118, 139, 150-1, 169, 205, 232, 234-7, 248, 271-286, 289, 290, 292-3, 295-6, 299-313, 323, 328-332, 334-5, 350, 361 —
    regrets the abandonment of SC and Georgia and, in doing so, implicitly criticises Cornwallis, 278;
    his letters to Cornwallis at Wilmington miscarried, 279
Ball, Burgess (III, 108), 236
Banister, John, 257n
Barkley, Andrew (III, 49), 60, 101-3, 208, 213, 215, 285
Barnes, ——, 353
Barras, Jacques-Melchior Saint-Laurent, Comte de, 135 —
    on the Wethersfield Conference and the dispatch of the French naval squadron to Boston, 128-9n
Barron, James, 253n, 256
Battle of Guilford, 16, 20, 30-1, 36, 39, 43 —
    Cornwallis's force, correlation of, 51n;
    'the sort of victory which ruins an army', 49
Beaufort, NC, the abode of revolutionary privateers, 307
Benson, George (I, 172), 280
Biggs, Robert (IV, 129), 51, 92
Bolling, Mary, 259n
Bolling IV, Robert, 258n
Bonet, Don Juan Bautista, 347n
Bowes, Frederick (IV, 51), 193-4
Brabazon, Edward, 80n, 83
Braddock, Edward, 201n
British strategy (*see also* 'Clinton, Sir Henry, KB', 'Cornwallis, Charles, Earl', and 'Phillips, William'), 89-90, 92-8, 105-6, 116, 118-120, 135, 139-143, 146, 165-6, 169, 286-7, 291
Brodhead, Daniel, 201n
Brodrick, The Hon Henry (I, 22), 275-6
Brown, Ebenezer, 138n
Brown, Thomas (I, 271), 5, 276, 281, 327, 336, 353, 357-361 —
    his operations in January, 358;
    makes a severe example of some murderers and plunderers, 358
Browne, William, 219n-221
Bruce, Andrew (II, 87), 84, 94
Bryan, Samuel (I, 168), 163

---

[1] The letter 'n' after the number of a page indicates the presence there of biographical or identifying information. Such information appearing in another volume is indicated in brackets immediately after a person's name.

Buchanan, James, 341
Burgoyne, John, 62-3
Butler, ——, 171
Butts, John, 260n

Cabaña, Fortaleza de San Carlo de la, 338n, 345, 349
Cagigal, Don Juan Manuel de, 346n
Calvert family, 223n
Camp, John (II, 145), 357
Campbell, John (I, 167), 329, 332
Campbell, William (II, 134), 107
Campbell of Caithness, William, 198n
Carlisle, Earl of: *see* 'Howard, Frederick'
Carne, Charles Loder (IV, 37), 304
Casas, Don Francisco, 341
Caswell, The Hon Richard (I, 60), 305-6, 309-310, 312
Cavalry —
    need for, and partial supply of, accoutrements, 88, 120-3, 180, 187, 198, 290;
    near 3,000 guineas subscribed by Charlestonians for equipping the South Carolina Royalist Regiment as dragoons, 291-2
Chads, Henry, 34n, 45, 53
Chaney, Jacob, 251n
Charlieu, ——, de, 19-20
Chastellux, François Jean de Beauvoir, Chevalier de, 133n
Chesnut, John, 262-3
Chewton, Viscount: *see* 'Waldegrave, George'
Claiborne, Richard, 260n-1
Clark, Elijah (I, 257), 327
Clarke, Alured (I, 330), 279, 295, 324, 339, 342-3, 350, 353-7, 361 —
    requests reinforcement from SC, 329-330, 332
Climate, 66
Clinton, Sir Henry, KB —
    his correspondence with Phillips (*see also* 'Phillips, William'), 7-64;
    his pain at Phillips' death, 120;
    his effective force at New York, 96, 143;
    his whole force, rank and file, fit for duty, 57;
    while unaware of Cornwallis's march to Virginia, declares that he cannot form a view of southern operations without the former's further advice, 92-4;
    deprecates Cornwallis's move to Virginia, 118;
    rules out solid operations in Virginia during the sickly months of summer, requisitions 3,000 troops and artillery for the defence of New York, and directs how Cornwallis's remaining force is to be employed, 3-4, 95-8;
    repeats his requisition, but this time for a raid on Philadelphia, 114-5;
    countermands his requisition and directs that a position be taken on Williamsburg Neck to protect ships of all sizes even if it requires Cornwallis's whole force, 5, 139-143;
    prefers small post at Mill Point to maintaining the post at Portsmouth, 141, 143;
    directs Cornwallis to be content with a strict defensive until operations can recommence after the sickly months of summer, 143;
    is ever aware that operations in the Chesapeake can be no longer secure than whilst the British are superior at sea, but expects timely warning of the contrary, 119-120;
    impresses on Arbuthnot the need to attend to the Chesapeake as the first object, 120;
    his criticism of Arbuthnot, 60;
    assumes Rodney will follow de Grasse if the latter comes to the coast of North America, 135, 142;
    his shortage of naval transports, 10, 13, 19, 98-103, 136, 139, 160, 162, 207, 218
Cochrane, The Hon Charles (VI, 39), 122
Colpoys, John, 149n, 214
Connolly, John, 63, 182 —
    his proposals to secure the transmontane territory, 200n-4
Constable, William, 264n
Contrecœur, Claude-Pierre Pécaudy, Seigneur de, 201n
Convalescents, employment of, 165, 275, 279, 285
Convention, Troops of —
    passport for flag vessel to carry necessaries for, 229-230, 235, 243-8;
    officers separated from the men, 241;
    officers ordered from Frederick, Maryland, to Hartford, Connecticut, 243;
    application for £2,000 in specie for the officers' relief, 243, 248
Cook, ——, 319
Cooke, Robert, 284
Cooper, Roe, 253n
Córdova, Don Luis de, 348n
Cornell, The Hon Samuel, 18n
Cornwallis, Charles, Earl —
    could so easily have returned overland

from Wilmington to SC, 5-6, 275, 277;
paroles near 3,000 men on his march to Halifax, 306;
arrives at Petersburg, 87;
orders Craig to evacuate Wilmington, 88;
his view of the situation in SC, 88, 286-7;
his view of further operations in NC, 90;
his views on the conduct of the war, 89-90, 169;
intends to commence offensive operations as soon as he hears a satisfactory account of the British and French fleets, 87-8;
having received a reinforcement from New York, sets out his plan for the Virginia campaign, 89;
relates the events of that campaign, 104-5;
examines Yorktown and Gloucester on 29th June, 169;
his views on a post there, 4, 106;
his views on the post at Portsmouth, 4, 89, 106;
decides to pass James River and retire to Portsmouth, 106;
will comply with Clinton's requisition for troops to defend New York or to raid Philadelphia, 106, 116, 137;
offers to return to SC but does not receive Clinton's consent, 106-7, 141, 285;
his naval transports, 174, 182;
authorises persons on parole to bring stragglers from his army to HQ, particularly those guilty of depredations, 269

Coulter, Andrew, 16, 17, 54
Craig, James Henry (III, 33), 46, 48, 66-7, 151, 190, 192, 205, 217, 279 —
is ordered by Cornwallis to evacuate Wilmington but obtains Balfour's and Rawdon's conditional permission to remain, 88, 107, 274, 285, 293, 300-1;
gives his reasons for wishing to stay, describes the loyalism prevalent in NC, and sets out his plans for offensive operations, 302-313
Croghan, George, 202n
Cruger, John Harris (I, 152 and 258), 5, 276-7, 284, 290-1, 293, 327 —
on the siege of Ninety Six, 281-2
Cunningham, ——, 304
Cunningham, Robert (I, 117), 362
Cuppiage, George, 163n

Dalling, John (II, 122), 87, 152, 315-9
Damer, The Hon George, 16, 20n, 184-5, 189, 191-2

Davies, William, 264n
Davis, William, 253n
De Lancey, Stephen, 334n
Despard, John (II, 235), 199
Destouches, Charles-René-Dominique Gochet, Chevalier, 39n
Dickinson, Jane, 224
Digby, Robert, 189n, 216
Dillon, Arthur Comte de, 19n-20
Doyle, John (I, 185), 287
Doyle, Wellbore Ellis (II, 119), 293
Drew, Thomas Haynes, 264n
Duncan, Henry (III, 50), 53, 61, 63, 95
Duncanson, Robertson (III, 330), 283
Dundas, Thomas (III, 55), 8, 13, 15, 67, 84, 117, 120, 138, 171, 179
Dunmore, Earl of: *see* 'Murray, John'
Duportail, Louis Le Bègue de Presle (III, 107), 133
Durnford, Andrew (I, 337), 335

Eastern shore of Virginia, 177n —
loyalists there seek protection, 181, 184, 186
Elliott, Richard, 258n
Elphinstone, The Hon George Keith (I, 16), 12, 293-4
England, Richard (I, 172), 184-5, 191, 196-9, 223
Eppes family, 222n
Escalona, Don Joaquin, 340
Estaing, Charles Hector Théodat, Comte d', 348
Evans, Henry Francis, 80n
Everitt, Charles Holmes (VI, 18), 146, 218
Ewald, Johann, 162n
Ewell, Charles or Thomas Winder, 237n, 240

Fage, Edward, 124n
Fairlie, James, 234n
Farley, Samuel, 326n
Fitzwilliams, ——, 220
Flags of truce, form of, 232, 235
Fleming, ——, 107
Floyer, ——, 330
Forbes, John, 201n
Forbes, Thomas, 329n-332, 337-352
Forts Granby, Motte, and Watson, and the British post at Orangeburg, surrender of, 5, 108, 110, 275-7, 288-290
Fraser, ——, 164
Fraser, Charles, 236n
Fraser, Simon (II, 357), 362
French expeditionary forces, 9-10, 12, 14, 15, 39, 41, 58, 62-3, 70, 75, 83-5, 128-131, 133-5, 167, 178, 216
Frietschie, Casper, 113-4n
Fuchs, Matthias von, 154-5n, 184, 191

Fyers, William, 12, 32n-4, 36-8, 54, 124
Gale, ——, 322
Gálvez, Don Bernado de (III, 305), 331-2, 337, 342, 344, 346-7, 349
Gee, Henry, 259n
Georgia (*see also* 'Augusta', 'Brown, Thomas', 'Clarke, Alured', 'Militia, royal', and 'Wright, Sir James, Bt') —
    murder in cold blood of Brown's rangers when taken prisoner, 357;
    address of the Royal Assembly congratulating Cornwallis on his victory at Guilford, 325-6;
    troops taken from Savannah for the defence of St Augustine, 326;
    garrison at Savannah much reduced and militia there worn out by constant duty, 326-8, 334;
    cold-blooded murder of loyalists in the Ceded Lands and its effect, 327;
    insufficient troops at Augusta to oppose enemy incursions, 327;
    Cruger can provide Brown with no assistance, 327;
    enemy threat to the Low Country, 327, 335;
    Clarke pressed to return to Savannah from St Augustine, 279;
    great part of country lost to the enemy, 274;
    Governor pleads for assistance, 277, 291;
    reinforced with the King's American Regiment, 279-280, 291-2;
    demands for rent by proprietors of houses occupied by the troops, 332-3n
Gerlach, ——, 244n-8
Germain, Lord George, 5, 72-3, 84-6, 150-1, 273-4, 276, 336, 339
Gibson, James or John, 256n
Giddes, Alexander, 182n, 243
Gimat, Jean-Joseph Sourbader de, 127n
Glasier, Beamsly (I, 355), 328-332, 342-3
Goode III, Robert, 209n
Goodrich, William, 80n
Goodwyn, ——, 259n
Gordon, ——, 344
Gordon, James, 79n
Gould, Paston, 106, 138, 141, 213, 285, 291-4n, 298-9 —
    the embarkation orders under which he is acting, 294, 296
Graham, John (I, 164), 85-6, 326n
Grandfield, ——, 180n
Grasse, François Joseph Paul, Comte de (VI, 68), 128-9, 135, 142

Graves, Thomas, 141-2, 145-6n, 149, 195, 214, 218-9 —
    supports establishment of posts at Old Point Comfort and Yorktown, 146
Greene, Nathanael (III, 10), 5, 11, 14, 25, 30-1, 36, 43, 52, 65, 92, 94, 106, 110-1, 118, 126, 128, 131, 134, 141, 222, 226, 230, 232, 240, 242, 249, 277, 287-291, 304-6, 309-313, 359 —
    his written instructions to Steuben in consequence of Cornwallis's march to Virginia, 107-8;
    is defeated at the Battle of Hobkirk's Hill, 273, 287;
    besieges Ninety Six, 281-2;
    raises the siege of Ninety Six, 139
Gregory, Isaac (II, 13), 30-1, 171
Grey, Charles, 20n
Grierson, James (II, 190), 327
Guichen, Luc Urbain de Bouëxic, Comte de, 348

Hagerty, Thomas, 107, 141
Haldane, Henry (II, 14), 167, 196-9, 213, 227-8, 269, 322-3
Haldimand, Sir Frederick (III, 22), 75
Hall, Thomas, 193n
Hamilton, James, 182, 241-2n, 243
Harden, William (IV, 177), 358, 361
Hardiman, ——, 222n
Hare, ——, 16n-24
Harrison, The Hon Benjamin, 40n-2
Hatch, Christopher, 79n
Hayes, John McNamara (I, 65), 293
Heth, William, 232-3n
Hill, John, 96n
Hoksley, ——, 182n
Hopper, William, 222n
Hospitals —
    at Havana, 337n, 349;
    at Wilmington, 309, 313
Howard, Frederick, Earl of Carlisle, 280n
Howard, John Eager, 20n
Howe, Richard, Viscount Howe (III, 126), 348
Hudson, Charles, 11, 53, 61, 63, 98, 125, 149, 163-5, 167-8, 170, 175, 177, 179, 183, 189, 190, 194-7, 207n-8, 210-2, 214-6, 218-9
Huntington, The Hon Samuel, 131n
Hutcheson, Robert, 270n

Indian Department, expenses of, 360-1
Innes, Alexander (I, 17), 120-3
Intelligence, 16-20, 29-31, 58, 75, 249-256, 304 —
    from Havana, 331-2, 337-352
Ions, Richard, 258

Jackson, Basil, 138n
Jarvis, Samuel, 31n
Jefferson, The Hon Thomas, 77n, 109, 229, 231-2, 244-8
Johnson, Henry, 163n, 190
Jones, Allen (III, 412), 126
Jones, Charles, 105n
Jones, Frank, 253
Jones, Joseph, 257n
Judkin, ——, 259n

Kelly, Hugh, 113-4n
Keppel, George or George Augustus, 123n
King, John, 22n
Kirkland, Moses (I, 236), 362
Knecht, Anthony (I, 212), 320
Knott, Elvinton, 173n
Knox, Henry, 133n

Lafayette, Marie Joseph Paul Yves Roch Gilbert du Motier, Marquis de, 3, 12, 13, 15, 17, 19, 20, 25, 29, 35-6, 40, 43-4, 65, 69, 84, 88, 96, 104, 106-111, 117, 123, 141, 165, 175-6, 179, 219-222, 229-232, 234-240, 249, 257, 260-2, 264, 287, 304 —
    his letter in furtherance of Greene's orders to Steuben, 108-9;
    his letter in May to Washington, 126-8
Langborn, William, 260-1n
Laurie, ——, 219
Lauzun, Armand Louis de Gontaut-Biron, Duc de, 19n, 75
Lawson, Robert, 109n, 128, 222
Lechmere, Nicholas (II, 92), 359, 361
Lee, Henry ('Light Horse Harry') (III, 252), 5, 273, 275-7, 287-8
Leslie, The Hon Alexander (III, 3-4), 3, 5, 8, 26, 54-5, 89, 92-3, 95, 102, 114-6, 118, 125, 137, 141, 147-150, 211-2, 215, 323, 329, 332, 359 —
    commands at Portsmouth, 160-199;
    is to command at Charlestown, SC, 169-170, 299;
    receives notice of his promotion to the local rank of lt general, 195
Lloyd, Richard, 341
Logan, Charles, 265n
Lowry, John, 252n, 256
Loyalist conspiracy in Maryland and Pennsylvania, discovery of, 113-4, 141
Luzerne, Anne-César, Chevalier de la, 128-9
Lyon, John, 177n

Mackie, Andrew and Richard, 170n
MacPherson, Donald, 276n, 289
MacPherson, Duncan, 124n, 180
Mag(g)ridge, ——, 311-2

Mallom, John (II, 213), 269
Mallory, Edward ('Ned'), 253n
March (Martz), Leonard, 262-3
Mariner, Magnus, 283
Marion, Francis (III, 4-5), 5, 273, 275-7, 287-8, 312, 327, 359
Marsh, George, 100n-1
Maryland —
    loyalist sentiment in, 250-2;
    armament at Annapolis, Baltimore, and Frederick, 249-251;
    eighteen months' men, 310
Mason, David, 258-260n
Mason, Littleberry, 258n
Mathew, Edward, 26n
Mathies, ——, 262n
Maury Jr, James, 229n, 231-2, 234, 238
Maxwell, Andrew (I, 252), 277, 362
Maxwell, William, 168n, 171, 173
McAlister, ——, 164
McArthur, Archibald (I, 87), 6, 287, 289, 336
McDonald, William, 339, 341
McKay (pronounced 'McKoy'), James (III, 427), 357-9
McKee, Alexander, 202n
McKenzie, ——, 189n, 283
McKinnon, Ranold, 359n
McNamara, James, 334n
Middleton, Charles, 100n-1
Militia, revolutionary —
    Maryland, 29;
    North Carolina, 30-1, 109;
    Overmountain, 107;
    South Carolina, 358;
    Virginia, 3, 14, 65, 96, 104, 107, 109, 110, 123-4, 126-8, 141, 163, 175, 222, 257
Militia, royal, in Georgia —
    fragility of, 357-8;
    worn out by constant duty in the Low Country, 327-8
Millar, Thomas (II, 94), 229, 231
Mister, Stephen, 250n
Mitchell, Nathaniel, 127n
Moncrief, James (I, 58), 12, 285-6, 302, 330, 335
Money, Margaret and John (II, 45), 268-9
Montagu, Lord Charles, 315n
Monteil, François-Aymar, Baron de, 338n, 345, 347
Moore, Philip (I, 164), 355-6
Morgan, Daniel (III, 11-12), 221, 359
Morrison, John (III, 125), 320
Morro, Castillo de los Tres Reyes del, 338n, 345, 349
Mühlenberg, John Peter Gabriel (III, 41), 108, 110-3, 126-7, 222, 257-8, 264
Muir, Francis, 128n

Murray, John, Earl of Dunmore, 202n
Mutzell, ——, 243n

Nairne, John or William (I, 320), 124, 166
Nash, The Hon Abner (II, 337), 31, 126
Navarro, Don Diego José, 337, 339-340n, 347
Navia, Don Victorio de, 337n, 343-4, 346-7
Necker, Jacques, 348n
Needham, The Hon Francis, 190n
Nelson, Robert, 225n
Nelson Jr, Thomas, 110n, 126
Nicholas, Wilson Cary, 113n
Nicolson, George, 262n
Ninety Six —
    enemy marching against, 108, 110;
    raising of siege, 139, 191
Noa, Tomás de, 351
Noble, Mungo, 244, 271-2n
Nowell, William, 251n
Nutt, George Anson, 241n-3, 248

Odell, William, 152, 285, 315-7n
O'Hara, Charles (III, 4), 92, 118, 141, 234, 238
Old Point Comfort —
    Clinton's references to post at, 4-5, 8, 39, 55-6, 139-143
Oliphant, David (II, 112), 242-3, 249
O'Reilly, ——, 183n-4, 191
Orendorf, Christian, 113
Overmountain settlers —
    attacked by native Americans, 359, 361;
    500 Holston inhabitants profess loyalty to the Crown, 360-1

Palmer, George, 35n
Parker, Josiah, 30n, 219-221
Pattison, George, 206, 208-9n, 210-1, 213
Paymaster at Charlestown, 322-3
Peacock, William, 189, 190, 192, 196, 215-6n, 217, 310, 313
Pensacola —
    Spanish preparations to take, 331-2, 346-7;
    Spanish investment of, 334, 353;
    native Americans aid the British, 353;
    capture of by the Spanish, 132
Perez, Pedro and Vicente, 351
Petition to the King from British merchants trading to South Carolina and action taken in consequence, 71-4
Phillips, William, 7-70, 93, 95, 118-9, 126, 132, 134, 140, 196, 198-9, 208, 229, 232-3, 241-7, 250, 265-7, 271-4, 287, 300, 302 —
    his detachment is embarked at New York, waiting to sail, and its strength, 84-5, 93;
    his written instructions from Clinton, 7-12;
    his disembarkation in Virginia, 13, 15, 24;
    his views on operations there and on the post at Portsmouth, 25-7, 36, 43-4, 48-50, 65;
    his views on the situation of the enemy, 35-6, 43-5;
    Clinton's responses, 39, 42, 45-7, 50-64;
    operations in favour of Cornwallis are to be Phillips' first object, but consideration later given to other operations, 51-4, 59-61, 64-5;
    embarkation of troops for desultory operations, 35, 43, 68-9;
    garrison to be left at Portsmouth while other operations proceed, 48;
    fortification etc of Portsmouth, 32-3, 35, 37-8, 154;
    employment of escaped slaves, 28;
    post on Elizabeth River only there to protect the Royal Navy, 54-6;
    sentiments of the inhabitants of Norfolk and Princess Anne Counties, 27;
    further reinforcement being sent from New York, and its strength, 52, 60, 70, 88, 93, 119, 132, 144, 151, 206;
    Phillips' letters to Cornwallis, 64-9;
    he falls ill, 69;
    his death, 87, 127, 259n, 304
Pickens, Andrew (I, 79), 5, 327
Pinckney, Charles Cotesworth (II, 111), 328-9n
Pleasants, Robert, 265-6n
Pleasants, Thomas, 262n
Poe, George, 113-4n
Porbeck, Friedrich von (III, 427), 324, 327, 334
Portsmouth —
    a dangerous post of severely limited utility, 4, 89, 106, 116;
    state of in May, 154;
    ordnance etc there in May, 156-160;
    three months' provisions for 8,000 men at, 187;
    operations of loyalist refugees in the vicinity of, 173;
    numbers of inhabitants flock in to offer their services, 272
Prevost, Augustine (I, 64), 343
Prevost, Augustine (I, 330), 360
Prisoners, British —
    delivery of under the cartel, arrangements for, 237-8, 240
Prisoners, enemy, and the cartel —
    ways to dispose of, 86, 164;
    consent to the export of tobacco from Virginia for the relief of at Charlestown, 231-8, 285;

cartel beginning to operate in South Carolina, 279;
dispatch of from Charlestown and their arrival in Virginia for exchange under the cartel, 179, 183, 189, 219, 223, 238, 240, 283-5;
rejection of proposal to enlist at Charlestown for service in the West Indies, 87, 152, 285, 314-9;
cartel forwarded to Clinton, 91;
cartel to operate in Virginia, 230;
prisoners at Portsmouth, 164, 173

Privateers, British etc, in Chesapeake Bay, depredations of, 91, 164, 250

Property and provisions —
appropriation of, 209-210, 257, 267-8;
provisions in store at Charlestown, Savannah, St Augustine, and Wilmington, 320-2

Punta, Castillo de San Salvador de la, 338n, 349

Quartermaster General's Department, Portsmouth, 196-9

Raids —
on Charlottesville, 104;
on the Point of Fork, 104;
on Bedford and Prince Edward Counties, 4, 138, 228

Rankin, ——, 113

Rankin, William, 53n, 59n-63, 89n, 105, 141n, 147n

Rawdon, Francis, Lord (I, 151-2), 5, 25, 88, 93, 118, 139, 150, 183, 279, 284-293 —
defeats Greene at the Battle of Hobkirk's Hill, 273, 287;
quits Camden and crosses the Santee, 276;
is five days within the Santee before a single man of the country comes near him, 290;
his strategy when within the Santee, 291;
severely criticises Gould and Stewart, 292-3;
marches to relieve Ninety Six, 281-2;
recounts events, and the circumstances surrounding them, from the Battle of Hobkirk's Hill to the commencement of his march on Ninety Six, 287-293;
his poor state of health, 106, 141, 169, 278, 285-6, 293, 300

Read, Jacob, 328-9n

Regiments, Anspach, 70, 89, 96, 114, 161, 175, 185, 187, 198, 206

Regiments or corps, British —
Brigade of Guards, 167, 169, 170, 172-3, 185, 191, 291, 294, 296-8;
3rd (The Buffs), 106, 291, 294-8;
7th (Royal Fusiliers), 18, 335;
17th Foot, 70, 89, 161, 175, 191, 293;
17th Light Dragoons, 96, 136;
19th, 106, 141, 291, 294, 296-8;
23rd (Royal Welch Fusiliers), 137;
30th, 106, 141, 291, 294, 296-8;
42nd, 25, 102;
43rd, 70, 89, 96, 114, 117, 160-1, 170, 173, 185, 187, 193, 198;
60th, 339, 341, 351;
71st, 1st Battalion, 18;
76th, 8-9, 24, 96, 114, 117, 161, 165, 167-8, 179, 185-6, 285;
80th, 24, 50, 77-8, 80, 96, 114, 117, 137-8, 161, 165, 168-171, 173, 179, 191, 285;
82nd, 279, 293, 303;
84th, 275;
Royal Artillery, 32, 78, 96, 114-5, 155-160, 185, 188;
Grenadiers, 17, 25, 102;
Light infantry, 9, 17, 24, 65, 70, 96, 114, 116-7, 175, 185, 303;
Pioneers, 138

Regiments or corps, British American —
American Legion (Arnold's corps), 163, 193n;
British Legion cavalry, 88, 109, 121-3, 137-8, 180, 184, 187, 198, 262;
King's American Regiment (Fanning's corps), 279-280, 291-2;
King's Rangers (Brown's corps), 327, 357-361;
Loyal American Regiment (Robinson's corps), 9, 24, 65, 78-9, 90, 163;
New York Volunteers, 77, 80;
North Carolina Highland Regiment (Martin's corps), 307;
Provincial light infantry (Watson's corps), 6;
Queen's Rangers (Simcoe's corps), 9, 24, 70, 77-8, 96, 104-5, 114, 116, 170, 173, 187;
Royal North Carolina Regiment (Hamilton's corps), 163, 279, 293, 303;
South Carolina Royalist Regiment (Innes's corps), 291-2

Regiments or corps, Continental, 3, 12, 17, 29, 35-6, 40-2, 65, 69, 96, 107-110, 117, 124, 126-7, 132, 175, 179, 201, 222, 260-1, 264, 310

Regiments or corps, Hessian, 24, 142, 275 —
von Bose, 180, 183, 187, 191, 198;
Erb Prinz (Prince Héréditaire), 8, 165, 169, 170, 172-3, 185, 187, 191, 198;

369

Regiments or corps, Hessian (*continued*)
    Grenadiers, 102;
    Jägers, 77-8, 80, 104, 162, 279, 293

Returns —
    of arms, ammunition etc captured by Arnold at Richmond, Westham, and Hood's Ferry, 81-3;
    of stores destroyed by Arnold at Richmond, 83;
    of ordnance, ammunition etc at Portsmouth in May, 156-160;
    of naval transports in Virginia at the end of June, 174;
    of the troop reinforcement arriving at Charlestown on 3rd June from Ireland, 297-8;
    of provisions in HM Magazine at Charlestown and issues therefrom, 18th to 31st March, 321-2;
    of prisoners at Havana, 352;
    of prisoners at Havana delivered up for exchange, 340-1

Rey, Don José Eugenio, 341
Riedesel, Friedrich Adolphus, the Baron (III, 17), 244-5
Robertson, George, 174n, 206-7
Robertson, James (I, 126), 114, 116, 120, 132, 134, 148, 152-3, 165, 314, 318
Robinson, Hugh, (VI, 101) 13, 15, 35-6, 205-6, 218
Rochambeau, Jean Baptiste Donatien de Vimeur, Comte de (II, 47) —
    at the Wethersfield Conference, 128-131, 133-4
Rochfort, George, 32n, 155, 160
Rodney, Sir George Brydges (I, 11), 10, 135, 142, 349
Rogers, John, 256n
Ross, Alexander (I, 73), 182, 279, 280, 235-6
Ross, David, 262-3n, 267-8
Royal Navy 9-11, 13-15, 145-6 —
    correspondence with naval officers in Virginia and South Carolina, 205-219;
    desultory water operations in Virginia, 219-223;
    Ships: *Amphitrite*, 49, 51, 57, 68, 92, 138, 165; *Assurance*, 183; *Bedford*, 145; *Blonde*, 208, 215-6; *Bonetta*, 14, 35, 149, 177, 179, 183, 214; *Camilla*, 101-2; *Carysfort*, 188-190, 192, 194, 196-7, 215, 285, 299, 303, 313; *Charon*, 137, 149, 179, 180, 218; *Chatham*, 86, 101; *Delight*, 208, 276; *Formidable*, 35, 115, 192; *Fowey*, 189, 190, 212, 217-8; *Foy*, 14, 35; *Galatea*, 101-2; *General Monk*, 14, 29; *Guadeloupe*, 13, 35, 189, 190, 218; *Hope*, 14, 29, 35, 77; *London*, 145, 149; *Loyalist*, 149, 218; *Medea*, 13, 15, 17, 23, 38, 49, 53, 68, 95; *Mentor*, 344; *Orpheus*, 137, 149, 179, 187-190, 192, 214; *Rambler*, 70, 77, 115, 192; *Richmond*, 9, 53, 57, 118, 144, 149, 164, 189, 193, 214, 278; *Roebuck*, 34, 66; *Romulus*, 84; *Royal Oak*, 144, 208; *Sandwich*, 350; *Savage*, 14, 35; *Solebay*, 145, 218-9; *Spitfire*, 35, 115, 193; *Swift*, 14, 19, 21-2, 35, 77, 214, 218; *Thames*, 13, 35; *Vulcan*, 14, 35, 218; *Warwick*, 183, 296

Rue, James, 262-3
Ruggles, Timothy, 121n
Rush, John, 138n
Rutherford, Andrew (IV, 167), 64, 66-7

St Augustine (*see also* 'Tonyn, Patrick') —
    strength of garrison, 326, 330, 332, 334, 342;
    fortifications in need of repair or strengthening, 342;
    province entirely without naval support, 343;
    requisition for provisions (*see also* 'Property and provisions'), 330;
    store of six months' provisions required for 1,500 men, 343;
    presents and provisions for Seminoles and other native Americans who visit, 336, 343, 353-7
St George, Hamilton Usher, 252-3n, 254-6
Sanderson, Joseph, 283
Saunders, John (III, 57), 274
Scott, Charles (I, 45), 232, 234-6, 238
Selden, Richard, 252n, 256
Shank, David, 78n
Shelby, Isaac (II, 109), 327
Simcoe, John Graves (I, 10), 3, 15, 53, 60, 63, 77-80, 104, 140, 171, 224-5, 234, 274
Sinclair, Arthur, 219n
Skelly, Francis, 180n, 182, 194
Skipwith, Sir Peyton, Bt 221n
Slaves, 28, 50, 164, 166, 183, 220-2, 256-7, 260, 265-8, 335, 347, 349 —
    rule of Cornwallis's army is to give up those who are willing to return and can conveniently be spared from the public service, 211
Smith, James, 360n
Smith, John (I, 60), 103
Solano y Bote, Don José, 346n-8
South Carolina (*see also* 'Balfour, Nisbet' and 'Cornwallis, Charles, Earl') —
    further evidence that Cornwallis could

so easily have returned overland from Wilmington to South Carolina, 5-6, 275, 277;
the state of affairs there, 272-300;
general revolt and universal disaffection, 276, 288;
great part of the country is lost to the enemy, 274;
the revolutionary irregulars murder in cold blood every royal militiaman who falls into their hands, 277, 287;
the ensuing terror and plight of the loyalists, 277-8;
the country may yet be regained but a very great additional force will be needed, 277-8;
want of every kind of naval assistance, 279;
arrival of three regiments, a detachment of the Guards, and recruits from Ireland, 138, 151, 284, 291, 297-8;
severe shortage of money to pay for much increased public expenditure, 279

Stapleton, ——, 139, 145, 150
Steuben, Freiherr Friedrich Wilhelm von (III, 223), 17, 104, 107, 110, 132, 220-2, 226, 234, 247, 264
Stewart, Alexander, 285, 292-3, 295n, 299-300
Stratton, James, 37n
Sueman, Peter, 113-4n
Sullivan, John, 130n
Sumner, Jethro (II, 100), 108, 126
Sumter, Thomas (I, 149), 277, 287, 290
Sutherland, Alexander (III, 121), 55, 124, 166-7, 195
Swords, Richard, 79n
Syme III, John, 227n-8
Symonds, Thomas (II, 129), 80, 83

Tarleton, Banastre (I, 154-7), 3-4, 92, 104, 106, 109, 126, 138, 151, 195, 219-222, 225-8, 262
Ternay, Charles Louis d'Arsac, Chevalier de (II, 47), 75
Thomas, William, 35n
Thompson, Benjamin, 121n-2
Tonken, Thomas, 98n-103
Tonyn, Patrick (I, 24), 329, 330, 332, 335-357
Torriano, Charles, 18n
Touche, Chevalier de la, 128-9n
Townsend, Gregory (I, 294), 5, 320-2, 330
Trail(e), Peter (II, 72), 330
Trepan, Lewis, 224
Tupper, Benjamin, 133n

Vallancey, George Preston (IV, 153), 170, 185, 196-9, 271-2

Vaughan, The Hon John (I, 11), 63, 86
Viomenil, Antoine Charles du Houx, Baron de, 39
Virginia campaign —
summary of, 3-6;
forces under Cornwallis's command, 3, 95;
forces under Lafayette's command, 3
Virginia twelve months' men, 104, 107
Voit von Salzburg, Freiherr August von, 172n
Vose, Elijah and Joseph, 132n

Waldegrave, George, Viscount Chewton (II, 119), 53, 61-2, 118, 120, 165, 168, 278-9, 306
Walter, Richard, 98n, 101-3
Washington, George, 56, 62, 96, 152, 202, 244, 249
— detaches Lafayette to Virginia, 84;
approves of Lafayette's determination not to engage the British, 132;
on the Battle of Hobkirk's Hill and Greene's plan of operations, 131;
his strategy, 40-2;
his situation as respects men, ammunition and clothing, 40-2, 63;
his force at West Point, 124;
at the Wethersfield Conference, 128-9, 133;
on the plan adopted there, 130-1, 133-4
Watson, John, 47
Watson, John Watson Tadwell (II, 199), 6, 273, 275-6, 278, 287-8, 293
Watt, ——, 220n, 222
Wayne, Anthony, 41, 88, 96, 104, 109, 111, 127, 132, 221-2, 249, 260-1, 264, 287
Webster, James (I, 9), 69, 87
Webster, Jonathan, 224
Weedon, George, 14n, 109, 110
Weeks, ——, 192n
Weir, Daniel (II, 118), 320
Weir, John, 242n-3, 248-9
White, Charles, 266-7
White, Jack, 221n
White, John, 29n
Williams, ——, 100n-1
Williams, ——, 253
Williams, Joseph, 251
Winstanley, Thomas (II, 317), 328-9n
Wood, James (III, 128), 242
Woodford, William (I, 376), 236
Wright, Sir James, Bt, —
laments Clarke's going to St Augustine, 324;
regrets that the military command in Georgia will fall on von Porbeck, 324, 334;
reports the unfavourable turn taken by events in April, 326-8;

Wright, Sir James, Bt (*continued*)
    expresses apprehensions for the safety of the Low Country, 335;
    his application is rejected for the issue of provisions to the royal militia from the King's Store, 333
Wylly, Alexander Campbell, 357n-8

Yorke, John (IV, 111), 278
Yorktown and Gloucester —
    Clinton's references to a post at, 4-5, 8, 39, 56, 95, 139-143;
    Cornwallis's views on such a post, 4, 106
Young, Henry, 261n

§ - §